TABLE OF CONTENTS

TABLE OF CONTENTS

TIME TO THE QUARTER-HOUR

TIME TO THE MINUTE

TIME REVIEW

TABLE OF CONTENTS

TABLE OF CONTENTS

TIME

Name________________________________

Face Clocks: Introduction

What is the best way to tell what time it is?

A clock!

There are all kinds of clocks.

Circle the ones you have seen.

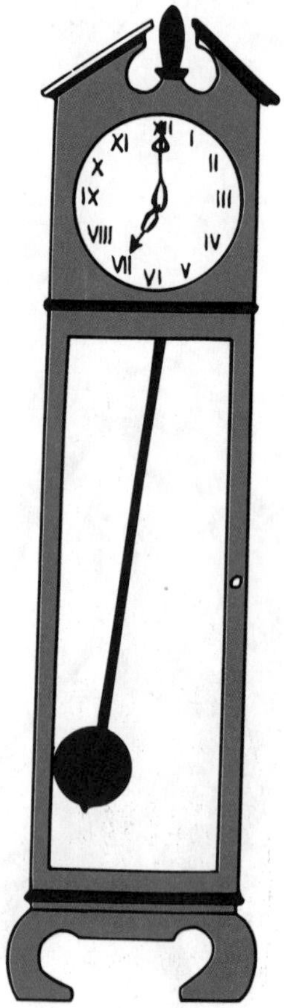

Name________________________________

Face Clocks: Identifying Parts

A clock can tell you what time it is.
A clock has different parts.
Read and **trace** each part of the clock.

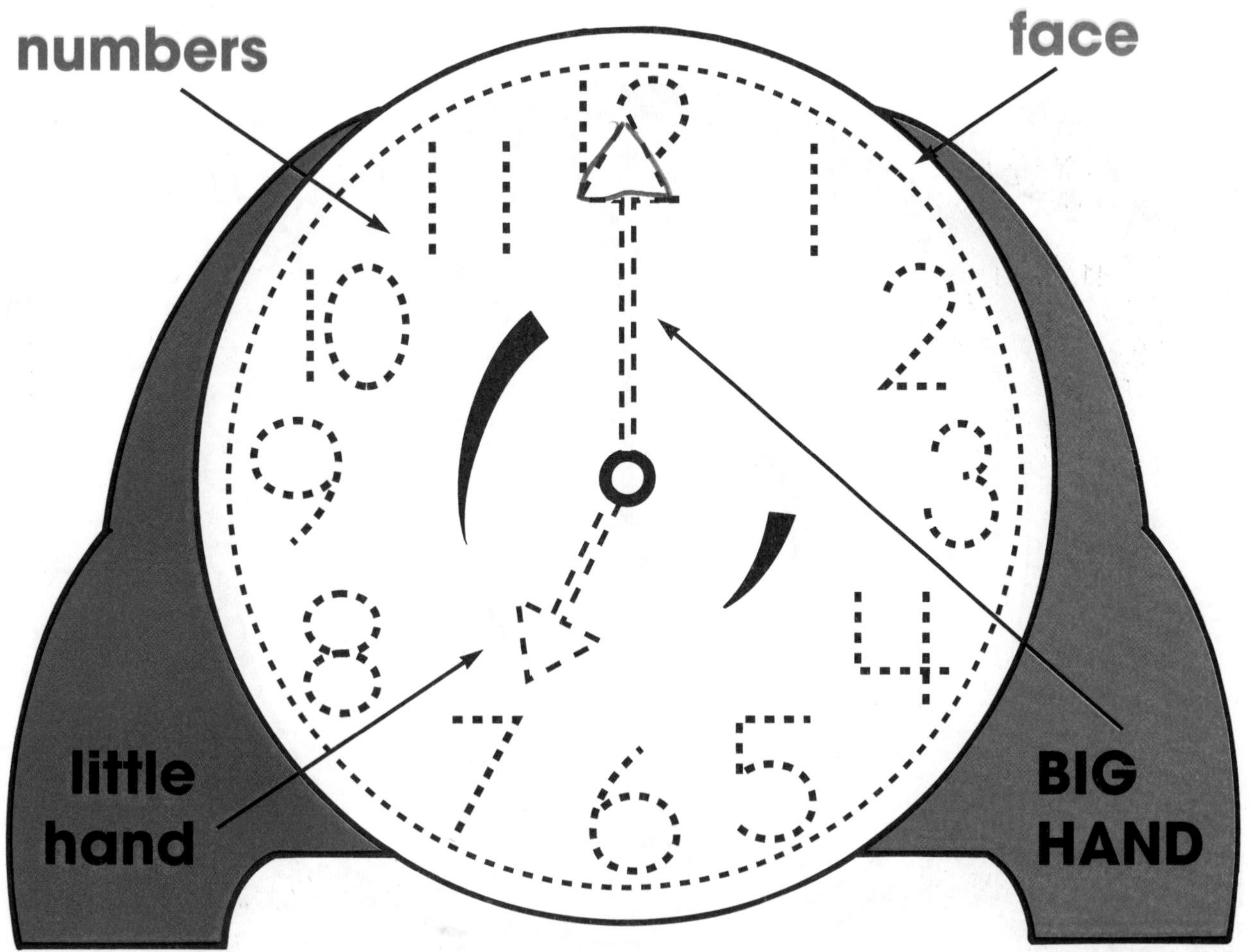

The **BIG HAND** is on **12**.
The **little hand tells the hour.**

Name____

Time to the Hour

Face Clocks: Identifying Parts

A clock face has numbers.
Trace the numbers on the clock

Tick Tock

12 11 1 10 2 9 3 8 4 7 6 5

Name____

Writing the Time

Hi! My name is **Tim Time**.
Learning to tell time is fun!
A clock tells us the time.

Write the numbers on the clock face.
Draw the **BIG HAND** to **12**.
Draw the **little hand** to **5**.

What time is it? 5:00 o'clock

Name ______________________________

Writing the Time

An **hour** is **sixty minutes** long.

It takes an **hour** for the **BIG HAND** to go around the clock.

When the **BIG HAND** is on **12**, and the **little hand** points to a number, that is **the hour**!

The **BIG HAND** is on the **12**. **Color** it **red**.

The **little hand** is on the **8**. **Color** it **blue**.

The **BIG HAND** is on ___12___.

The **little hand** is on ___8___.

It is ___8___ o'clock.

Name________________________________

Writing the Time

Color the **little hour hand** red.

Fill in the blanks.

The **BIG HAND** is on __12__.
The **little hand** is on __3__.

It is __3__ o'clock.

The **BIG HAND** is on ________.
The **little hand** is on ________.

It is __________ o'clock.

The **BIG HAND** is on ________.
The **little hand** is on ________.

It is __________ o'clock.

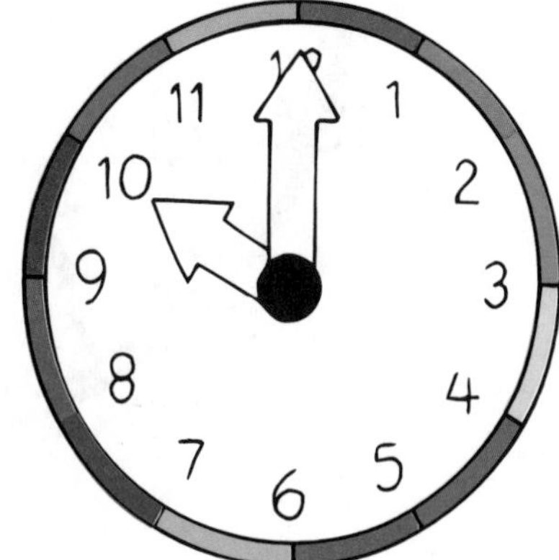

The **BIG HAND** is on ________.
The **little hand** is on ________.

It is __________ o'clock.

Name ________________________________

Drawing the Hour Hand

If the **BIG HAND** is on **12**,
it is easy to tell the time.
Look and see the hour.
Trace the **little hand** to make the hour **10 o'clock.**

The **BIG HAND** is on ________.
The **little hand** is on ________.

It is ____________ **o'clock.**

Name____

Drawing the Hour Hand

Draw the **little hour hand** on each clock.

8 o'clock

1 o'clock

7 o'clock

Name____

Drawing the Hour Hand

Draw the **little hour hand** on each clock.

2 o'clock

10 o'clock

9 o'clock

Name______________________________

Drawing the Hour Hand

Draw the **little hour hand** on each clock.

4 o'clock

11 o'clock

5 o'clock

Name________________________________

Drawing the Hour Hand

Draw the **little hour hand** on each clock.

6 o'clock

12 o'clock

3 o'clock

Name ____________________

Circling the Hour Hand

Circle the **little hour hand** on each clock.

What time is it? Write the time below.

___3___ o'clock

___8___ o'clock

___4___ o'clock

___12___ o'clock

___10___ o'clock

___5___ o'clock

Name______________________________

Practice

Here's the Scoop!

Draw the **little hour hand** on each clock.

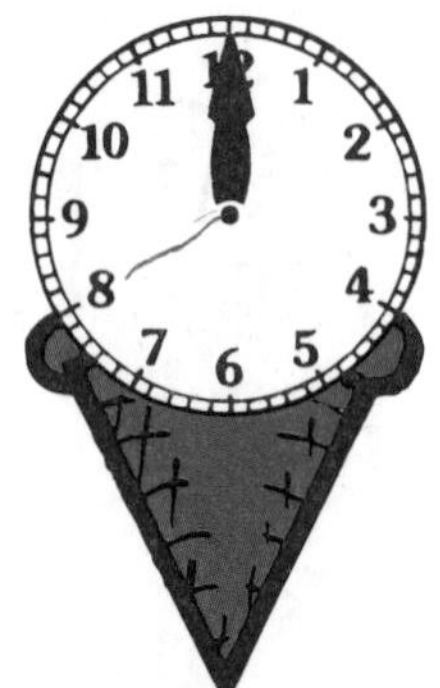

8 o'clock

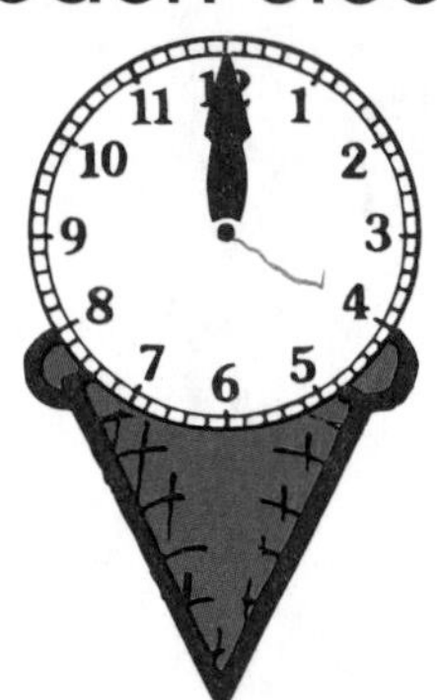

4 o'clock

2 o'clock

6 o'clock

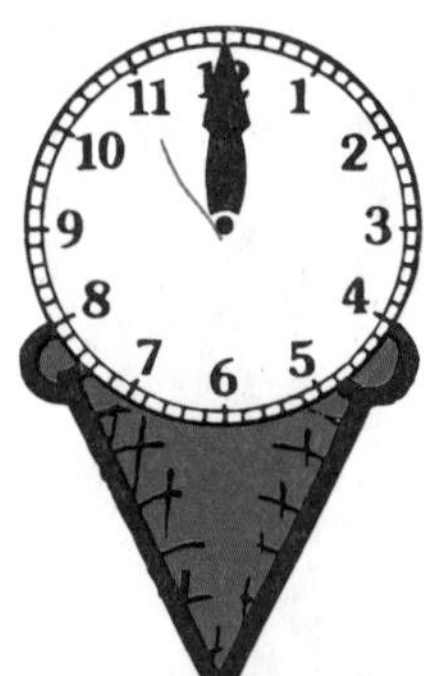

11 o'clock

3 o'clock

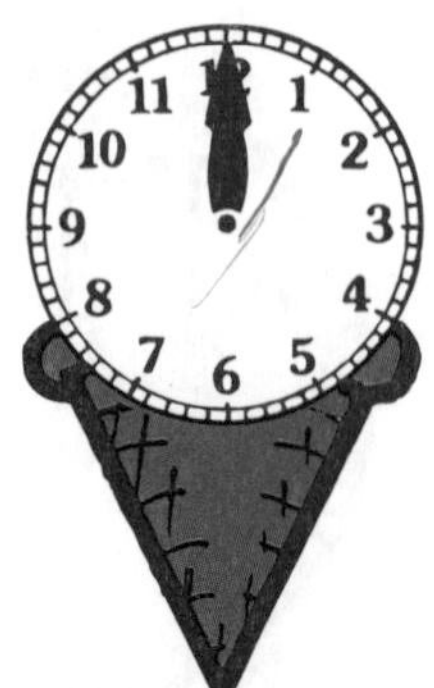

1 o'clock

5 o'clock

7 o'clock

Name______________________________

Practice

What is the time?

_____ o'clock

_____ o'clock

_____ o'clock

_____ o'clock

_____ o'clock

_____ o'clock

_____ o'clock

_____ o'clock

_____ o'clock

_____ o'clock

_____ o'clock

_____ o'clock

Name___________________________________

Practice

What is the time?

_____ o'clock  _____ o'clock  _____ o'clock

_____ o'clock  _____ o'clock  _____ o'clock

_____ o'clock  _____ o'clock  _____ o'clock

_____ o'clock  _____ o'clock

Name________________________________

Practice

What is the time? It's Clown Time!

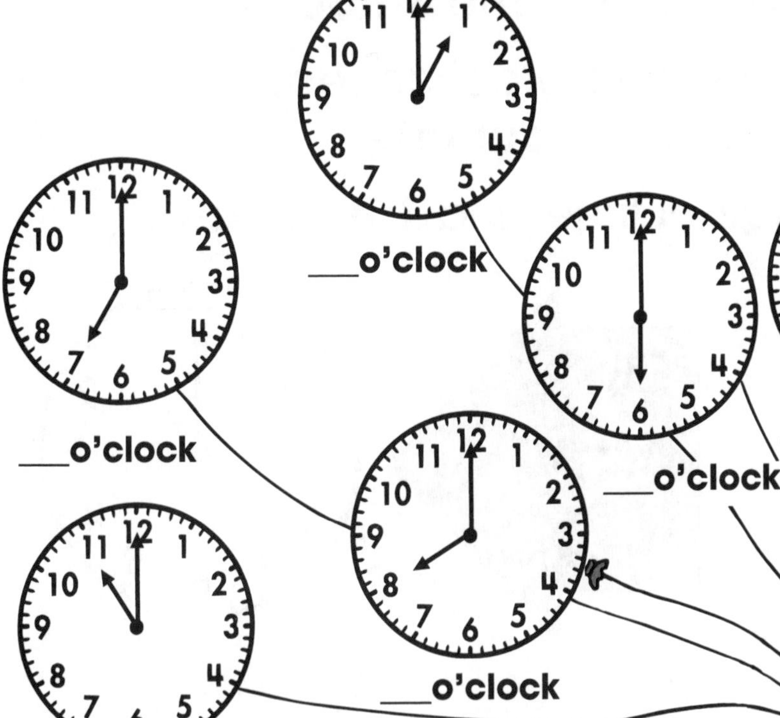

___o'clock

___o'clock

___o'clock

___o'clock

___o'clock

___o'clock

___o'clock

___o'clock

___o'clock

___o'clock

Name________________________________

Writing the Time: One Hour Later

When I go to my friend's house to play, Mom says to come home **1 hour later**.

Tim Time needs to practice reading the clock **1 hour later**.

Write the original time and **1 hour later**.

7:00 ________________ 8:00 ________________

________________ ________________

Name____

Writing the Time: One Hour Later

Place the hands on the clocks to show **1 hour later**. **Write** the times.

One hour later

________________________ ________________________

One hour later

________________________ ________________________

One hour later

________________________ ________________________

Name______________________________

Time Poems

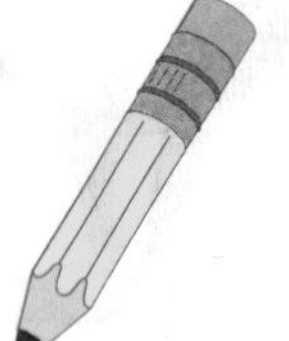

Read each poem.
Draw a line to the clock that matches.

A. It is 7 o'clock.
Time to rise and shine.
First it will rain,
Then turn out fine.

B. It is 10 o'clock.
We are at the pool.
We're happy today
Because there is no school!

C. It is 4 o'clock.
It is time to play!
We will see friends
Outside today.

Name________________________________

Time Poems

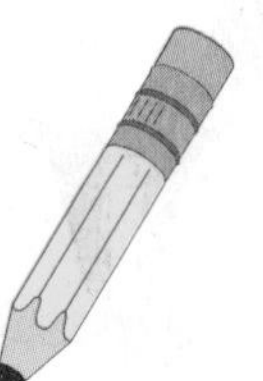

Read each poem.
Draw a line to the clock that matches.

A. It is 2 o'clock.
Now it is dark night.
I am in bed,
All tucked in tight.

B. It is 12 o'clock,
And time to eat.
Have a sandwich,
Then a treat!

C. It is 5 o'clock.
Night is almost here.
Evening shadows
Are very near.

Name________________________________

Time Poems

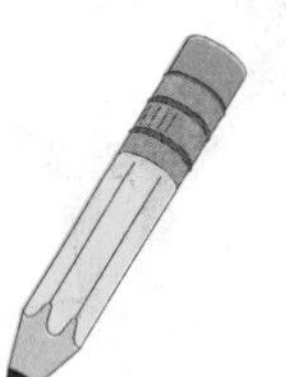

Read each poem.
Draw a line to the clock that matches.

A. It is 8 o'clock.
Now dinner is done.
Time for homework
And then some fun.

B. It is 11 o'clock,
And I am in bed
With a pillow
Underneath my head.

C. It is 3 o'clock.
We are out the door,
To run and play,
Then play some more.

Name________________________________

Digital Clocks: Introduction

Meet my friend **Digital Clock**.
He tells **time with numbers**.
First, he tells the **hour**, then the **minutes**.

Draw the **little hour hand** on this face clock below to read **10 o'clock**.

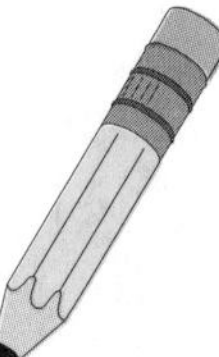

Both clocks show that it is **10 o'clock**.

Make a **green circle** around the kinds of clocks you have at home.

Name________________________________

Matching Digital and Face Clocks

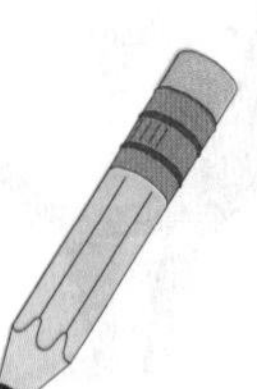

Trace the time on the **digital clocks**.

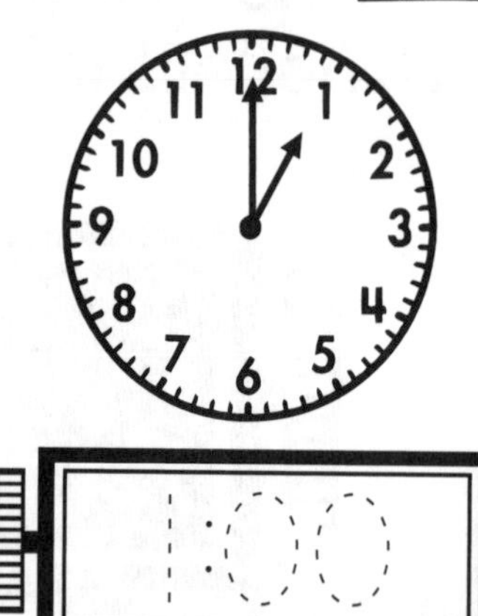

Match the clocks.

Name________________________________

Matching Digital and Face Clocks

Long ago, there were only **wind-up clocks.** Today, we also have **electric** and **battery clocks.** We may soon have **solar clocks**!

Match these digital and face clocks.

Name________________________________

Digital Clocks

Write the time on the digital clocks.

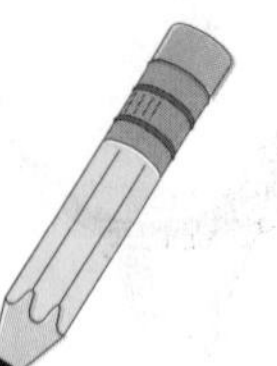

4:00

:

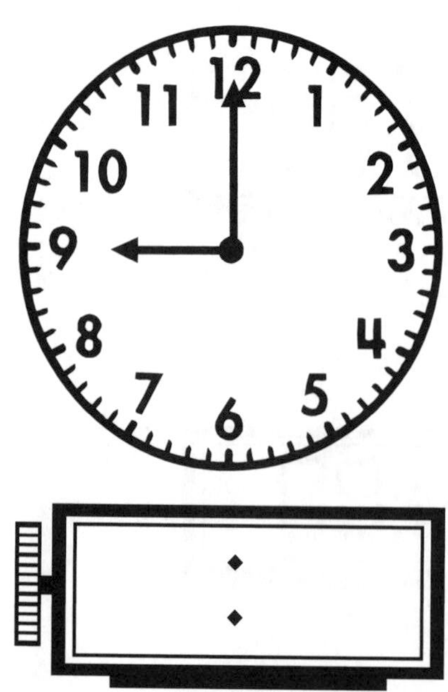

:

:

Name________________________________

Digital Clocks

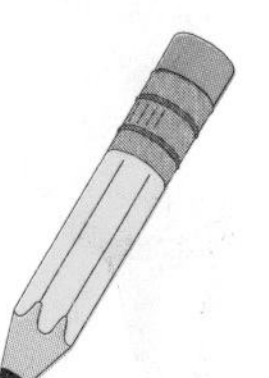

Write the time on the digital clocks.

Name________________________________

Write the time on the digital clocks.

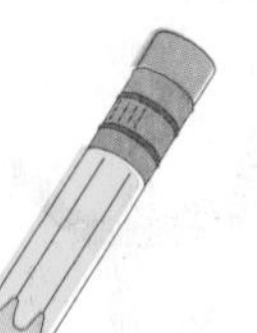

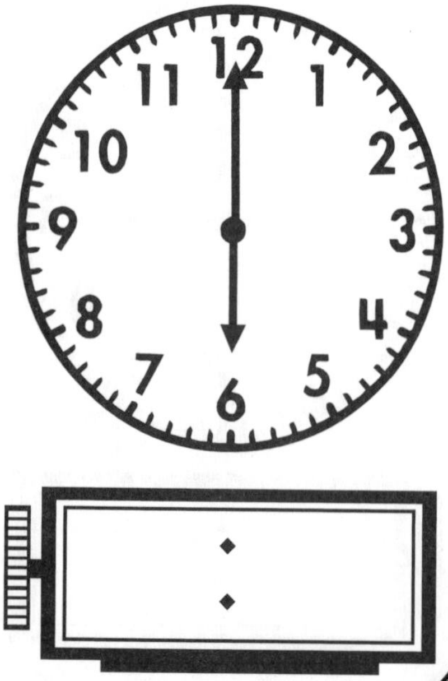

Name________________________________

Drawing the Hour Hand: Matching Digital and Face Clocks

Look at the digital clock.
Say the time.
Draw the **little hour hand** on each face clock.

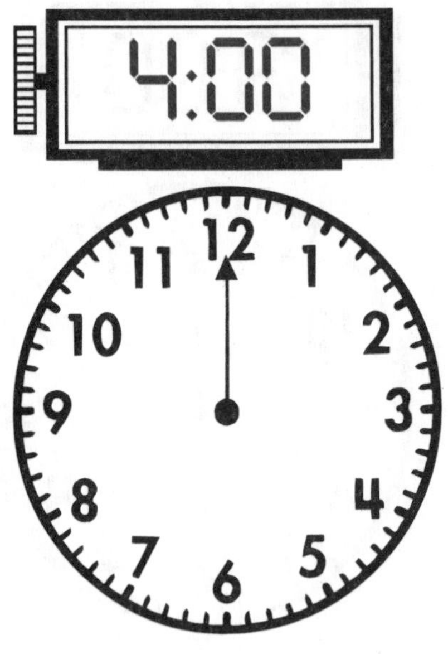

8:00

Name____

Drawing the Hour Hand: Matching Digital and Face Clocks

Look at the digital clock.
Say the time.
Draw the **little hour hand** on each face clock.

Name ____________________

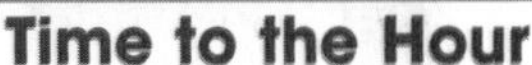

Time Two Ways

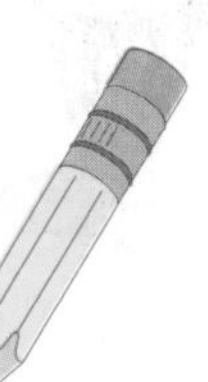

Show each time **two ways**.
Draw the hands on each clock face.
Write the time on each digital clock.

A. Bessie Bear gets up at **6 o'clock**.

B. Bernie Bear eats breakfast at **7 o'clock**.

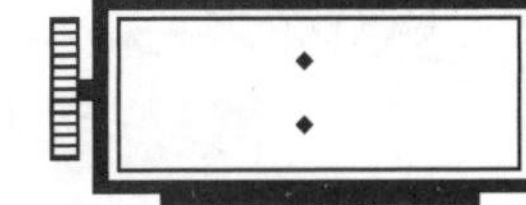

C. What time do you get up on school mornings?
Draw it here!

Name____________________

Time Two Ways

Show each time **two ways**.
Draw the hands on each clock face.
Write the time on each digital clock.

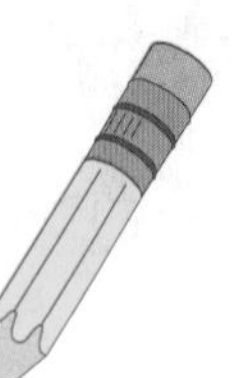

A. Randy Rabbit leaves for school at **8 o'clock**.

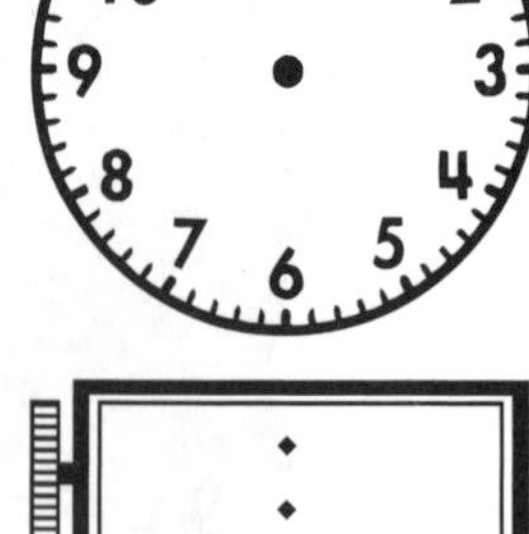

B. Rebecca Rabbit goes out to recess at **10 o'clock**.

C. What time do you go out for recess?
Draw it here!

Name________________________________

Time Two Ways

Show each time **two ways**.
Draw the hands on each clock face.
Write the time on each digital clock.

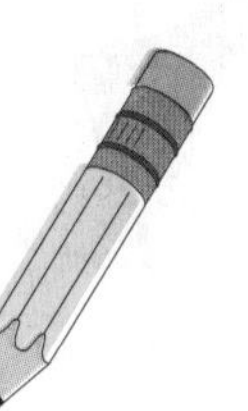

A. Fernando Frog eats lunch at **12 o'clock.**

B. Fanny Frog goes to the library at **1 o'clock**.

C. What time do you eat lunch?
Draw it here!

Name____

Time Two Ways

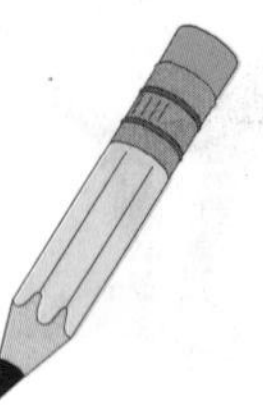

Show each time **two ways**.
Draw the hands on each clock face.
Write the time.

A. At **9 o'clock,** Frog goes for a swim.

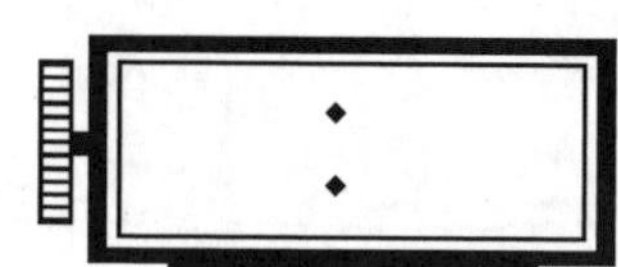

B. At **11 o'clock,** Frog sits on a lily pad.

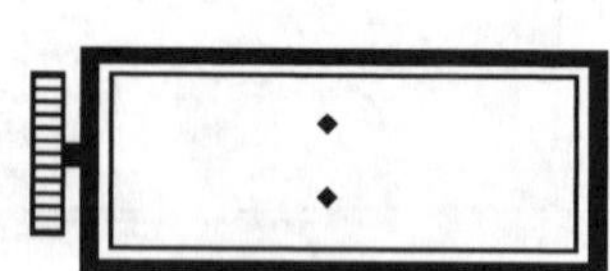

C. At **12 o'clock,** Frog eats a sandwich.

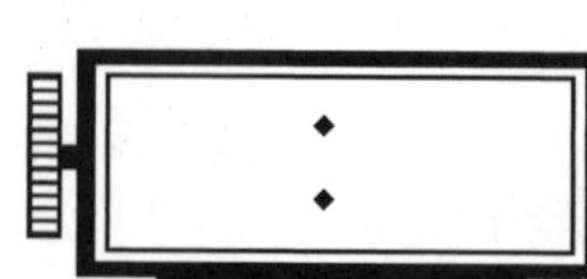

Name______________________________

Time Stories

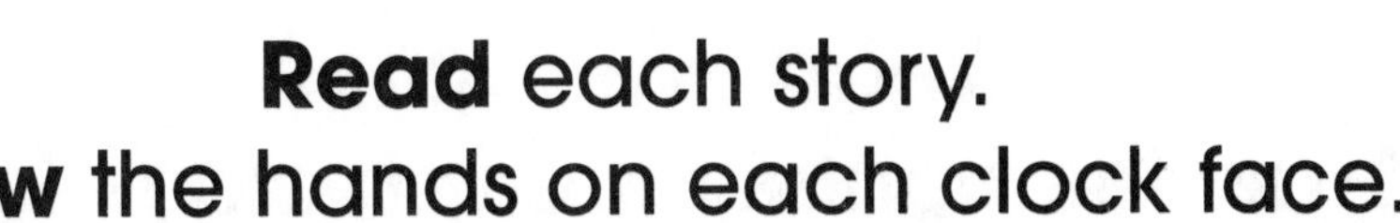
Read each story.
Draw the hands on each clock face.

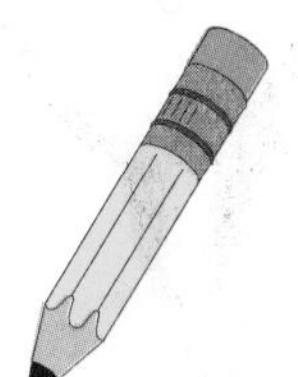

A. At **11:00**, Mouse starts to cook. Yum-Yum! Cheese soup is good.

B. At **12 o'clock**, Mouse sets the table. Uh – oh! He drops a spoon.

C. At **7:00**, Mouse reads a book. What a funny story!

D. Time for bed. It is **9 o'clock**, and Mouse is sleepy.

Name ____________________________________

Time Stories

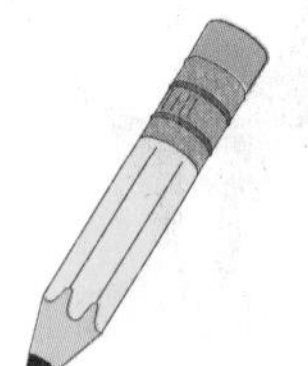

Read each story.
Draw the hands on each clock face.

A. Rabbit is hungry. It is **6 o'clock**—time for supper and some carrot stew.

B. At **8:00,** Rabbit washes the dishes. Scrub, scrub, the pot is sticky.

C. Rabbit works in his garden. It is **4 o'clock,** and he is picking lettuce.

D. At **5:00,** Rabbit makes a lettuce salad. What a tasty meal!

Name ________________________________

Time to the Half-Hour: Introduction

This clock face shows the time gone by since 8 o'clock.

Thirty minutes or **half an hour** has gone by.

There are 3 ways to say time to the half-hour. We say **seven thirty, thirty past seven** or **half past seven**.

Half-hour later

9:00 ________________ 9:30 ________________

30 ________ minutes past ____9____ o'clock

Half-hour later

________________ ________________

________ minutes past ________ o'clock

Name ____________________

Writing Time on the Half-Hour

Half-hour later

____________________ ____________________

__________ minutes past __________ o'clock

Half-hour later

____________________ ____________________

__________ minutes past __________ o'clock

What is your dinner time?

Circle the time you eat.

Name______________________________

Writing Time on the Half-Hour

What time is it?

half past 2

half past 9

half past 4

half past 12

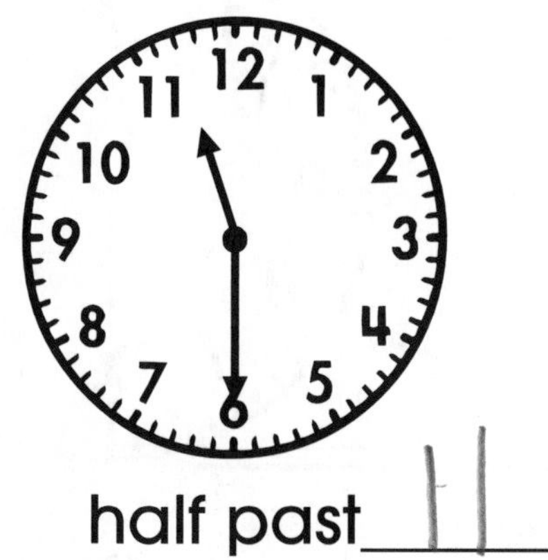

half past 11

half past 1

Name________________________________

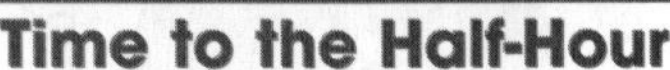

Writing Time on the Half-Hour

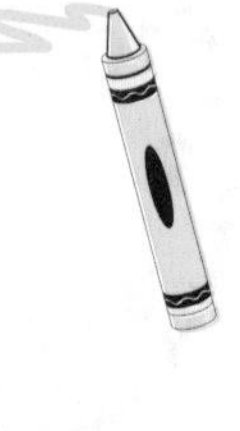

Trace the **BIG MINUTE HAND** green.
Trace the **little hour hand** yellow.
Write the time on the line.

h 5:30

6:30

11:30

2:30

Name________________________________

Writing Time on the Half-Hour

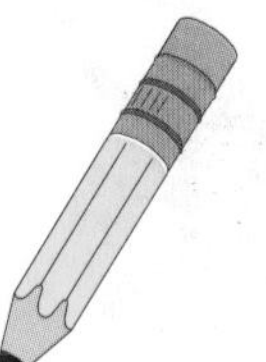

Who **"nose"** these times?
Write the time under each clock.

Color the noses.

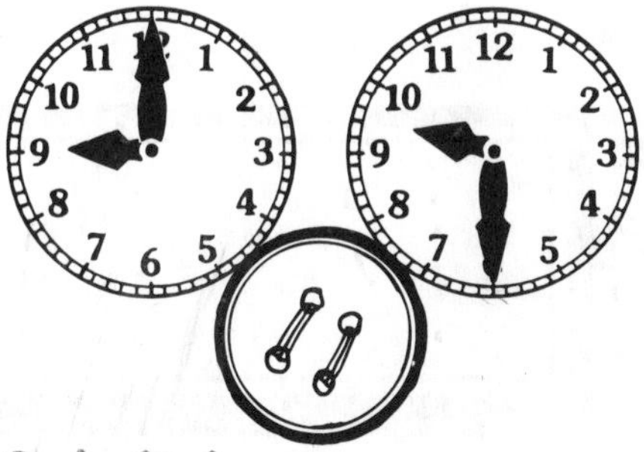

9:00 9:30 2:00 2:30

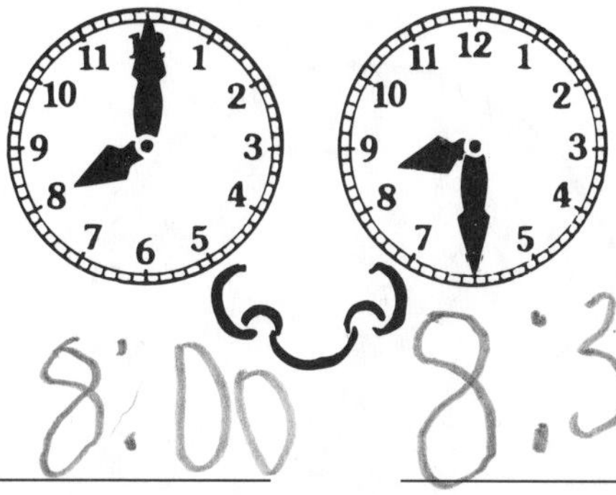

5:00 5:30 8:00 8:30

1:00 1:30 11:00 11:30

Name_______________________________________

Matching Digital and Face Clocks

These digital numbers got lost.
Put them in the right clocks on this page
and page 47.

6:30	12:30	3:30	8:30	9:30	5:30

Name______________________________

Matching Digital and Face Clocks

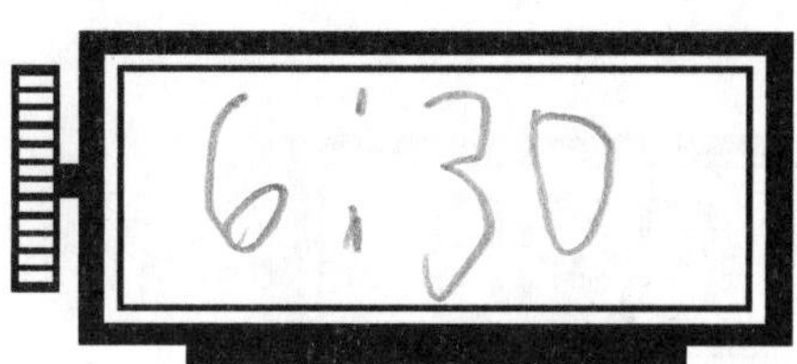

Name____________________

Drawing the Hour Hand

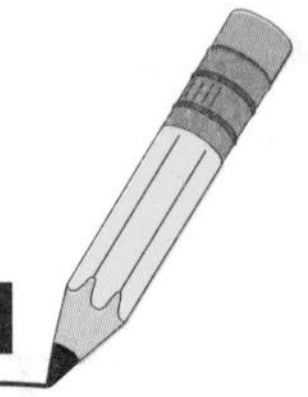

Say the time.
Draw the **little hour hand**
on each clock.

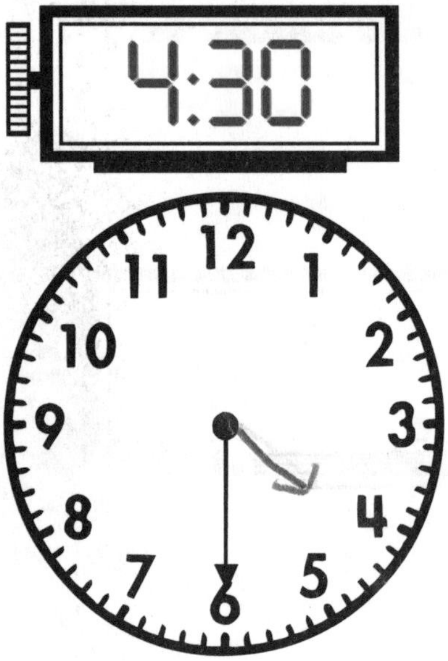

4:30

11:30

8:30

12:30

Name________________________________

Drawing the Hour Hand

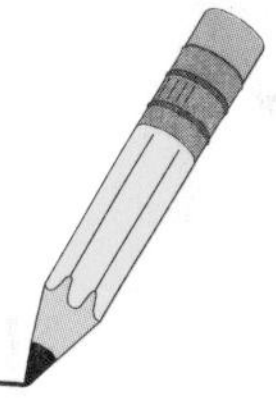

Say the time.
Draw the **little hour hand** on each clock.

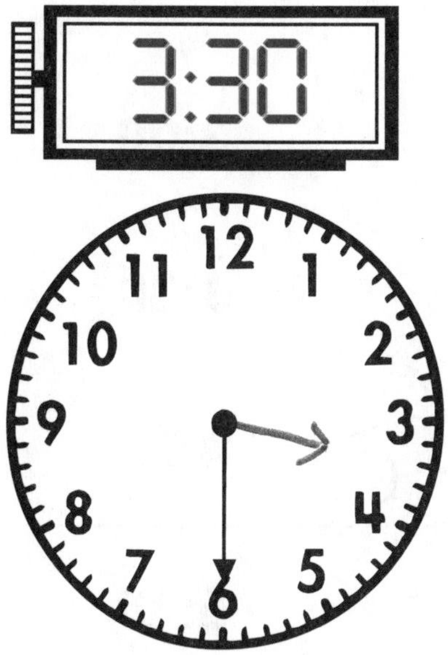

3:30

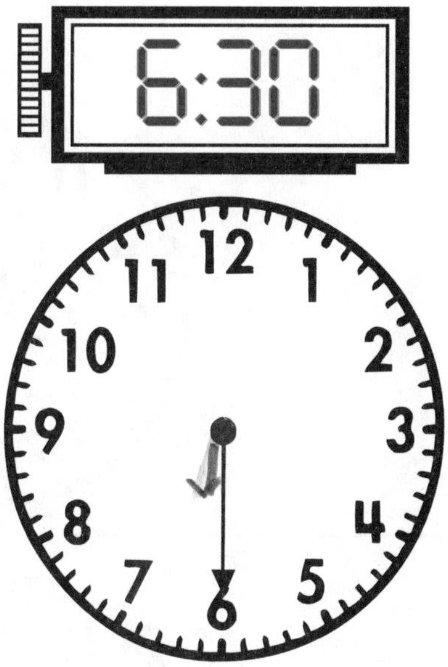

6:30

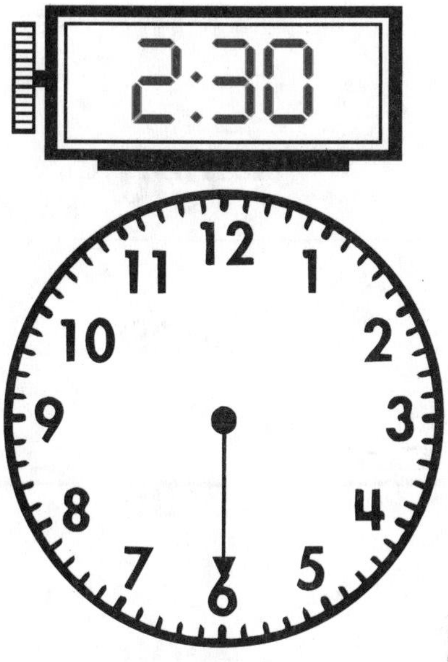

2:30

9:30

Name________________________________

Telling Time: Hour and Half-Hour

I'm mixing the **hour time** and **half-hour** time. See if I can fool you! **Draw a line** from the clock to the correct time.

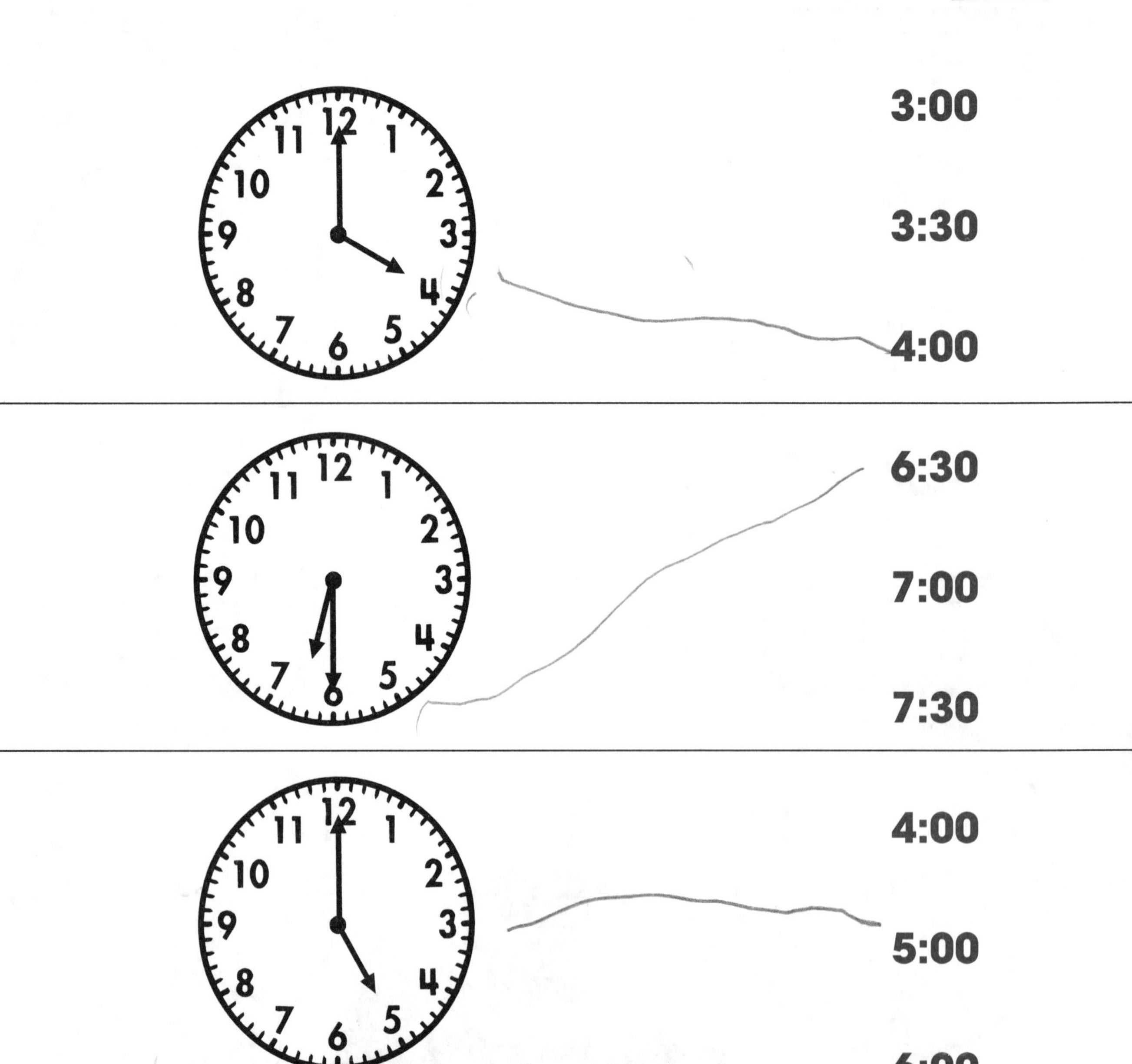

Name ______________________

Telling Time: Hour and Half-Hour

8:00

4:30

5:00

12:00

10:30

1:00

9:30

10:30

10:00

Good Work!

half past __1__

half past __9__

Name______________________________

Writing the Time: Practice

Space Time

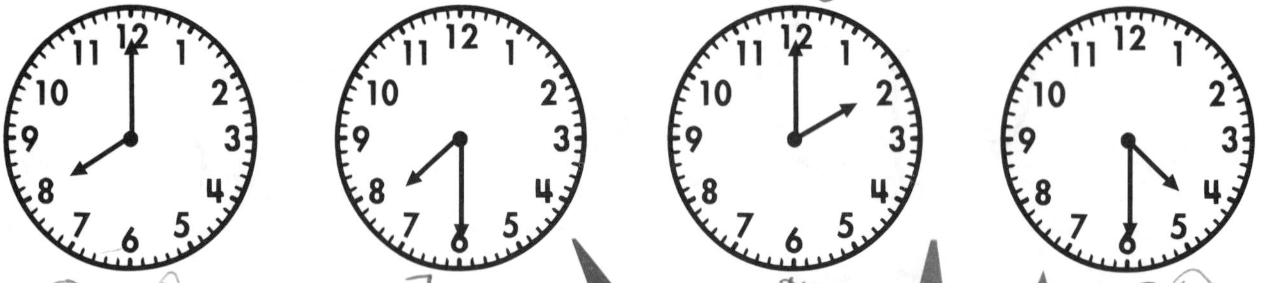

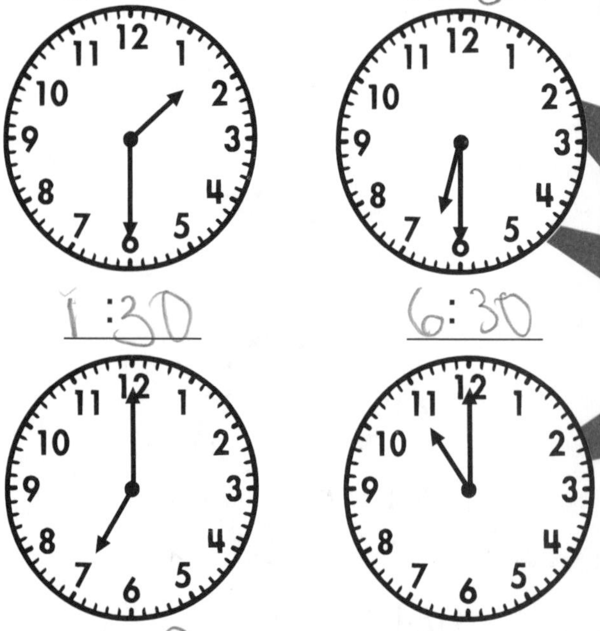

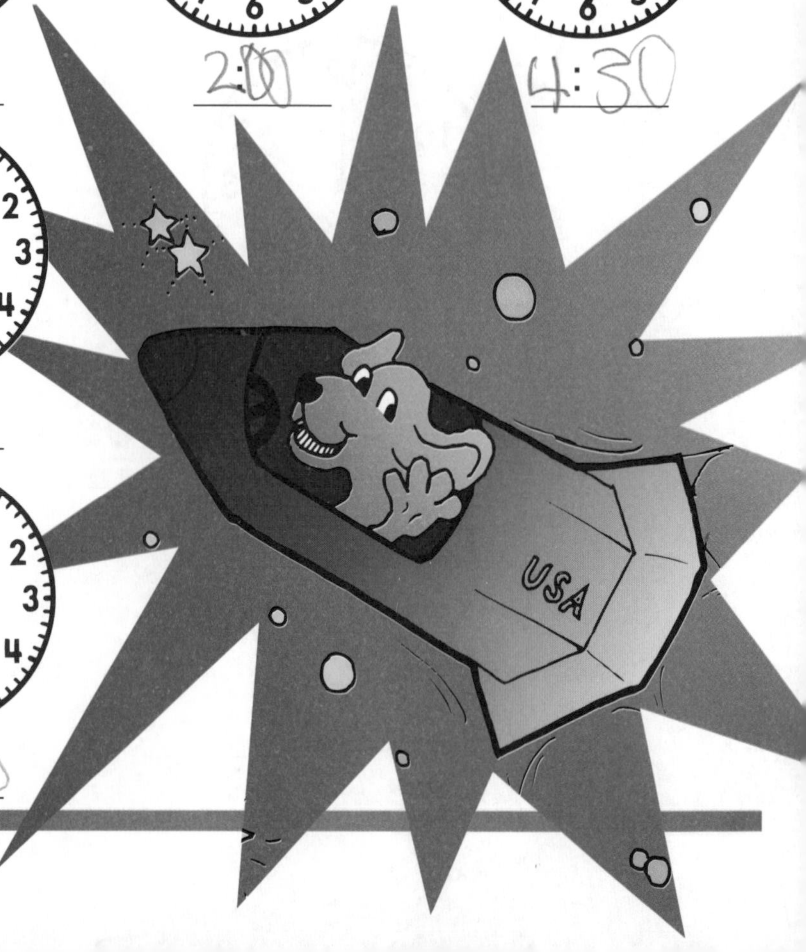

What time is it?

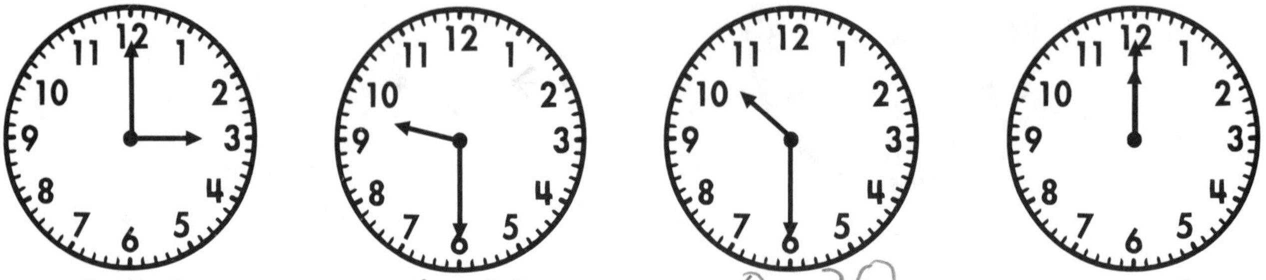

Name ______________________________

Writing the Time: Practice

Sock Clocks

Draw the hands on the sock clocks.

1:30

7:00

4:30

10:00

3:30

9:30

4:00

2:30

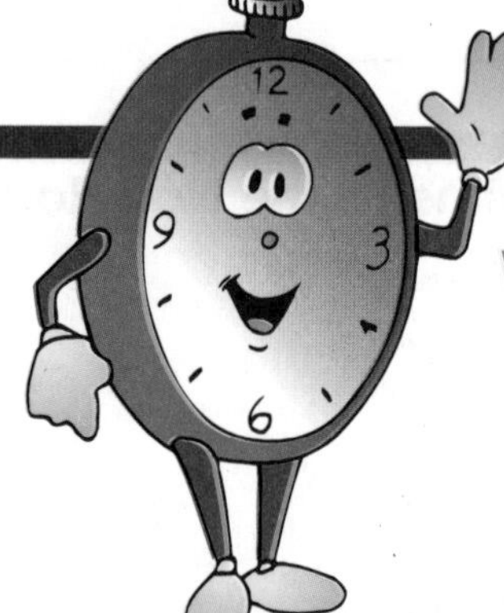

Name________________________________

Writing the Time: Practice

You Are My Sunshine

What time is it?

3:00 9:30 8:00 7:30

1:30 6:30 10:30 12:00

7:00 11:00 2:00 4:30

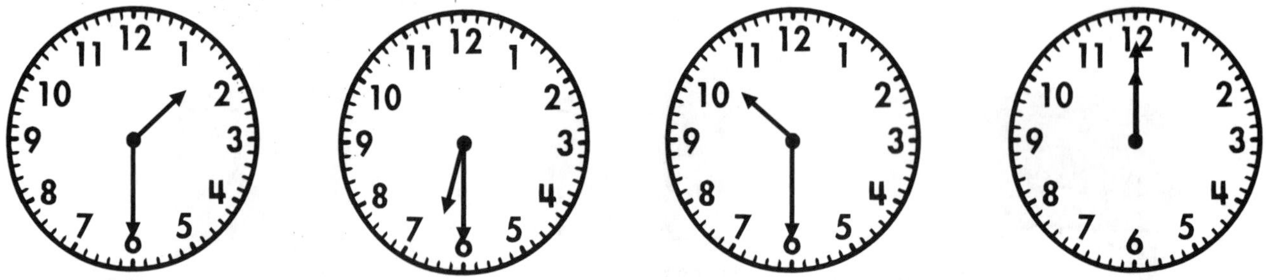

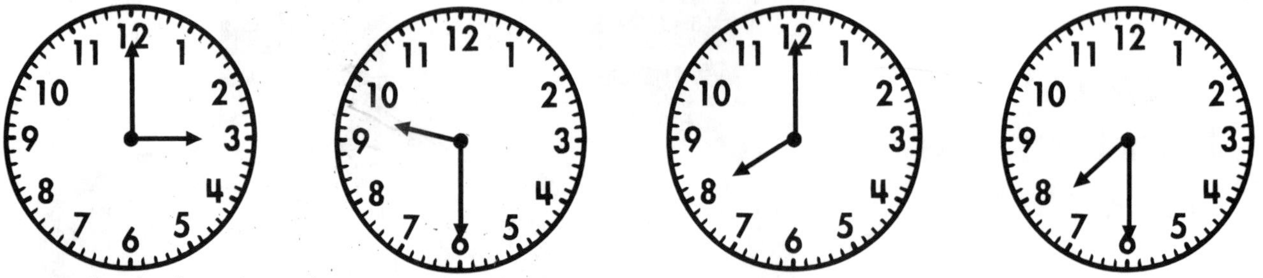

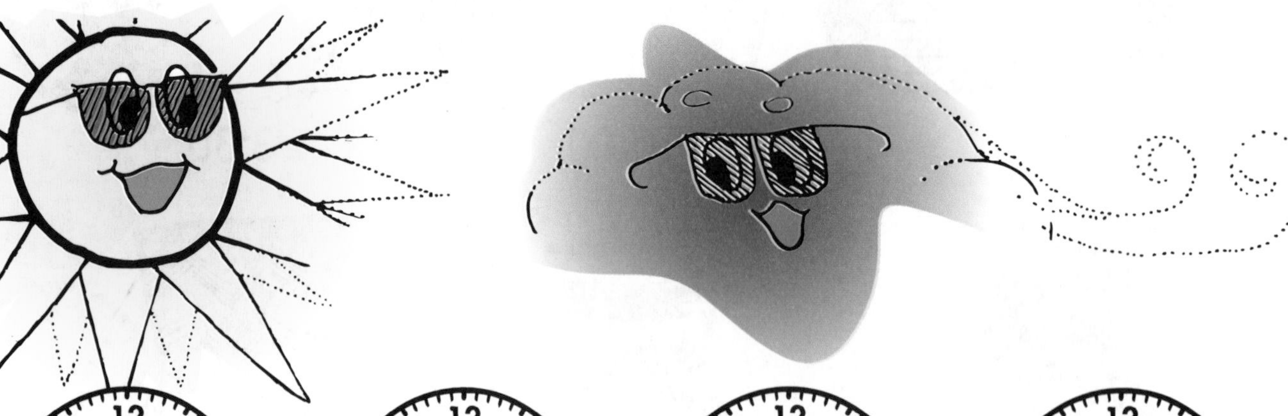

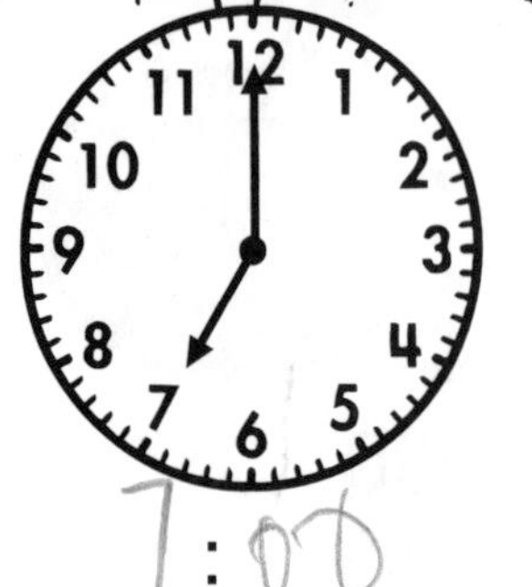

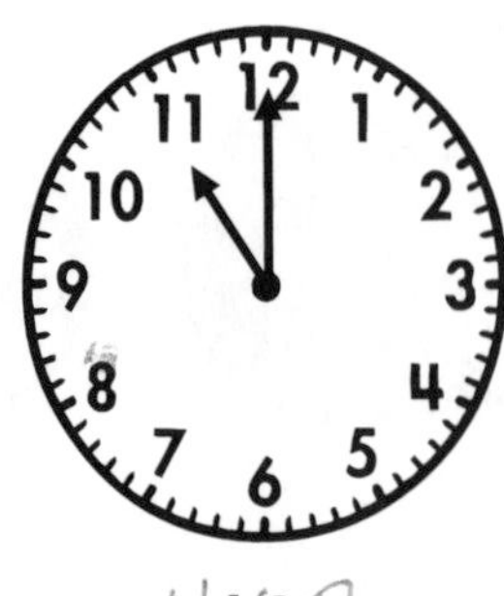

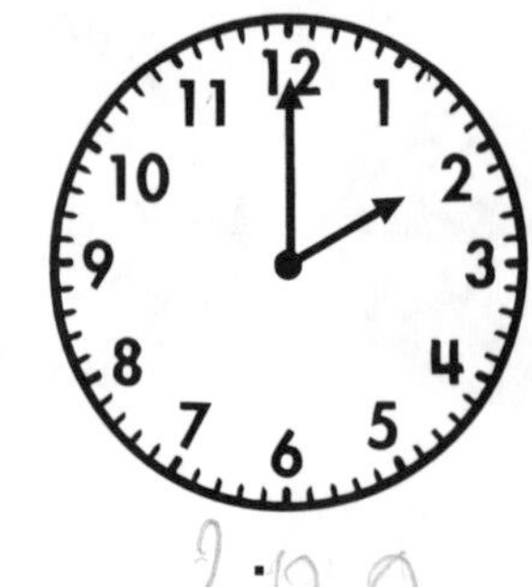

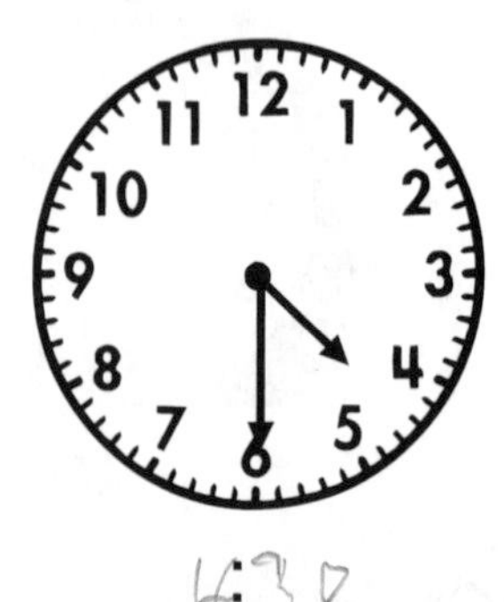

Name_______________________________

Matching Digital and Face Clocks

Time Lines

Match each clock to the correct time.

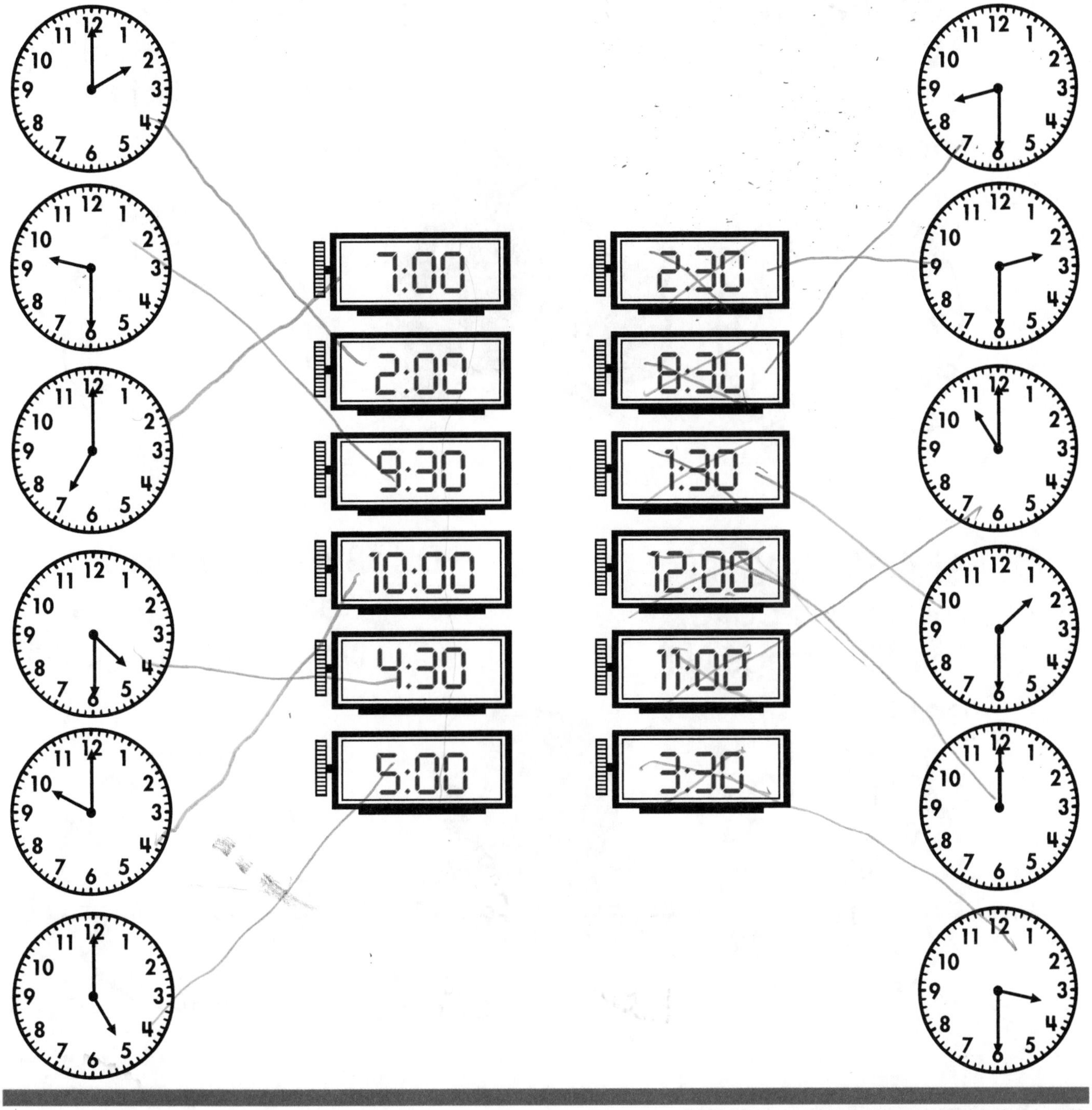

7:00

2:00

9:30

10:00

4:30

5:00

2:30

8:30

1:30

12:00

11:00

3:30

Name________________________________

Time Stories

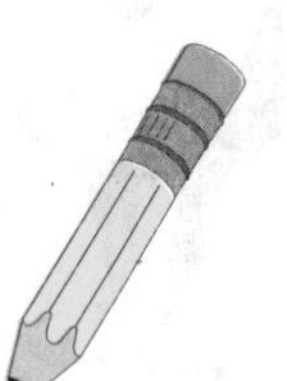

Read each story.
Draw the hands on each clock face.

A. Hop, hop. It is **10:30**, and Frog is going to the market.

B. At **11:30**, Frog heads home. She has a basket of tasty treats.

C. At **4:30**, Frog is making a cake. The little frogs will eat it.

D. By **7:30**, Frog's cake is all gone. My, that was good!

Name________________________________

Time Stories

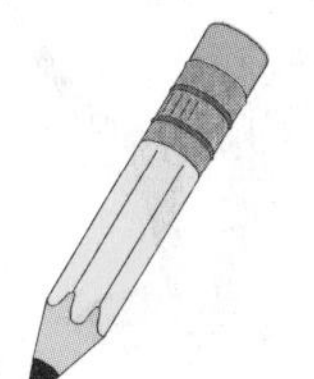

Read each story.
Draw the hands on each clock face.

A. It is **5:30**, and the sun is coming up. Bird is ready for the day.

B. At **6:30**, Bird is looking for breakfast. Watch out, worms!

C. Bird is resting after breakfast. It is **9:30** and almost time for flying practice.

D. At **12:30**, Bird naps before lunch. Flying is hard work!

Name____________________

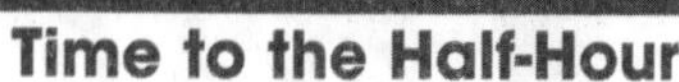

Time Lapse: Hours

Can you tell how much time has passed?

3:00 6:00

If it started snowing at **3:00** and snowed until **6:00**, it snowed three hours.

What time did the spider start spinning the web? 1:00

What time did she finish? 3:00

1:00 3:00

The spider took two hours to spin the web.

Name ______________________

Time Lapse: Hours

Dad went to the grocery store.

5 : 00 6 : 00

Dad took one hour to buy groceries.

The teacher taught math class.

1 : 00 2 : 00

Math lasted one hour.

Write how much later.

five hours

Name________________________________

Time Lapse: Hours

It is important to get home when your parents expect you!

Steve went to play baseball at **3:30.** Mom told him to be home in **2 hours.**

He should be home at _____ : _______ .

Show the time on this watch.

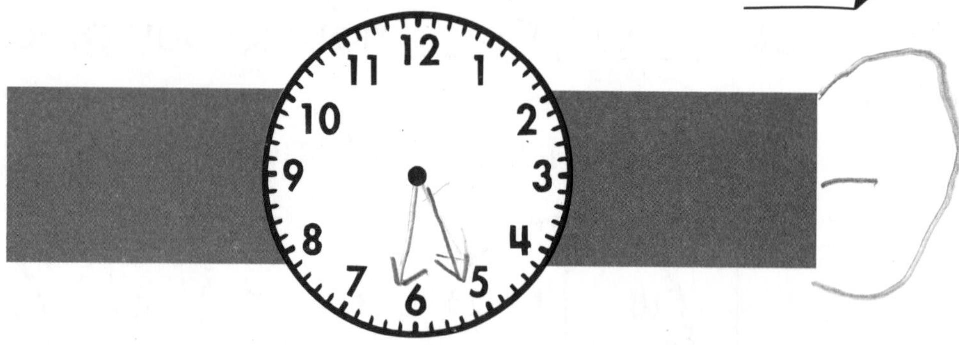

Tiffany went to Latonia's house to ride bikes at **10:00.** Dad asked her to be home in **3 hours.**

She should be home at _____ : _________.

Show the time on this watch.

Name____________________

Time Lapse: Hours

Kristen took her sister to the movies at **7:30**. Mom said she would meet them in **2 hours**.

She will meet them at __9__ : __30__.

Show the time on this clock.

Latrissa went to the library for story hour. She got there at **1:00**. She stayed **1 hour**.

Story hour should be over at __2__ : __00__.

Show the time Latrissa left for home.

Name ____________________

Drawing the Hour Hand: A Half-Hour Later

Draw the hands on each clock face.

A. At **7:00**, Bill turns on the TV.

What time is it one half-hour later?

B. At **4:00**, we all jump in the car.

What time is it one half-hour later?

C. At **12:00**, Julio and Nathan are ready to eat.

What time is it one half-hour later?

Name ____________________

Drawing the Hour Hand: A Half-Hour Later

Draw the hands on each clock face.

A. At **8:00**, it starts to rain.

What time is it one half-hour later?

B. At **11:00**, the sun comes out.

What time is it one half-hour later?

C. At **3:00**, we skip home from school.

What time is it one half-hour later?

Name________________________________

Drawing the Hour Hand: A Half-Hour Later

Draw the hands on each clock face.

A. At **6:30**, a fire engine roars down the street.

What time is it one half-hour later?

B. At **11:30**, everyone is playing in the schoolyard.

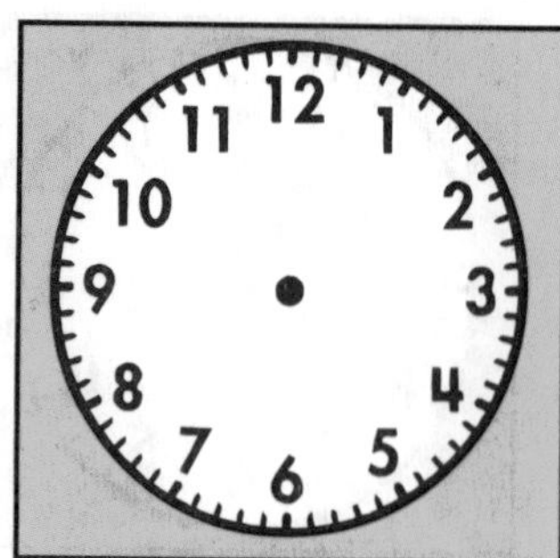

What time is it one half-hour later?

C. **At 5:30**, my dog gets out of the yard.

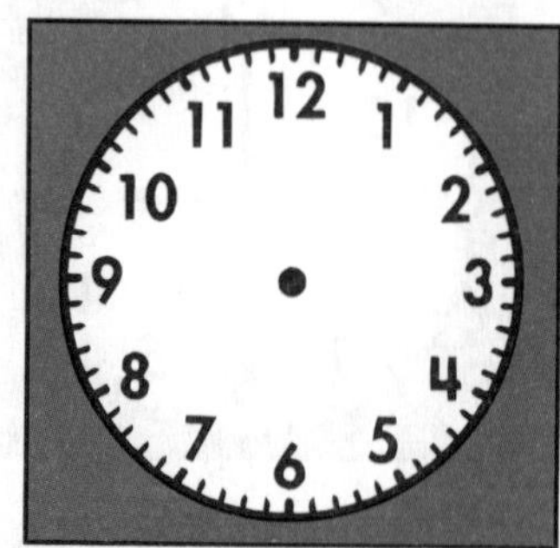

What time is it one half-hour later?

Name______________________________

Time Stories

Read each story.
Draw the hands on each clock face.

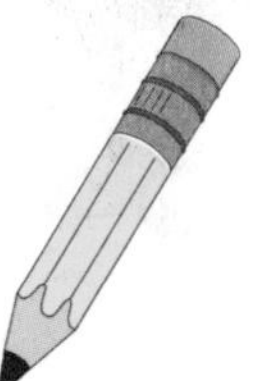

A. Tom makes a HUGE sandwich at **1:00**. He finishes the whole sandwich **one half-hour** later. What time does Tom finish the sandwich?

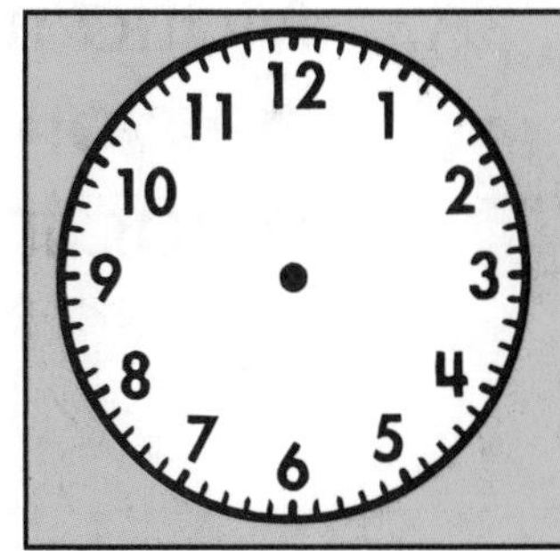

B. Tom gets home from school at **3:00**. He goes out to play **30 minutes** later. What time does Tom go out to play?

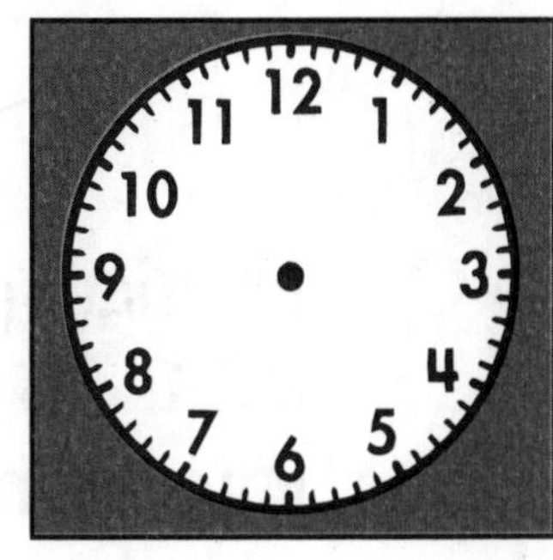

C. Tom goes to bed at **8:30**. He falls asleep **one half-hour** later. What time does Tom fall asleep?

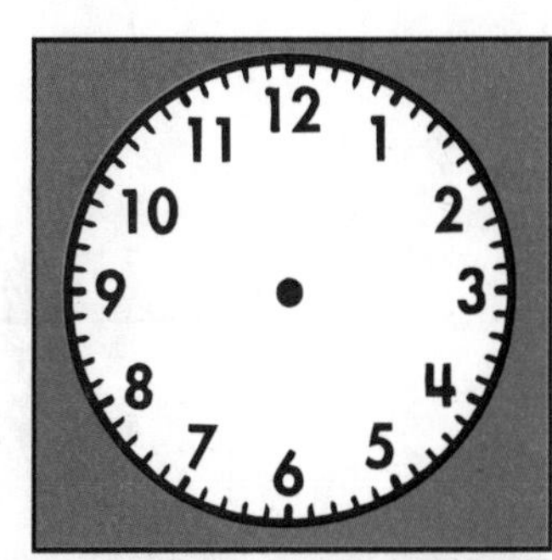

Name________________________________

Time Stories

Read each story.
Draw the hands on each clock face.

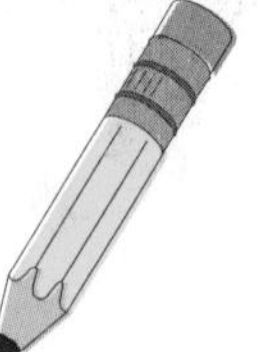

A. Maria makes a lunch at **7:00**. She gets on the bus **30 minutes** later. What time does she get on the bus?

B. Maria helps make dinner at **5:30.** Everyone eats it **one half-hour** later. What time does everyone eat?

C. Maria's family plays a game at **8:30**. They stop playing **30 minutes** later. What time do they stop playing?

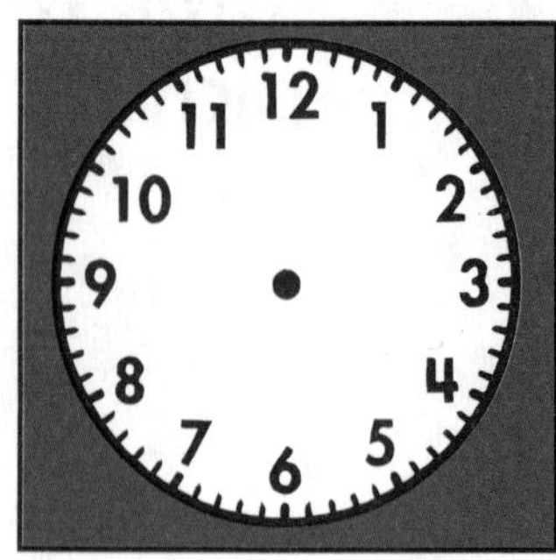

Name____

Time Stories

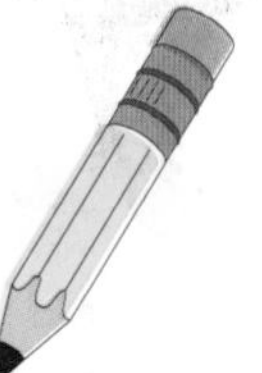

Read each story.
Draw the hands on each clock face.

A. Li goes for a walk at **10:30**. He comes back with three friends **30 minutes** later. What time does he come back with his friends?

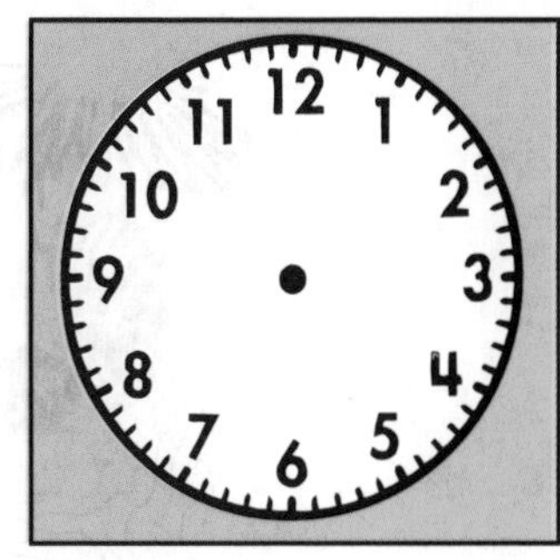

B. Li gets on his bike at **3:30**. He reaches the library **one half-hour** later. What time does he get to the library?

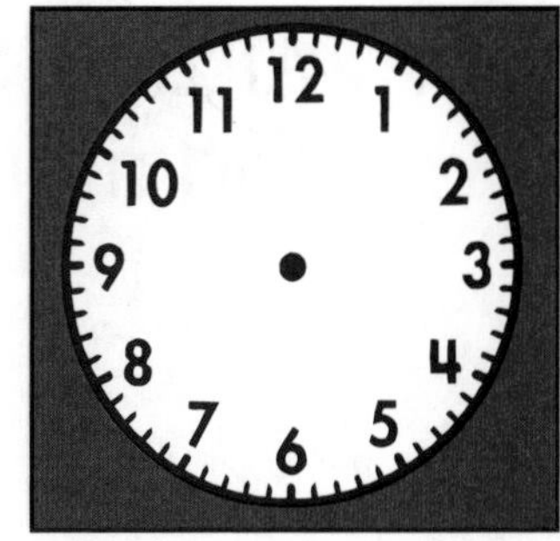

C. Li starts home at **5:00**. He gets home **30 minutes** later. What time does he get home?

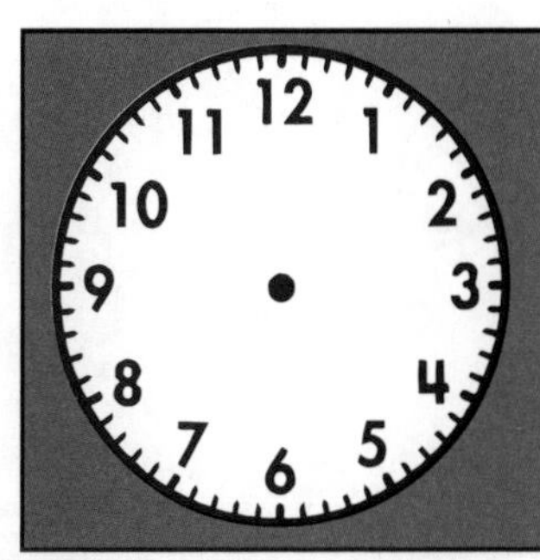

Name________________________________

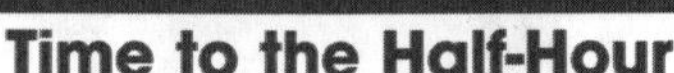

Time Two Ways

Draw the hands on each clock face.
Write the time.

A. At **1:30**, Squirrel hides seven nuts.

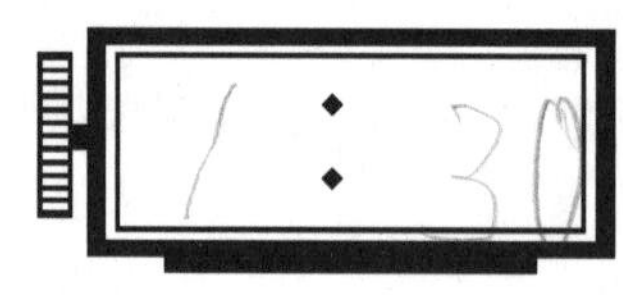

B. At **2:00**, Squirrel runs down the tree to find more nuts.

C. By **3:30**, Squirrel is ready for a long rest.

Name____

Time Two Ways

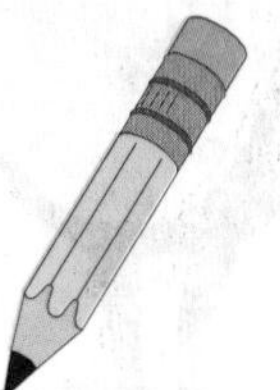

Draw the hands on each clock face.
Write the time.

A. At **5:30**, Toad hops over to visit Frog.

B. At **6:00**, Frog and Toad are sipping Fine Fly Tea.

C. At **7:30**, Toad heads home, full of tea and bug cakes.

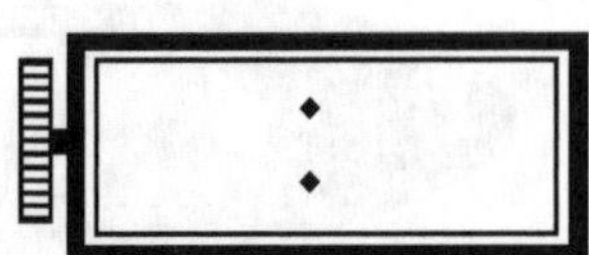

Name________________________________

Time Two Ways

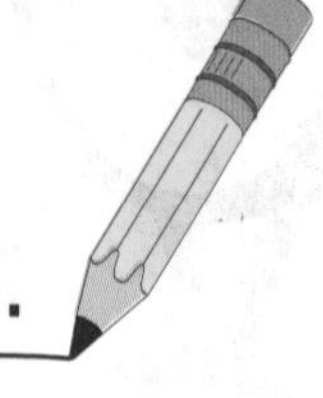

Draw the hands on each clock face.
Write the time.

A. Maria Mouse gets to the library at **11 o'clock**. She leaves the library at **11:30**.

Gets to library **Leaves the library**

B. Marcus Mouse gets to Pizza Palace at **3 o'clock**. He finishes his pizza at **3:30.**

Gets to Pizza Palace **Finishes pizza**

Name________________________________

Time Two Ways

Draw the hands on each clock face.
Write the time.

A. Tim Toad begins planting the garden at **9 o'clock**. He finishes planting at **9:30**.

Begins planting **Finishes planting**

B. Tara Toad starts roller-skating at **10 o'clock**. She stops roller-skating **30 minutes after 10 o'clock**.

Starts roller-skating **Stops roller-skating**

Name________________________________

Time Two Ways

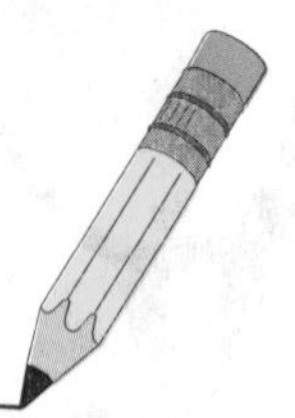

Draw the hands on each clock face.
Write the time.

A. Ricardo Raccoon starts his lunch at **12:00.** He finishes his lunch **30 minutes after 12:00.**

Starts lunch **Finishes lunch**

B. Rachel Raccoon sits down at the computer at **7:00**. She gets up from the computer a **half-hour after 7:00**.

Sits down **Gets up**

Name____________________________________

Time Stories

Read the story.
Write the time two ways.

Choose a time for everyone to eat lunch!

Bear is going on a picnic today with his brother and sister. They leave for the park at **9:00**. They get to the park at **10:00**. Bear helps carry the food to a picnic table. Then he gets out his kite. Bear flies his kite at **10:30**. Later, at ____________ , everyone has a picnic lunch!

Put the story in order by writing what time Bear did each thing.

A. **Leave for the park**

B. **Get to the park**

C. **Fly kite**

D. **Eat lunch**

Name________________________________

Time Stories

Read the story.
Write the time two ways.
Choose a time for everyone to go home!

Pig wakes up at **7:00**. Pig's grandmother is taking her to the zoo today! They get to the zoo at **10:30**. They walk and walk. They stop to eat at **12:30**. They walk some more. Pig and her grandmother don't get home until ____________ . They had a wonderful day!

Put the story in order by writing what time Pig did each thing.

A. ________________

B. ________________

C. ________________

D. ________________

Name ____________________

Time Stories

Read the story.
Write the time two ways.
Choose a time for everyone to wake up!

It's a hot summer day. Frog and Turtle begin to walk to the lake at **11:00**. They jump into the cold water at **12:30**. They swim and dive. Then they enjoy lunch at **1:30**. They fall asleep after lunch. Later, at ________ , Frog and Turtle wake up. They hurry home!

Put the story in order by writing what time Frog and Turtle did each thing.

A. ____________________

B. ____________________

C. ____________________

D. ____________________

Name________________________________

Time Puzzles

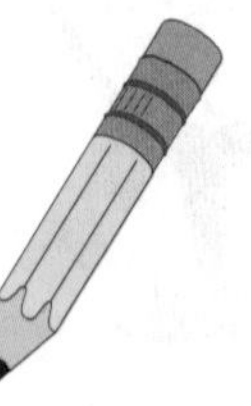

Read each "time clue."
Draw the hands on each clock.
Write the time.

A. It's dark outside.
Everyone is asleep.

B. Ring, ring!
Time to get up.

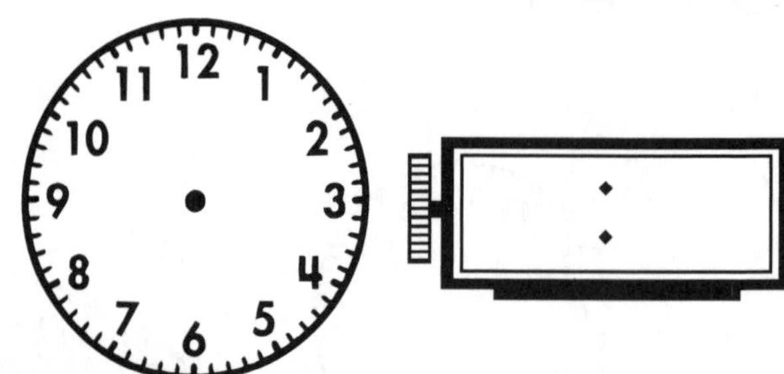

C. Here comes the school bus.
Run, so you won't
be late!

D. I'm hungry! Soon it will
be time for lunch.

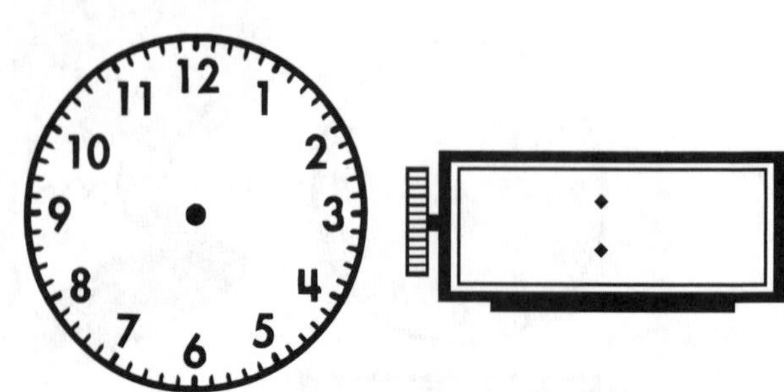

Name____________________

Time Puzzles

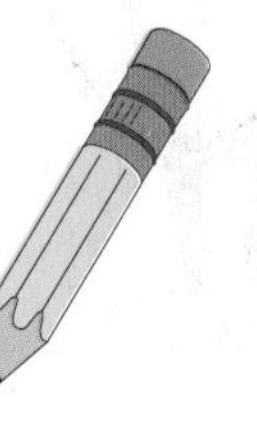

Read each "time clue."
Draw the hands on each clock.
Write the time.

A. School is out!
We're going home.

B. Here comes the mail!
I hope I get a letter.

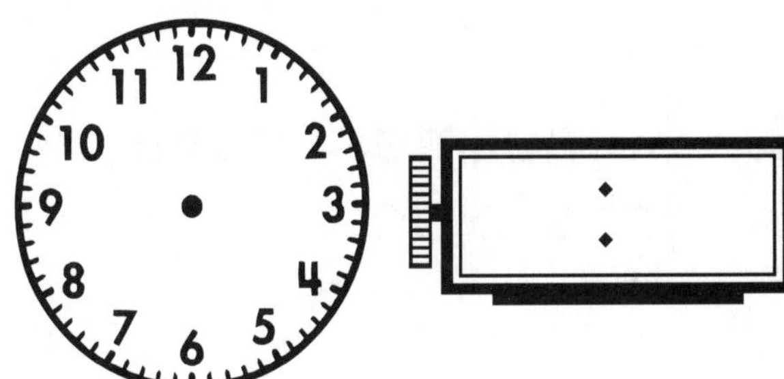

C. It's getting dark.
Time to go inside.

D. It's light tonight.
Look, a big full moon!

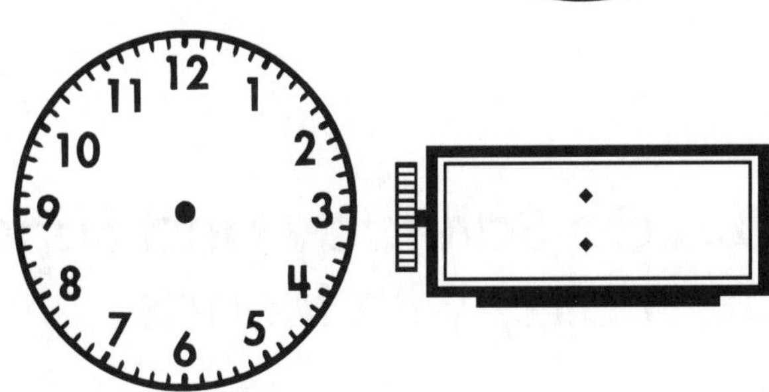

Name________________________________

Time Puzzles

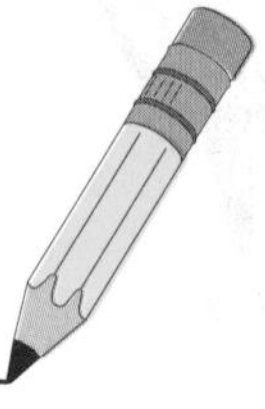

Read each "time clue."
Draw the hands on each clock.
Write the time.

A. Sometimes I have homework to do.

B. Sometimes I have jobs to do.

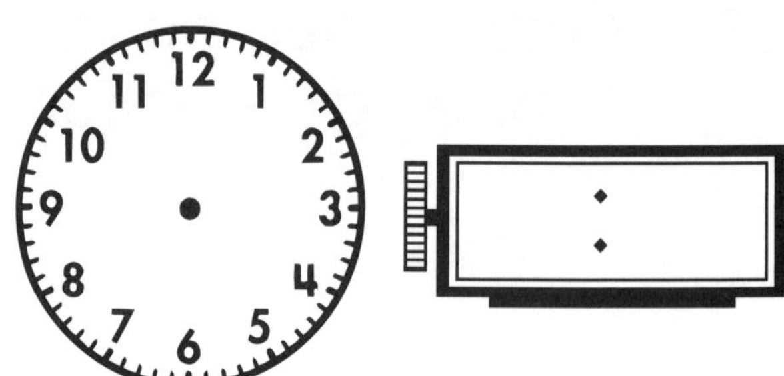

C. The best time is when I can do just what I want to do.

D. On Saturday and Sunday, I play with friends.

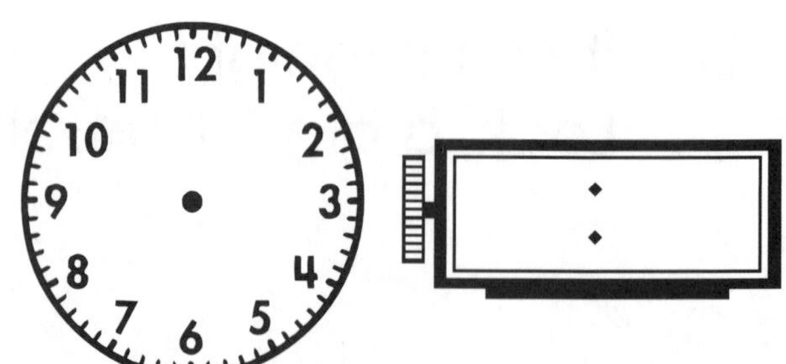

Name ____________________________

Time to the Quarter-Hour: Introduction

Each **hour** has **60** minutes.
An **hour** has **4 quarter-hours**.
A **quarter-hour** is **15 minutes**.

This clock face shows a quarter of an hour.

From the **12** to the **3** is **15 minutes.**

From the 12 to the 3 is 15 minutes.

___15___ minutes after ___8___ o'clock

is ___8:15___

Name________________________________

Telling Time

Each **hour** has **4 quarter-hours.**
A **quarter-hour** is **15 minutes.**

Write the times.

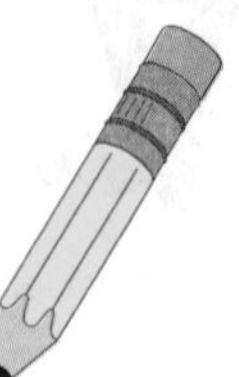

One Quarter-Hour later

9:00 ____________ 9:15 ____________

15 ______ minutes past ______ 9 ______ o'clock

One Quarter-Hour later

____________ ____________

__________ minutes past ______________ o'clock

Name________________________

Telling Time

Draw the hands. Write the times.

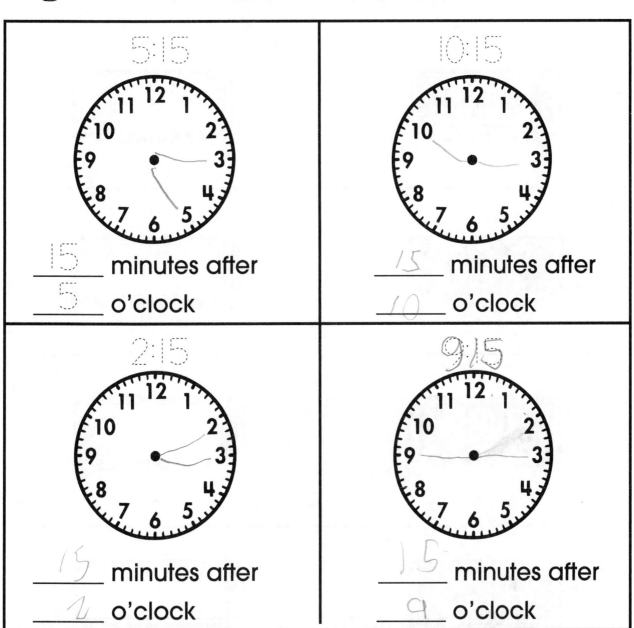

5:15 15 minutes after 5 o'clock	10:15 15 minutes after 10 o'clock
2:15 15 minutes after 2 o'clock	9:15 15 minutes after 9 o'clock

Name____________________

Digital Clocks

Your **digital clock** has quarter-hours, too!
It also shows **15 minutes**.

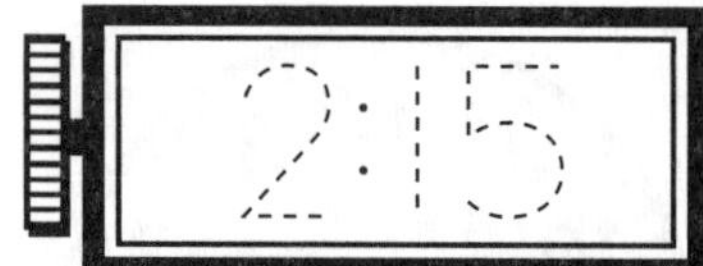

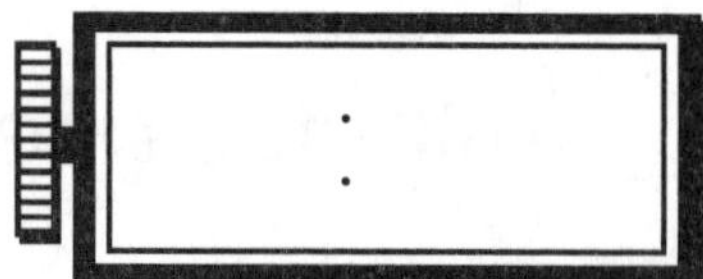

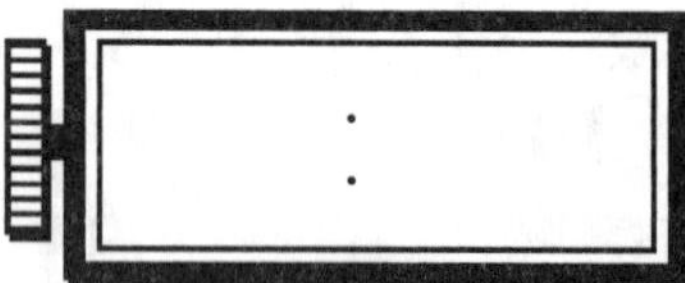

Name________________________________

Digital Clocks

Circle the correct digital time.

15 minutes past 6 is my dinner time.

6:15

Draw the minute hand with an **orange** crayon.

Draw the hour hand with a **purple** crayon.

_____ minutes after _____ o'clock

Name______________________________

Telling Time

Count the numbers by 5's
to see how many minutes have passed.

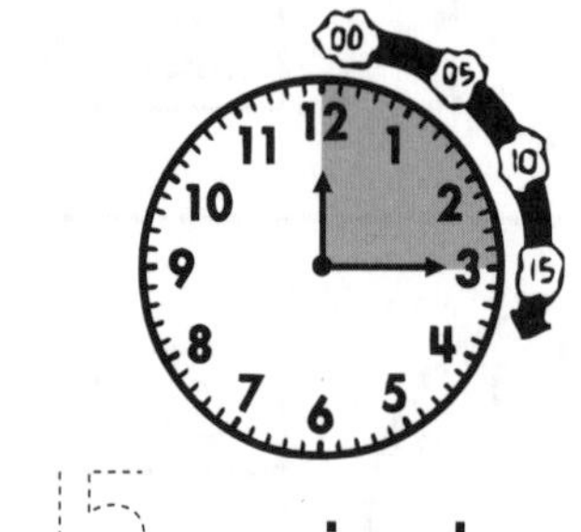

15 minutes

after 12

30 minutes

after 12

45 minutes

after 12

Name ____________________________________

Telling Time

Can you speak **"clock time?"**

1. **"Quarter after"** means 15 minutes after the hour.
2. **"Half past"** means 30 minutes after the hour.
3. **"Quarter to"** means 15 minutes until the next hour.

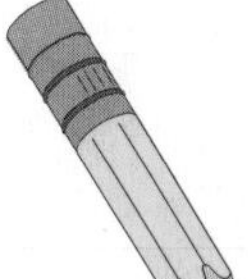

Write the quarter-hours from this time.

___8___ o'clock

quarter past ________

half past ________

quarter to ________

next hour: ______ o'clock

Name________________________________

Telling Time

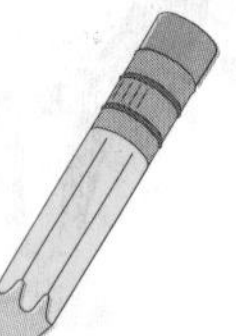

Write the time on the digital clocks.

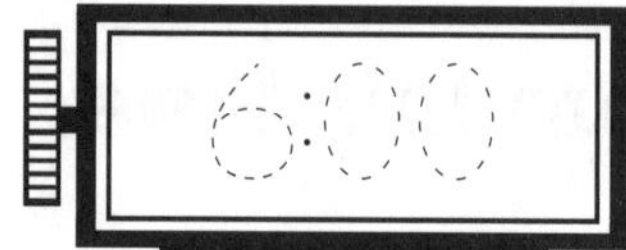

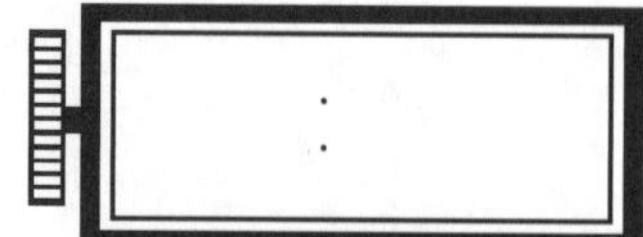

Name________________________________

Telling Time

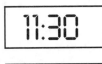

Circle the time.

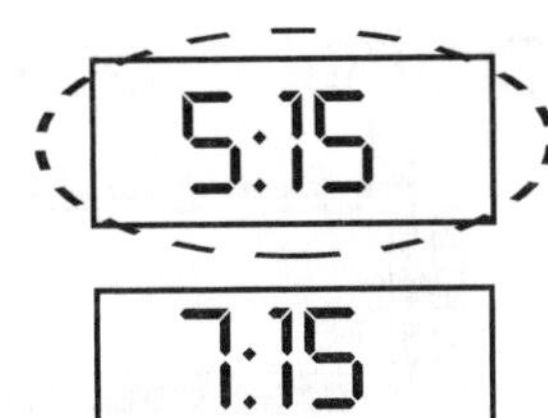

7:15

11:30

10:45

12:45

9:45

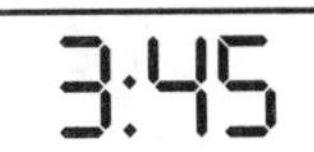

7:30

6:45

10:00

6:15

6:45

10:30

10:45

4:45

4:15

This pie bakes until a **quarter past 4.**

Name ____________________

Telling Time

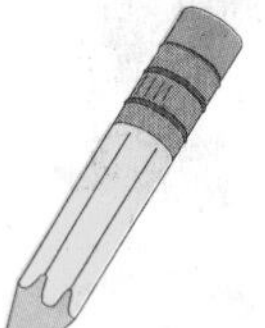

Write the time on the digital clocks.

__45__ minutes after

__3__ o'clock

______ minutes after

______ o'clock

______ minutes after

______ o'clock

______ minutes after

______ o'clock

Name________________________

Time Two Ways

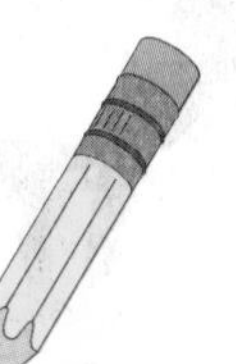

Draw the hands on each clock face.
Write the time.

A. Marta **begins** writing a letter **at 3:30.**
She **stops 30 minutes later.**

Stops

:

B. Arnold **begins** drying dishes **at 8:00.**
He **stops 15 minutes later.**

Begins

Stops

:

C. Write your own time story.

Begins

:

Stops

:

Name________________________________

Time Two Ways

Draw the hands on each clock face.
Write the time.

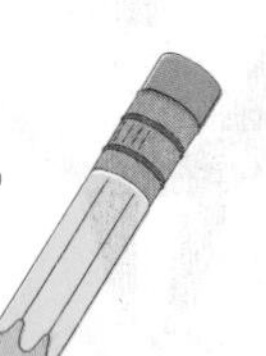

A. Darius **begins** throwing balls for the dog **at 5:00.**
He **stops 15 minutes later.**

Begins

:

Stops

:

B. Olga **begins** playing frisbee **at 4:15.**
She **stops 15 minutes later.**

Begins

:

Stops

:

C. Write your own story.

____

____

____

Begins

:

Stops

:

Name________________________________

Time Two Ways

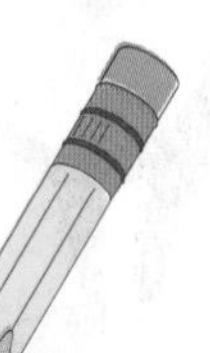

Draw the hands on each clock face.
Write the times.

A. Alberto **begins** working in the yard **at 10:00**.
He **stops 45 minutes later**.

Begins

[:]

Stops

[:]

B. Darlene **begins** playing catch **at 2:30**.
She **stops 15 minutes later.**

Begins

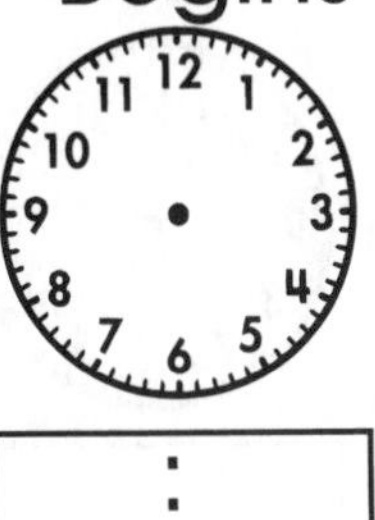

[:]

Stops

[:]

C. Write your own story.

____

____

____

Begins [:]

Stops [:]

Name________________________________

Time Two Ways

Draw the hands on each clock face.

Write the times.

A. Lucia **begins** practicing for the play **at 3:00.** She **stops 45 minutes later.**

Begins

[:]

Stops

[:]

B. Ann **begins** sorting her baseball cards **at 7:30.** She **stops 15 minutes later.**

Begins

[:]

Stops

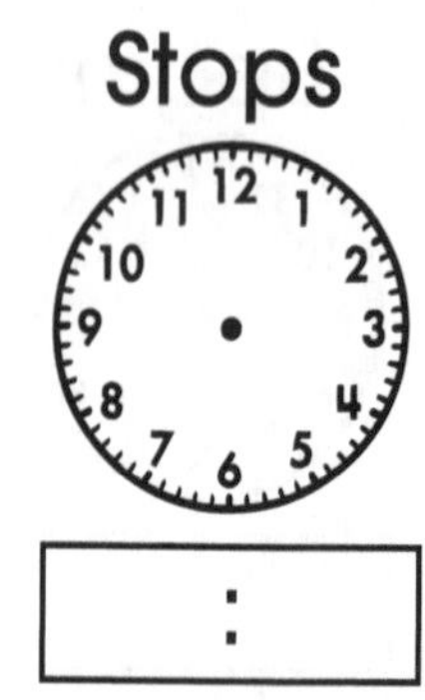

[:]

C. **Solve this time puzzle.**

When did Ray begin biking?

Ray biked **for 30 minutes.**

He stopped biking **at 5:30.**

Began

[:]

Stopped

[:]

Name________________________________

Time Two Ways

Draw the hands on each clock face.

Write the times.

A. Jake **begins** playing a game **at 1:30.**
He **stops 45 minutes later.**

Begins

[:]

Stops

[:]

B. Nicole **begins** swim practice **at 4:45.**
She **stops 15 minutes later.**

Begins

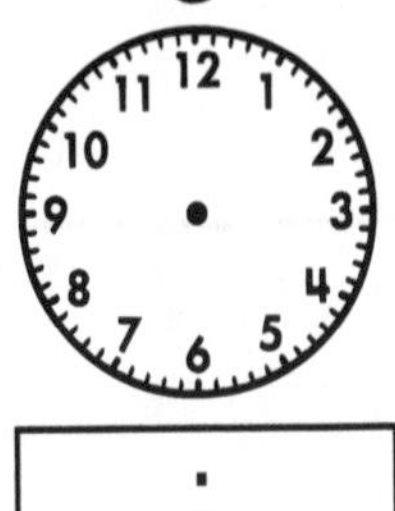

[:]

Stops

[:]

C. **Solve this time puzzle.**
When did Jill begin working in the recycling center? Jill worked in the recycling center **for 45 minutes**. She stopped working **at 7:45.**

Began

[:]

Stopped

[:]

Name______________________________

Time to the Minute Intervals: Introduction

Each number on the clock face **stands for 5 minutes.**

Count by 5's beginning at 12
Write the numbers here:

00 05 10 15 20 25

It is 25 minutes after 8 o'clock. **It is written 8:25.**

Count by 5's.

00 ____ ____ ____ ____ ____ ____ ____

It is ____ minutes after ____ o'clock.

____ : ____

Name______________________________

Time to the Minute Intervals: Introduction

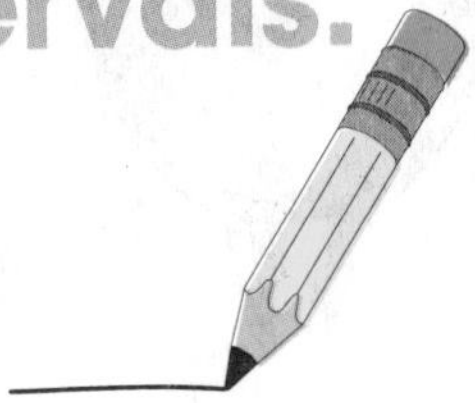

Write the time both ways.

00 _____ _____

_____ minutes after _____ o'clock

_____ : ________

---

00 _____ ______ ______ ______

_____ minutes after _____ o'clock

_____ : ________

---

00 _____ ______ ______ _______ ______ ______

______ _______

_____ minutes after _____ o'clock

_____ : ________

---

00 _____ ______ ______ ______ ______ ______

______ ______ ______ ______ ______

_____ minutes after _____ o'clock

_____ : ________

Circle the clocks with times **between 3 o'clock and 9 o'clock.**

Name________________________________

Telling Time by 5 Minutes

(Use with page 97)

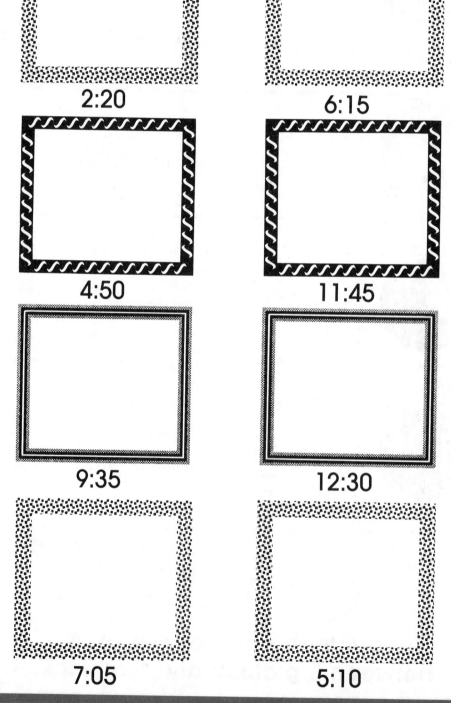

2:20

6:15

4:50

11:45

9:35

12:30

7:05

5:10

Name________________________________

Telling Time by 5 Minutes

These clock faces got lost from their clocks.
Can you help put them together again?

Read the time on each clock face.
Find the clock on page 96 with the correct time.
Cut out the face and glue it on the clock.

This page left blank for cutting lesson on reverse side.

Name ______________________________

Drawing the Minute Hand

This clock lost its minute hand!
Can you help it?

Read the time.
Draw the minute hand with a pencil.
Color over it with a **red** crayon.

2:05

___5___ minutes after ___2___ o'clock

Name______________________________

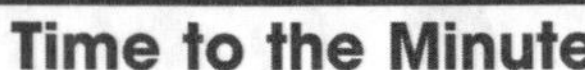

Drawing the Minute Hand

Draw and color the minute hand.

12:25

11:15

5:30

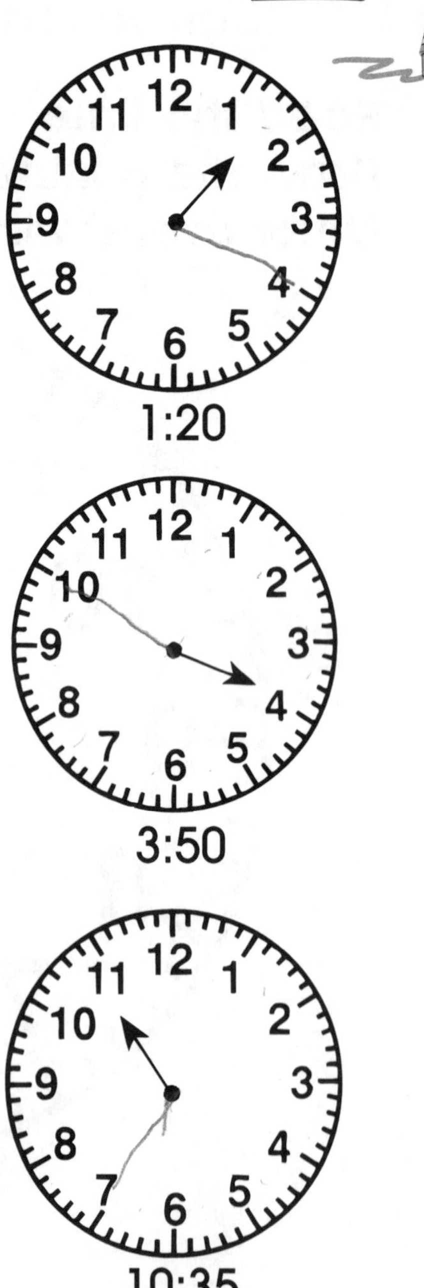

1:20

3:50

10:35

Name ______________________

Drawing the Minute Hand

Fish Time

Draw the hands on these fish clocks.

7:45

8:05

11:15

3:20

5:55

1:50

12:10

10:25

4:40

Name________________________________

Drawing the Minute Hand

Cartoon Time!
Draw the clock hands to show the time you watch these cartoons.

Space Bunny
7:35

Car Wars
8:45

The Snuffs
5:15

Fun Runner
9:00

Scare Bears
2:40

Magic Elf
11:30

Tummy Bears
3:20

Monster Time
12:10

Sunny Funnies
1:05

What is your favorite cartoon? ______________________

What time does it come on? ______________________

Name ____________________________________

Digital Clocks

Can you read a digital clock?
First read the hour.
Then read the minutes.

This clock is read **four twenty**
or twenty minutes past 4 o'clock.

Match the digital and face clocks.

Name____________________

Digital Clocks

Circle the words to match the times.

five twenty  five fifty

six twenty-five  six thirty-five

seven ten  seven twenty

one fifty-five  eleven fifty-five

Name________________________________

Matching Digital and Face Clocks

Clock Tower Times

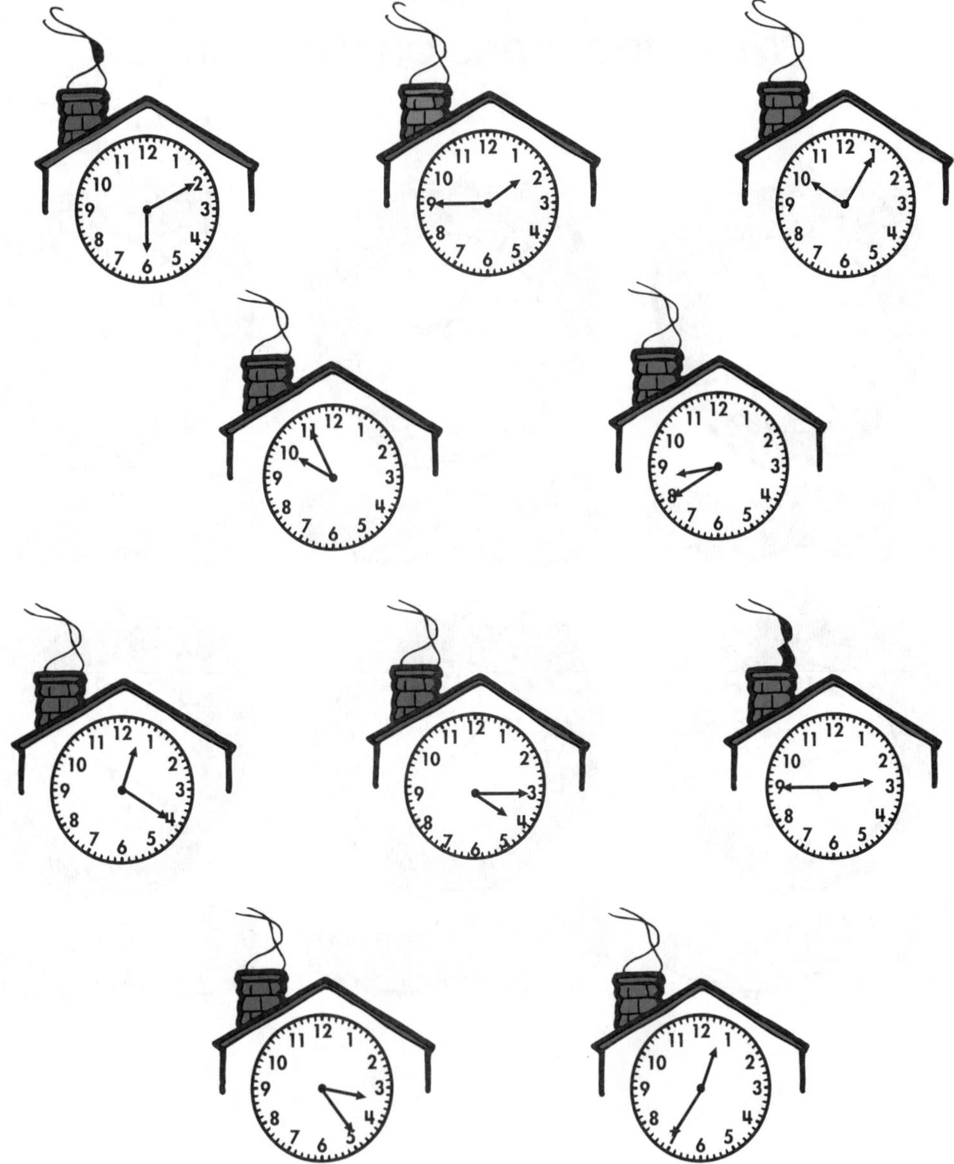

Cut out and glue under the correct clock.

12:35	8:40	4:15	9:55	10:05
6:10	1:45	12:20	2:45	3:25

Name______________________________

Writing the Time

Apple Time

Write the times on the worms.

Name________________________________

Writing the Time

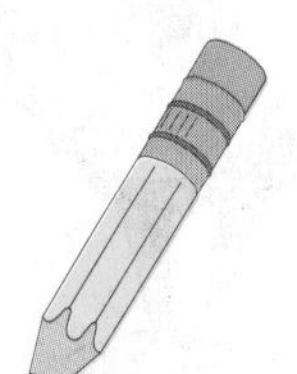

Turtle Time

What time is it?

____

____

____

____

____

____

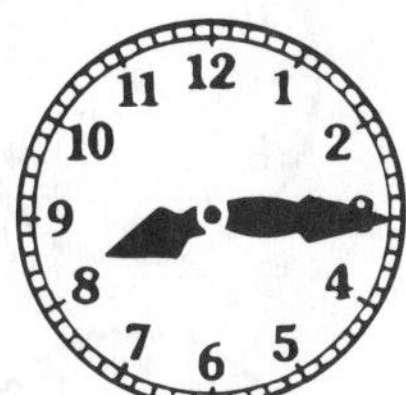

____

____

____

____

____

Name______________________________

Drawing Clock Hands

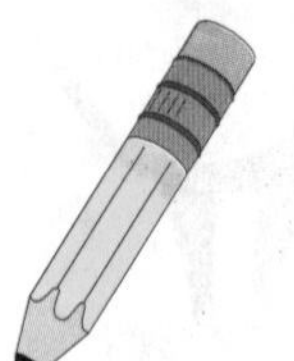

As Easy as 1, 2, 3!
Draw the hands. **Write** the time.

Three thirty

Five forty-five

Eleven twenty

Eight ten

Two fifty-five

Nine forty

Name____________________

Time Two Ways

Draw the hands on each clock face.
Write the time.

A. 30 minutes after 6:00

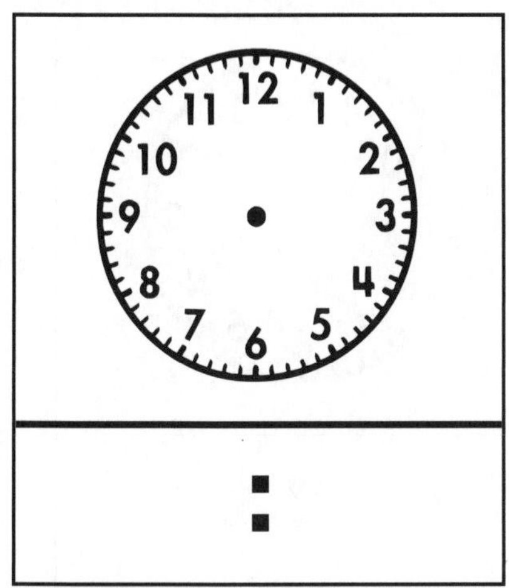

B. 20 minutes before 6:00

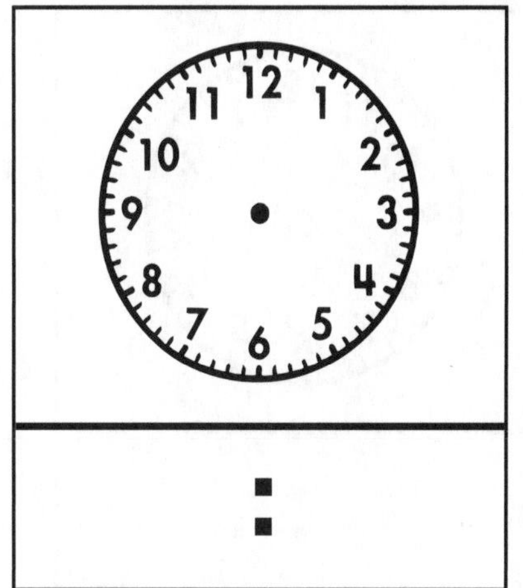

C. Exactly 6 o'clock

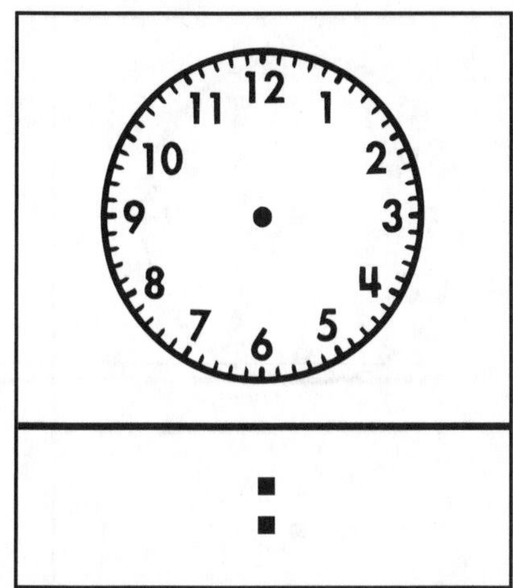

D. 20 minutes after 6:00

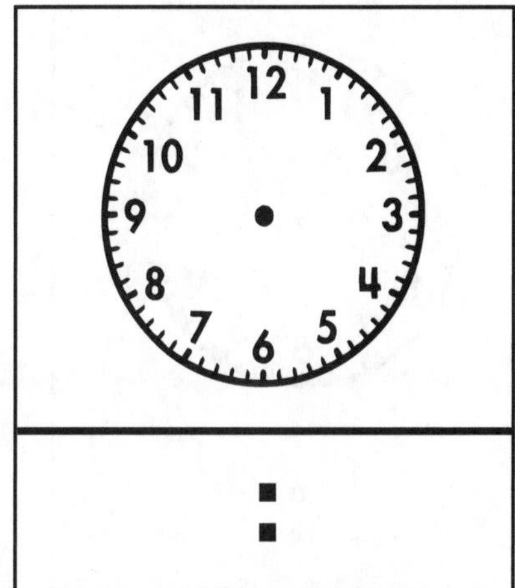

Name________________________________

Time Two Ways

Draw the hands on each clock face.
Write the time.

A. Exactly noon or midnight

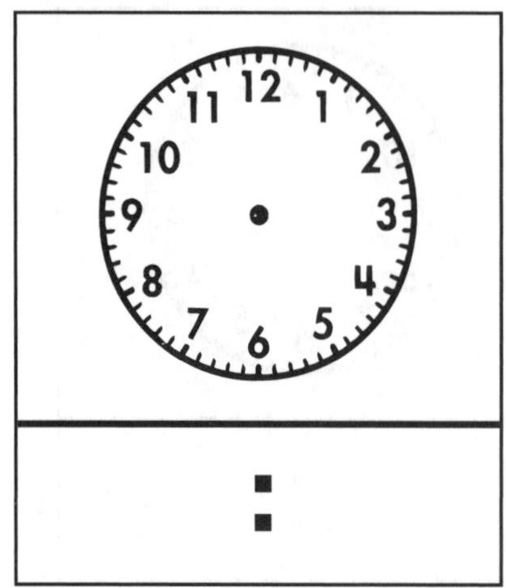

B. Quarter past 12:00

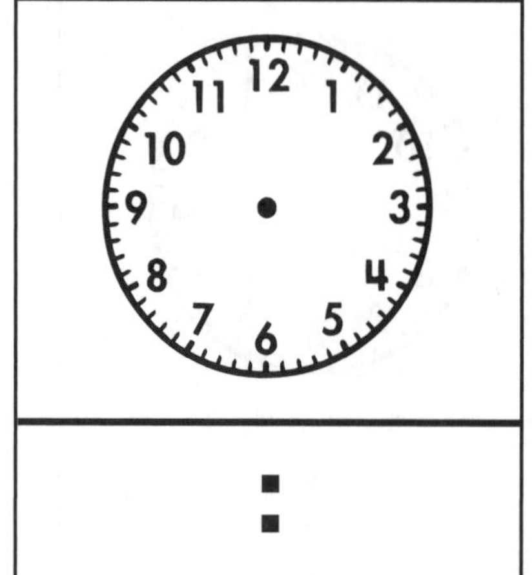

C. 15 minutes before 12:00

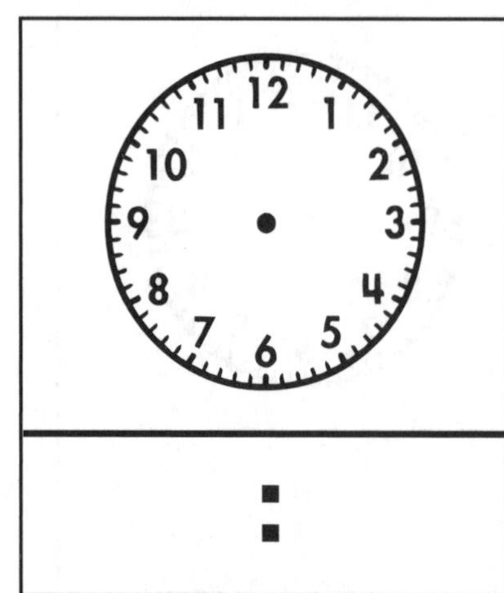

D. Half past 12:00

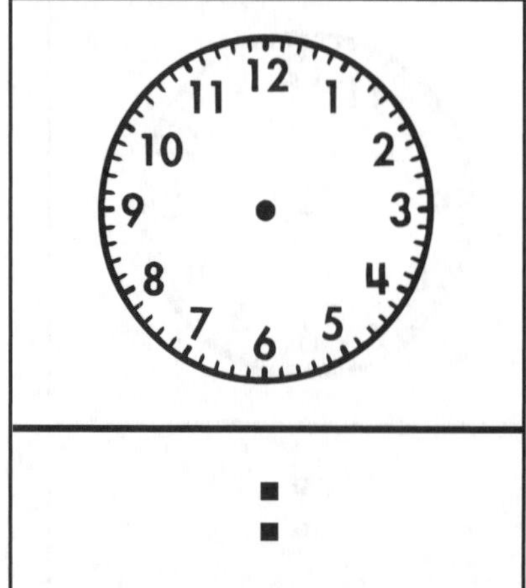

Name_______________________________

Time Two Ways

Draw the hands on each clock face.
Write the time.

A. 2 hours past midnight

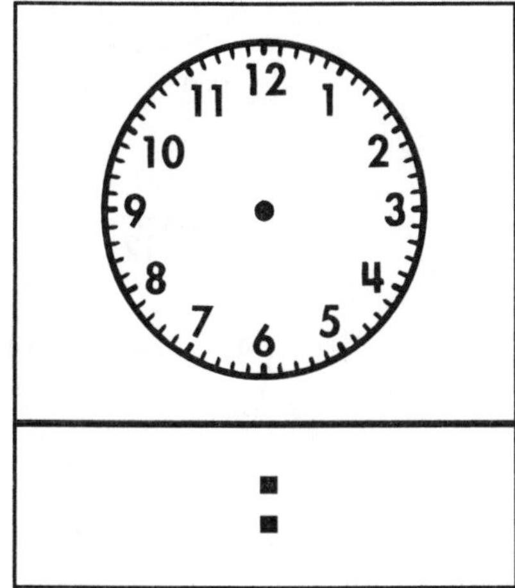

B. 10 minutes after 2:00

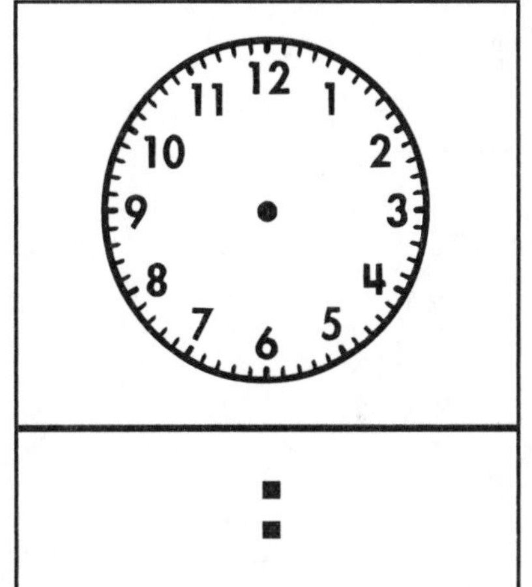

C. 45 minutes after 2:00

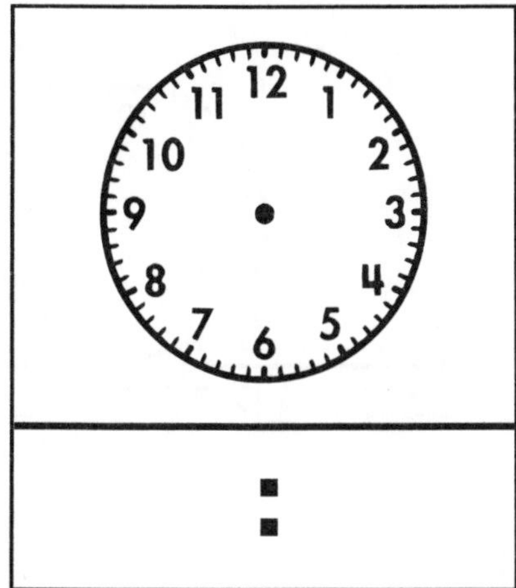

D. 50 minutes before 3:00

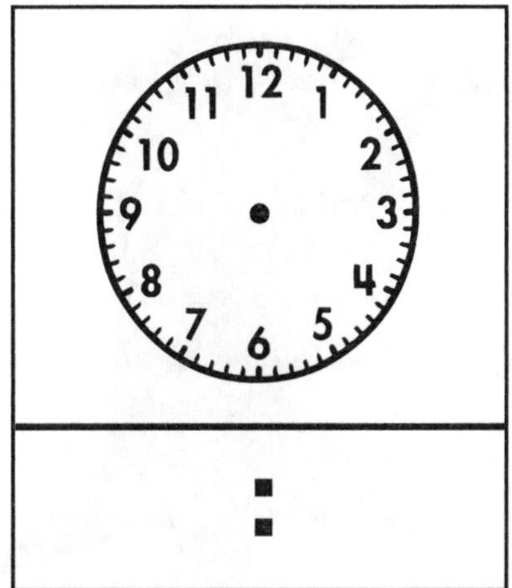

Name________________________________

Writing Familiar Times: Family "Time Tree"

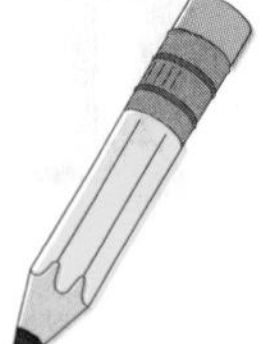

Write the time.
Draw the hands on each clock.

I get up at ______.

I go to bed at ______.

Lunch is at ______.

Dinner is at ______.

School starts at ______.

School ends at ______.

Recess is at ______.

I play at ______.

Name ______________________

Time Lapse: Minutes

Our school had an "end-of-school picnic."
We really had fun!

How much time did each activity take?

1. Jimmy played darts from 1:20 till 1:40.
   He played for __20__ minutes.

2. Marietta rode a pony for 15 minutes.
   She began at 1:00.
   She finished at _____ : _________.

3. She had so much fun, she rode
   another 15 minutes.
   She finished at _____ : ________ .

Name____________________________________

Time Lapse: Minutes

4. Tim worked at the snow cone booth. The first clock shows the time he started. He worked 1 hour and 30 minutes. **Show the time** he finished on the second clock.

5. Andrea won the juggling contest. She kept the balls in the air for 5 minutes. She began juggling at 1:25. She finished at _____ : ________.
Circle the clock which shows the correct time.

Keep it up!

Write the time.

____________ ____________ ____________ ____________

Name____

Drawing Clock Hands

Show the Times

Read each story.

Draw the hands on each clock face.

A. Frog sees a fly at 1:00. He catches the fly and eats it 60 minutes later.

Sees fly **Eats fly**

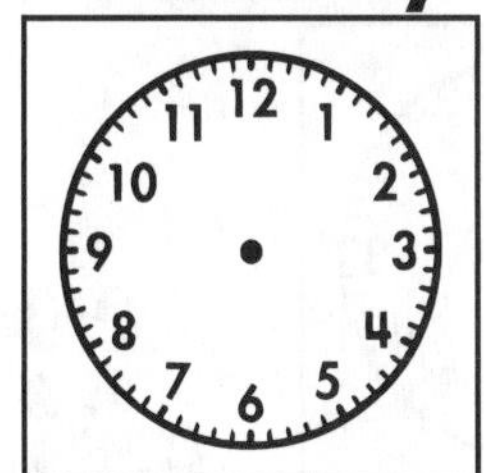 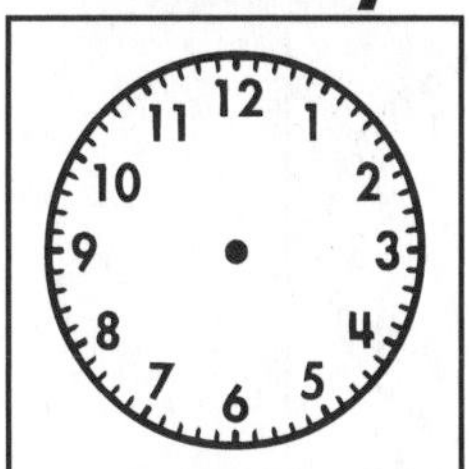

B. Frog hops out of the water at 2:00.
Frog hops back in the water 40 minutes later.

Hops out **Hops back in**

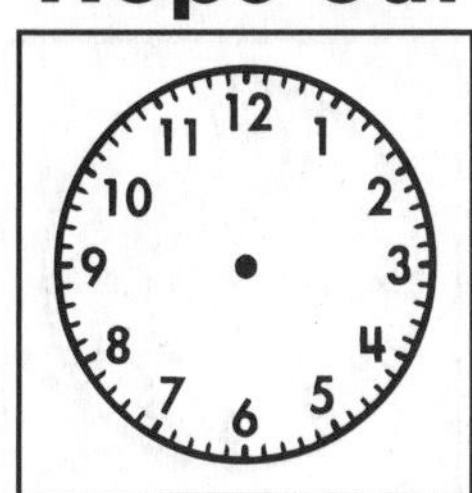 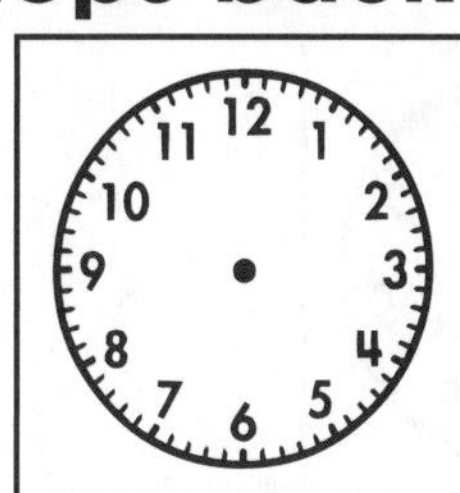

C. Frog sits on a lily pad at 3:00.
He swims away 45 minutes later.

Sits on lily pad **Swims away**

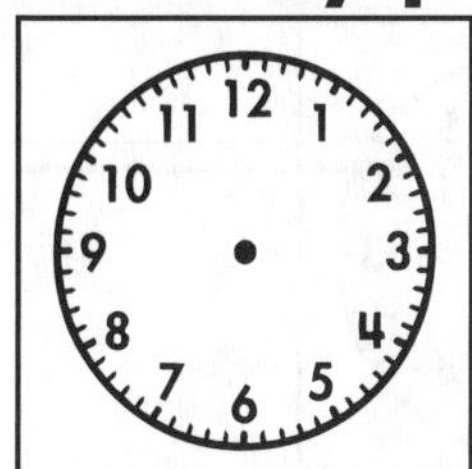 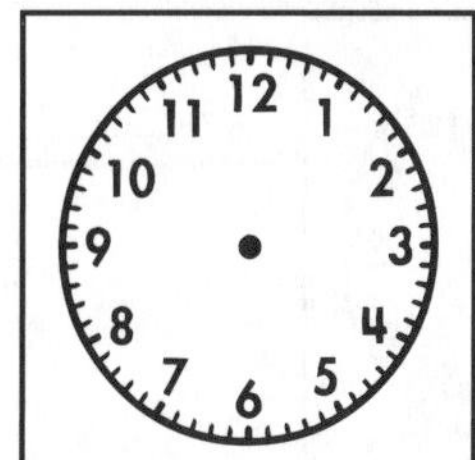

Name________________________________

Drawing Clock Hands

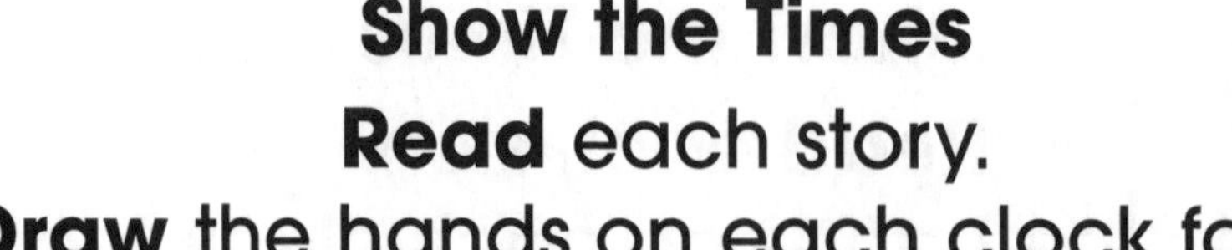
Show the Times

Read each story.

Draw the hands on each clock face.

A. Rabbit hops into his garden at 6:00. He finishes working in the garden one and one-half hours later.

Hops in garden **Finishes work**

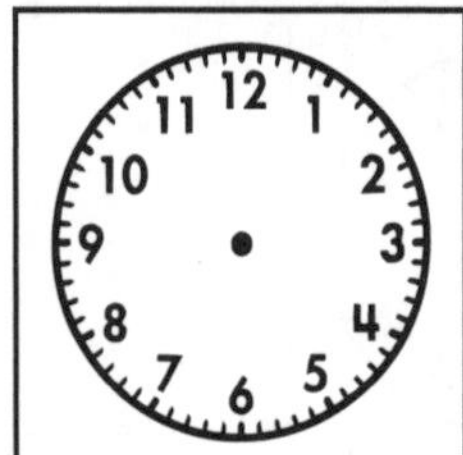

B. Rabbit gets out lettuce and carrots at 8:30. He finishes eating 45 minutes later.

Gets out lettuce & carrots **Finishes eating**

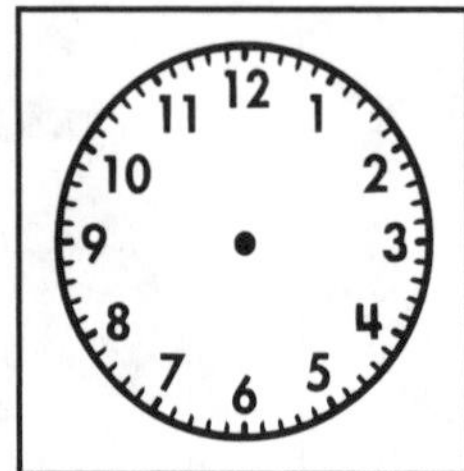

C. Rabbit lies down for a nap at 4:00. He wakes up and hip-hops away 55 minutes later.

Lies down **Wakes up**

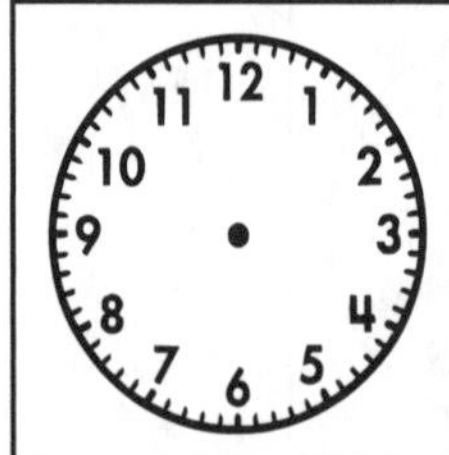
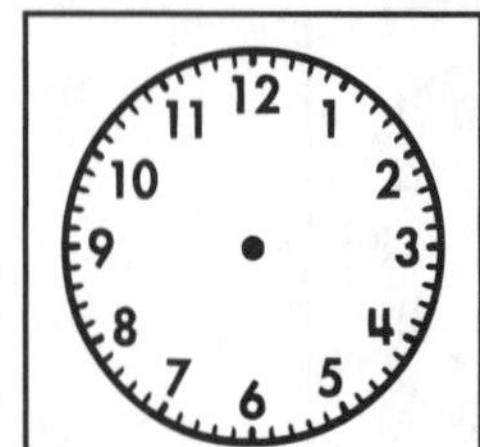

Name ____________________________________

Drawing Clock Hands

Show the Times

Read each story.

Draw the hands on each clock face.

A. Pig takes a mud bath at 9:00.
Pig showers off 15 minutes later.

Takes mud bath **Showers off**

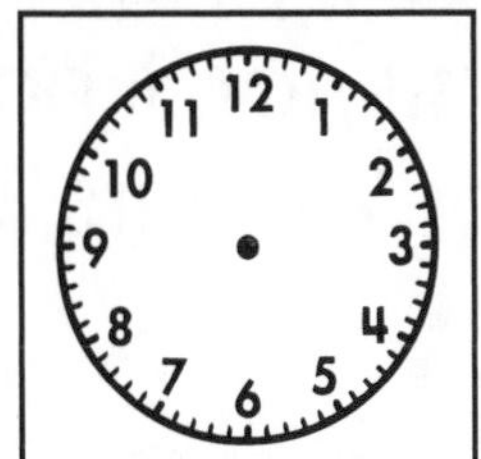 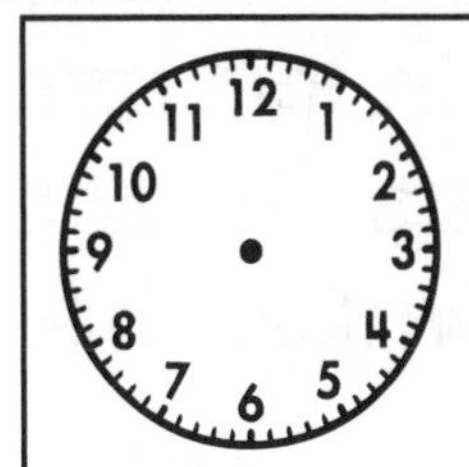 

B. On Monday, Pig begins cleaning at noon.
Her house is clean and neat 90 minutes later.

Begins cleaning **House is clean**

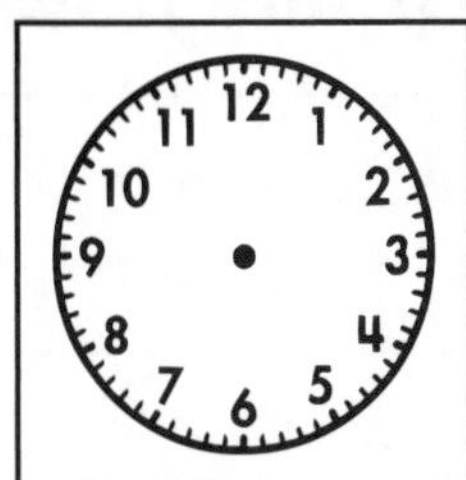 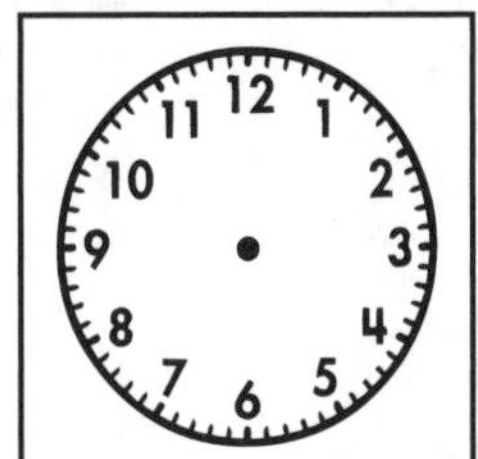

C. On Tuesday, Pig goes to the market at 12:45.
She comes home with a basket full of goodies 30 minutes later.

Goes to market **Comes home**

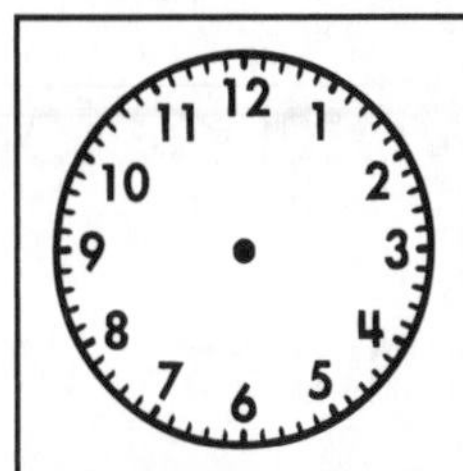 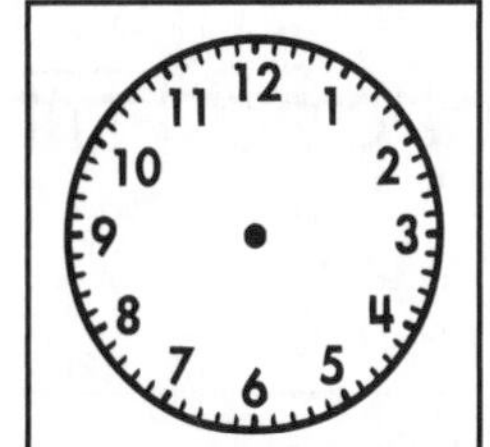

Name________________________________

Time Stories

Read the story.
Write the times on each digital clock.

Val and Phil Camp Out

Val and Phil go out to the backyard at 6:00. They put up their tent. This takes them 1 hour and 30 minutes. They get in the tent and talk for 1 hour. Then they fall asleep. They sleep for 2 hours, until a dog barks and wakes them up.

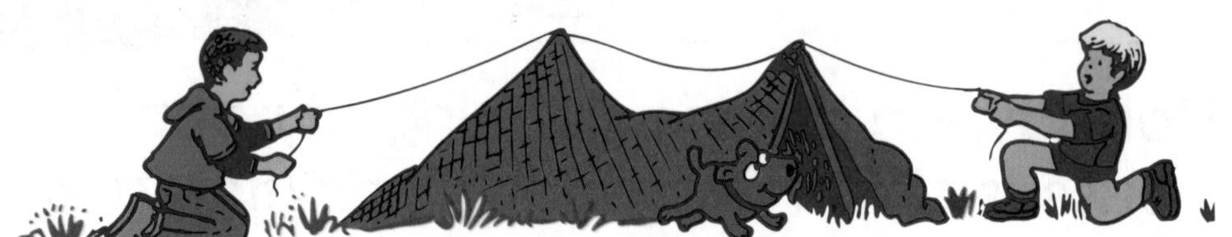

A. Go to backyard

[:]

B. Finish putting up tent

[:]

C. Fall asleep

[:]

D. Dog barks

[:]

E. How long are Val and Phil in the yard before the dog wakes them up?

________ hours ______________ minutes

Name 

Time Stories

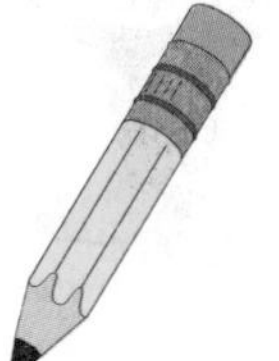

Read the story.
Write the times on each digital clock.

Mike and Maria Go Skating

Mike and Maria leave home at 3:30. They ride their bikes to the ice-skating rink. This takes one half-hour. They skate and leave the rink 2 hours later. They get on their bikes and arrive home 40 minutes after leaving the rink.

A. Leave home

:

B. Get to rink

:

C. Leave rink

:

D. Arrive home

:

E. How long does Mike & Maria's trip to the skating rink and back take?

_________ hours _______________ minutes

Name ______________________

Time Stories

Read the story.
Write the times on each digital clock.

Joe and José Go Skating

Joe and José put on roller skates at 8:30. They skate for 2 hours, then stop to rest. They rest for one half-hour, then start skating again. They reach the park 1 hour and 45 minutes later.

A. Put on roller skates

[:]

B. Stop to rest

[:]

C. Start skating again

[:]

D. Get to park

[:]

E. How long does Joe and José's trip to the park take?

________ hours ____________ minutes

Name ____________________________

Time Stories

Read each time story.
Write the time on each clock.

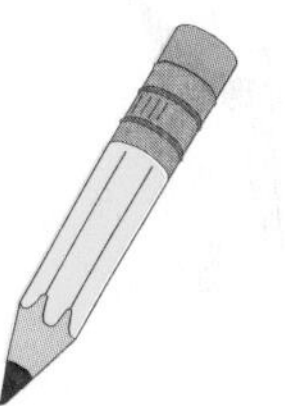

Andrea took her dog for a walk. They left home at 5:30. They walked for 20 minutes. What time did they get home?

A. Leave home **B. Get home**

Rhiannon and her mother were making cookies. They put the cookies in the oven at 7:15. After 10 minutes they took the cookies out of the oven. Yum! What time did they take them out?

C. Cookies in oven **D. Cookies out of oven**

Solve the time puzzle.
When did Anita begin playing ping-pong? Anita played ping-pong with her brother for 30 minutes. They stopped playing at 4:30.

E. Begin playing **F. Stop playing**

Name________________________________

Time Stories

Read each time story.
Write the time on each clock.

Benito went for a ride on the roller coaster. He got on the roller coaster at 2:30. He rode for 15 minutes. What time did he get off?

A. Start ride **B. Get off**

Valerie and her sister went hiking. They started hiking at 9:00. They hiked for one hour and 30 minutes. What time did they stop hiking?

C. Start hike **D. Finish hike**

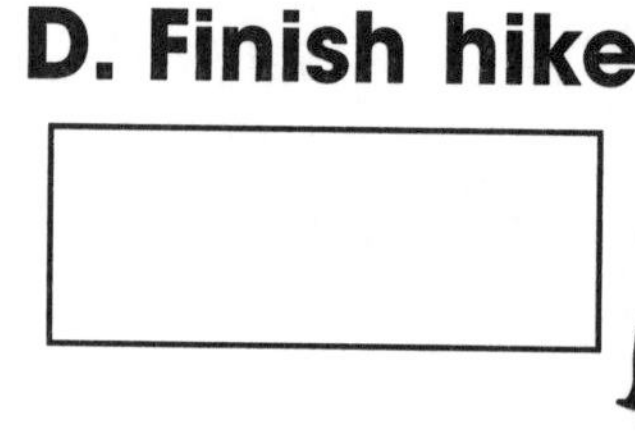

Solve this time puzzle.
When did Ben and his mother get on the subway?
Ben and his mother rode the subway for 20 minutes.
They got off the subway at 4:30.

E. Get on **F. Get off**

Name____________________

Time Stories

Read each time story.
Write the time on each clock.

Andrea and her sister walked by the lake. They started walking at 2:15. They walked for one hour and 15 minutes. What time did they stop walking?

A. Start walking **B. Stop walking**

Berta gave her dog Maria a bath. She started washing Maria at 7:40. Maria hates baths. It took Berta 50 minutes to wash the dog. They both got wet! When did she finish?

C. Start bath **D. Finish bath**

Solve this time puzzle.
When did Sergei start playing frisbee? Sergei played frisbee with his brother for 40 minutes. They stopped playing at 7:30.

E. Start playing **F. Stop playing**

Name ____________________

Time Puzzles

Write any time that fits the time clues.

A. Between 11:00 and 12:00

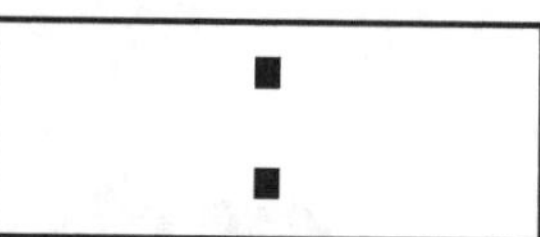

B. Between 30 minutes after 2:00 and 3:00

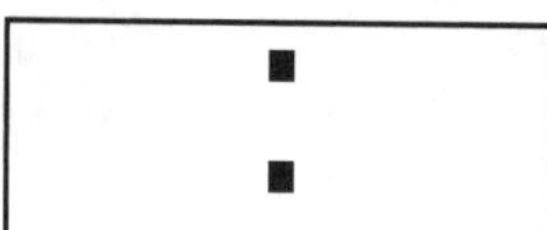

C. After quarter-past 7:00 and before 8:00

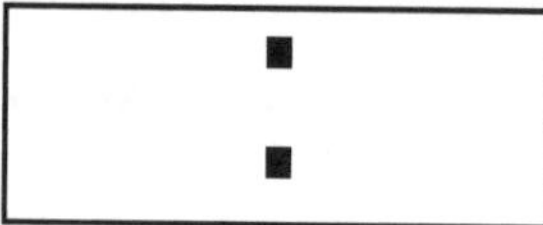

D. **Make up** your own time clues.
Ask a friend to solve your time puzzle!

____

____

____

Name________________________________

Time Puzzles

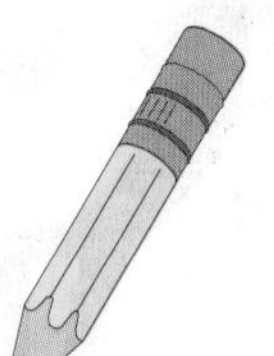

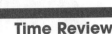

Write any time that fits the time clues.

A. Between 4:15 and 5:15

[:   ]

B. After 6:00 and before quarter to 7:00

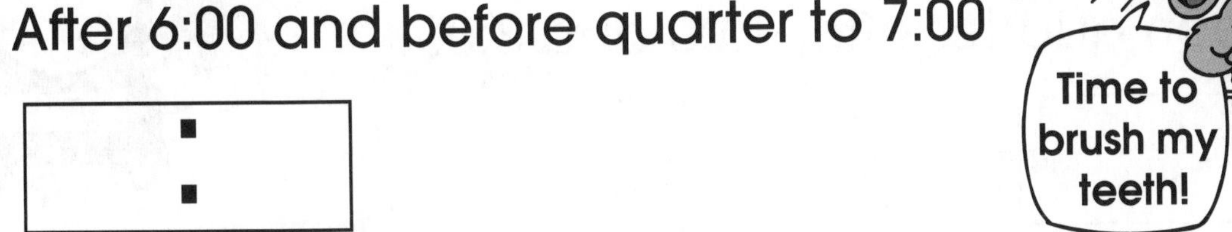

[:   ]

C. Between noon and 1:00

[:   ]

D. **Make up** your own time clues.
Ask a friend to solve your time puzzle!

____

____

____

Name________________________________

Time Puzzles

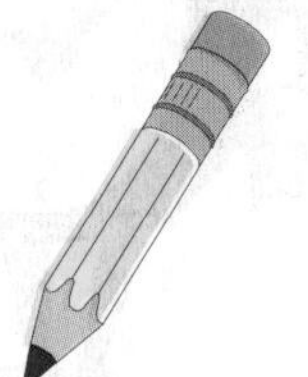

Write any time that fits the time clues.

A. After 3:00 and before 3:40

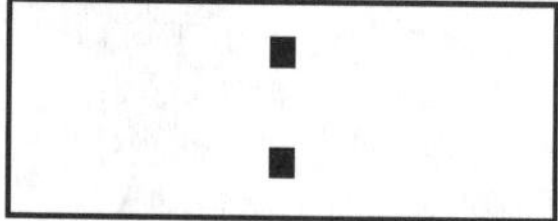

B. Between quarter after 1:00 and 3:00

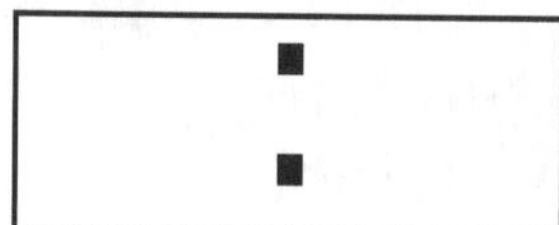

C. Before 9:00 and after 8:20

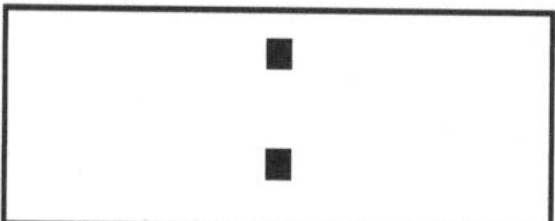

D. **Make up** your own time clues.
Ask a friend to solve your time puzzle!

____

____

____

Name________________________________

Time Stories

Read the story. **Write** the time on each clock.

Story Times

Erin and her brother Harry were shopping for dinner. First they went into the bakery at 5:00 to buy fresh bread. This took 5 minutes. Next they walked to the market for vegetables and cereal. This took them 20 minutes. Then they walked next door for a treat at Fanny's Famous Fudge. This took them 15 minutes. Then they met their brother Andrew outside.

A. Go into bakery

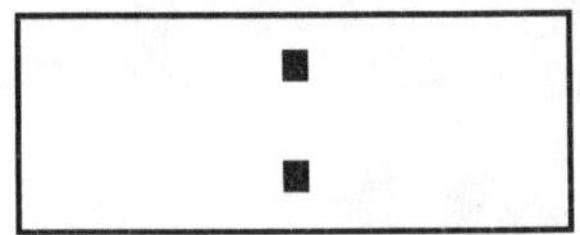

C. Leave bakery

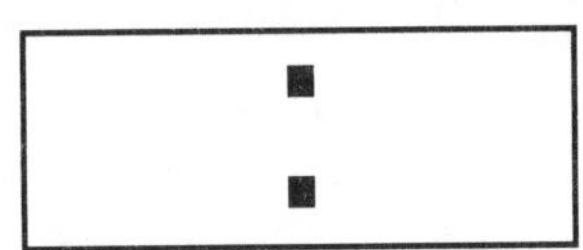

B. Leave market

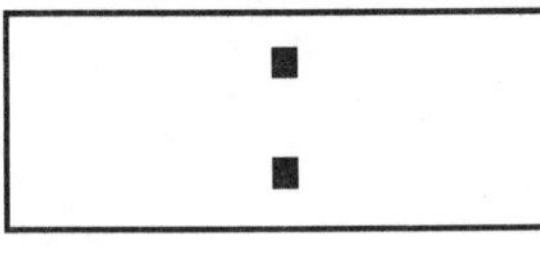

D. See Andrew

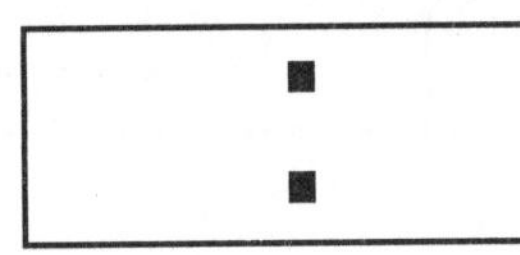

E. How long had Erin and Harry been shopping when they saw Andrew?

____

F. Make up your own story about shopping. What do you do, and how long does each thing take? Make up a starting time. Use your clock to find the ending time.

Name________________________________

Time Stories

Read the story. **Write** the time on each clock.

Story Times

Hanna and Shawn got to the fair at 3:00. They threw balls at the clown's pocket for 10 minutes. No luck! Then they rode the Big Dipper for 30 minutes. They got wet! After this they ate pizza for 15 minutes. Then they saw their friend Mary.

A. Go to fair

B. Stop throwing balls

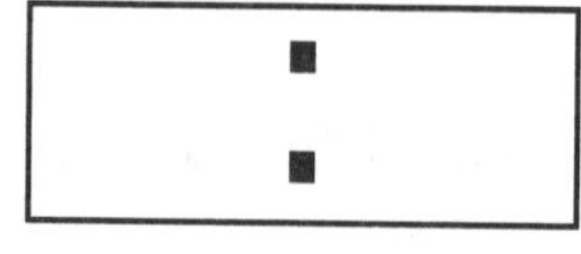

C. Stop riding Big Dipper

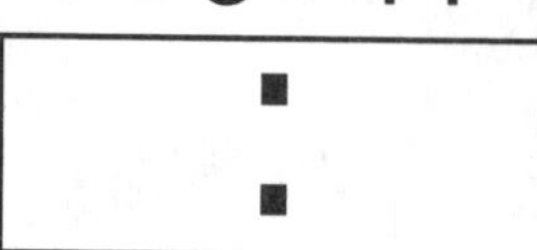

D. See Mary

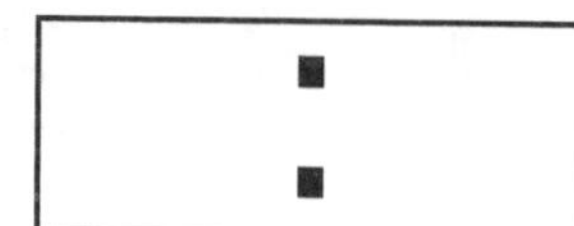

E. How long had Hanna and Shawn been at the fair when they saw Mary?

____

F. Make up your own story about being at a fair. What do you do, and how long does each thing take? Make up a starting time. Use your clock to find the ending time.

Name________________________________

Time Stories

Read the story. **Write** the time on each clock.

Story Times

A. Valerie and Angela got off the bus at the mall. It was 12:30. First they went to Toby's Toys & Games. They looked at toys for 20 minutes. Then they spent 40 minutes walking to Yummy Yogurt and having a snack. Then they looked at shoes in The Shoe Factory for 15 minutes. They met Angela's sister outside the Shoe Factory.

A. Go to mall

[:]

B. Leave toy store

[:]

C. Leave Yummy Yogurt

[:]

D. See Angela's sister

[:]

E. How long had Valerie and Angela been at the mall when they saw Angela's sister?

____

F. Make up your own story about being at a mall. What do you do, and how long does each thing take? Make up a starting time. Use your clock to find the ending time.

Name______________________________

Telling Time: Using Charts

BIG TEN MOVIES:

Mark's Great Adventure	12:15	3:00	5:30
The Mad Hatter Returns	12:45	3:30	5:45
Morris and the Magic Van	1:30	4:15	6:45

Use the chart.
Write the time that each pair went to a movie.

A. Barry and his brother went to the movie that began closest to 4:00.
Movie: ________________________
Began at: ________________________

B. Andrea and her friend went to the movie that began closest to 1:00.
Movie: ________________________
Began at: ________________________

C. Ismelda and her mom went to the movie that began closest to 6:00.
Movie: ________________________
Began at: ________________________

D. **Make up** your own time puzzle about Big Ten Movies.

Name ____________________

Telling Time: Using Charts

Gull Air	10:45	12:10	1:45
Far West Airlines	9:25	10:10	11:40
Swift Flights	12:30	1:15	2:20

Use the chart.
Write the time that each pair took a flight.

A. Teresa and her aunt flew on the plane that left closest to 10:30.
Airline: ____________________
Left at: ____________________

B. Kelly and her mother flew on the plane that left closest to 11:00.
Airline: ____________________
Left at: ____________________

C. Leticia and her father flew on the plane that left closest to 12:15.
Airline: ____________________
Left at: ____________________

D. **Make up** your own time puzzle about the Main Airport.

Name____________________

Telling Time: Using Charts

BAYSIDE AQUARIUM

SATURDAY FEEDINGS:

Otters	2:00	3:30	5:00
Dolphins	11:30	3:15	5:20
Sharks	2:30	4:00	5:45

Use the chart.
Write the time that each pair went to a feeding.

A. Francisco and José went to the feeding that was closest to 3:00.
Animal: ____________________
Feeding at: ____________________

B. Alex and Shannon went to the feeding that was closest to 6:00.
Animal: ____________________
Feeding at: ____________________

C. Kim and Amanda went to the feeding that was closest to 5:30.
Animal: ____________________
Feeding at: ____________________

D. **Make up** your own time puzzle about the Bayside Aquarium.

MONEY

IN GOD WE TRUST
LIBERTY
1990

LIBERTY
IN GOD WE TRUST

LIBERTY
IN GOD
WE TRUST
1990

IN GOD WE TRUST
LIBERTY · 1990

LIBERTY
IN GOD WE TRUST
1990

Name ____________________

Pennies: Introduction

Hi! I am Mary Money.

It is important to learn about **money**.

This is a **penny**.

It is worth **1 cent.**
It has **2 sides.**

front

back

This is the **cent symbol.**
Trace it.

Color the pennies **brown.**

Name ________________________________

Pennies: Introduction

Find each penny. **Color** it **brown.**

Good work!

How many pennies did you find? 5 ________

Name ____________________

Counting Pennies

Count my pennies.

__3__ pennies = __3__ ¢

__5__ pennies = __5__ ¢

__1__ penny = __1__ ¢

Name____________________________

Counting Pennies

Each candy costs 1¢.

Cut out each money box
and **glue** it beside the candy it will buy.

2¢

3¢

4¢

Name________________________________

Counting Pennies

Henny Penny

1 penny  1 cent

How much money?

Example:

 = 5 ¢

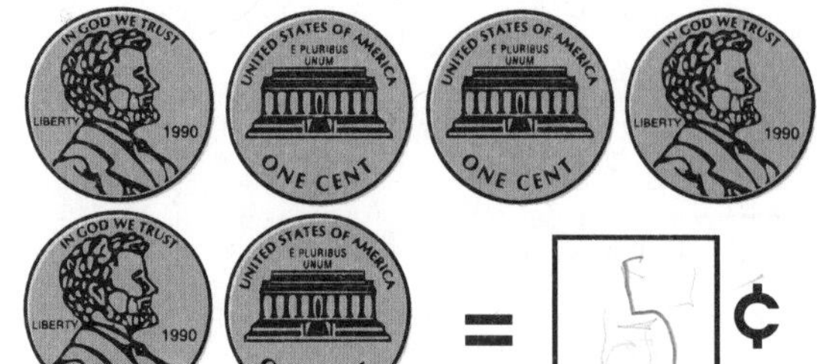 = ¢

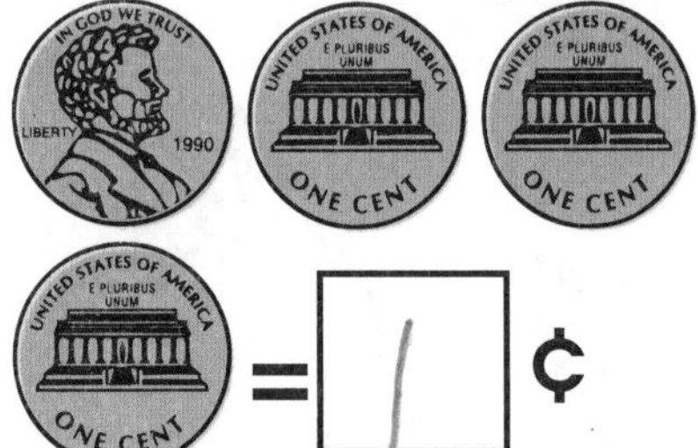 = ¢

 = ¢

Name________________________________

Counting Pennies

Penny Penguin

Count the pennies.
How many cents?

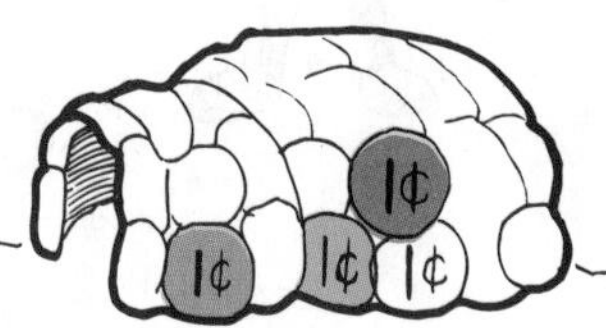

Example:

    = 4¢ 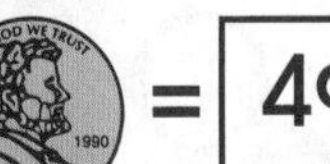

        = 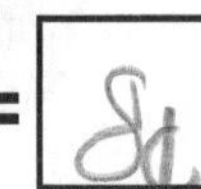

     = 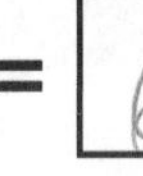 

  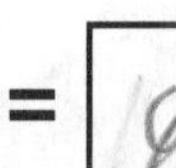 =

   =  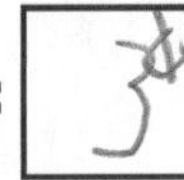

    =   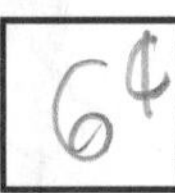

       =  

  = 

         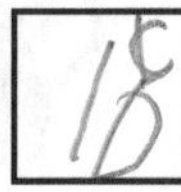 =

Name________________________________

Counting Pennies

You're Blooming Good!

Count the pennies on the flowers.
Write the cents in the center.

Example:

4¢

Name________________________________

Counting Pennies

Penny Pinchers

Draw a line from the pennies to the right numbers.

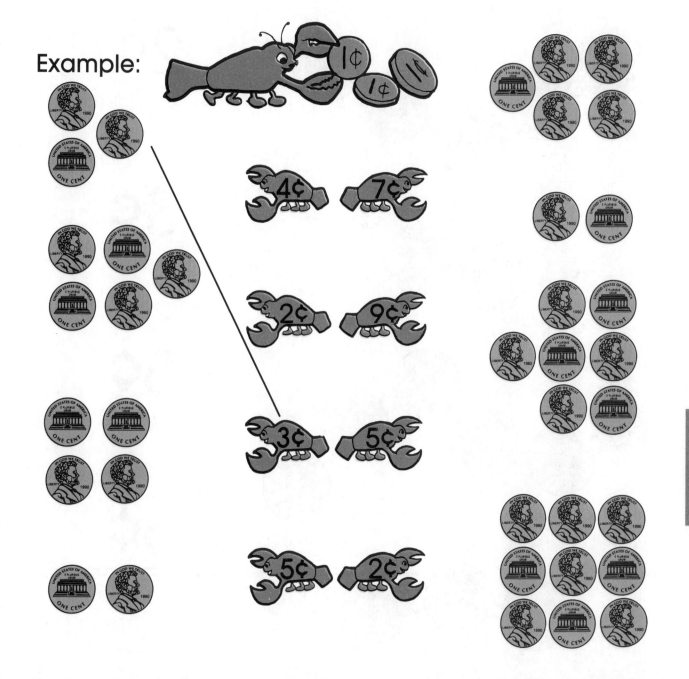

Example:

1¢ 1¢ 1¢

4¢ 7¢

2¢ 9¢

3¢ 5¢

5¢ 2¢

Name____________________________

Counting Pennies

Count the pennies in each chain.
Draw a line to the number of pennies.

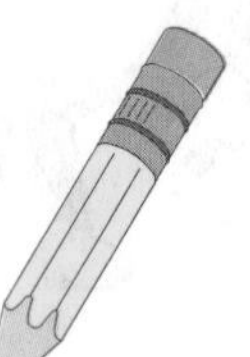

2¢

3¢

5¢

6¢

Name ______________________________

Counting Pennies

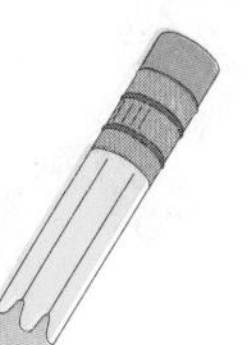

Count the pennies in each triangle.

__________________ ¢ __________________ ¢

____________________________ ¢

Don't knock the pennies down!

Name ____________________

Counting Pennies

I put my pennies in bags.

Write the number of pennies on each bag.

Color each penny.

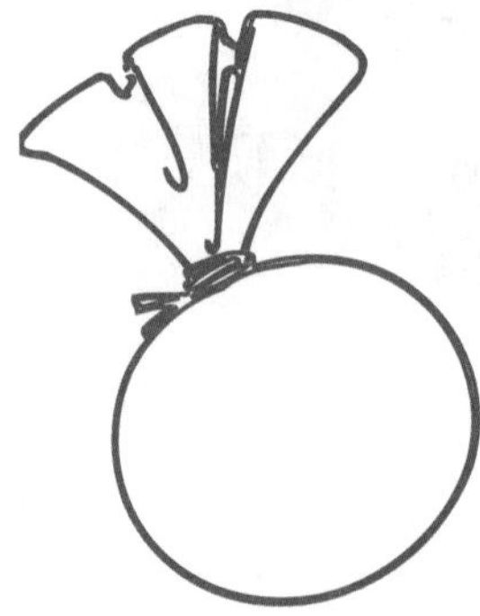

Name______________________________

Counting Pennies

Count the pennies in each group.
Match it to the correct bag.

5¢

3¢

1¢

Don't lose your penny bag!

2¢

4¢

Name ______________________________

Counting Pennies

I love to go to the amusement park and ride rides.

Count the pennies.
Write the number of pennies on the line.
Color each ride.

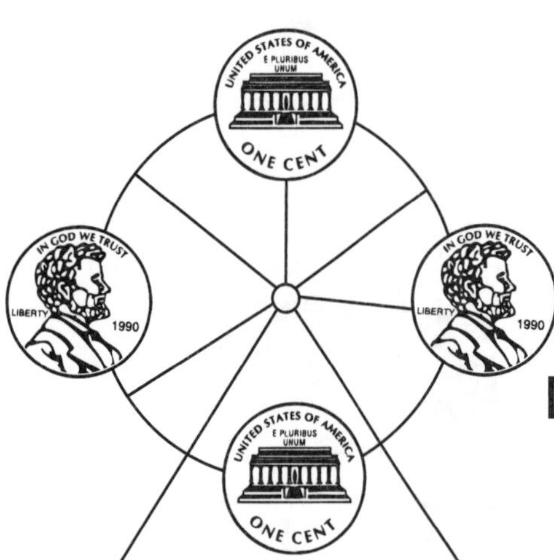

______________¢

Do you like the ferris wheel?

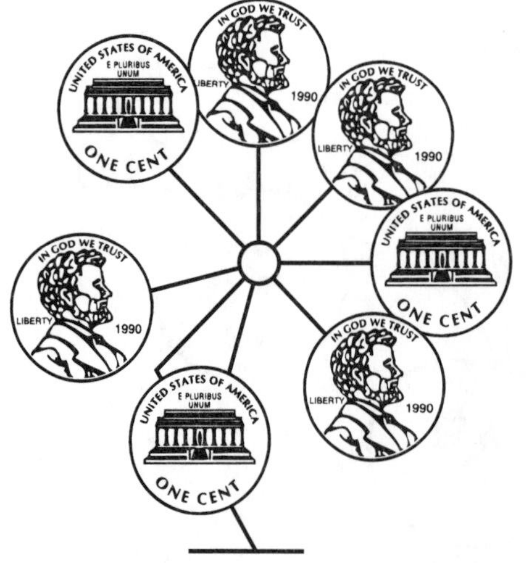

______________¢

...the tilt-a-whirl?

Name ____________________

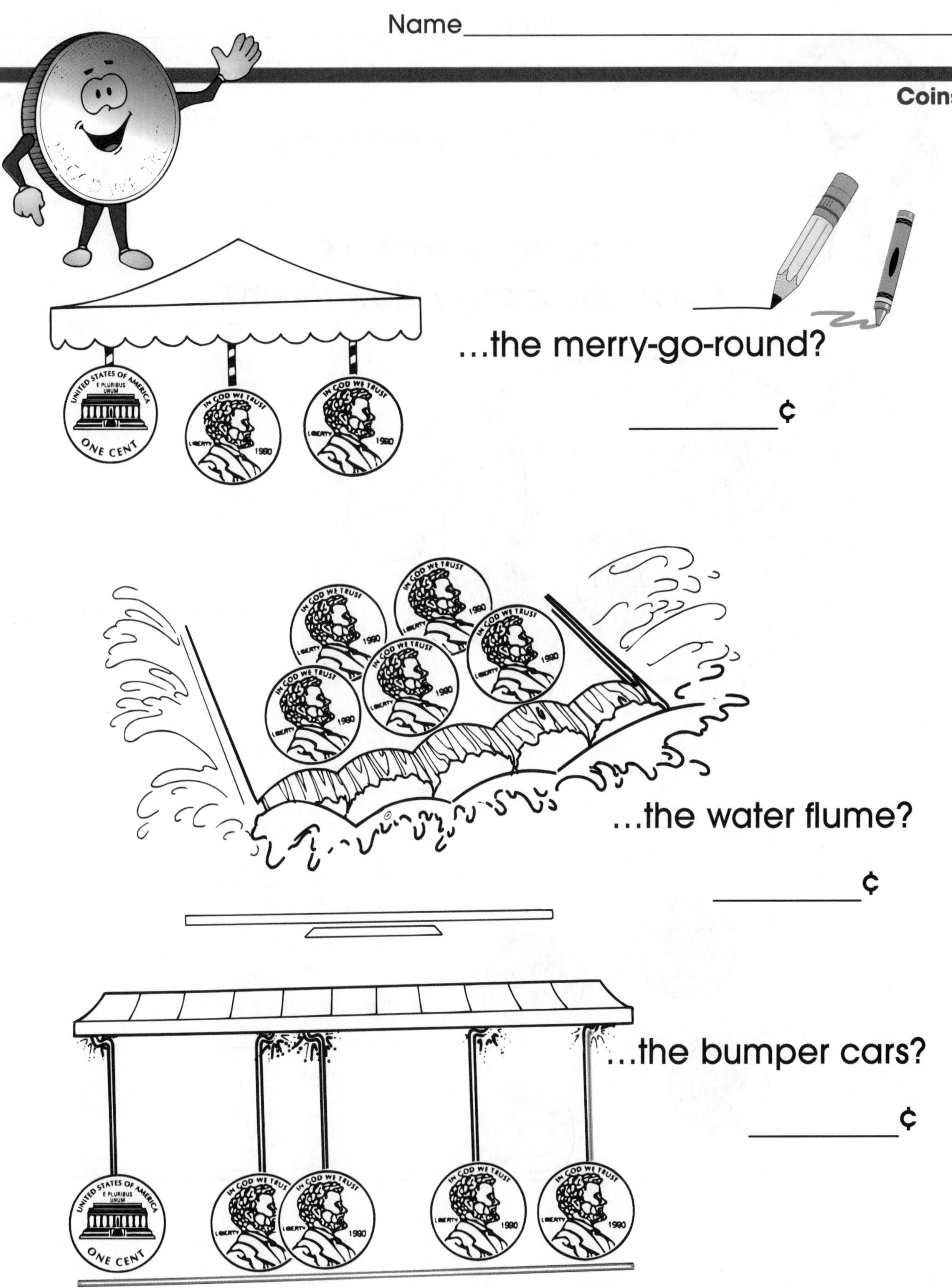

...the merry-go-round?

______ ¢

...the water flume?

______ ¢

...the bumper cars?

______ ¢

Name_______________________________________

A **penny** is worth **1¢**.

Count the money. How much? ________

A.

____________¢

B.

____________¢

Name________________________________

Counting Pennies

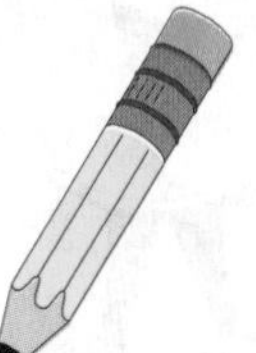

Count the money. How much?

A.

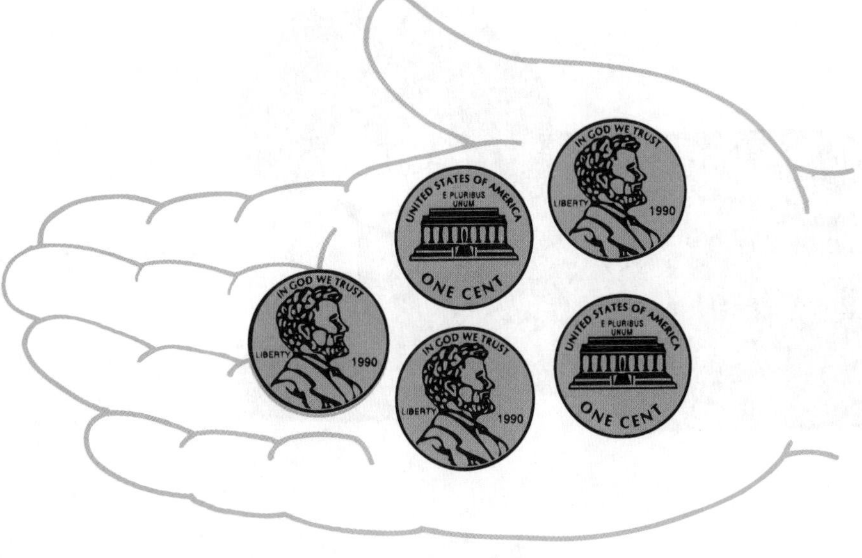

__________¢

B.

__________¢

Name________________________

Counting Pennies

Who Has More Money?

Count the money.
Write the amount.

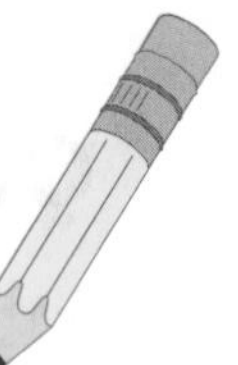

A.

__________ ¢

B.

__________ ¢

C. **Circle** the answer.
Who has more money?

Name______________________________

Nickels: Introduction

Meet another **money friend.**
Let's hear it for the **Nickel!**

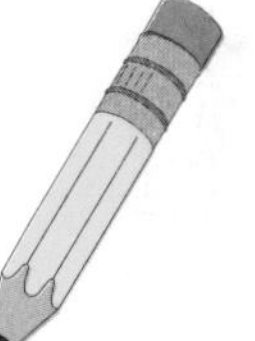

Look at the two sides of a nickel.
Color the nickels silver.

front

back

_____ nickel = _____ pennies

_____ nickel = _____ cents

_____ nickel = _____ ¢

5¢ = ____¢ + ____¢ + ____¢ + ____¢ + ____¢

=

Name ____________________

Counting with Nickels and Pennies

A **nickel** is worth **5¢**.
Count the money.

How much? ______

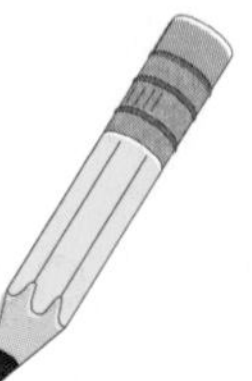

A.

______ ¢

B.

______ ¢

Both of these bags hold 5¢!

Name______________________________

Counting with Nickels and Pennies

Here are my friends, **Penny** and **Nickel**.
You can count them together!

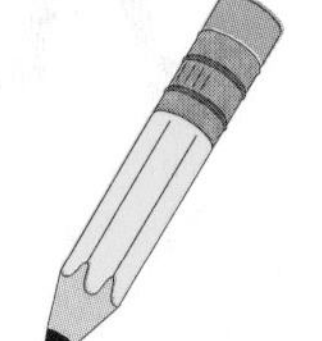

Remember: They both have a front and back!

Here is a **penny**.
Color it **brown**.

And here is a **nickel**.
Color it **silver**.

1 penny = ______ cent

1 penny = ______ ¢

1 nickel = ______ cents

1 nickel = ______ ¢

Make the cent symbol here: ______

Name____________________

Counting with Nickels and Pennies

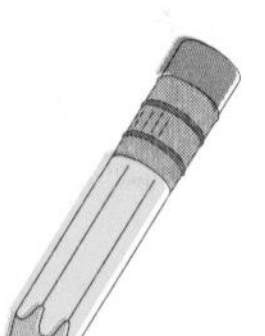

Count this money.

Begin by saying 5 for the nickel and **add** 1 for each penny.

<table>
<tr><td>1.</td><td>   </td><td>= ______¢</td></tr>
<tr><td>2.</td><td> </td><td>= ______¢</td></tr>
<tr><td>3.</td><td></td><td>= ______¢</td></tr>
<tr><td>4.</td><td>   </td><td>= ______¢</td></tr>
</table>

Keep your money in a **safe place** so it won't get lost!

Name ____________________

Counting with Nickels and Pennies

Count the money.

Start with the nickel. Then **count** the pennies.

Write the amount.

________ ¢

________ ¢

________ ¢

________ ¢

________ ¢

________ ¢

Name____

Counting with Nickels and Pennies

Count the money.
Start with the nickel. Then **count** the pennies.
Write the amount of money.

A.

____________¢

B.

____________¢

Name____

Counting with Nickels and Pennies

Who Has More Money?

Count the money.
Write the amount.

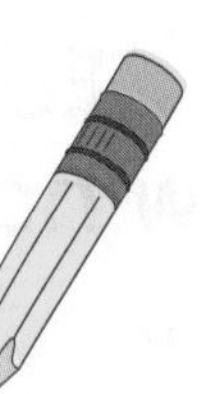

A.

____________¢

B.

____________¢

C. **Circle** the answer.
Who has more money?

Name________________________________

Counting with Nickels and Pennies

Each **nickel** is worth **5 cents**. ______

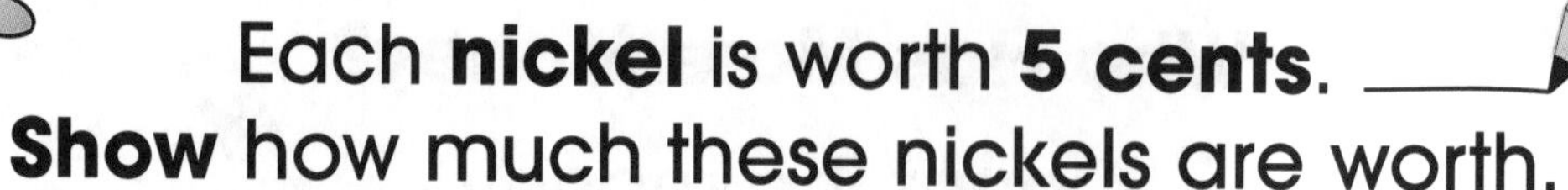

Show how much these nickels are worth.

= _____¢

= _____¢

= _____¢ = ________¢

= _____¢

= _____¢

= _____¢ = ________¢

= _____¢

= _____¢

= _____¢

= _____¢ = ________¢

12 ¢

B.

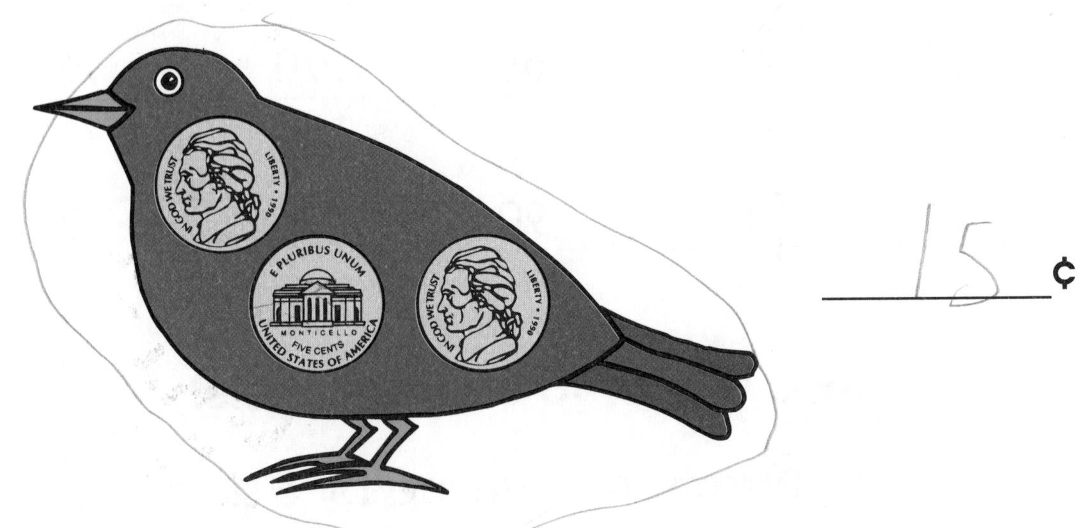

15 ¢

C. **Circle** the answer.
Who has more money?

Name____________________

Nickels: Counting By Fives

Let's count my nickels to see if we have enough to buy something!

Count by 5's.

See how far you can count.

5 ,	10 ,	15 ,	20 ,	25 ,
30 ,	35 ,	40 ,	45 ,	50 ,
55 ,	60 ,	65 ,	70 ,	75 ,
80 ,	85 ,	90 ,	95 ,	100 ,

This is how to count nickels!

Practice counting by 5's!

Name ________________________________

Nickels: Counting By Fives

Nickel Pickles

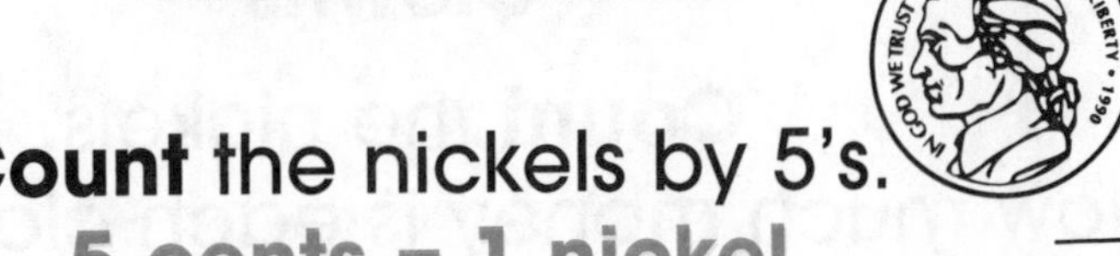

Count the nickels by 5's.

5 cents = 1 nickel

Write the amount.

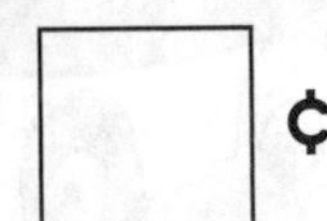

☐ ¢

Count 5, 10, 15.

☐ ¢

Count ____, ____.

☐ ¢

Count ____, ____, ____,

____, ____.

☐ ¢

Count ____, ____, ____, ____,

____, ____, ____.

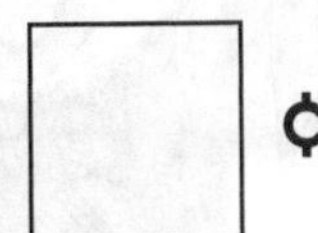

☐ ¢

Count ____, ____, ____,

____.

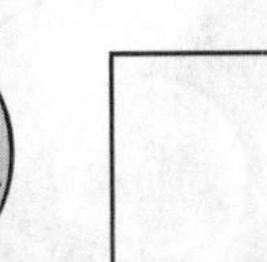

☐ ¢

Count ____, ____, ____,

____, ____, ____.

Name_______________

Nickels: Counting By Fives

Clowns

Count the nickels.
How much money is each clown worth?

_______ ¢

_______ ¢

_______ ¢

_______ ¢

Name________________________________

Nickels: Counting By Fives

Feed the Meter

Count the nickels.
Write the money in the meter.

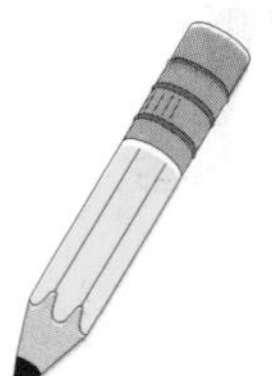

Example:

Name________________________________

Nickels: Counting By Fives

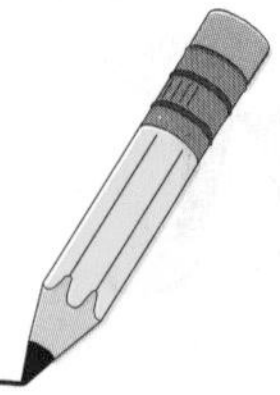

Five Hive

How much money is in each hive?

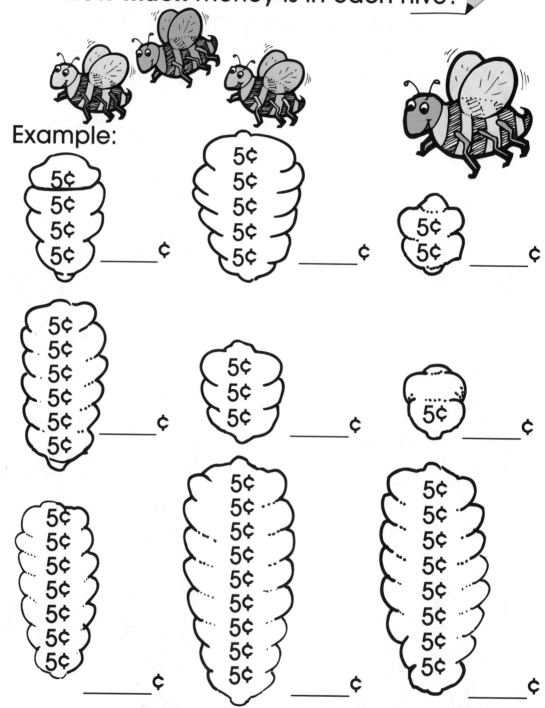

Example:

5¢
5¢
5¢
5¢ ______¢

5¢
5¢
5¢
5¢
5¢ ______¢

5¢
5¢ ______¢

5¢
5¢
5¢
5¢
5¢
5¢ ______¢

5¢
5¢
5¢ ______¢

5¢ ______¢

5¢
5¢
5¢
5¢
5¢
5¢
5¢ ______¢

5¢
5¢
5¢
5¢
5¢
5¢
5¢
5¢
5¢ ______¢

5¢
5¢
5¢
5¢
5¢
5¢
5¢
5¢ ______¢

Name________________________________

Counting with Nickels and Pennies

Money Bunnies

Count the coins.

Write the amount under each bunny's carrot.

Example:

______¢

______¢

______¢

______¢

______¢

______¢

Name________________________________

Counting with Nickels and Pennies

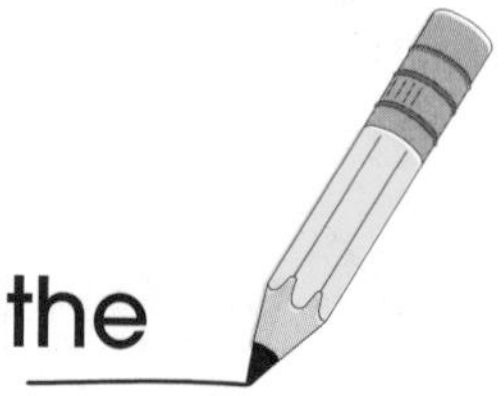

Hooting about Money

Count the coins.
Draw a line to match each owl with the same amount of money.

Example:

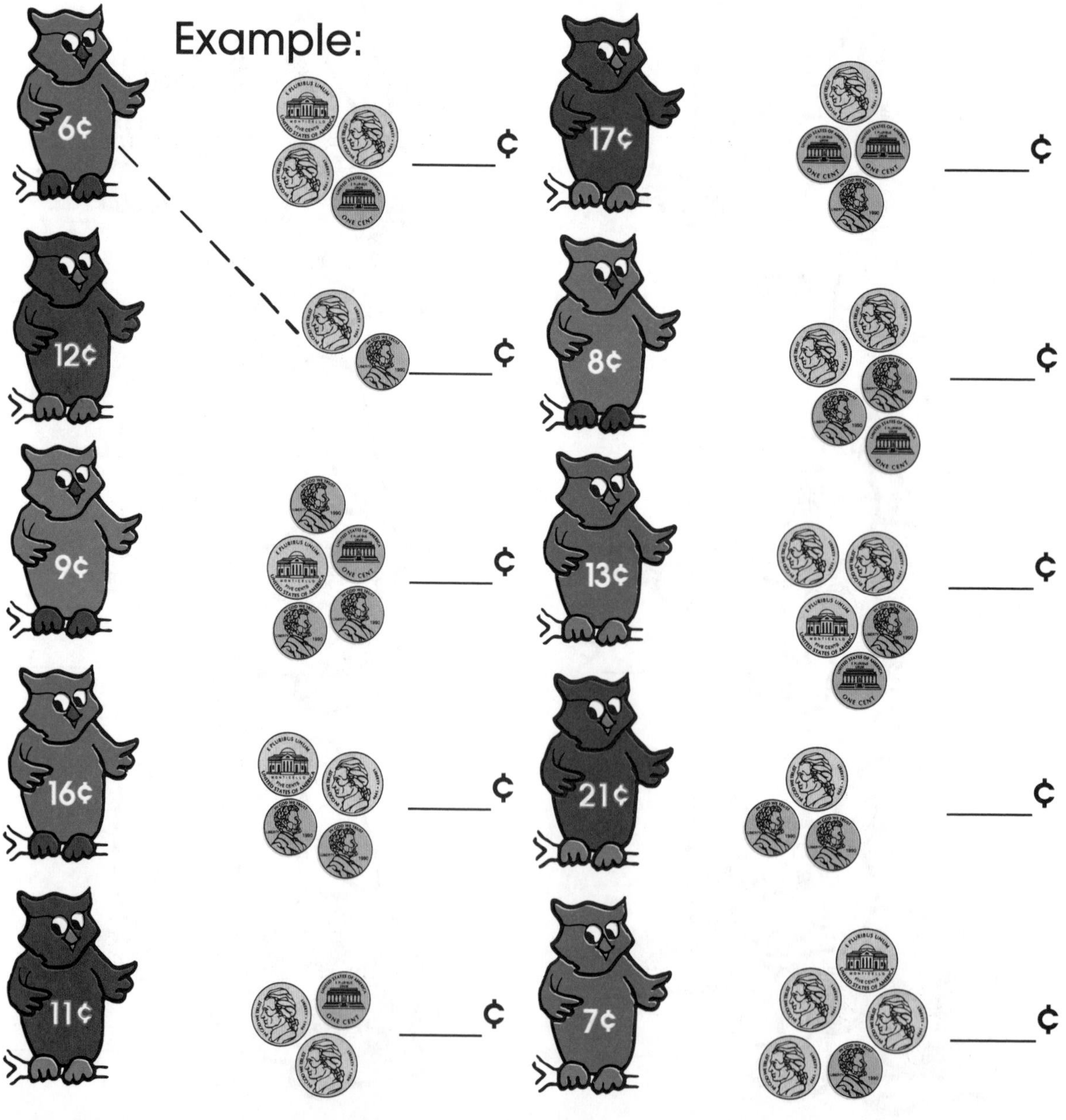

Owl	Coins		Owl	Coins	
6¢		____¢	17¢		____¢
12¢		____¢	8¢		____¢
9¢		____¢	13¢		____¢
16¢		____¢	21¢		____¢
11¢		____¢	7¢		____¢

Name________________________________

Counting with Nickels and Pennies

"Cent"-erpillars

Count the coins on each "**cent**"-erpillar.

Example:

______ ¢ ______ ¢

______ ¢ ______ ¢

______ ¢ ______ ¢

______ ¢ ______ ¢

______ ¢ ______ ¢

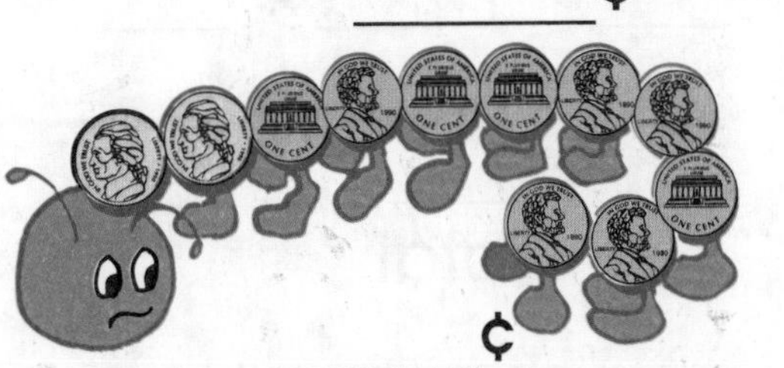

Name________________________________

Counting with Nickels and Pennies

Count the money.
Start with nickels. Then **count** the pennies.

A. _____¢ _____¢ _____¢ _____¢ = _____¢
Total

B. _____¢ _____¢ _____¢ _____¢ _____¢ _____¢ _____¢

= _____¢
Total

C.     

_____¢ _____¢ _____¢ _____¢ _____¢

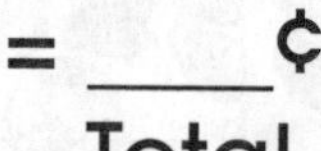

= _____¢
Total

Name____________________

Counting with Nickels and Pennies

Look at the price on each toy.
Color it if there are enough nickels.

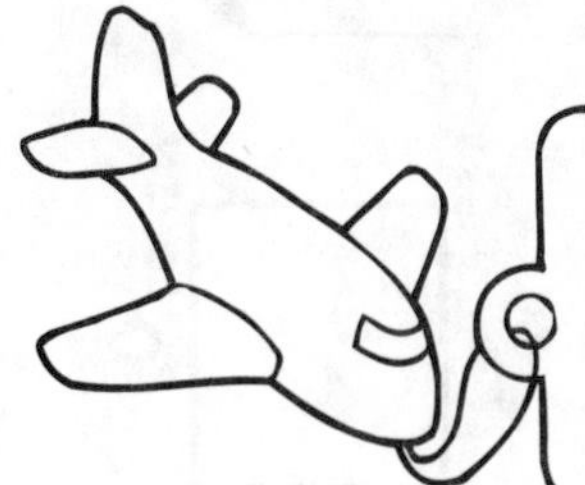

25¢

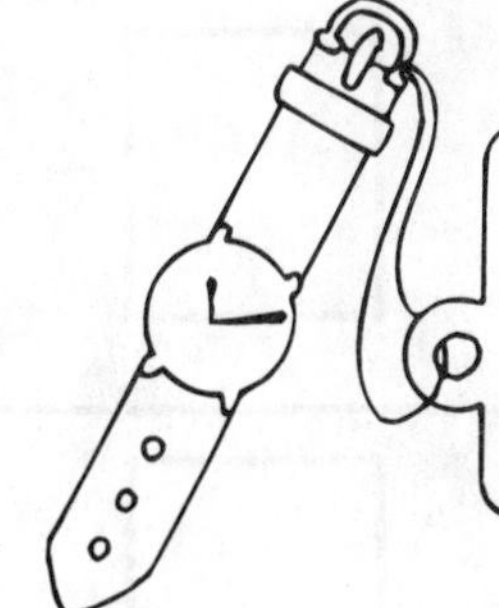

30¢

20¢

35¢

Good counting!

Name________________________________

Adding with Nickels and Pennies

Adding money is **fun and easy!**

Write how much money there is in all.

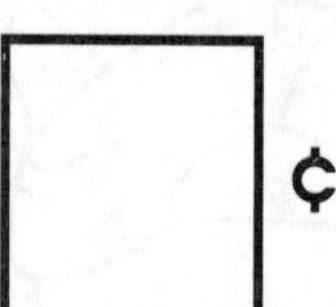

¢

\+ ¢

¢ in all

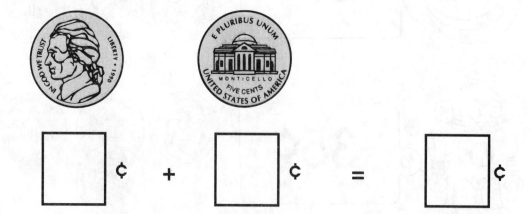

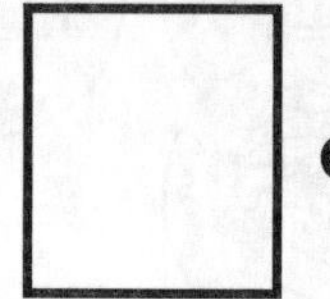 ¢ +  ¢ = 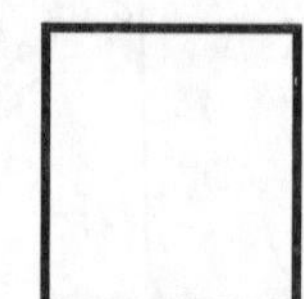 ¢

Name________________________________

Adding with Nickels and Pennies

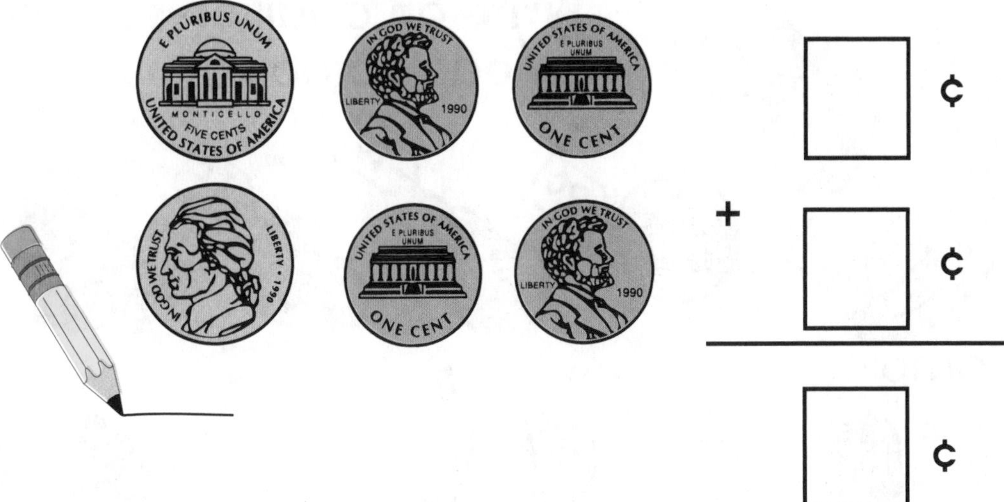

Draw groups of pennies and nickels here.
Write an addition sentence using the coins you drew. **Color the coins.**

You are catching on!

Name________________________________

Adding with Nickels and Pennies

Go Bananas over Money!

Write an addition sentence for each problem.

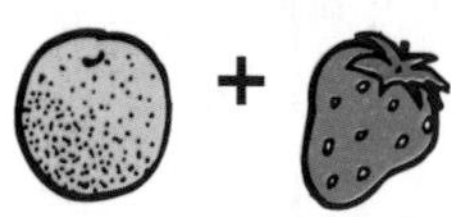

2¢ + 1¢ = 3¢

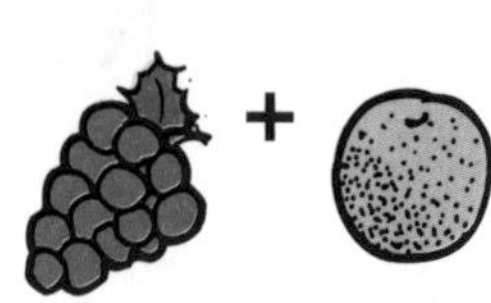

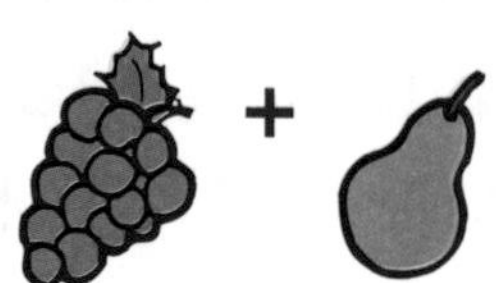

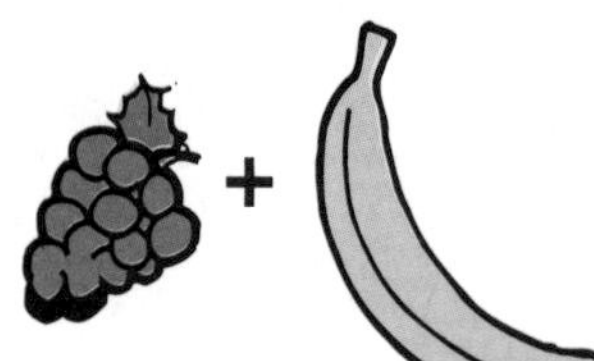

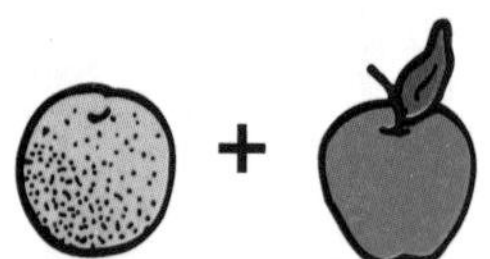

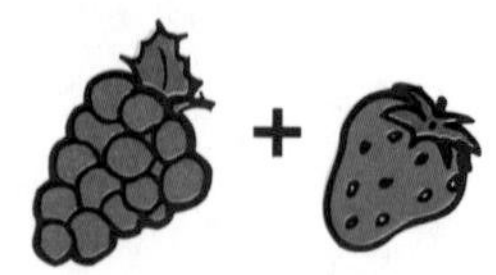

Name ____________________________________

Adding with Nickels and Pennies

Kristen is having a birthday party. Let's see what she bought for her 3 friends.

These are for her friends.

1. For Cassie, she bought the  and the .

   She paid ________¢.

2. For Terri, she bought the  and the .

   She paid ________¢.

3. For Lauren, she bought the 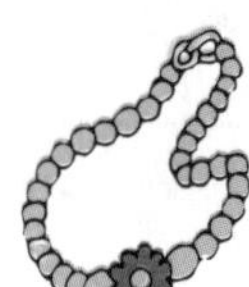 and the .

   She paid ________¢.

Name________________________________

Adding with Nickels and Pennies

Every birthday party needs balloons.
Draw one for each girl, including Kristen.

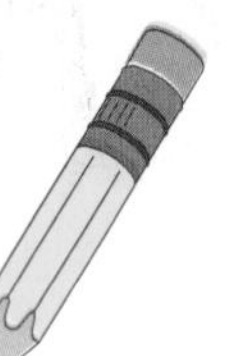

They cost 5¢ each. **Count** by 5's. She paid ______ ¢.

She also bought bubble wands.
Draw one for each girl.

They cost 2¢ each. **Count** by 2's. She paid _____ ¢.

Finally! The presents!
Color the presents.

Name________________________________

Dimes: Introduction

You have met some of my friends – Penny and Nickel.
Now, meet Dime!

My friend Dime is small, but quite strong. It can buy more than Penny or Nickel.

front

back

Each side of a dime is different. It has ridges on its edge. Color the dime silver.

=

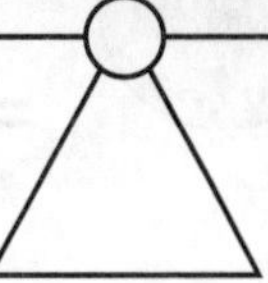

__________ dime = __________ pennies

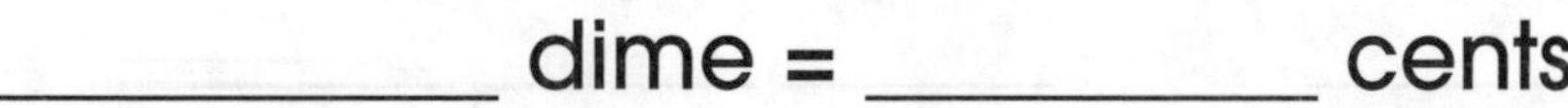

__________ dime = __________ cents

__________ dime = __________ ¢

Name ____________________

Counting with Dimes and Pennies

When Dime and his penny friends go together, they are easy to count.

 +   = ______¢

Say ______ ______ ______

Always begin with the dime, then add the pennies.

 +    = ______¢

______ ______ ______ ______

 +  = ______¢

______ ______

 +   

______ ______ ______ ______

   = ______¢

______ ______ ______

Name ____________________

Counting with Dimes and Pennies

Who Has More Money?

Count the money. **Write** the amount.

A.

_______ ¢

B.

_______ ¢

Name ______________________

Coins

Dimes: Counting By Tens

Counting Dimes

Come march with my dime friends and me!

Count by 10's.

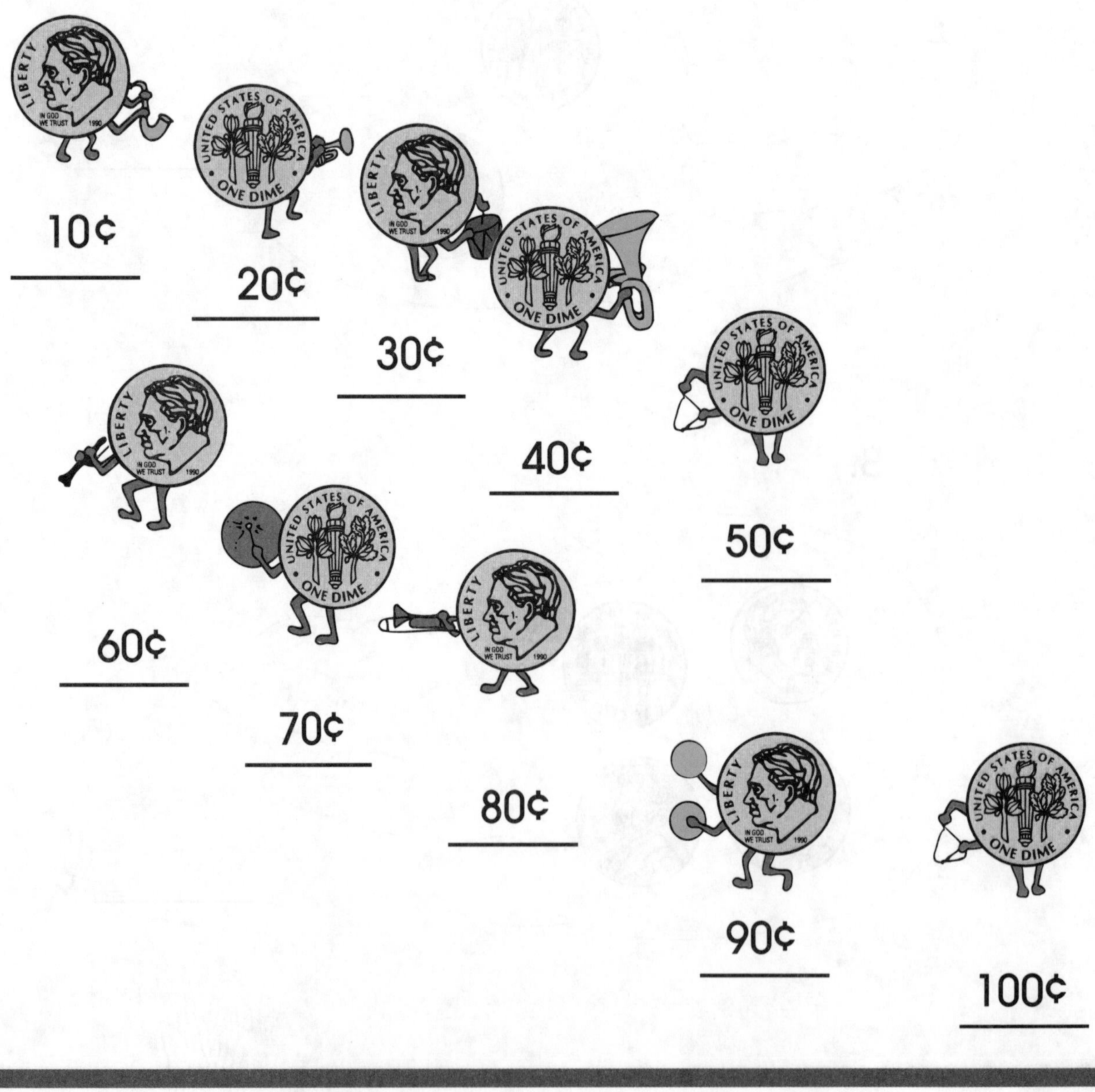

10¢ ____

20¢ ____

30¢ ____

40¢ ____

50¢ ____

60¢ ____

70¢ ____

80¢ ____

90¢ ____

100¢ ____

Name________________________________

Dimes: Counting By Tens

Count by 10's. **Write** the number.
Circle the group with more.

_______¢ or _______¢

_______¢ or _______¢

_______¢ or _______¢

You can count fast by tens!

Name________________________________

Counting with Dimes and Pennies

Dime Climbs

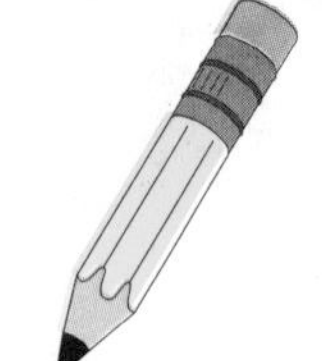

Count the dimes by tens. Then **count** the pennies.
How much?

33¢ ______

______

______

______

______

______

______

______

______

Name ______________________________

Counting with Dimes and Nickels

Do you like to do tricks?

I want to show you a trick about counting dimes and nickels.

Look carefully at these dimes and nickels. **Circle** two nickels, then two more, until all the nickels are circled.

Then **count** by 10's to see how much money is here.

I see ________ ¢

Name______________________________

Counting with Dimes and Nickels

Count the money.
Start with dimes, then **count** the nickels.

Write the amount.

A.

_____¢ _____¢ _____¢ _____¢ _____¢ _____¢
Total

B.

_____¢ _____¢ _____¢ _____¢ _____¢ _____¢

_____¢ _____¢ _____¢ _____¢
Total

I'm counting my money.
10¢, 20¢, 30¢, 35¢,
40¢, 45¢, 50¢...

C. **Solve** this puzzle.
What coins does
Raccoon have?

Name____________________

Counting with Dimes, Nickels and Pennies

Count the money.
Start with the dime.

Write the amount.

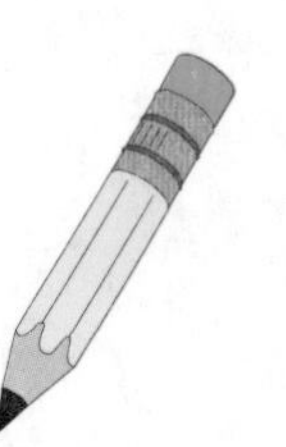

A.

_______¢

B.

_______¢

C. **Circle** the answer.
Who has more money?

Name____________________

Counting with Dimes, Nickels and Pennies

Count the money.
Start with the dime.
Write the amount.

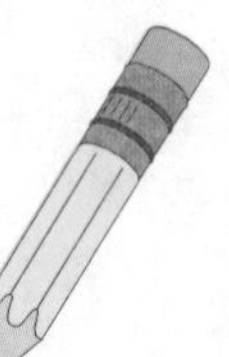

A. ________¢

B. ________¢

C. ________¢

Name________________________________

Counting with Dimes, Nickels and Pennies

Count the money.
Start with the dime.
Write the amount.

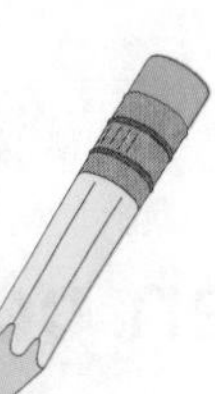

A.

________¢

B.

________¢

Name________________________________

Counting with Dimes, Nickels and Pennies

Count the money.
Start with the dime.
Then **count** the nickels and pennies.

Write the amount.

A.

________¢

B.

________¢

Name ____________________

Counting with Dimes, Nickels and Pennies

Count the money.
Start with the dime.
Then **count** the nickels and pennies.

Write the amount.

A.

________ ¢

B.

________ ¢

Name________________________________

Counting with Dimes, Nickels and Pennies

Count the money.
Start with the dimes.

Write the amount.

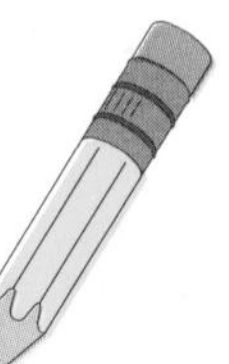

A.

________¢

B.

________¢

Name ______________________

Counting with Dimes, Nickels and Pennies

Count the money.

Write the amount.

A.

______ ¢

B.

______ ¢

Name________________________________

Counting with Dimes, Nickels and Pennies

Money Belts

Count the money on each belt.
Write the amount under the belt.

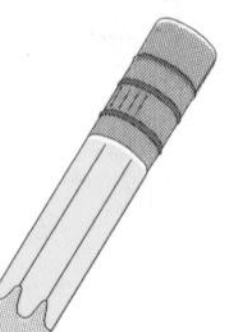

Example: 10 15 16

16¢

_____¢

_____¢

_____¢

_____¢

_____¢

_____¢

_____¢

_____¢

_____¢

_____¢

Name________________________________

Counting with Dimes, Nickels and Pennies

The children made block towers.

Circle the block in each set with the greater amount.

1.

2.

3.

4.

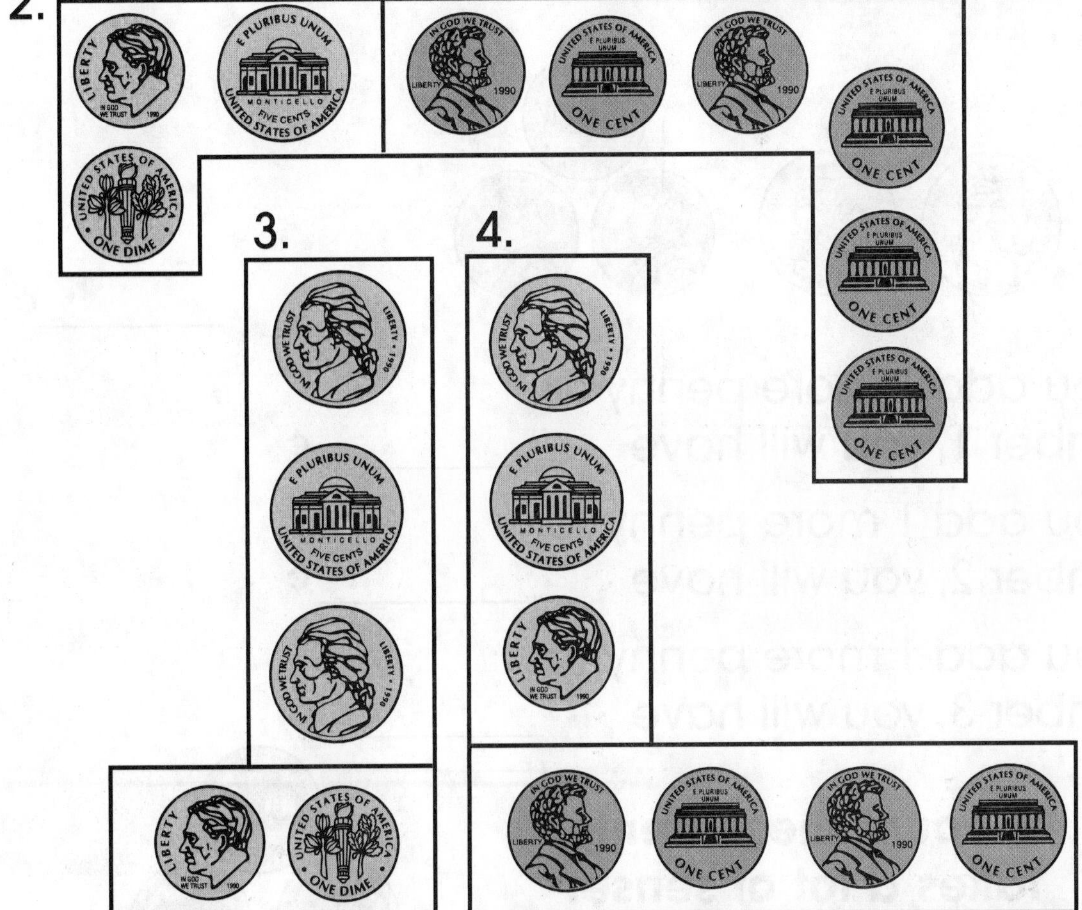

Name ____________________

Counting with Dimes, Nickels and Pennies

Write how many cents.

1.     ________¢

2.    ________¢

3.    ________¢

If you add 1 more penny to number 1, you will have ________¢

If you add 1 more penny to number 2, you will have ________¢

If you add 1 more penny to number 3, you will have ________¢

To count these cents takes a lot of sense!

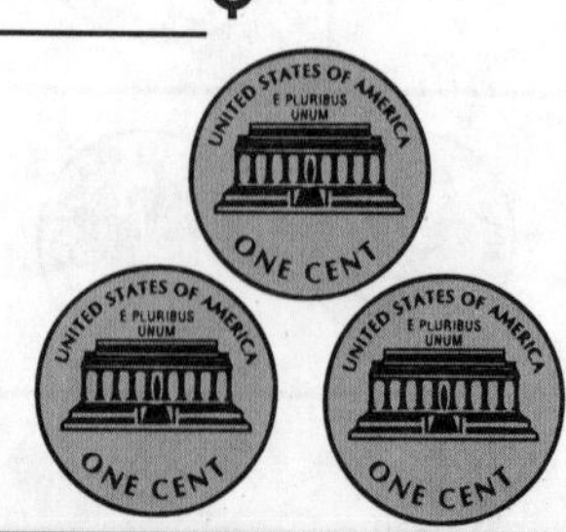

Name______________________________

Counting with Dimes, Nickels and Pennies

(Use with page 194)

There is a bake sale at school today.
Be sure to bring Mary Money along!

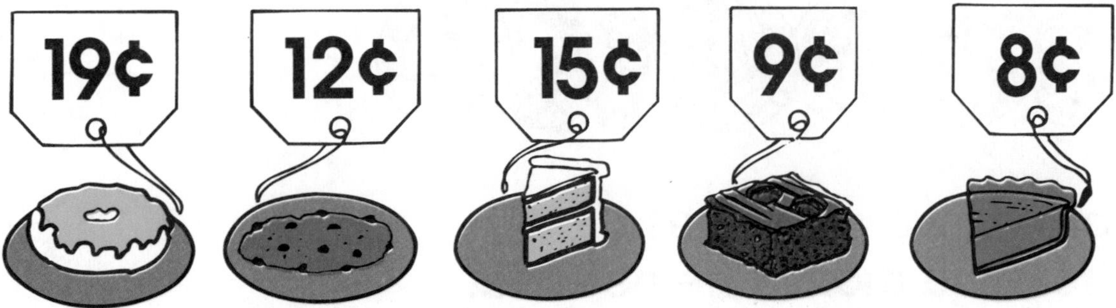

Decide which one you want.

In the space below, draw enough money to pay for it.

Name ____________________

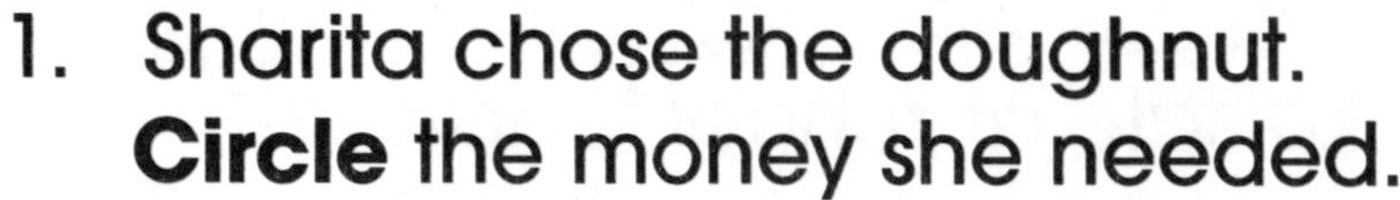

Counting with Dimes, Nickels and Pennies

(Use with page 193)

1. Sharita chose the doughnut.
   Circle the money she needed.

______ ¢

2. Robert loves brownies.
   Circle the money he needed.

______ ¢

3. Tom had 3 of these.
   He had ______ ¢. He spent it all on something good. **Draw** it here.

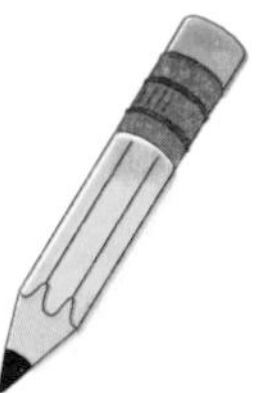

Yum!

Name ___________________________

Counting with Dimes, Nickels and Pennies

"Sir Circle" counts coins!
How much money?
Count the coins.
Circle the set with more money.

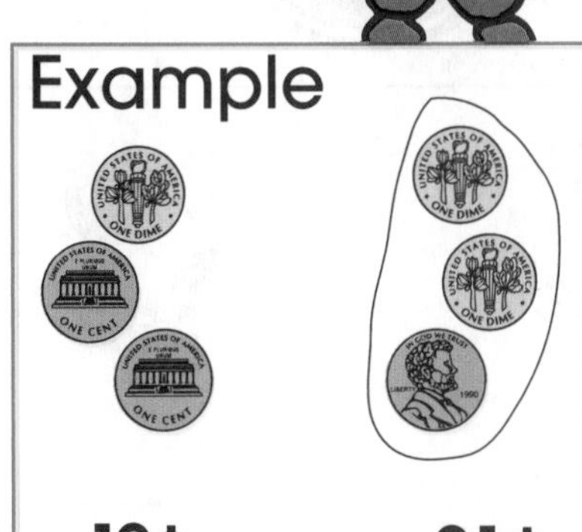

Example

12¢ 21¢

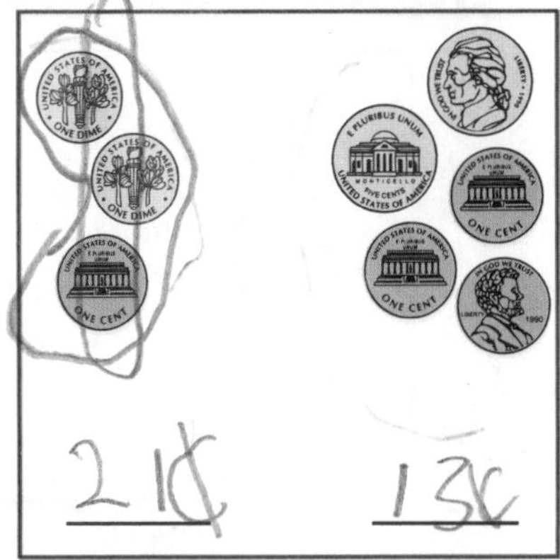

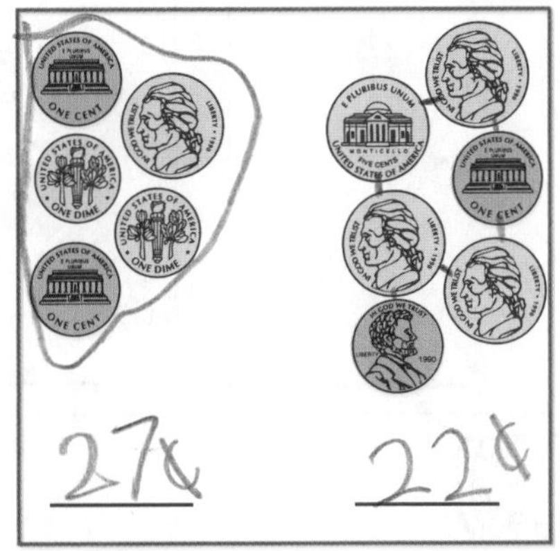

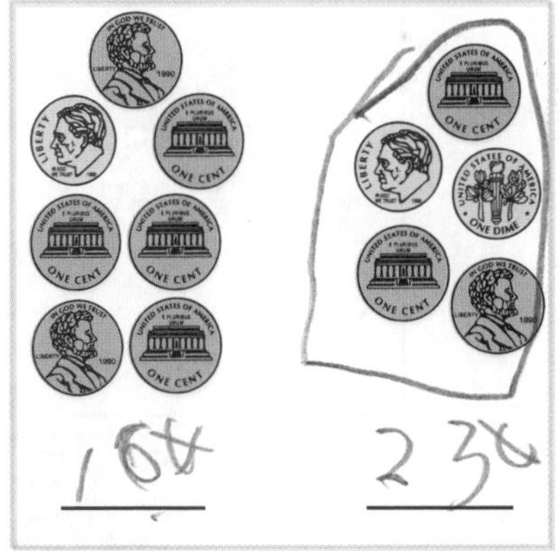

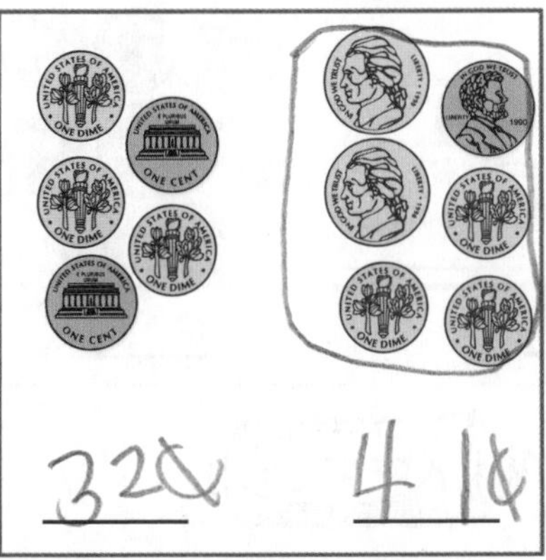

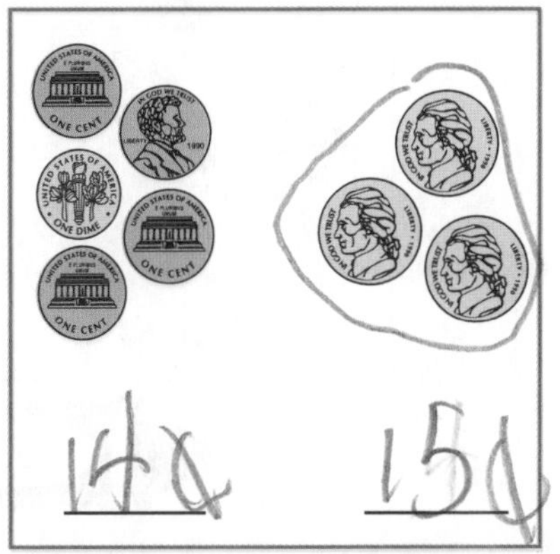

Name______________________________

Counting with Dimes, Nickels and Pennies

Colorful Coins

Count the coins. Use the right color to circle the set of coins with the most money.

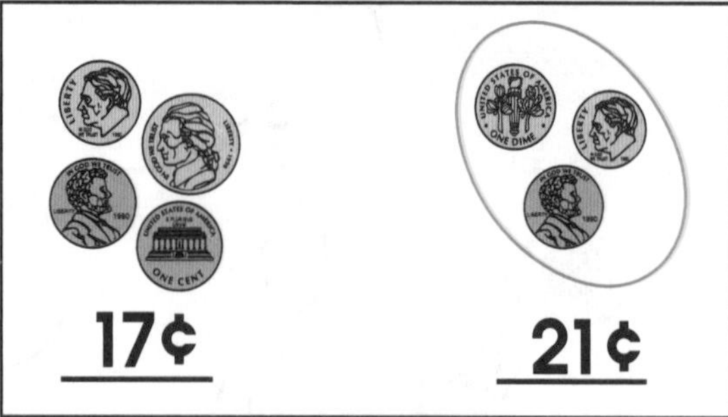

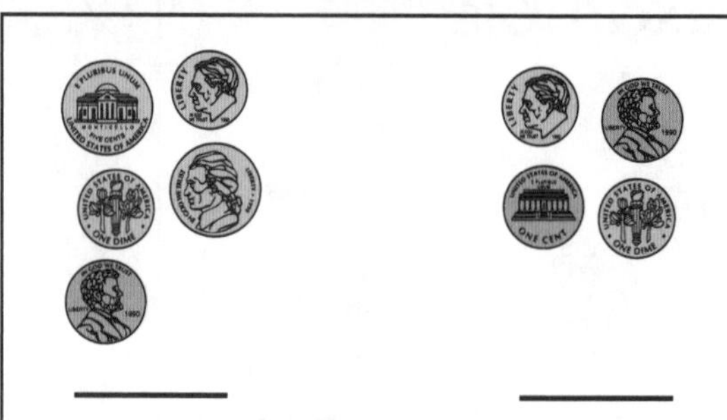

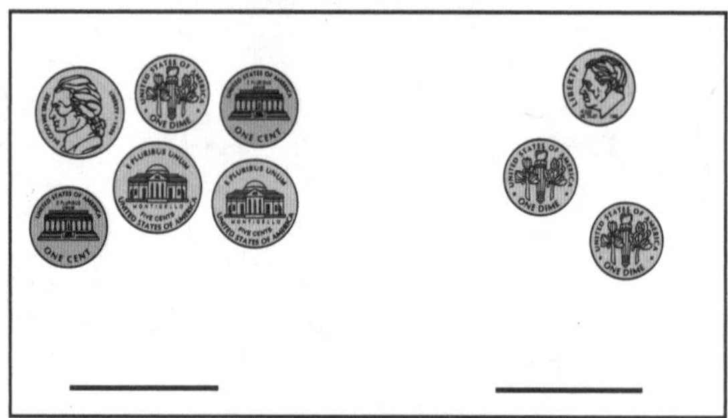

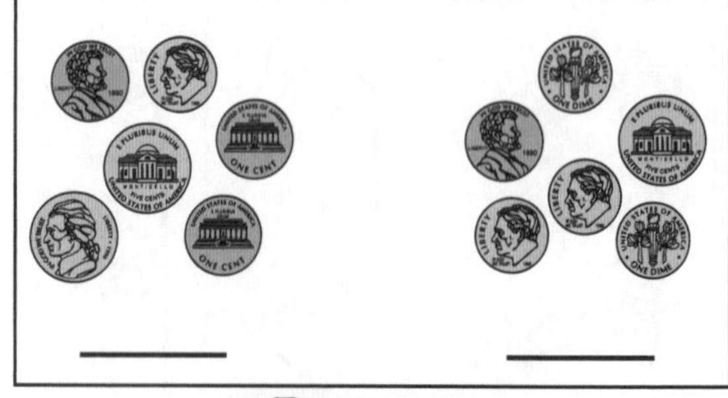

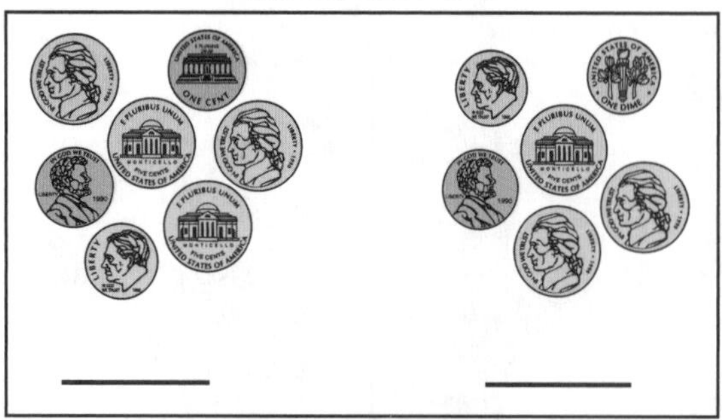

Name ______________________________

Counting with Dimes, Nickels and Pennies

Count the money.

Start with dimes. Then count the nickels and pennies.

A.

____¢ ____¢ ____¢ ____¢ ____¢ ____¢

Total

B.

____¢ ____¢ ____¢ ____¢

____¢ ____¢ ____¢ ____¢

Total

Name ____________________

Counting with Dimes, Nickels and Pennies

Buy and Buy

Circle the coins to equal the right amount.

Example:

Name______________________________________

Counting with Dimes, Nickels and Pennies

Smart Shoppers

Circle the coins to show the right amount.

Example:

Name___________________________________

Counting with Dimes, Nickels and Pennies

Join the Coins

Draw a line from the coins to the right amount.

Example:

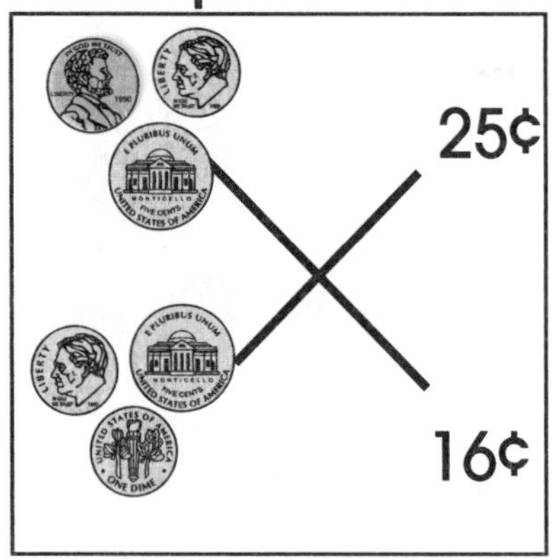

25¢

16¢

26¢

13¢

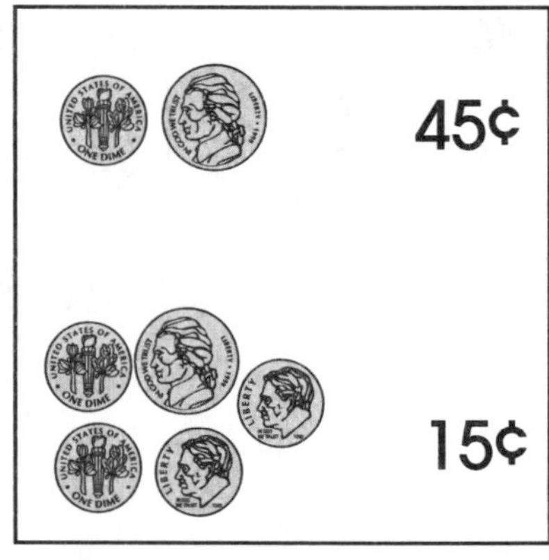

45¢

15¢

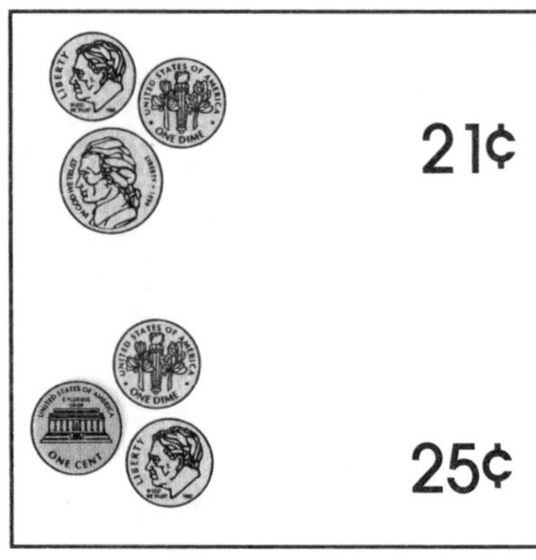

21¢

25¢

20¢

18¢

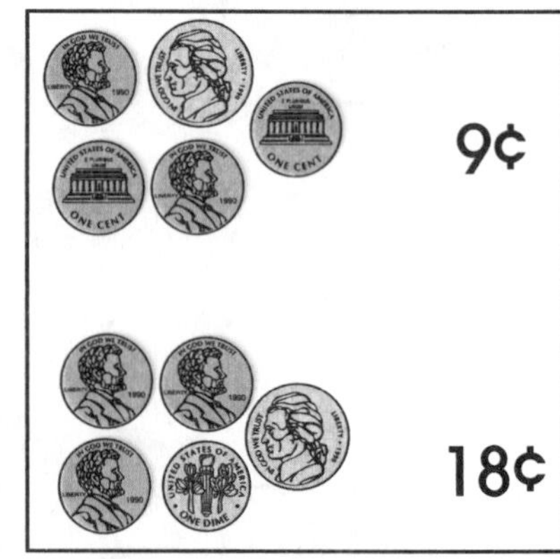

9¢

18¢

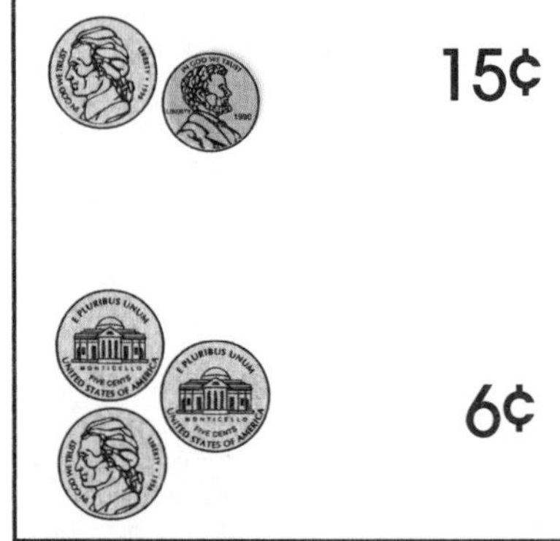

15¢

6¢

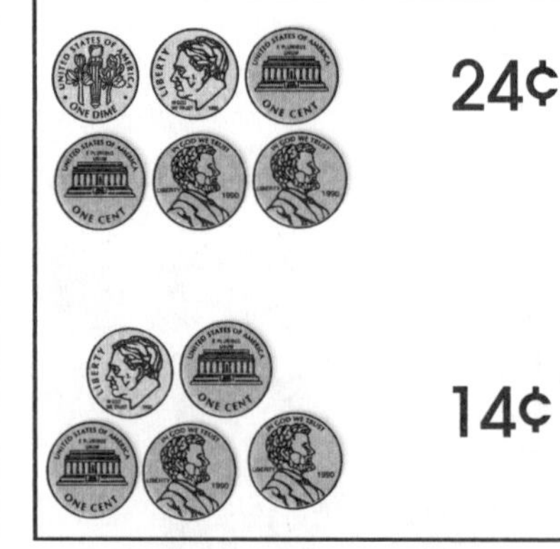

24¢

14¢

15¢

17¢

Name________________________________

Subtracting with Dimes, Nickels and Pennies

Earning money is fun! So is spending it!
See what the children buy with their money.

"X" the coins needed.
Write how much money is left.

José wants

He has

______¢
is left

Catherine wants

She has

______¢
is left

Name___________________________________

Subtracting with Dimes, Nickels and Pennies

Andrew wants

He has

_______¢
is left

Sherry wants

She has

_______¢
is left

Robert wants

He has

Can Robert buy the truck? _________

Name______________________________

Subtracting with Dimes, Nickels and Pennies

Pay the exact amount for each toy.

A.        

Coins left: __________

Money left: __________¢

B.         

Coins left: __________

Money left: __________¢

C. **Choose** a price between 30¢ and 40¢.
Write the price on the robot's tag.

Coins left: __________

Money left: __________¢

Name ______________________________

Quarters: Introduction

Presenting...
the Quarter!

Our first president,
George Washington, is on the **front**.
The American **eagle** is on the **back**.

front

back

__________ quarter = __________ pennies

__________ quarter = __________ cents

__________ quarter = __________ ¢

Count these nickels by 5's.

Is this another way to make 25¢?

yes no

Name________________________________

Follow each path to see how many quarters Mike and Maria found.

The **bananas** cost **25¢** each. How many can they buy?

Mike Monkey

Maria Monkey

BANANAS 25¢

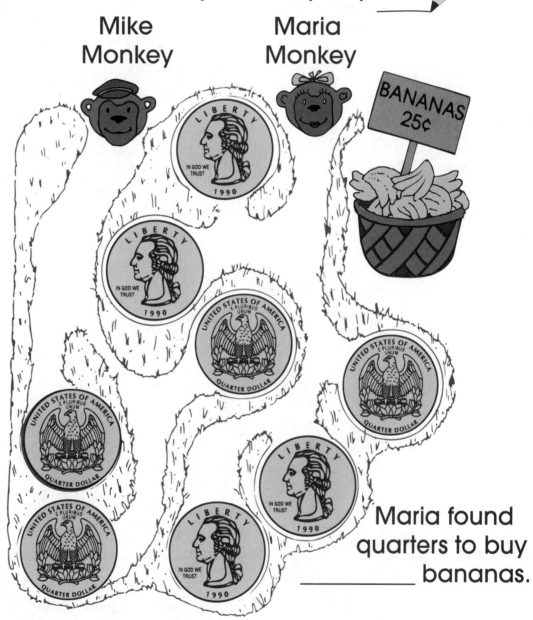

Maria found quarters to buy __________ bananas.

Mike found quarters to buy __________ bananas.

Name____

Quarters: Combinations of 25 Cents

These are all ways to make **25¢**.

Color each coin.

2 dimes, 1 nickel

5 nickels

25 pennies

Name ____________________

Quarters: Combinations of 25 Cents

Count the money.
Write the amount.
A **quarter** is worth **25¢**.

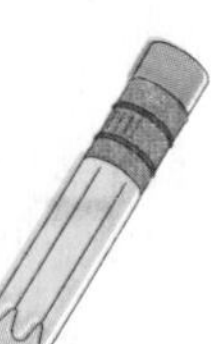

A.

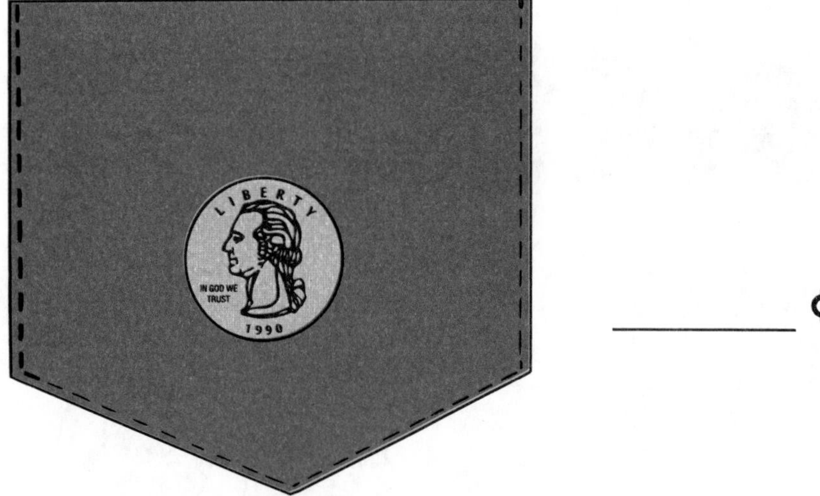

_________ ¢

B.

_________ ¢

Both of these pockets **show 25¢**.

Name________________________________

Quarters: Combinations of 25 Cents

It costs 25¢ to catch a fish.

Circle each group of coins that makes 25¢.

How many fish can I catch?

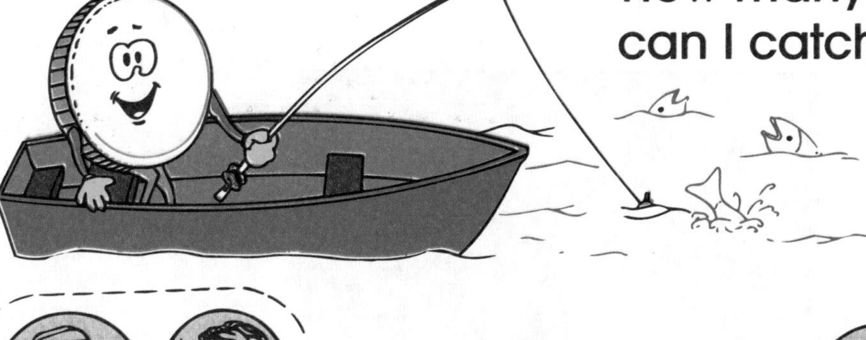

Draw and **color** the fish I can catch.

Name________________________________

Quarters: More or Less Than 50 Cents

The tooth fairy left 2 quarters for your shiny baby tooth.

How much money do you have?

Each quarter is worth 25¢.

Two quarters = 50¢

Color each toy you can buy.

Name________________________________

Quarters: More or Less Than 50 Cents

Some children had fun spending the allowance they earned. The boys bought some cars.

Terry paid 5¢ for each **blue** car.
Color Terry's cars **blue**.

How much did Terry pay for the **blue** cars?

__________¢

Lucas liked the **red** cars. They were the same price. **Color** his cars **red**.

How much did Lucas pay for the **red** cars?

__________¢

Which boy paid more? ______________

Name ______________________________

Quarters:
More or Less Than 50 Cents

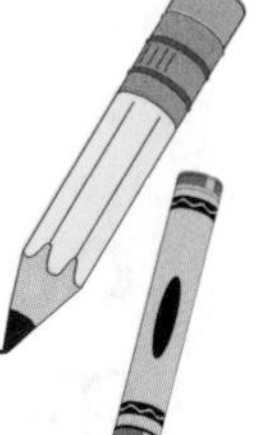

Patty bought some pears at the store.
She paid **25¢** for **each pear**. **Color** the pears.

25¢ each

Draw the quarters she spent.

How much money did she spend? ______¢

Jennifer bought these bananas. She paid **10¢** for **each one**. **Color** the bananas.

Draw the dimes she spent.

How much money did she spend? ______¢

Which girl spent less? ____________

Name______________________________

Counting with Quarters

These are some machines that use quarters.

Color each machine you have to put quarters into.

Circle the number of quarters you need.

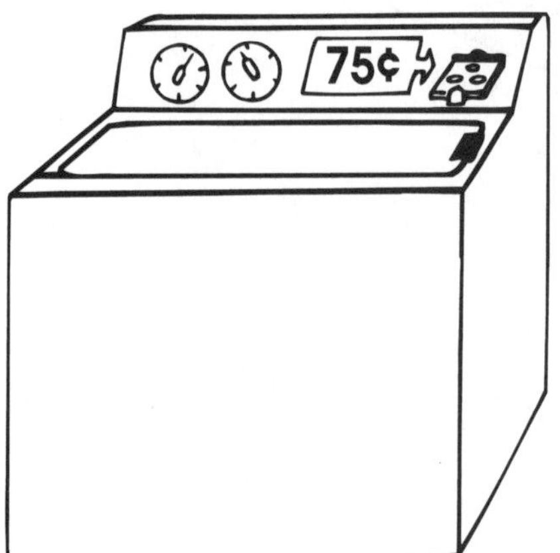

I need __________ quarters to wash clothes.

I need __________ quarter(s) to make a phone call.

Name______________________________

Counting with Quarters

75¢

Drinks

I need _____ quarters to buy a drink.

$1.00

I need _____ quarters to buy a comic book.

50¢

I need _____ quarters to buy a frozen fruit bar.

Hurry! It's melting!

Name ______________________________

Counting with Quarters, Dimes, Nickels and Pennies

Count the money.
Start with the quarters. Then **count** the dimes, nickels and pennies.

A.    

25¢	35¢	40¢	41¢
			Total

B.     

25¢	35¢	36¢	37¢	38¢

39¢	40¢
	Total

Name________________________________

Counting with Quarters, Dimes, Nickels and Pennies

Count the money.
Write the amount.
A **quarter** is worth **25¢**.

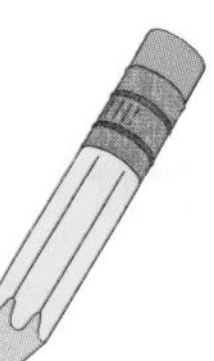

A.   

_______¢ _______¢ _______¢ _______¢
Total

B.   

_______¢ _______¢ _______¢ _______¢
Total

C. **Put** more than 50¢ in the bank. **Show** the coins.

_______¢
Total

Name ______________________________

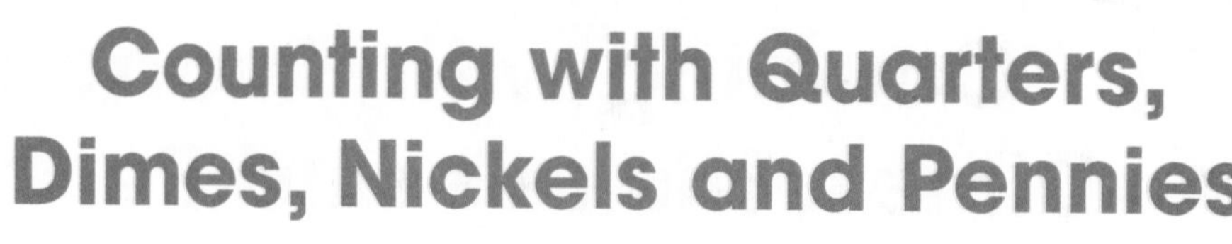

Counting with Quarters, Dimes, Nickels and Pennies

Count the money.
Start with the quarters. Then **count** the dimes, nickels and pennies.

A.

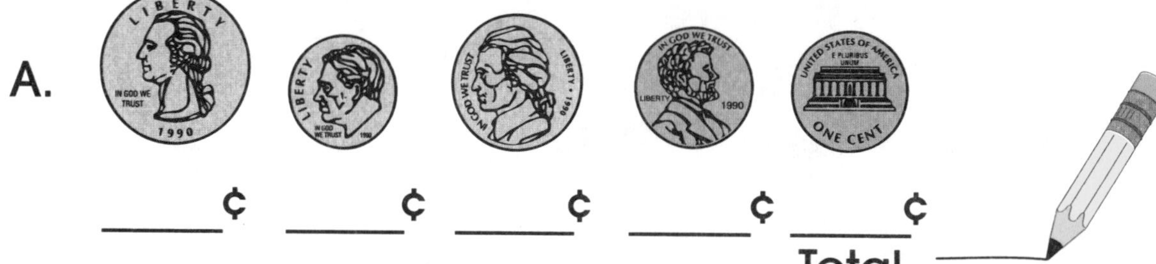

_____¢ _____¢ _____¢ _____¢ _____¢
Total

B.

_____¢ _____¢ _____¢ _____¢ _____¢ _____¢

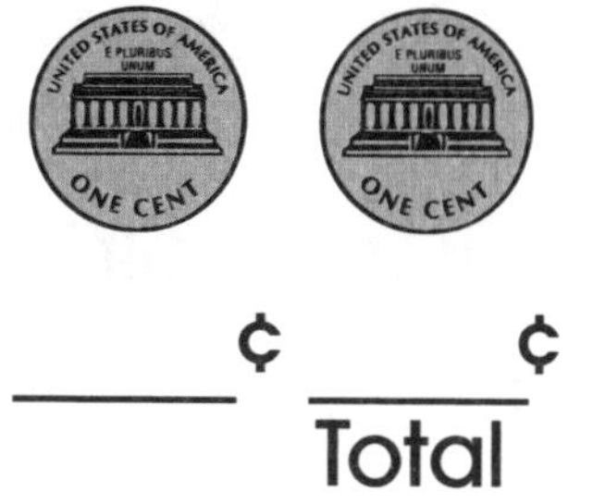

_____¢ _____¢
Total

C. **Solve** this puzzle.
What coins does Lizard have?

I'm counting my money.
25¢, 35¢, 45¢, 55¢, 60¢, 65¢, 66¢, 67¢.

Name________________________________

Counting with Quarters, Dimes, Nickels and Pennies

Count the money.

Start with the quarter.

Write the amount.

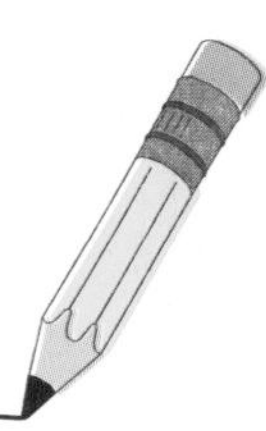

A.

__________ ¢

B.

__________ ¢

Name____________________

Count the money.

Start with the quarter.

Write the amount.

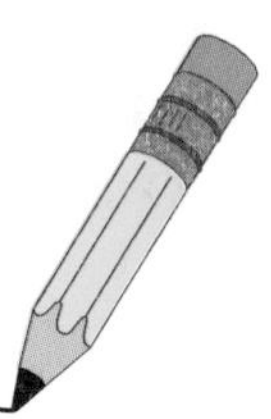

A.

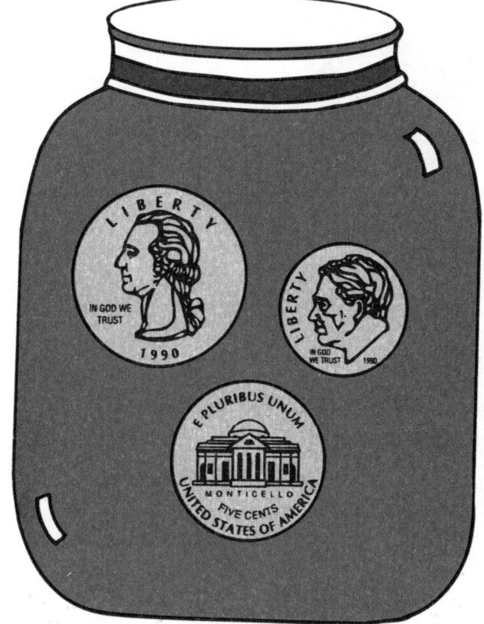

________¢

B.

________¢

Name________________________________

Counting with Quarters, Dimes, Nickels and Pennies

Match the money with the amount.

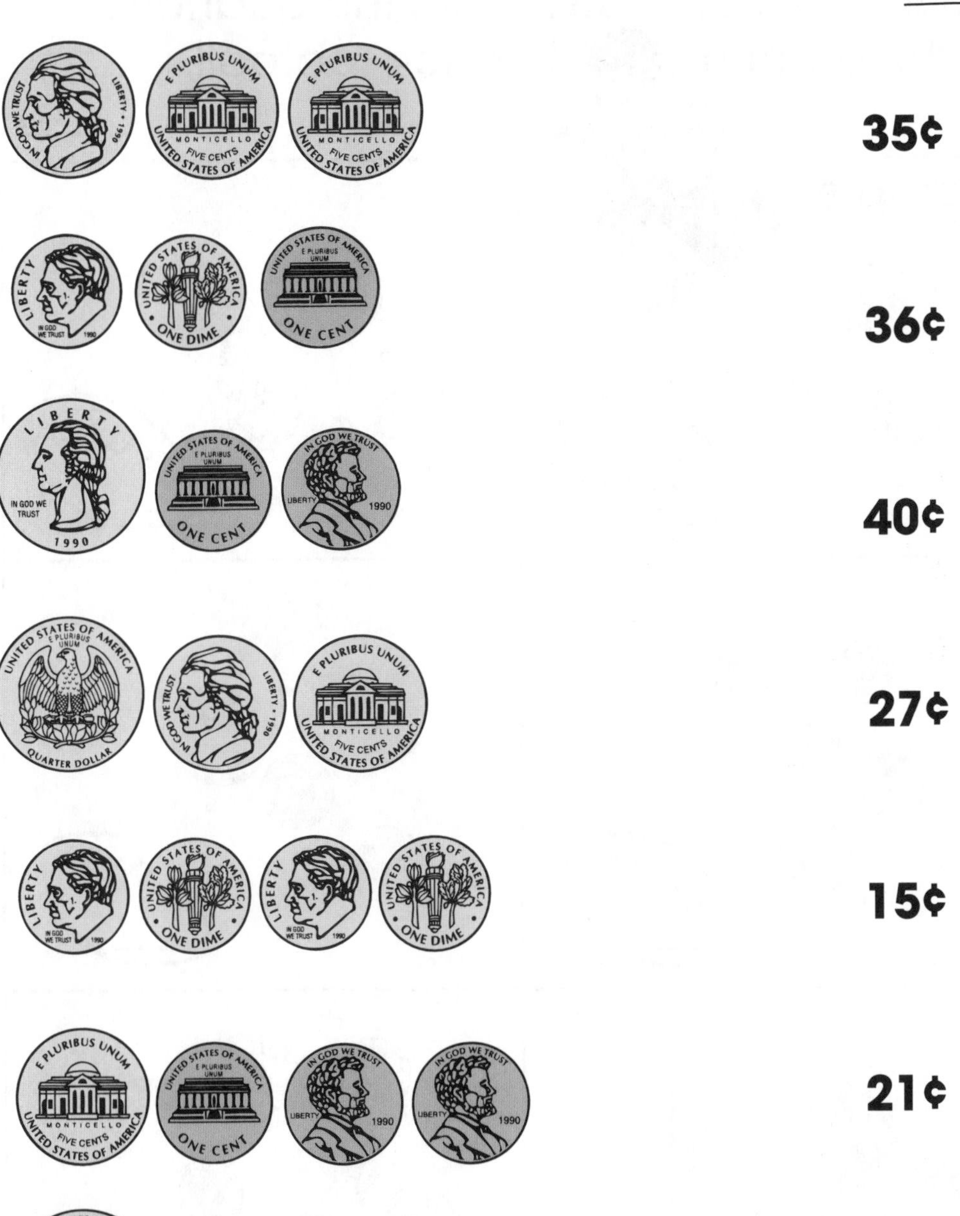

35¢

36¢

40¢

27¢

15¢

21¢

8¢

Good work!

Name____________________

Counting with Quarters, Dimes, Nickels and Pennies

Quarterback Attack

Count the coins. **Start** with the quarters. **Write** the amount in each football.

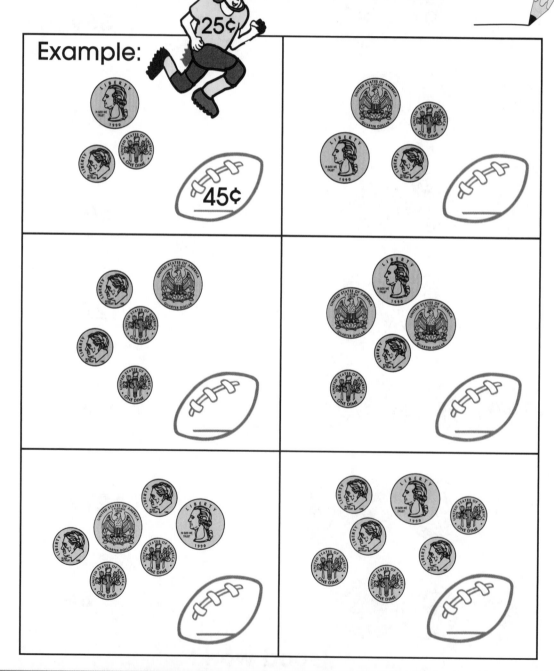

Example:

Name____

Counting with Quarters, Dimes, Nickels and Pennies

(Use with page 222)

Carolyn and Marilyn are going to the beach for their vacation.

The twins wanted to buy some things to take along. They emptied their piggy banks.

Name____________________________________

Counting with Quarters, Dimes, Nickels and Pennies

(Use with page 221)

Cross off the money Carolyn and Marilyn used for:

Color the pails **pink**.

Cross off the money they used for:

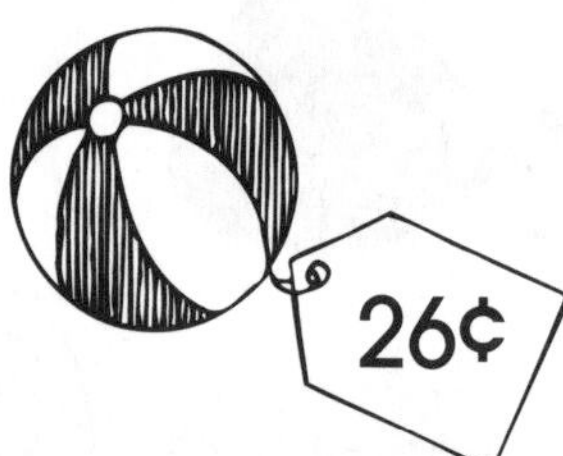

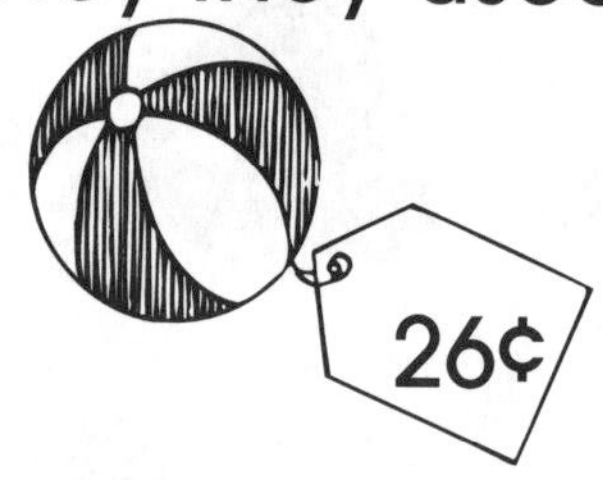

Color the beach balls **red** and **yellow**.

Cross off the money they used for:

Color the beach towels **blue** and **green**.

Cross off the money they used for:

Color the sunglasses.

Did they have enough money?__________

Name________________________________

Counting with Quarters, Dimes, Nickels and Pennies

You Make "**Cents**"

Count the coins.

Do you have enough money to buy each toy?

Example:	**You have...**		yes or no
58¢		51¢	no
47¢		______	______
75¢		______	______
43¢		______	______
98¢		______	______
32¢		______	______
26¢		______	______
45¢		______	______

Name________________________________

Counting with Quarters, Dimes, Nickels and Pennies

It is fun to buy things to keep your hair looking great!

20¢

32¢

How many of each coin do you need? **Write** 1, 2, 3 or 4.

	Quarters	Dimes	Nickels	Pennies

Name________________________________

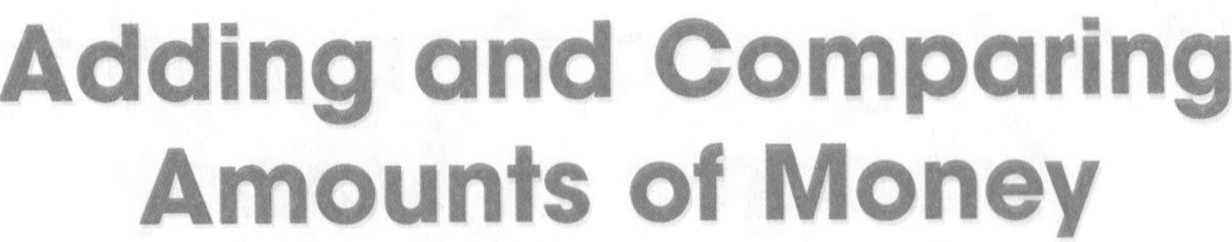

Adding and Comparing Amounts of Money

(Use with page 226)

Christopher was a good shopper.
He looked for the best prices when he bought school supplies.

Circle and **color** the one he bought.

________¢

or

________¢

Name_______________________________

Adding and Comparing Amounts of Money

(Use with page 225)

________¢

or

________¢

________¢

or

________¢

Draw the coins you think he spent for this notebook. Good job, Chris! **Spend wisely!**

How much? ________¢

Name____

Adding Nickels and Pennies

(Use with page 229)

You know how to add numbers when they are in a problem. **Can you add money the same way?**

When Gerald earns money and saves it in his bank, Mother always gives him 7¢ more because he is 7 years old. Gerald washed the dishes. He was given this money.

Cut and **glue** the 7¢ Mom gave him on this page and page 228.
Write the number problem.

25
7
32

This page left blank for cutting lesson on reverse side.

Name________________________________

Adding Dimes and Nickels

(Use with page 227)

Gerald mopped the kitchen floor for 2 dimes, then put wax on it for 2 more dimes.

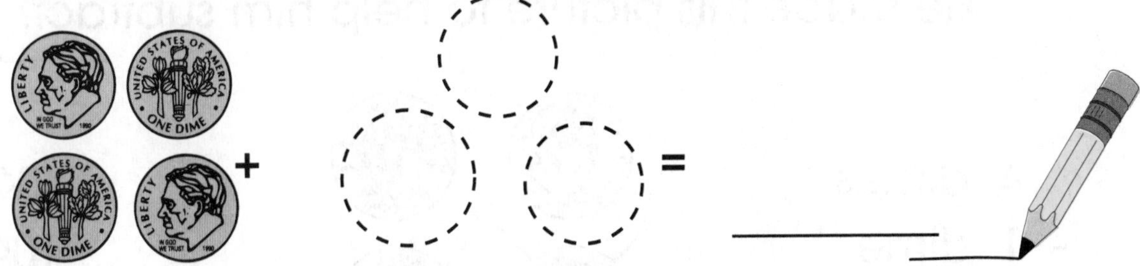

He watered all the plants.

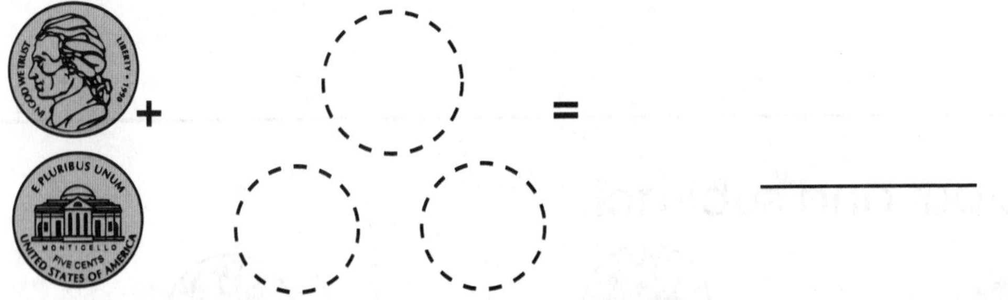

He folded the clothes from the dryer and put them away.

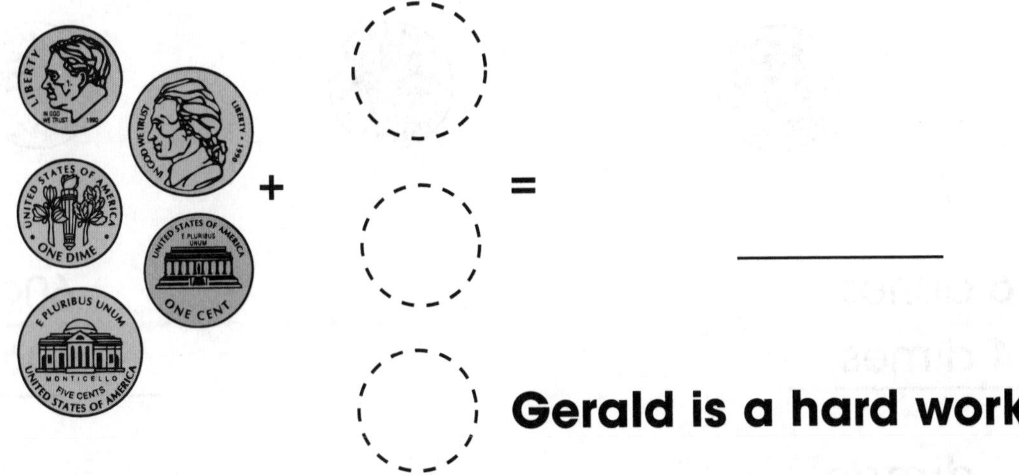

Gerald is a hard worker!

Name____________________________________

Coins

Subtracting for Change

Adam wanted to know how much change he would have left when he bought things.

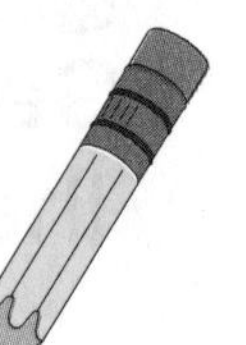

He made this picture to help him subtract.

4 dimes
- 1 dime
____
3 dimes

40¢
- 10¢
____
30¢

Cross out and subtract.

6 dimes
- 4 dimes
____
dimes

60¢
- 40¢
____

Name ______________________________

Subtracting for Change

Pay the exact amount for each toy.
Cross out the coins you use.

How much is left? ________

A.

Coins left: ______________

Money left: _______ ¢

B.

Coins left: ______________

Money left: _______ ¢

C.

Coins left: ______________

Money left: _______ ¢

Name ______________________

Subtracting for Change

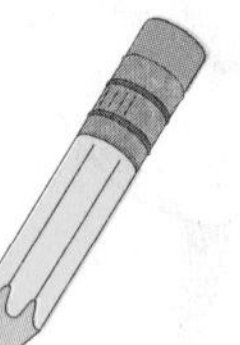

Cross out. **Write** the problem.

Adam wants:	Adam has:	
	  	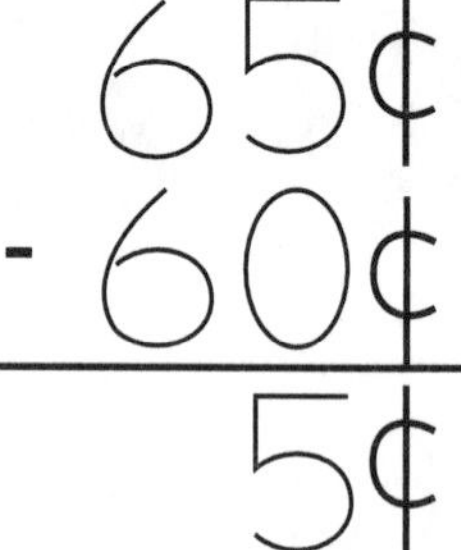
	 	¢ - ¢ ______ 
		¢ - ¢ ______ 

Name________________________________

Subtracting from 50 Cents

Maria went to the store to buy
a birthday gift for her best friend.

Maria took 50¢ to the store.
She looked at these things.

Circle the things she could buy.

Name___________________________

Subtracting from 50 Cents

Maria wanted to know how much change she would get back from each toy.

50¢
- ¢
_____

50¢
- ¢
_____

50¢
- ¢
_____

50¢
- ¢
_____

Color the toy you think Maria chose.

Name______________________________

Making Exact Amounts of Money

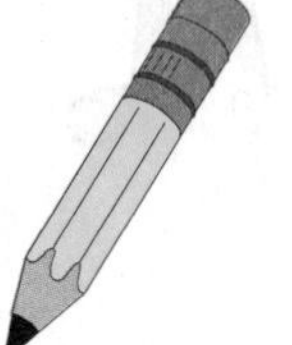

Use dimes, nickels and pennies.
Pay the exact amount for each toy.

A. What coins did you use?

______ dimes ______ nickels

______ pennies

B. What coins did you use?

______ dimes ______ nickels

______ pennies

C. **Solve** this puzzle.

What coins did Cat use to pay for the ball?

______ dimes ______ nickels

______ pennies

Name________________________________

Making Exact Amounts of Money

Use dimes, nickels and pennies.
Pay the exact amount for each toy.

A. What coins did you use?

______ dimes ______ nickels

______ pennies

B. What coins did you use?

______ quarters ______ dimes

______ nickels ______ pennies

C. **Solve** this puzzle.

What coins did Alligator use to pay for the toothbrush?

______ dimes ______ nickels

______ pennies

Name______________________________

Making Exact Amounts of Money

Use quarters, dimes, nickels and pennies.
Pay the exact amount for each toy.

A. What coins did you use?

______ quarters ______ dimes

______ nickels ______pennies

B. What coins did you use?

______ quarters ______ dimes

______nickels ______ pennies

C. **Solve** this puzzle.

What coins did Bird use
to pay for the pilot wings?

I used 6 coins
to pay.
PILOT
WINGS
30¢

______ quarters ______ dimes

______ nickels ______ pennies

Name________________________________

Making Exact Amounts of Money

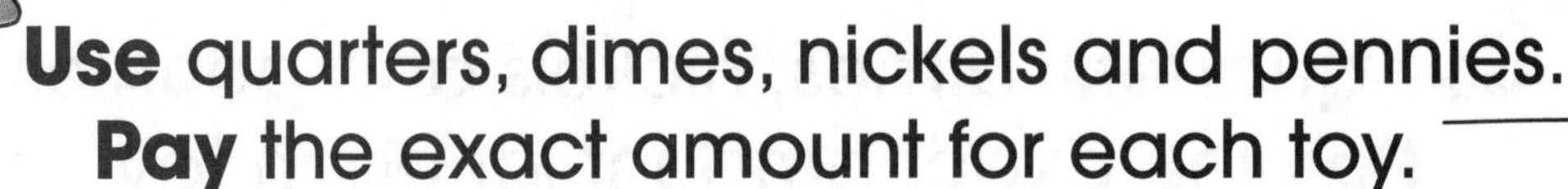

Use quarters, dimes, nickels and pennies.
Pay the exact amount for each toy.

A. What coins did you use?

______ quarters ______ dimes

______ nickels ______ pennies

B. What coins did you use?

______ quarters ______ dimes

______ nickels ______ pennies

C. **Solve** this puzzle.

What coins did Frog use to pay for the bow tie?

______ quarters ______ dimes

______ nickels ______ pennies

Name____________________________

Making Exact Amounts of Money

Use quarters, dimes, nickels and pennies.
Pay the exact amount for each toy.

A. What coins did you use?

______ quarters ______ dimes

______ nickels ______ pennies

B. What coins did you use?

______ quarters ______ dimes

______ nickels ______ pennies

C. **Solve** this puzzle.

What coins did Rabbit use to pay for the watch?

______ quarters ______ dimes

______ nickels ______ pennies

Name______________________________

Making Exact Amounts of Money and Change

Use the coins shown.
Pay the exact amount for each toy.
How much do you have left?

A.        

Coins left: ______________

Money left: ________¢

B.        

Coins left: ______________

Money left: ______¢

C.         

Choose a price between 42¢ and 58¢. **Write** the price on the tag.

Coins left: ______________

Money left: ______¢

Name____________________________________

Making Exact Amounts of Money and Change

Use the coins shown.
Pay the exact amount for each toy.

A.

Coins left: ______________

Money left: _______¢

B.

Coins left: ______________

Money left: _______¢

C. **Solve** this puzzle.

How much money does Turtle have left?

Coins left: ________________

Money left: _______¢

27¢
I had 2 dimes, 2 nickels and 2 pennies. Now I have one coin left.

Name________________________________

Making Exact Amounts of Money and Change

Use the coins shown.
Pay the exact amount for each toy.

A.          

Coins left: ______________

Money left: ______¢

B. 

Coins left: ______________

Money left: ______¢

C. **Solve** this puzzle.

How much money does Squirrel have left?

60¢
I had 2 quarters, 3 dimes and 1 nickel. I paid for the sunglasses. Now I have one coin left.

Coins left: ______________

Money left: ______¢

Name ______________________________

Problem-Solving with Money

(Use with page 244)

To be a good problem-solver,
you must **read the problem carefully**.

Think: What do I want to know?

Solve these problems.

1.

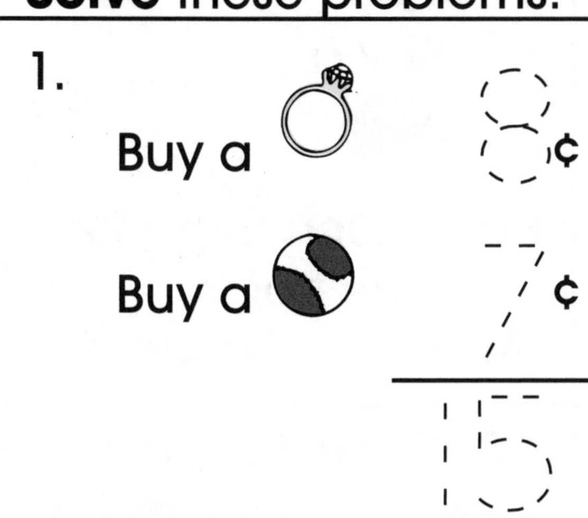

How much for both the ring and the ball?

Subtract

2.

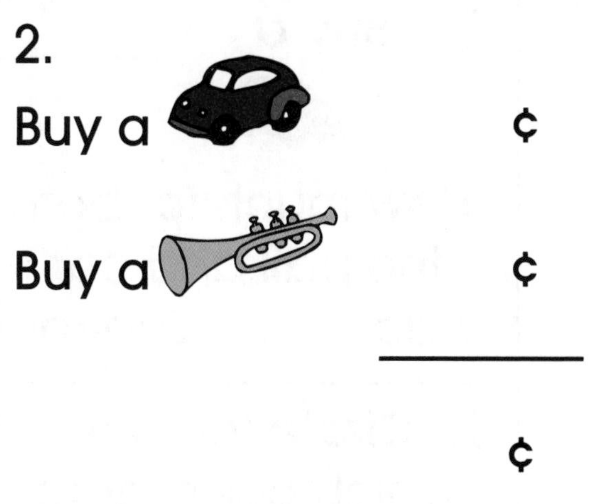

How much more for the car?

Add

Name________________________________

Problem-Solving with Money

(Use with page 243)

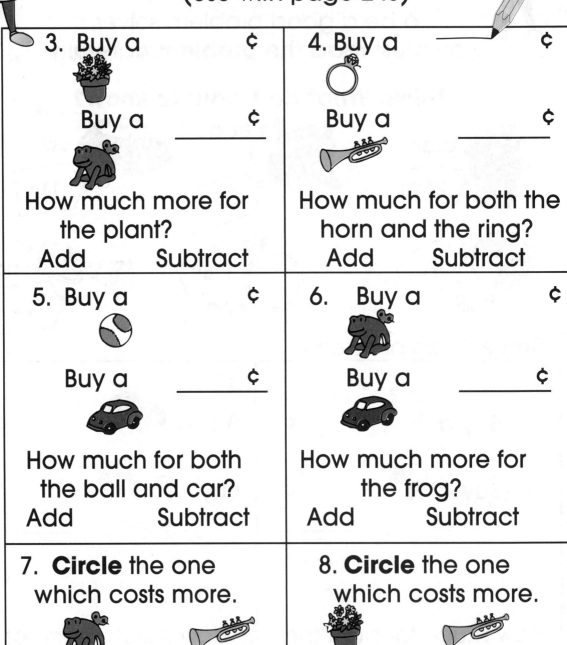

3. Buy a ¢

   Buy a ______ ¢

   How much more for the plant?

   Add Subtract

4. Buy a ______ ¢

   Buy a ______ ¢

   How much for both the horn and the ring?

   Add Subtract

5. Buy a ¢

   Buy a ______ ¢

   How much for both the ball and car?

   Add Subtract

6. Buy a ¢

   Buy a ______ ¢

   How much more for the frog?

   Add Subtract

7. **Circle** the one which costs more.

8. **Circle** the one which costs more.

Buy a , a  and a .

How much for all?

______ ¢ + ______ ¢ + ______ ¢ = ______ ¢

Name ______________________________

Problem-Solving with Money

How Much?

Draw the coins you use.
Write the number of coins on each blank.

A. 9¢

5 1 1 1 1

_______ dimes
_______ nickels
_______ pennies

B. 11¢

_______ dimes
_______ nickels
_______ pennies

C. 14¢

_______ dimes
_______ nickels
_______ pennies

D. Find another way to pay for the 14¢

_______ dimes
_______ nickels
_______ pennies

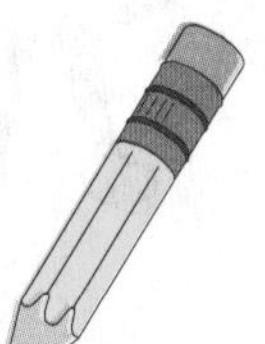

Name ____________________________

Problem-Solving with Money

How Much?

Draw the coins you use.
Write the number of coins on each blank.

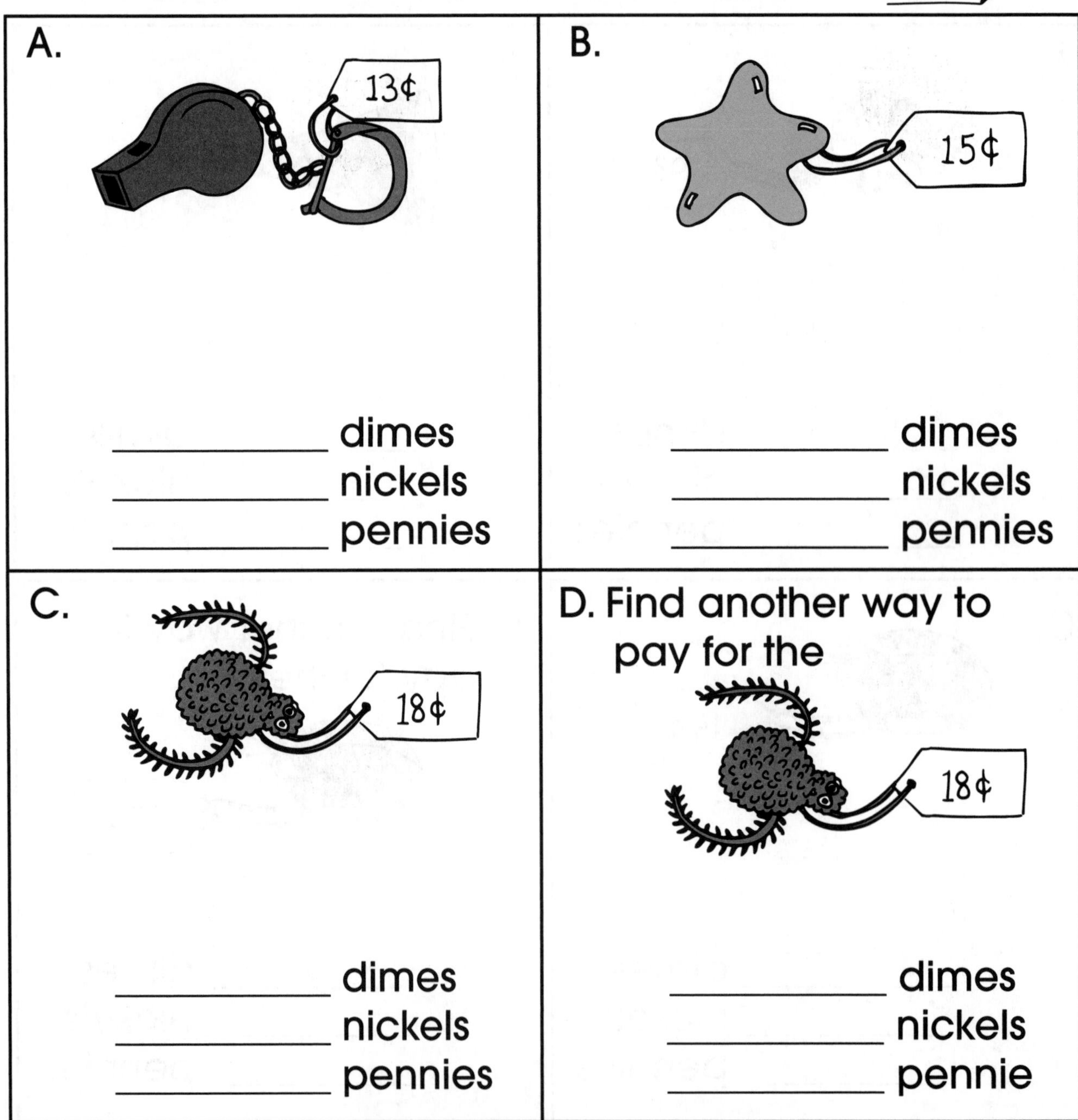

A.

13¢

_______ dimes
_______ nickels
_______ pennies

B.

15¢

_______ dimes
_______ nickels
_______ pennies

C.

18¢

_______ dimes
_______ nickels
_______ pennies

D. Find another way to pay for the

18¢

_______ dimes
_______ nickels
_______ pennie

Name ____________________

Problem-Solving with Money

How much?

Draw the coins you use.
Write the number of coins on each blank.

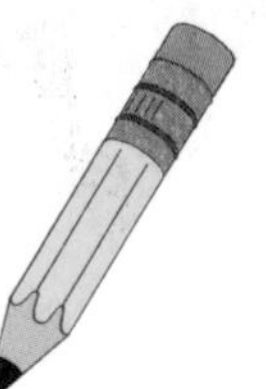

A.

______ quarters
______ dimes
______ nickels
______ pennies

B.

______ quarters
______ dimes
______ nickels
______ pennies

C.

______ quarters
______ dimes
______ nickels
______ pennies

D. Find another way to pay for the

______ quarters
______ dimes
______ nickels
______ pennies

Name ___________________________________

Problem-Solving with Money

How Much?

Draw the coins you use.
Write the number of coins on each blank.

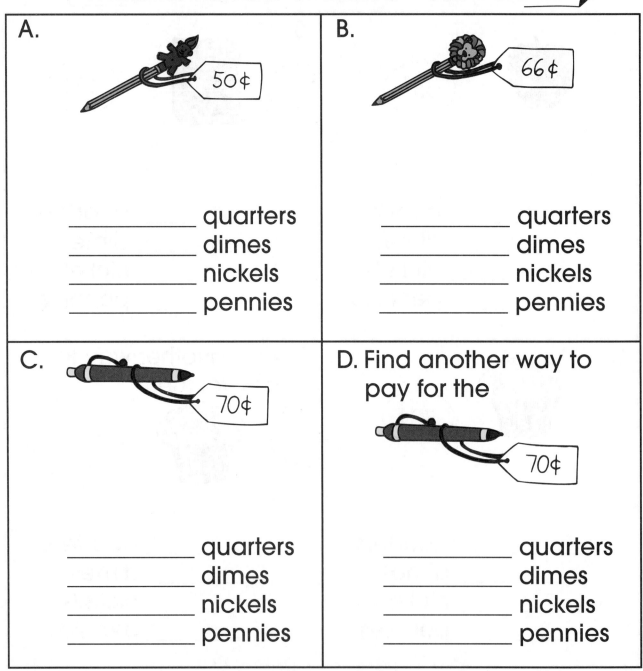

A.

50¢

_______ quarters
_______ dimes
_______ nickels
_______ pennies

B.

66¢

_______ quarters
_______ dimes
_______ nickels
_______ pennies

C.

70¢

_______ quarters
_______ dimes
_______ nickels
_______ pennies

D. Find another way to pay for the

70¢

_______ quarters
_______ dimes
_______ nickels
_______ pennies

Name ________________________________

Making Exact Amounts of Money: Two Ways to Pay

Find two ways to pay.
Show what coins you use.

A.

__________ quarters
__________ dimes
__________ nickels
__________ pennies

B.

__________ quarters
__________ dimes
__________ nickels
__________ pennies

C.

__________ quarters
__________ dimes
__________ nickels
__________ pennies

D.

__________ quarters
__________ dimes
__________ nickels
__________ pennies

Name ______________________________

Making Exact Amounts of Money: Two Ways to Pay

Find two ways to pay.
Show what coins you use.

A.

_______ quarters
_______ dimes
_______ nickels
_______ pennies

B.

_______ quarters
_______ dimes
_______ nickels
_______ pennies

C.

_______ quarters
_______ dimes
_______ nickels
_______ pennies

D.

_______ quarters
_______ dimes
_______ nickels
_______ pennies

Name ______________________________

Making Exact Amounts of Money: Two Ways to Pay

Find two ways to pay.
Show what coins you use.

A.

_________ quarters
_________ dimes
_________ nickels
_________ pennies

B.

_________ quarters
_________ dimes
_________ nickels
_________ pennies

C.

_________ quarters
_________ dimes
_________ nickels
_________ pennies

D.

_________ quarters
_________ dimes
_________ nickels
_________ pennies

Name________________________________

Making Exact Amounts of Money: How Much More?

Count the coins.
Find out how much more money you need to pay the exact amount.

A.  

How much money do you have? ______ ¢

How much more money do you need? ______ ¢

B.      

How much money do you have? ______ ¢

How much more money do you need? ______ ¢

C. **Solve** this puzzle.

How much more money does Frog need?

______ ¢

I have 1 quarter, 2 nickels, and 15 pennies. I need one more coin to buy the plane.
55¢

Name________________________________

Making Exact Amounts of Money: How Much More?

Count the coins.
Find out how much more money you need to pay the exact amount.

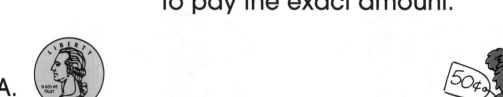

A. 

How much money do you have? ______ ¢

How much more money do you need? ______ ¢

B. 

How much money do you have? ______ ¢

How much more money do you need? ______ ¢

C. **Solve** this puzzle.

How much more money does Monkey need?

______ ¢

I have 1 quarter and 4 dimes. I need one more coin to pay for the banana-van.
75¢

Name______________________________

Half-Dollars: Introduction

Introducing the Half-Dollar

Meet another one of my money friends... the **Half-Dollar!**

front

back

The half-dollar is worth 50¢.

Look at each side of the half-dollar. **Color** them silver.

_____ half-dollar = _________ pennies

_____ half-dollar = _________ cents

_____ half-dollar = _________ ¢

Name ______________________________

Half-Dollars: Introduction

These are some ways to make a half dollar:

Color each coin.

1 half-dollar

2 quarters

10 nickels

5 dimes

50 pennies

Name________________________________

Counting Half-Dollars, Quarters, Dimes, Nickels and Pennies

Count the money.
Write each amount.
A **half-dollar** is worth **50¢** or **$.50**

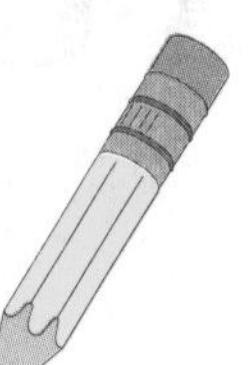

A.

______ ______ ______ ______¢

B.

______ ______ ______ ______ ______¢

C. **Draw** between 50¢ and 90¢ in the jar.

Name ____________________

Counting Half-Dollars, Quarters, Dimes, Nickels and Pennies

Count the money.
Write each amount.

A. 

______ ______ ______ ______ ¢

B. 

______ ______ ______ ______ ______ ______ ¢

C. **Draw** more than 80¢ in the pocket.

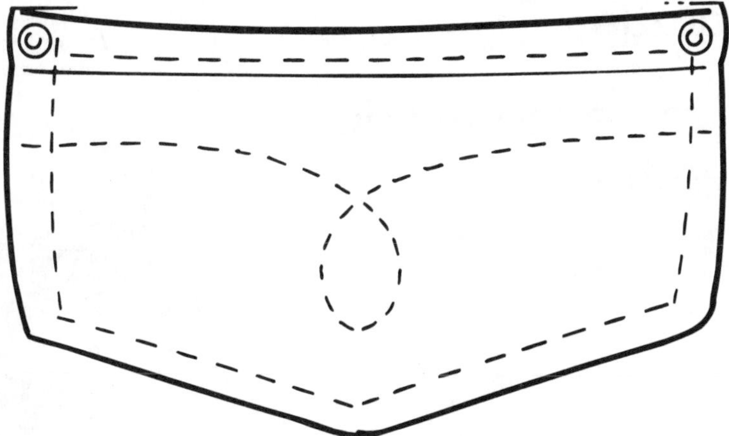

Name________________________________

Counting Coins: How Much More?

Count the coins.
Find out how much more money you need to pay the exact amount.

A.  

90¢

How much money do you have? ______ ¢

How much more money do you need? ______ ¢

B. 

99¢

How much money do you have? ______ ¢

How much more money do you need? ______ ¢

C. **Solve** this puzzle.

How much more money does Alligator need?

______ ¢

I have 1 half-dollar and 1 quarter. I need one more coin to pay for the jump rope.
76¢

Name ____________________

Counting Coins: How Much More?

Count the coins.

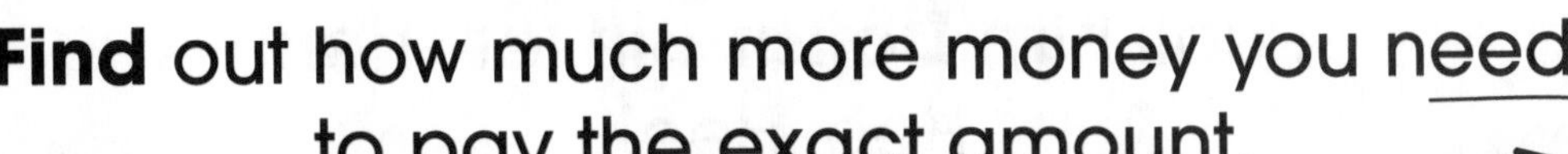

Find out how much more money you need to pay the exact amount.

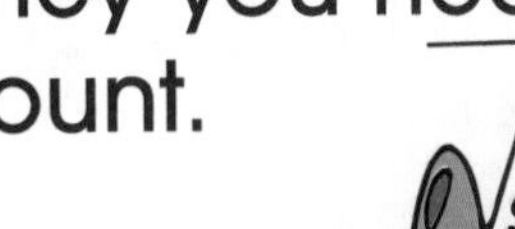

A.  

How much money do you have? ______ ¢

How much more money do you need? ______ ¢

B.       

How much money do you have? ______ ¢

How much more money do you need? ______ ¢

C. **Solve** this puzzle.

How much more money does Raccoon need?

______ ¢

I have 1 half-dollar, 1 quarter, 2 dimes, 1 nickel and 4 pennies. I need one more coin to buy the spyglass.
$1.09

Name________________________________

Dollar Bills: Introduction

Introducing the Dollar

Meet my friend, William Dollar.
I call him **Dollar Bill** for short!
Hee, Hee!

This is a **dollar bill**.

It has **2 sides**.

Color them green.

1 dollar = $1.00

1 dollar = 

1 dollar =  pennies

1 dollar = ______ cents

Name ______________________________

Dollar Bills: Introduction

Long ago, people got tired of carrying heavy coins in their pockets, **so... dollar bills were made!**

This is the **dollar sign**: **$**
It is an S with a line through it.

There is also a period between the dollars and the cents: $1.00

Name____________________

Dollar Bills: Introduction

There are many ways to make a dollar.

1 dollar bill

2 half-dollars

4 quarters

100 pennies

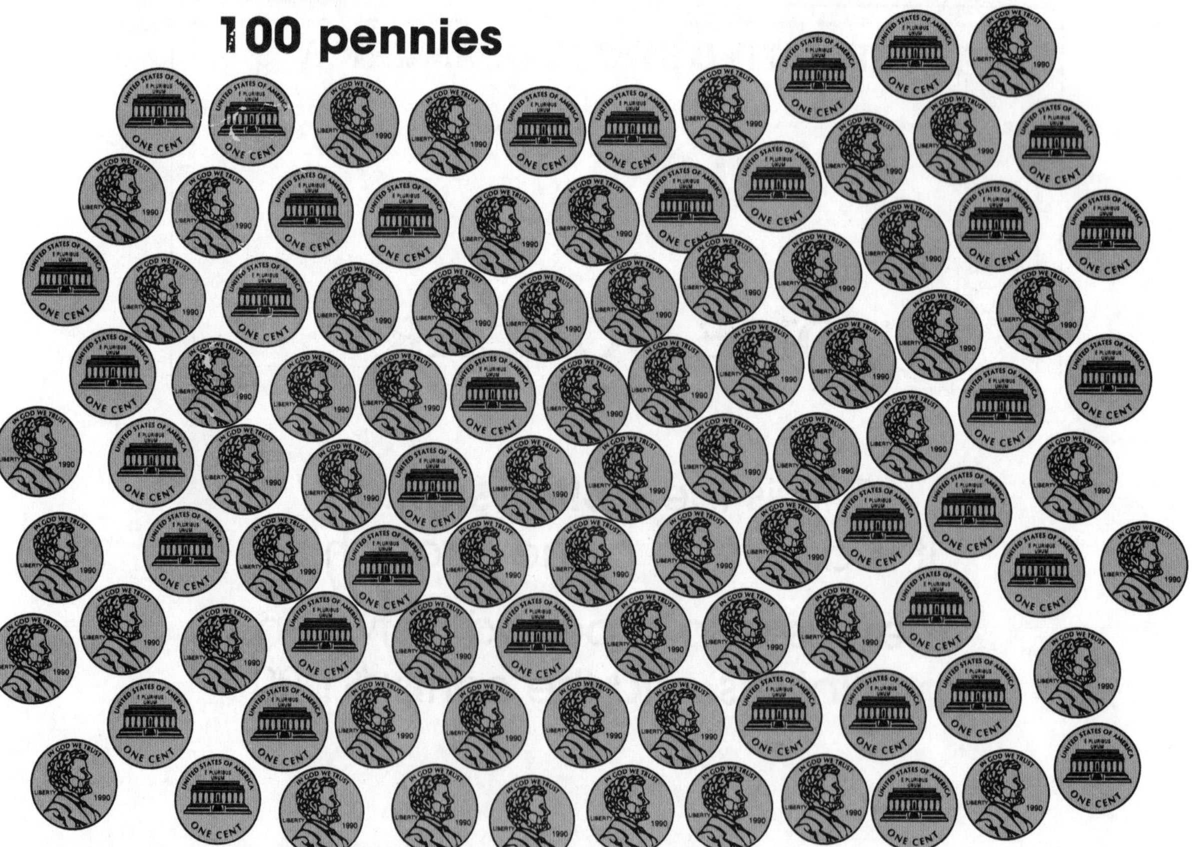

Name____________________________________

Dollar Bills: Introduction

Here are some more ways
to make a dollar!

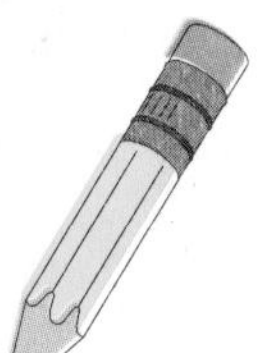

Count each set of coins.
If it equals one dollar, **write** $1.00 on the line.

Count by 10's with dimes. ____________

Count by 5's with nickels. ____________

It's a lot easier to carry **1 dollar bill** than **20 nickels!**

Name________________________________

Counting with Dollar Bills and Coins

Writing Dollar Amounts

A few **dollar tips** for you...

1. Drop the ¢ sign.
2. Add the $ sign.
3. Use a . (period) between the dollars and cents.

Write the amount of dollars and cents.

1. 

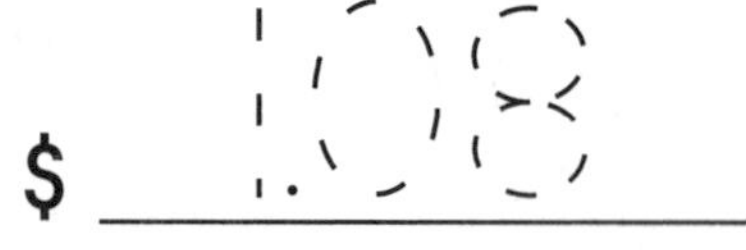

2. 

$ _____._________

Name ____________________

Counting with Dollar Bills and Coins

Count the money.
Write each amount.

A one-dollar bill  is worth 100¢ or $1.00.

A.  

____ ____ $ 1.25

B.   

____ ____ ____ $ ________

C. **Draw** about $2.00 in the bank. **Use** a one-dollar bill.

Name________________________________

Counting with Dollar Bills and Coins

Count the money.
Write each amount.

1.

$____.______

2.

$____.______

3.

$____.______

4.

$____.______

Name________________________________

Matching Dollar Amounts

Count the money.
Draw a line to match.

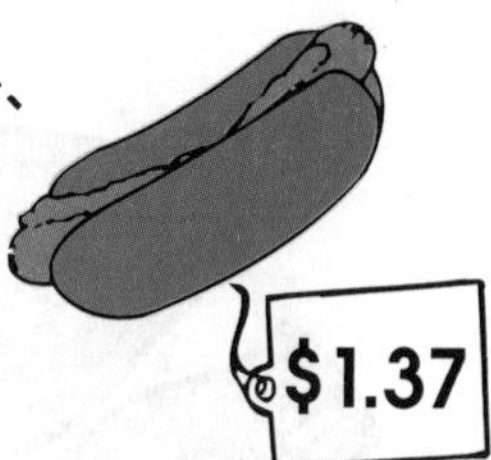

Name________________________________

Matching Dollar Amounts

A Good Match

Count the money.
Draw a line to match.

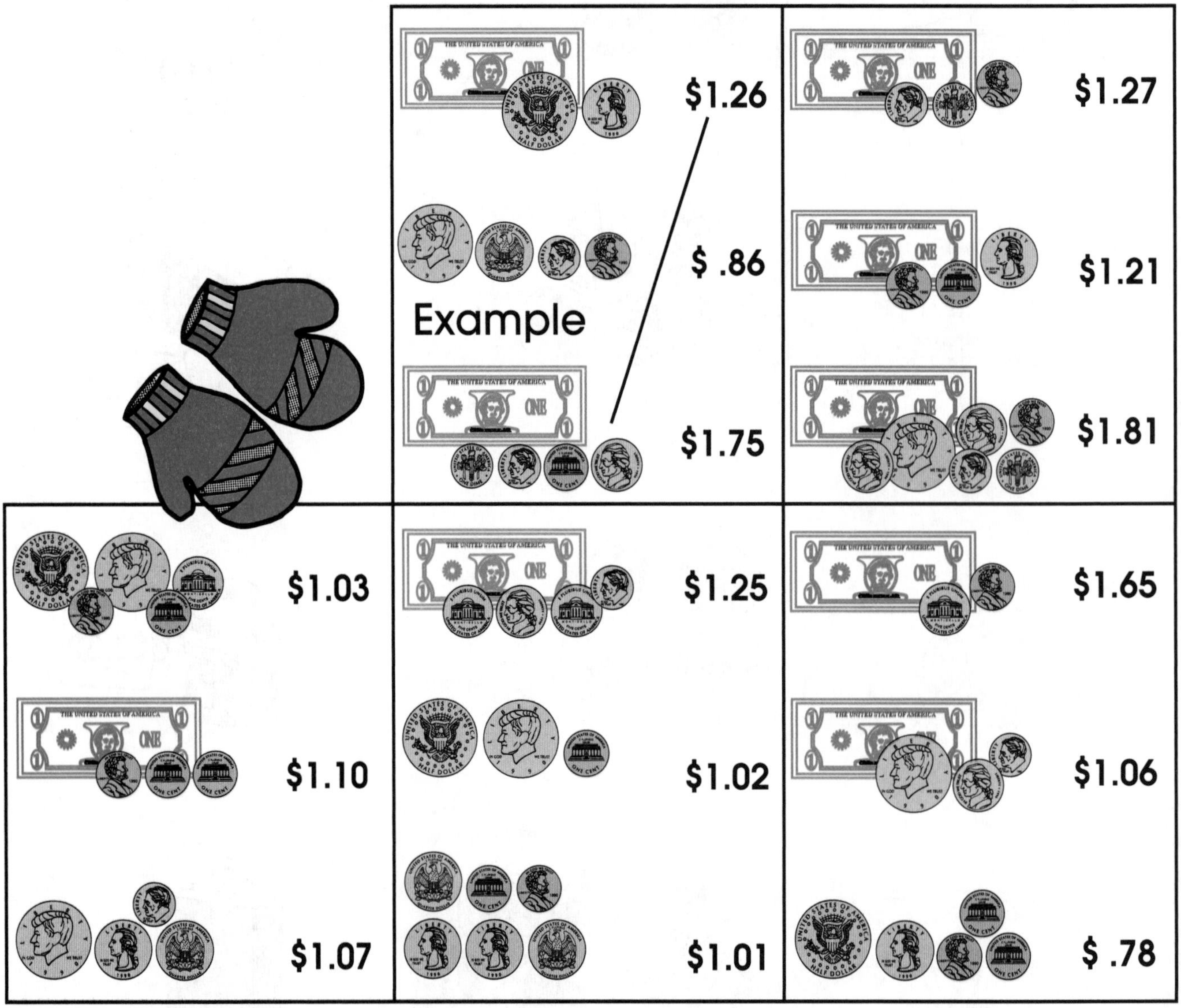

$1.26	$1.27
$ .86	$1.21
Example $1.75	$1.81

$1.03	$1.25	$1.65
$1.10	$1.02	$1.06
$1.07	$1.01	$ .78

Name________________________________

Counting Dollar Bills and Coins: How Much More?

Count the coins and bills.
Find out how much more money you need to pay the exact amount.

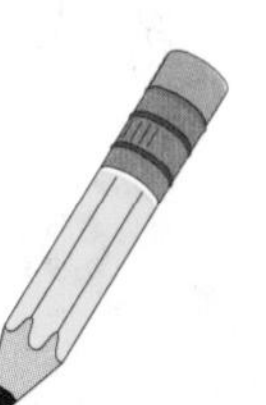

A. 

How much money do you have? ______¢

How much more money do you need? ______¢

B. 

How much money do you have? ______¢

How much more money do you need? ______¢

C. **Solve** this puzzle.

How much more money does Anteater need?

______¢

I have 1 dollar bill, 1 quarter, 1 dime and 1 penny. I need one more coin to buy the flashlight.
$1.61

Name________________________________

Estimating Amounts of Money

We estimate, or round up or down, to make a quick guess about money.

Circle the amount that is closer to the amount on the tag. **This is an estimate.**

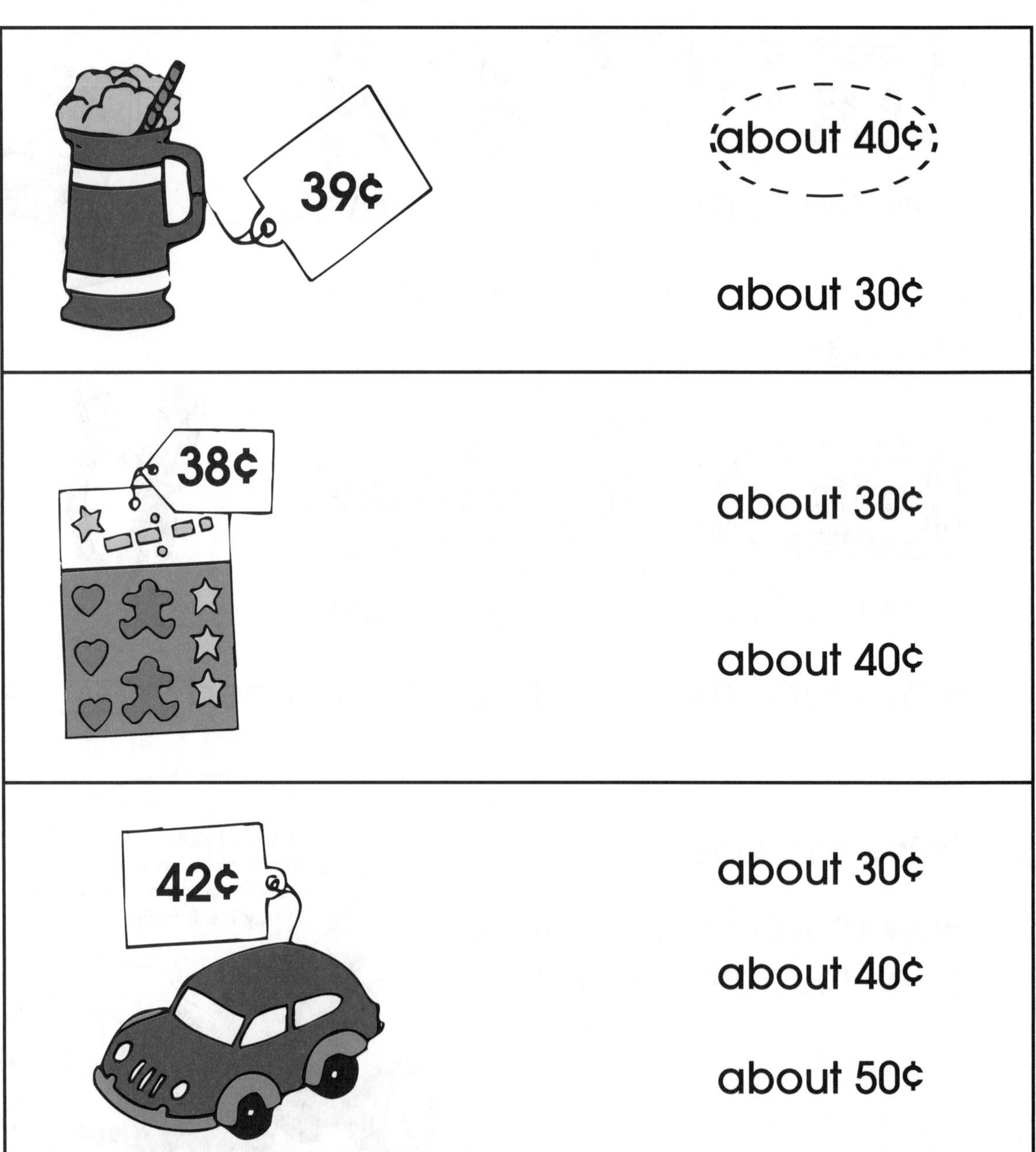

Name___________________________

Estimating Amounts of Money

Circle the best estimate.

about 50¢

about $1.40

about $1.50

about $2.00

about $3.00

about $4.00

about $1.00

about $2.00

about $3.00

about $3.00

about $4.00

Name________________________________

Adding and Subtracting Amounts of Money: Using Estimation

Using estimation makes it much easier to add or subtract in your head.

These foods are for sale in the lunchroom.

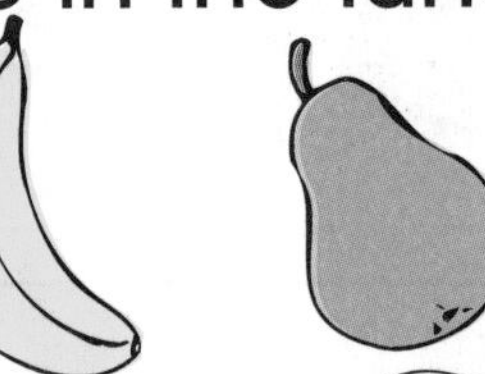

You have this much money:

You want the  **Round or estimate** the cost. _____ ¢

Do you have enough money?______

The  and 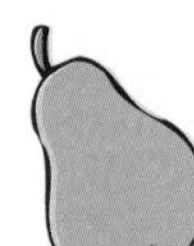 look good.

Add the estimated prices.

You probably have enough!

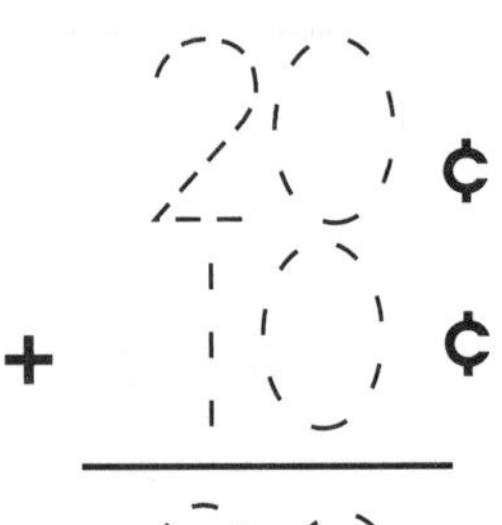

Name ______________________________

Adding and Subtracting Amounts of Money: Using Estimation

You have this money:

You have ________ cents. 

If you buy , will you have enough left to buy a ?

yes no

money you have = ________¢

estimated milk = - ________¢

________¢

You have this money:

You want to buy 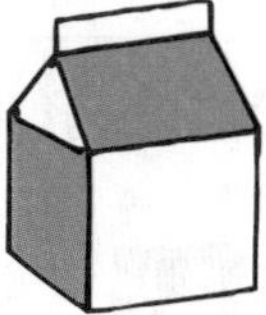 and an .

Estimate.

Do you have enough money? ________________

Which other fruit can you buy to have with your milk?

____

Name______________________________

Adding and Subtracting Amounts of Money: Making Change

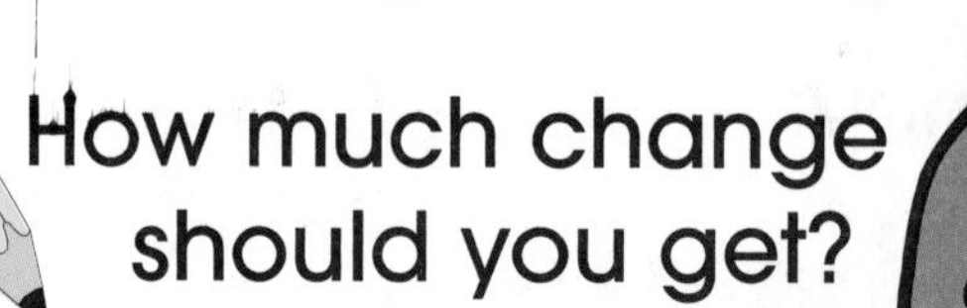

How much change should you get?

Example:

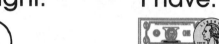

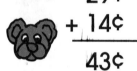

Bought:    29¢ + 14¢ = 43¢ **I have:**  55¢ - 43¢ = 12¢ Change 12¢	**Bought:**  56¢ + 27¢ **I have:** 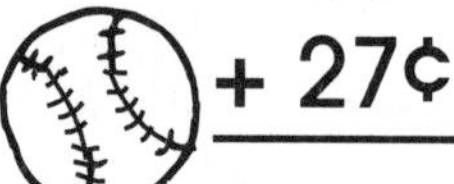 Change ☐
Bought:  61¢ + 59¢ **I have:**  Change ☐	**Bought:**   \$ .78 +\$ .69 **I have:** Change ☐
Bought: 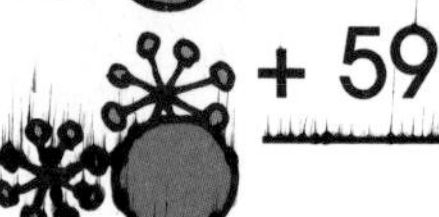   \$ .59 +\$ .86 **I have:**  Change ☐	**Bought:**    \$ .66 + \$ .75 **I have:**  Change ☐

Name________________________________

Adding and Subtracting Amounts of Money: Making Change

Lunch Money

How much change?

Example:

Lunch:	I have:
59¢ + 17¢ = 76¢	115¢ − 76¢ = 39¢
	Change 39¢

Lunch:	I have:
$ .86 + $ .15	
	Change

Lunch:	I have:
$0.75 + $ .16	
	Change

Lunch:	I have:
$ .66 + $1.26	
	Change

Lunch:	I have:
77¢ + 54¢	
	Change

Lunch:	I have:
64¢ + 89¢	
	Change

Name____

Making Change: Money Puzzles

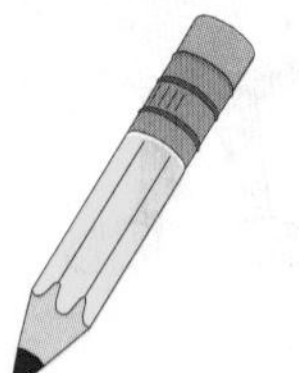

Solve the puzzles.
Show how much change you get.

A. Use 2 quarters. Pay  What change will you get? _______	B. Use 1 quarter, 2 dimes and 2 nickels. Pay  What change will you get? _______
C. Use 3 quarters and 1 dime. Pay  What change will you get? _______	D. Use 3 quarters and 2 nickels. Pay  What change will you get? _______

Name________________________________

Making Change: Money Puzzles

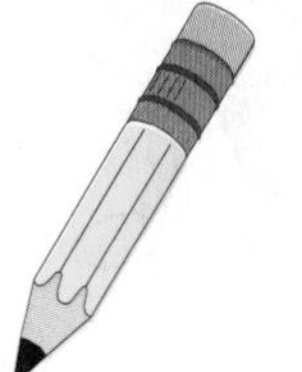

Solve the puzzles.
Show how much change you get.

A. Use 1 one-dollar bill. Pay  75¢ What change will you get? _______	B. Use 1 half-dollar and 2 quarters. Pay 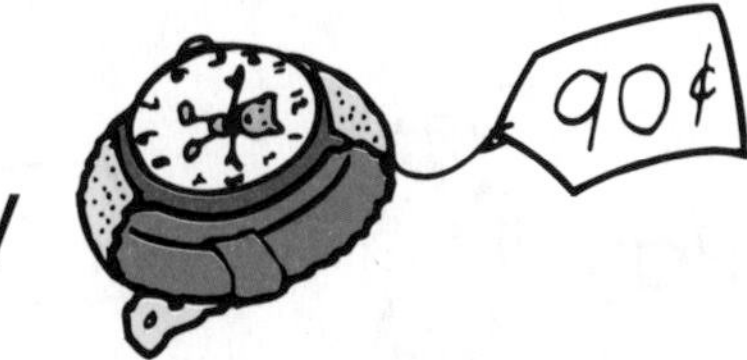 90¢ What change will you get? _______
C. Use 1 one-dollar bill and 1 quarter. Pay  $1.10 What change will you get? _______	D. Use 2 half-dollars, 1 quarter and 1 dime. Pay  $1.30 What change will you get? _______

Name______________________________

Making Change: Money Puzzles

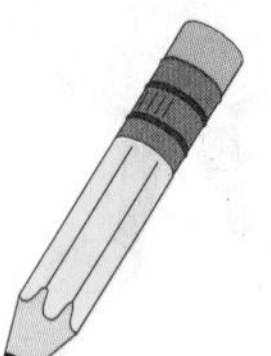

Solve the puzzles.
Show how much change you get.

A. Use 3 half-dollars. Pay  What change will you get? _______	B. Use 1 one-dollar bill, 2 quarters and 1 dime.  Pay What change will you get? _______
C. Use 1 one-dollar bill, 1 half-dollar and 1 quarter.  Pay What change will you get? _______	D. Use 1 one-dollar bill and 2 half-dollars. Pay  What change will you get? _______

Name ____________________

Making Change: Money Puzzles

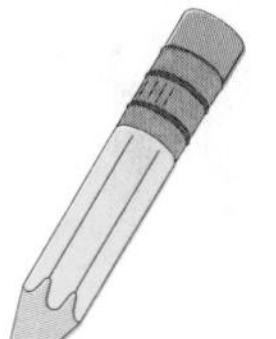

Solve the puzzles.
Show how much change you get.

A. Use 2 one-dollar bills.	B. Use 2 one-dollar bills.
 Pay	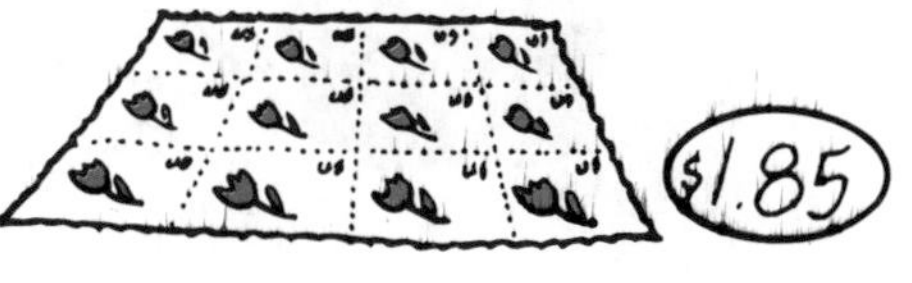 Pay
What change will you get? _______	What change will you get? _______
C. Use 3 one-dollar bills.	**D. Use 3 one-dollar bills.**
Pay 	Pay 
What change will you get? _______	What change will you get? _______

Name ______________________________

Making Change: Money Puzzles

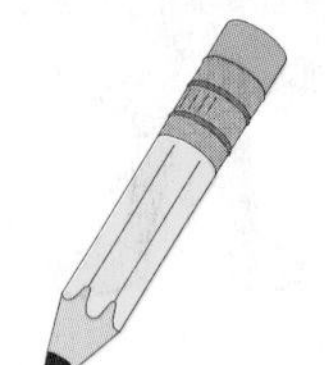

Solve the puzzles.
Show how much change you get.

A. Use 4 one-dollar bills.

Pay

What change will you get? ________

B. Use 5 one-dollar bills.

Pay

What change will you get? ________

C. Use 3 one-dollar bills.

Pay

What change will you get? ________

D. Use 2 one-dollar bills.

Pay

What change will you get? ________

Name ____________________

Making Exact Amounts of Money

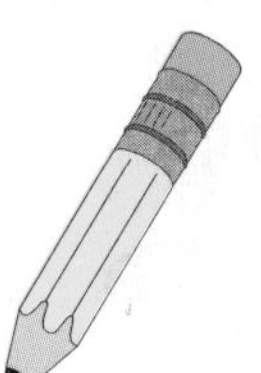

Pay for each toy.
Show what coins you use.

A. 60¢

_______ quarters
_______ dimes
_______ nickels

B. 55¢

_______ quarters
_______ dimes
_______ nickels

C. **Write** the price.

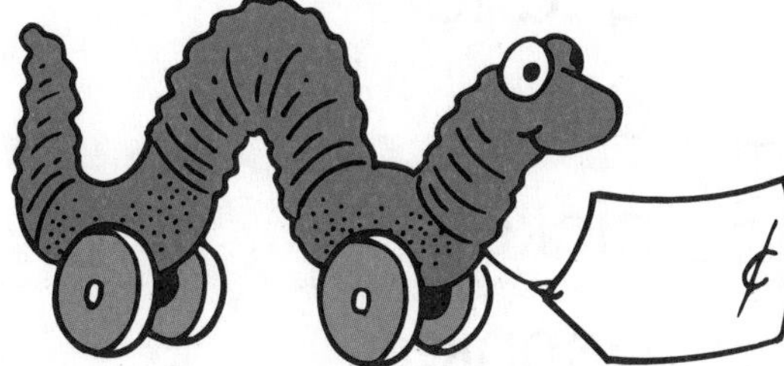

_______ quarters
_______ dimes
_______ nickels

Name____________________________

Making Exact Amounts of Money

Pay for each snack.
Show what coins you use.

A.

_________ quarters
_________ dimes
_________ nickels
_________ pennies

B.

_________ quarters
_________ dimes
_________ nickels
_________ pennies

C. **Write** the price.

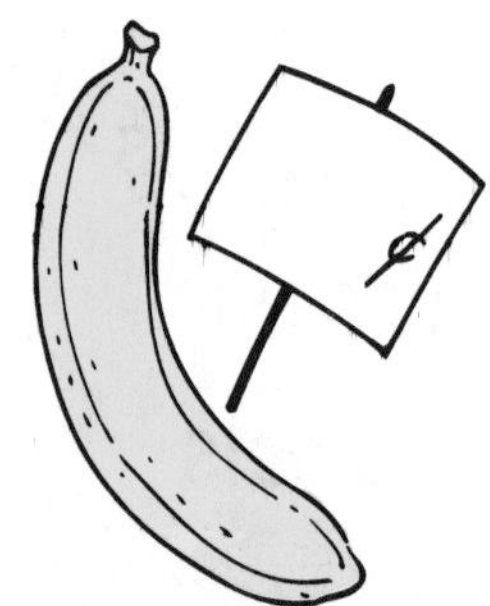

_________ quarters
_________ dimes
_________ nickels
_________ pennies

Name ____________________

Making Exact Amounts of Money

Pay for each robot.
Show what coins you use.

A.

_________ half-dollars
_________ quarters
_________ dimes
_________ nickels
_________ pennies

B.

_________ half-dollars
_________ quarters
_________ dimes
_________ nickels
_________ pennies

C. **Write** the price.

_________ half-dollars
_________ quarters
_________ dimes
_________ nickels
_________ pennies

Name________________________________

Making Exact Amounts of Money

Pay for each animal.
Show what coins you use.

A.

__________ half-dollars
__________ quarters
__________ dimes
__________ nickels
__________ pennies

B.

__________ half-dollars
__________ quarters
__________ dimes
__________ nickels
__________ pennies

C. **Write** the price.

__________ half-dollars
__________ quarters
__________ dimes
__________ nickels
__________ pennies

Name ____________________

Making Exact Amounts of Money

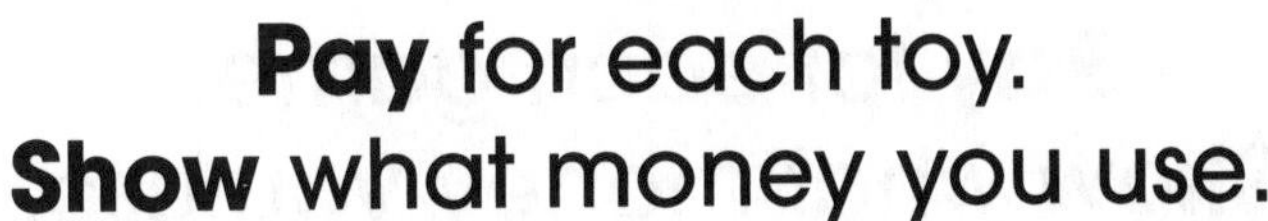

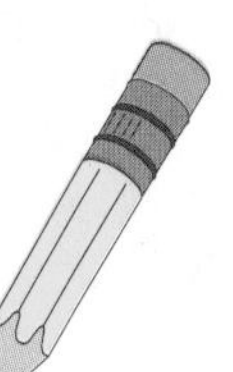

Pay for each toy.
Show what money you use.

A.

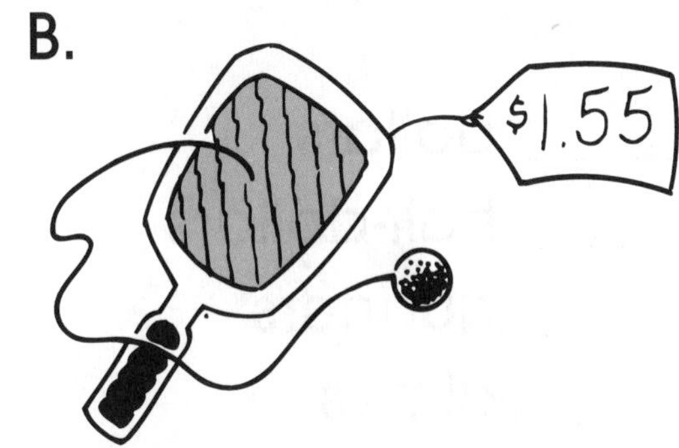

_______ dollars
_______ half-dollars
_______ quarters
_______ dimes
_______ nickels
_______ pennies

B.

_______ dollars
_______ half-dollars
_______ quarters
_______ dimes
_______ nickels
_______ pennies

C. **Write** the price.

_______ dollars
_______ half-dollars
_______ quarters
_______ dimes
_______ nickels
_______ pennies

Name ____________________

Making Exact Amounts of Money

Pay for each game.
Show what money you use.

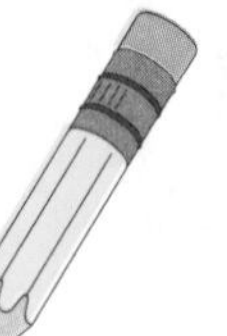

A.

_________ dollars
_________ half-dollars
_________ quarters
_________ dimes
_________ nickels
_________ pennies

B.

_________ dollars
_________ half-dollars
_________ quarters
_________ dimes
_________ nickels
_________ pennies

C. **Write** the price.

_________ dollars
_________ half-dollars
_________ quarters
_________ dimes
_________ nickels
_________ pennies

Name________________________________

Review

Using Combinations of Coins to Pay

How Would You Pay?
Pay for each cookie.
Use as few coins as you can.

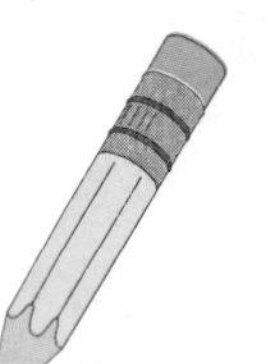

	Quarter	Dime	Nickel	Penny	Number of Coins Used
A. 28¢	1			3	4
B. 39¢					
C. 49¢					
D. Write the price. ¢					

Name________________________________

Review

Using Combinations of Coins to Pay

How Would You Pay?
Pay for each toy.
Use as few coins as you can.

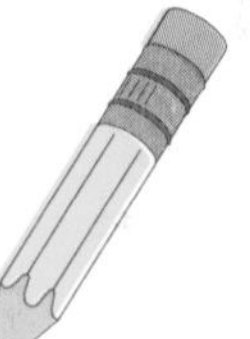

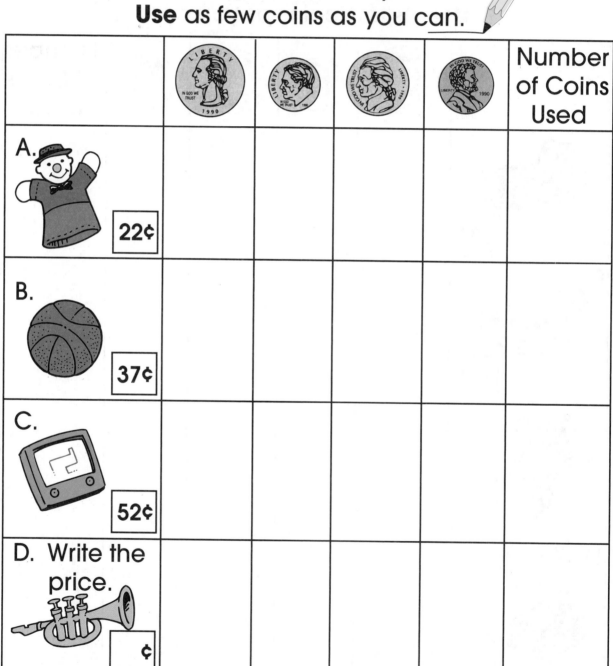

	(quarter)	(dime)	(nickel)	(penny)	Number of Coins Used
A. 22¢					
B. 37¢					
C. 52¢					
D. Write the price. ____¢					

Name________________________________

Review

Using Combinations of Coins to Pay

How Would You Pay?

Pay for each book.

Use as few coins as you can.

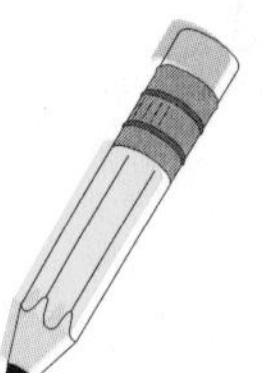

	Quarter	Dime	Nickel	Penny	Number of Coins Used
A. SUPER 75¢					
B. SPORT 80¢					
C. Monster 97¢					
D. Write the price. MAGIC ___¢					

Name________________________________

Review

Using Combinations of Coins to Pay

How Would You Pay?

Pay for each snack.
Use as few coins as you can.

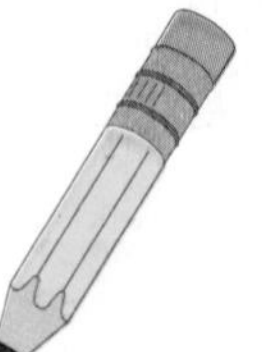

	Half dollar	Quarter	Dime	Nickel	Number of Coins Used
A. $1.05					
B. 95¢					
C. 85¢					
D. Write the price.					

Name____________________________________

Review

Using Combinations of Coins to Pay

How Would You Pay?

Pay for each mask.

Use as few coins and bills as you can.

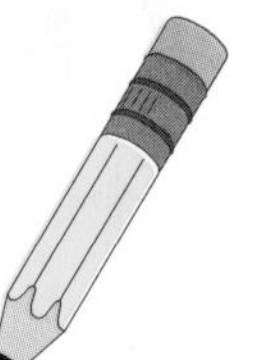

	one dollar bill	quarter	dime	nickel	Number of Coins Used
A. $1.75					
B. $1.95					
C. $2.50					
D. Write the price.					

Name________________________________

Review

Making Exact Amounts of Money Two Ways

Find two ways to pay for each thing.
Pay the exact amount.

A.

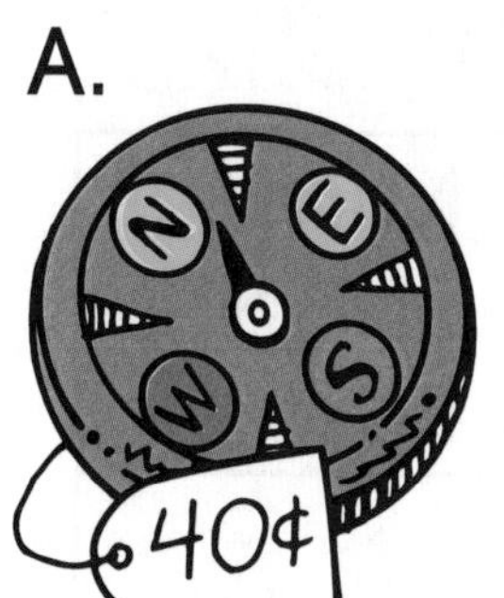

	Dimes	Nickels	Pennies
Way 1	4		
Way 2		8	

B.

	Dimes	Nickels	Pennies
Way 1			
Way 2			

C. **Write** a price for the magnifying glass.

	Dimes	Nickels	Pennies
Way 1			
Way 2			

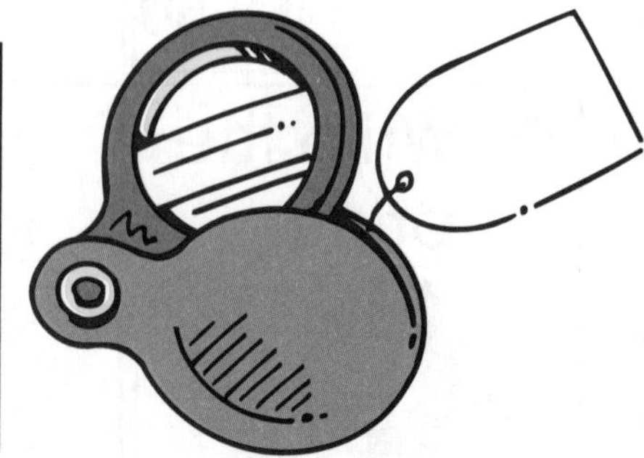

Name________________________________

Making Exact Amounts of Money Two Ways

Find two ways to pay for each thing.
Pay the exact amount.

A.

	Quarters	Dimes	Nickels	Pennies
Way 1				
Way 2				

B.

	Quarters	Dimes	Nickels	Pennies
Way 1				
Way 2				

C. **Write** a price for the game.

	Quarters	Dimes	Nickels	Pennies
Way 1				
Way 2				

Name________________________________

Review

Making Exact Amounts of Money Two Ways

Find two ways to pay for each thing.
Pay the exact amount.

A.

STICK-ON JEWELS $1.25

	Half-Dollars	Quarters	Dimes	Nickels	Pennies
Way 1					
Way 2					

B.

$1.50

	Half-Dollars	Quarters	Dimes	Nickels	Pennies
Way 1					
Way 2					

C. **Write** a price for the robot.

	Half-Dollars	Quarters	Dimes	Nickels	Pennies
Way 1					
Way 2					

Name ______________________________

Review

Making Exact Amounts of Money Two Ways

Find two ways to pay for each thing.
Pay the exact amount.

$1.00

A.

	$1 Bills	Half-Dollars	Quarters	Dimes	Nickels
Way 1					
Way 2					

B. $1.65

	$1 Bills	Half-Dollars	Quarters	Dimes	Nickels
Way 1					
Way 2					

C. **Solve** this puzzle.
What's missing in each way?

	$1 Bills	Half-Dollars	Quarters	Dimes	Nickels
Way 1	2			2	
Way 2		4	1		

Name____________________

Review

Making Exact Amounts of Money Two Ways

Find two ways to pay for each thing.
Pay the exact amount.

A. $5.60

	$1 Bills	Half-Dollars	Quarters	Dimes	Nickels	Pennies
Way 1						
Way 2						

B. $5.95 JUMBO MARKERS

	$1 Bills	Half-Dollars	Quarters	Dimes	Nickels	Pennies
Way 1						
Way 2						

C. $6.72 WHITE SHARK ACTION VIDEO

Solve this puzzle.
What's missing in each way?

	$1 Bills	Half-Dollars	Quarters	Dimes	Nickels	Pennies
Way 1	5	1				12
Way 2	4		1			7

Name ______________________________

Review

Estimating Amounts of Money

Snacks

Use the coins shown.
If you spend all your money, which snacks can you buy? **First**, estimate. **Then**, check.

A.

I think I can buy: ______________________

I can buy: ______________________________

B.

I think I can buy: ______________________

I can buy: ______________________________

C. **Solve** this puzzle.

Ahmad had 1 quarter, 1 dime, 1 nickel and 10 pennies. He bought two snacks. He has less than 10 cents left. What snacks did he buy? ____________________

Name____________________________________

Review

Estimating Amounts of Money

Pet Treats

Use the coins shown.
If you spend all your money, which pet treats can you buy? **First**, estimate. **Then**, check.

A.

I think I can buy: ____________________
I can buy: __________________________

B.

I think I can buy: ____________________
I can buy: __________________________

C. **Solve** this puzzle.
Ismelda had 3 half-dollars. She bought 3 pet treats. She has less than 20 cents left.
What treats did she buy?____________________

Name ____________________

Review

Estimating Amounts of Money

Fun Fair Tickets

Use the coins and bills shown.
If you spend all your money, what tickets can you buy? **First,** estimate. **Then**, check.

A.   

I think I can buy: ____________________

I can buy: ____________________

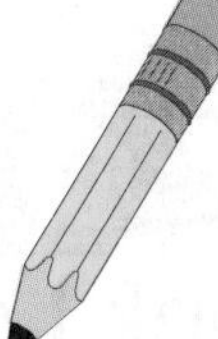

B.  

I think I can buy: ____________________

I can buy: ____________________

C. **Solve** this puzzle.
Larry and Leticia had 2 one-dollar bills and 3 half-dollars. They bought 6 tickets. They used all of their money. What tickets did they buy?

____

Name________________________________

Review

Estimating Amounts of Money

Kassie's Cafe

Hamburger........65¢	Milk......................35¢
Cheeseburger...75¢	Chocolate Milk...45¢
Burrito...............60¢	Apple Juice........50¢
Small Pizza........80¢	Berry Juice..........85¢
Super Salad......40¢	Dream Bar..........25¢

Use the coins and bills shown.
If you spend all your money, what can you buy?
First, estimate. **Then,** check.

A.

I think I can buy:________________________

I can buy: ___________________________

B.

I think I can buy:________________________

I can buy: ___________________________

C. **Solve** this puzzle.
Tina had 1 one-dollar bill, 1 half-dollar and 2 quarters. She bought three things. She has less than 25 cents left. What did Tina buy?____________________

Name ____________________

Review

Estimating Amounts of Money

Use the coins and bills shown.
If you spend all your money, what can you buy?
First, estimate. **Then,** check.

A. 

I think I can buy: ____________________
I can buy: ____________________

B. 

I think I can buy: ____________________
I can buy: ____________________

C. **Solve** this puzzle.
Martin had 3 one-dollar bills.
He bought three gifts. He has less than 25 cents left.
What did Martin buy? ____________________

Name______________________________

Review

Making Exact Amounts and Change

Pay the exact amount.
What change do you get back?

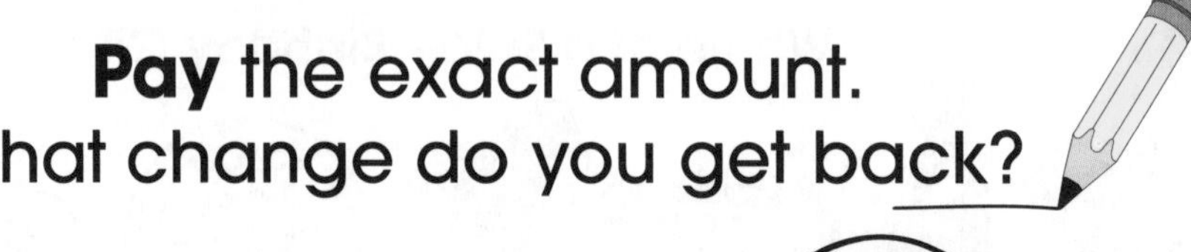

A. 

Amount you get back:

________________ ¢

B. 

Amount you get back:

________________ ¢

C. 

Amount you get back:

________________ ¢

Name______________________________

Review

Making Exact Amounts and Change

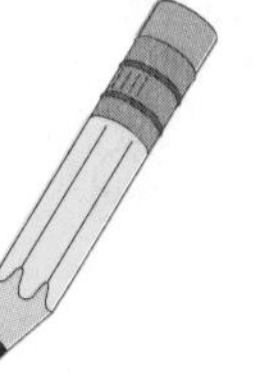

Pay the exact amount.
What change do you get back?

A.   

Amount you get back:

________________ ¢

B.  

Amount you get back:

________________ ¢

C.  

Choose a price between
75¢ and 90¢. **Write** the price.
Amount you get back:

________________ ¢

Name________________________________

Review

Making Exact Amounts and Change

Pay the exact amount.
What change do you get back?

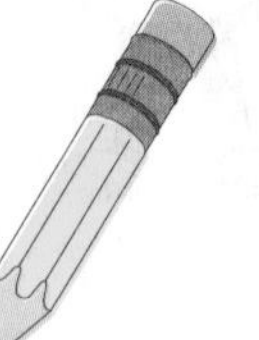

A.    

Amount you get back:

______________¢

B.  

Amount you get back:

______________¢

C.  

Choose a price between $1.15 and $1.28. **Write** the price.

Amount you get back:

______________¢

Name________________________________

Review

Making Exact Amounts and Change

Pay the exact amount.
What change do you get back?

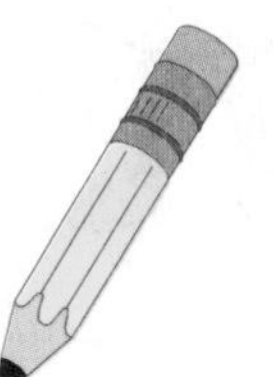

A.  

Amount you get back: __________ ¢

B.   

Amount you get back: __________ ¢

C. **Solve** this puzzle.

What did Abby pay?
Write the amount on the tag.

I had 2 one-dollar bills.
I paid for the kite. I got
back a quarter, 1 dime
and 1 penny.

Name______________________________________

Review

Making Exact Amounts and Change

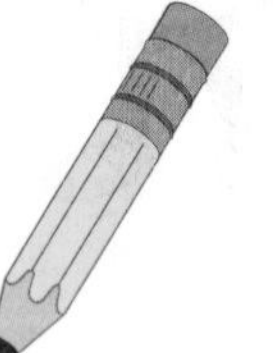

Pay the exact amount.
What change do you get back?

A.   

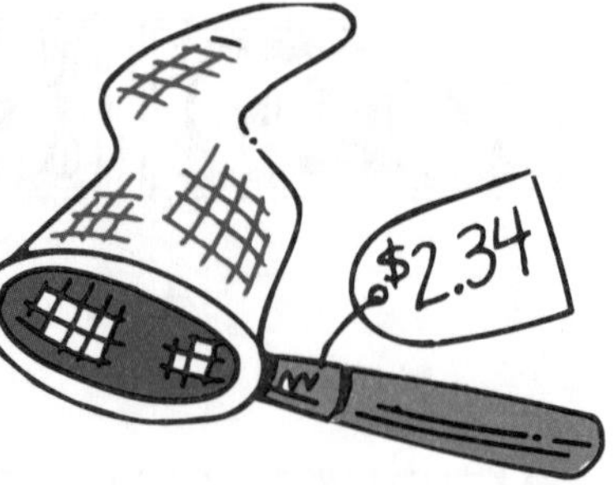

Amount you get back: $__________

B.  

Amount you get back: $__________

C. **Solve** this puzzle.

What did Dominic pay?
Write the amount on the tag.

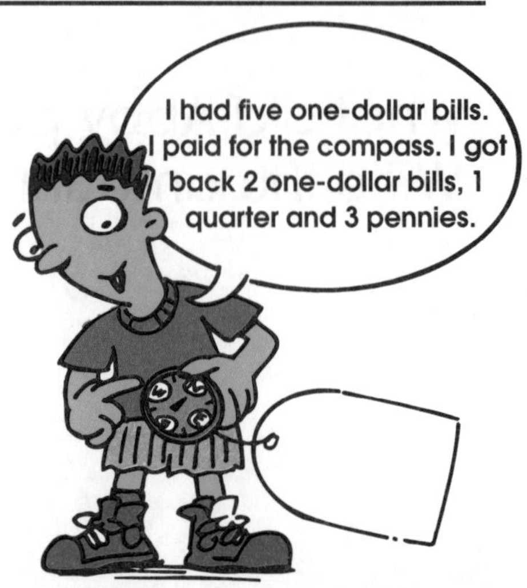

I had five one-dollar bills. I paid for the compass. I got back 2 one-dollar bills, 1 quarter and 3 pennies.

Name________________________________

Money Puzzles

Solve the puzzles.
Draw the coins.

A. There are 4 coins in the bag. Together they are worth less than 50¢. What coins could they be?	B. There are 4 coins in the bag. Two are worth more than 25¢ each. Two are worth less than 10¢ each. What coins could they be?
C. There are 5 coins in the bag. Together they are worth more than 90¢. What coins could they be?	D. There are 6 coins in the bag. Together they are worth between 75¢ and $1.00. What coins could they be?

Name________________________________

Money Puzzles

Solve the puzzles.
Draw the coins.

A. There are 5 coins in the bank. Together they are worth $1.00 exactly. What coins could they be?	B. There are 6 coins in the bank. Together they are worth between 80¢ and $1.20. What coins could they be?
C. There are 6 coins in the bank. Two are worth more than 10¢ each. Four are worth less than 10¢ each. All together they are worth more than $1.00. What coins could they be?	D. There are 6 coins in the bank. Four are worth more than 10¢ each. Two are worth less than 25¢ each. All together they are worth less than $1.50. What coins could they be?

Name______________________________

Review

Using Combinations of Coins to Pay

Use the coins shown to make each amount.

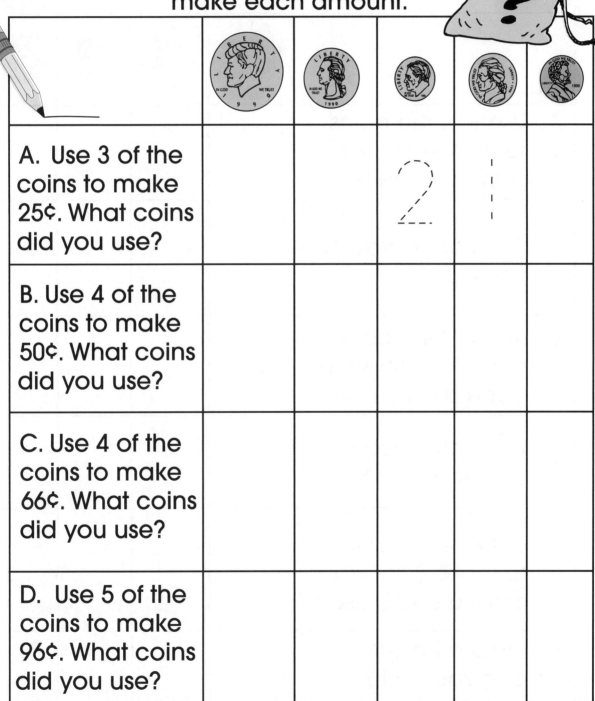

A. Use 3 of the coins to make 25¢. What coins did you use?			2	1	
B. Use 4 of the coins to make 50¢. What coins did you use?					
C. Use 4 of the coins to make 66¢. What coins did you use?					
D. Use 5 of the coins to make 96¢. What coins did you use?					

Name______________________________

Review

Using Combinations of Coins to Pay

Use the coins shown to make each amount.

A. Use 3 of the coins to make 60¢. What coins did you use?				
B. What other way can you do it?				
C. Use 4 of the coins to make 40¢. What coins did you use?				
D. What other way can you do it?				
E. Use 4 of the coins to make 80¢. What coins did you use?				
F. What other way can you do it?				

Name____________________

Review

Money Story Puzzles

Solve the money story puzzles.

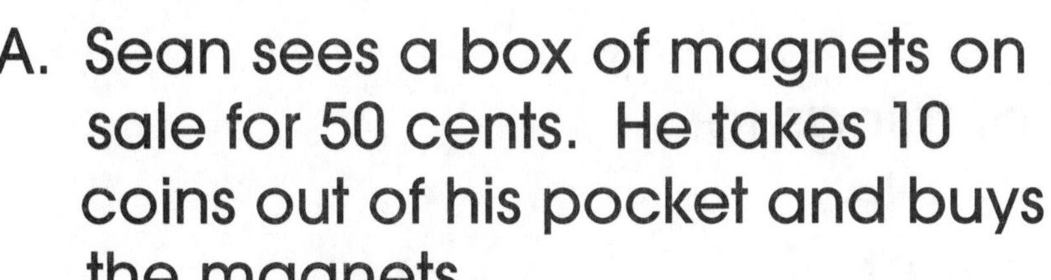

A. Sean sees a box of magnets on sale for 50 cents. He takes 10 coins out of his pocket and buys the magnets.

What coins could they be?

B. Tonia sees a small bag of jacks for 58 cents. She takes 9 coins out of her pocket to pay.

What coins could they be?

C. Dustin sees a toy hammer. He wants to buy it for his little brother. He pulls six coins out of his pocket and pays 75 cents.

What coins could they be?

Name________________________________

Money Story Puzzles

Solve the money story puzzles.

A. Matt buys a box of things for doing magic tricks. He takes an even number of coins out of his pocket and pays 65 cents.

What coins could they be?

B. Stacey buys a poster for 70 cents. She uses an odd number of coins to buy it.

What coins could they be?

C. **Write** a money story puzzle about buying the stuffed whale.

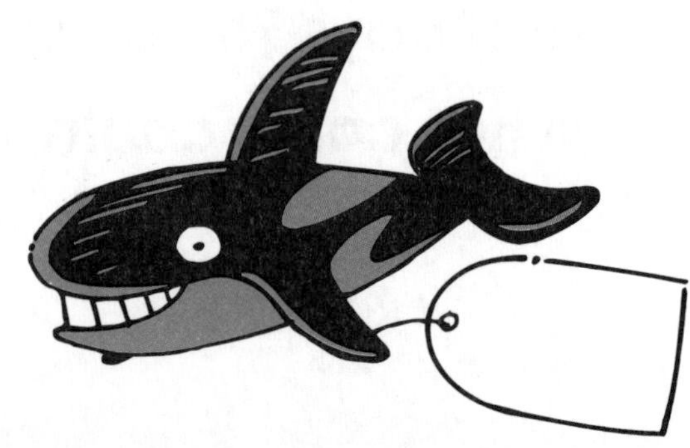

Name________________________________

Money Story Puzzles

Solve the money story puzzles.

A. Amber put coins into her bank for a long time. She saved $6.25 in all. Amber saved $3.55 more than her sister Holly.

How much did Holly save?

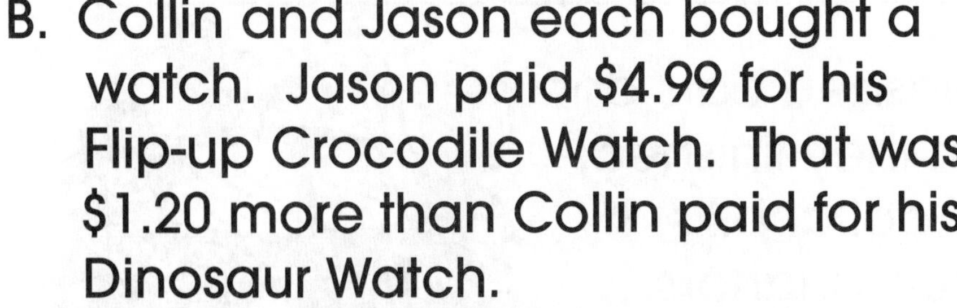

B. Collin and Jason each bought a watch. Jason paid $4.99 for his Flip-up Crocodile Watch. That was $1.20 more than Collin paid for his Dinosaur Watch.

How much did Collin pay?

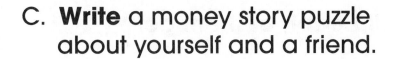

C. **Write** a money story puzzle about yourself and a friend.

Name____

Review

Money Story Puzzles

Solve the money story puzzles.

A. Darci and Kara fed the horses at the fair. Kara's mother gave the girls 3 one-dollar bills, 3 quarters, 5 dimes and 3 nickels. Darci and Kara divided the money equally.

How much money did each of them get?

____

B. Josh and Ben washed cars one Saturday. When they finished, they had 3 one-dollar bills, 1 1 half dollar, three quarters, 2 dimes and 1 nickel in their money box. The boys divided the money fairly.

How much money did each of them get?

____

C. **Write** a money story puzzle about earning money and dividing it equally.

Name________________________________

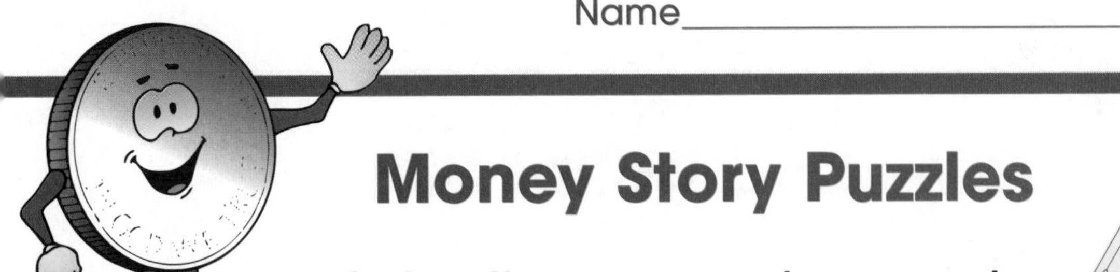

Review

Money Story Puzzles

Solve the money story puzzles.

A. Eric and Alicia took all the coins out of their pockets. They put the coins together and paid 65 cents for a bag of corn chips. Alicia paid 15 cents more than Eric.

How much did each of them pay?

B. Two friends put their money together and bought a package of stickers for $1.60. Rachel paid 20 cents more than Amanda.

How much did each girl pay?

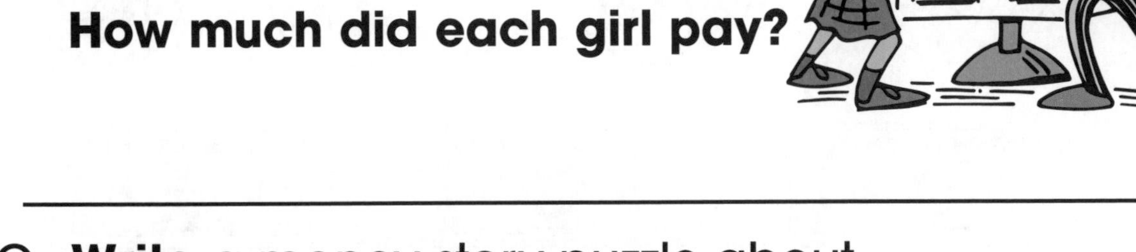

C. **Write** a money story puzzle about buying something with a friend.

Name________________________________

Review

Coins and Dollar Bills

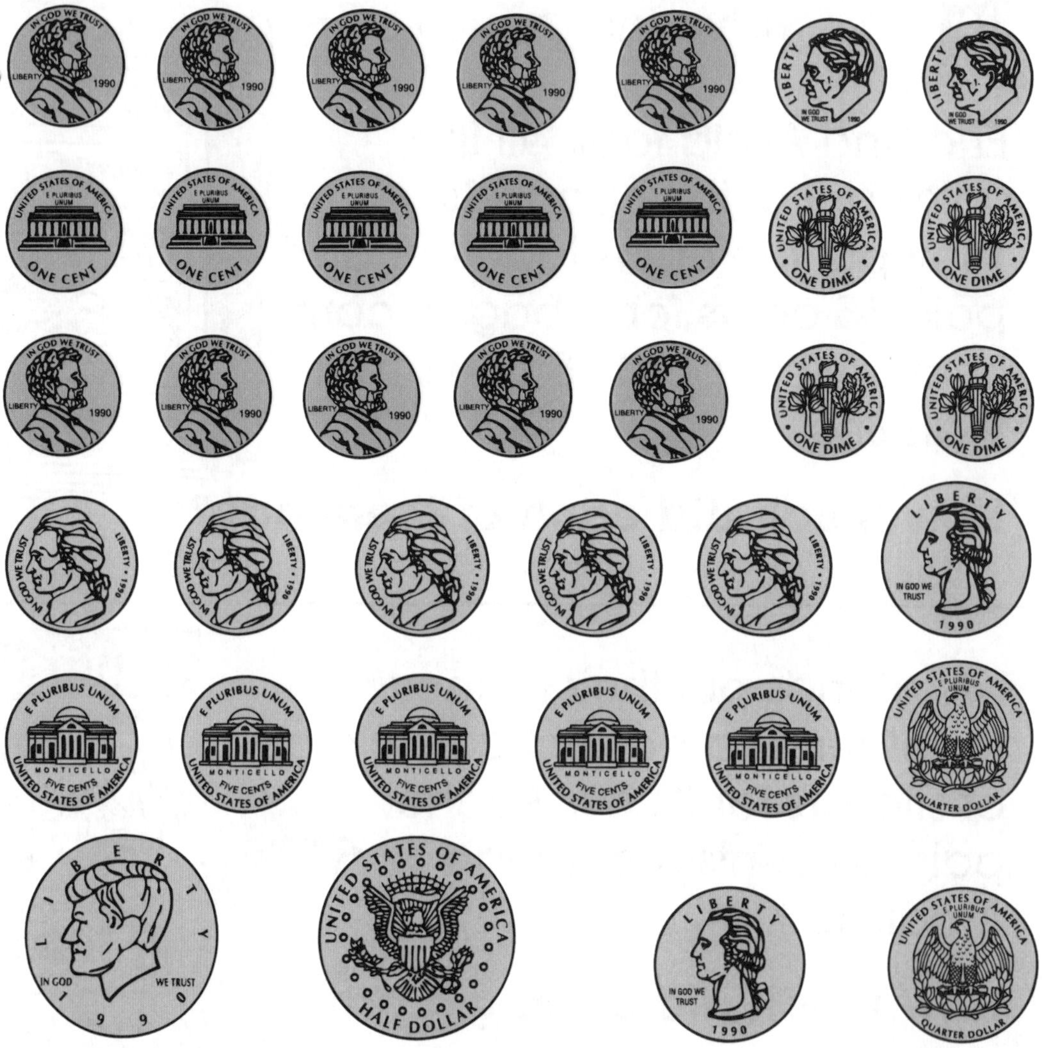

Name________________________________

Review

Time Award Certificates

Champion Time Teller!

____

name

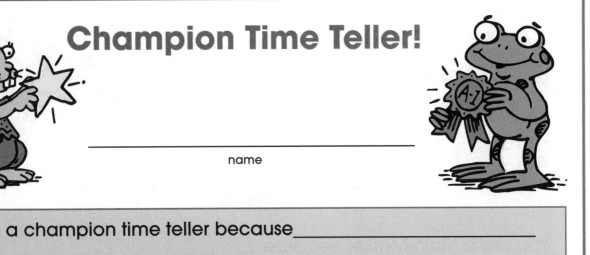

You are a champion time teller because________________________

____

Nice Going!

Signed______________________________ Date__________

____

name

Wonderful Work!

You are wonderful because________________________

____

Way to Go!

Signed______________________________ Date__________

Name ____________________

Money Award Certificates

Math Marvel!

____
name

You are a Math Marvel because ____________________
____

Marvelous Job!

Signed ____________________ Date ____________

____
name

Wonderful Work!

You are a Money Expert because ____________________
____

Awesome Work!

Signed ____________________ Date ____________

Answer Key - Time

Name____________________

Time to the Hour

Face Clocks: Introduction

What is the best way to tell what time it is?
A clock!
There are all kinds of clocks.
Circle the ones you have seen.
Answers will vary.

8:00

Page 6

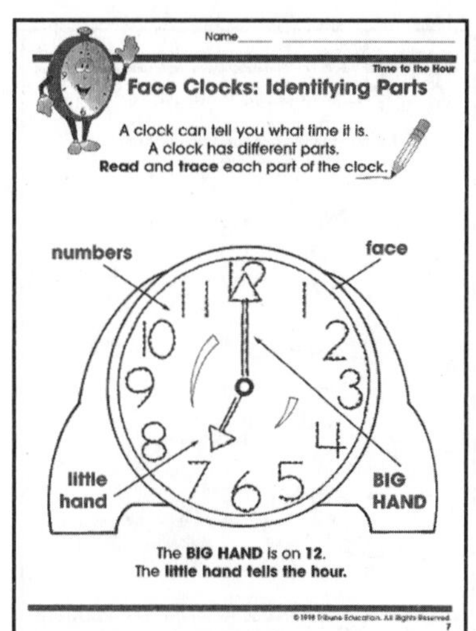
Name____________________

Time to the Hour

Face Clocks: Identifying Parts

A clock can tell you what time it is.
A clock has different parts.
Read and **trace** each part of the clock.

numbers
face
little hand
BIG HAND

The **BIG HAND** is on **12**.
The **little hand tells the hour.**

Page 7

Name____________________

Time to the Hour

Face Clocks: Identifying Parts

A clock face has numbers.
Trace the numbers on the clock.

Tick
Tock

Page 8

Name____________________

Time to the Hour

Writing the Time

Hi! My name is **Tim Time**.
Learning to tell time is fun!
A clock tells us the time.

Write the numbers on the clock face.
Draw the **BIG HAND** to **12**.
Draw the **little hand** to **5**.

What time is it? __5__ o'clock

Page 9

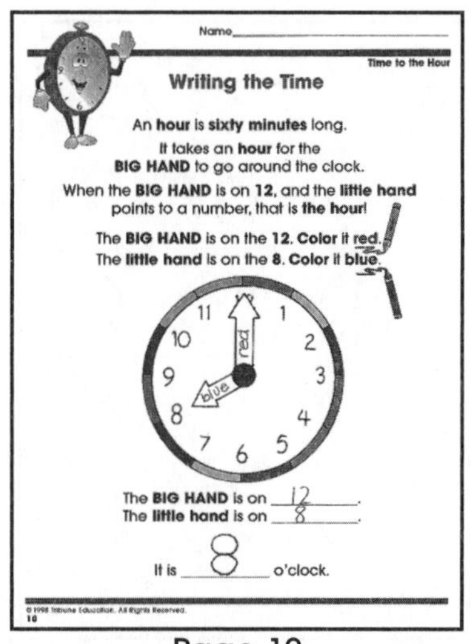
Name____________________

Time to the Hour

Writing the Time

An **hour** is **sixty minutes** long.
It takes an **hour** for the
BIG HAND to go around the clock.
When the **BIG HAND** is on **12**, and the **little hand** points to a number, that is **the hour!**

The **BIG HAND** is on the **12**. **Color** it **red**.
The **little hand** is on the **8**. **Color** it **blue**.

The **BIG HAND** is on __12__.
The **little hand** is on __8__.

It is __8__ o'clock.

Page 10

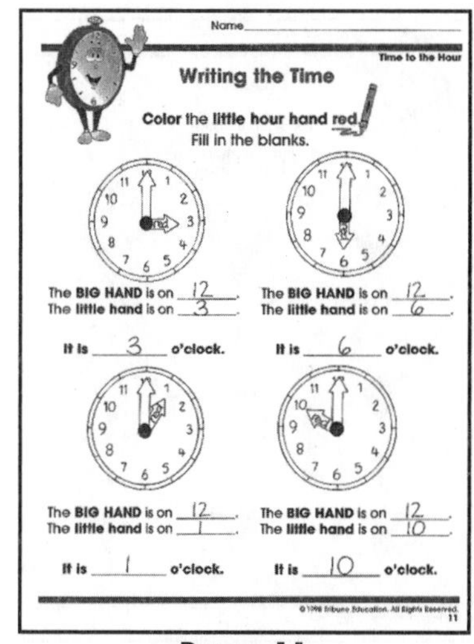
Name____________________

Time to the Hour

Writing the Time

Color the **little hour hand red**.
Fill in the blanks.

The **BIG HAND** is on __12__.
The **little hand** is on __3__.
It is __3__ **o'clock.**

The **BIG HAND** is on __12__.
The **little hand** is on __6__.
It is __6__ **o'clock.**

The **BIG HAND** is on __12__.
The **little hand** is on __1__.
It is __1__ **o'clock.**

The **BIG HAND** is on __12__.
The **little hand** is on __10__.
It is __10__ **o'clock.**

Page 11

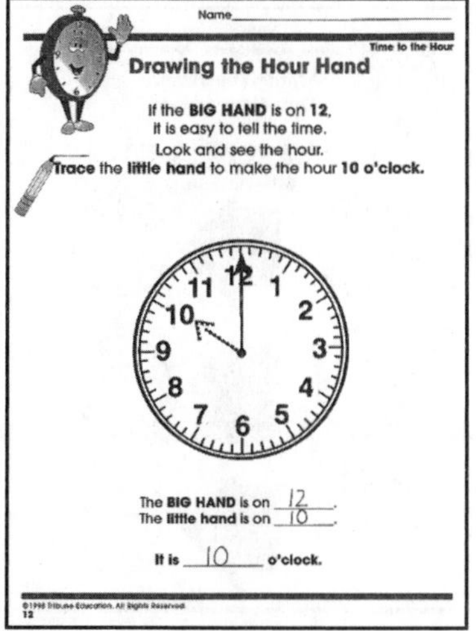
Name____________________

Time to the Hour

Drawing the Hour Hand

If the **BIG HAND** is on **12**,
it is easy to tell the time.
Look and see the hour.
Trace the **little hand** to make the hour **10 o'clock.**

The **BIG HAND** is on __12__.
The **little hand** is on __10__.
It is __10__ **o'clock.**

Page 12

Name____________________

Time to the Hour

Drawing the Hour Hand

Draw the **little hour hand** on each clock.

8 o'clock
1 o'clock
7 o'clock

Page 13

Name____________________

Time to the Hour

Drawing the Hour Hand

Draw the **little hour hand** on each clock.

2 o'clock
10 o'clock
9 o'clock

Page 14

Page 15

Page 16

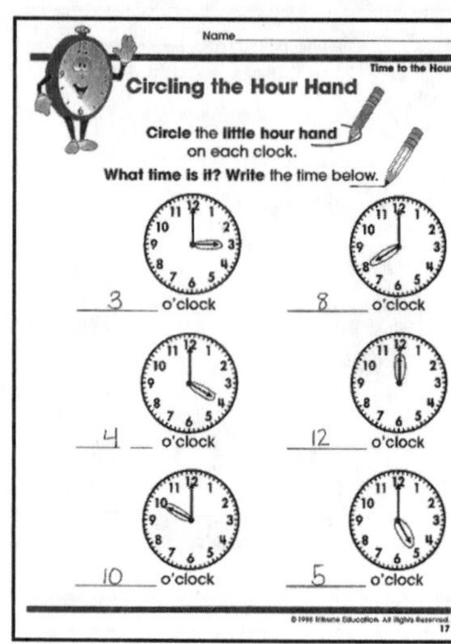

Circling the Hour Hand
Circle the little hour hand on each clock.
What time is it? Write the time below.
3 o'clock
8 o'clock
4 o'clock
12 o'clock
10 o'clock
5 o'clock

Page 17

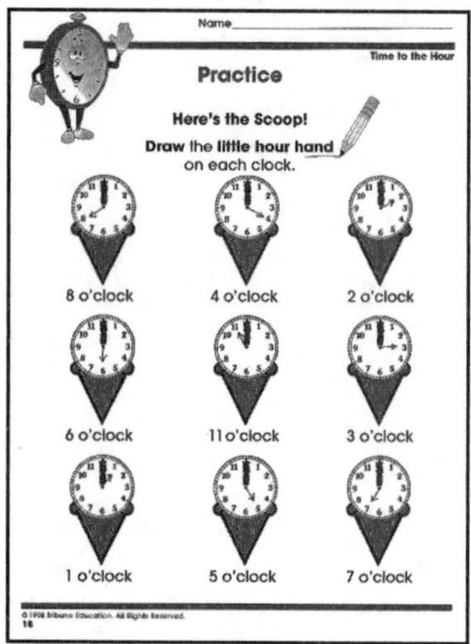

Page 18

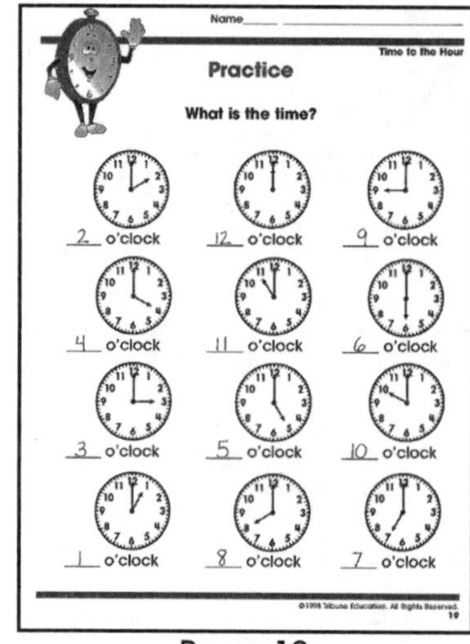

Page 19

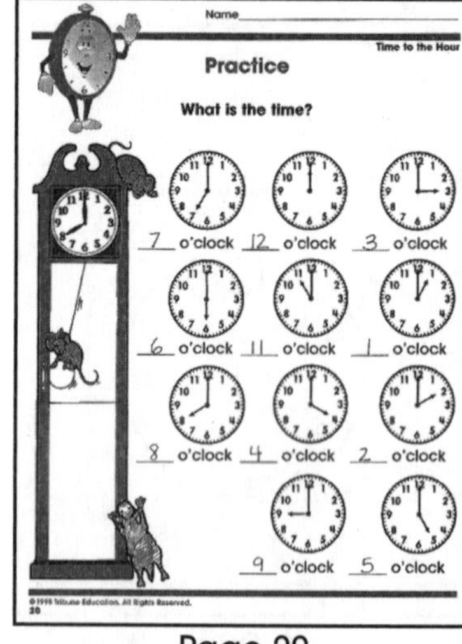

Page 20

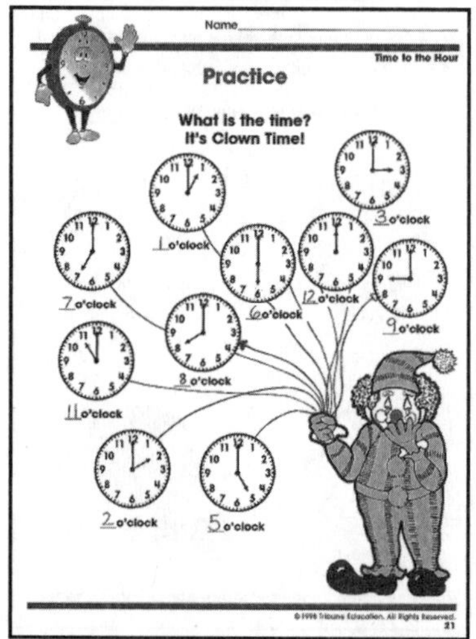

Page 21

Page 22

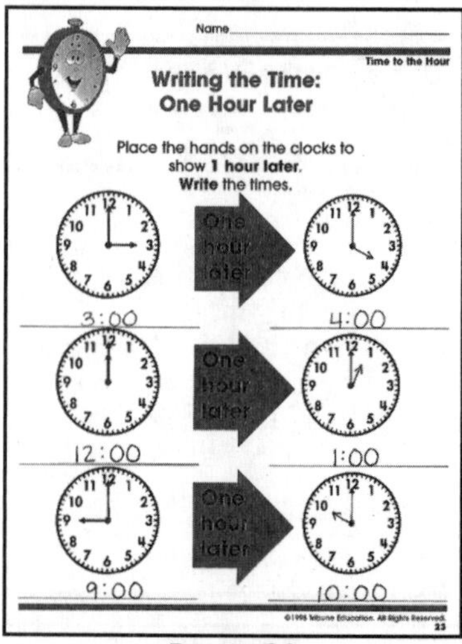

Writing the Time: One Hour Later
Place the hands on the clocks to show 1 hour later.
Write the times.
One hour later
3:00
4:00
One hour later
12:00
1:00
One hour later
9:00
10:00

Page 23

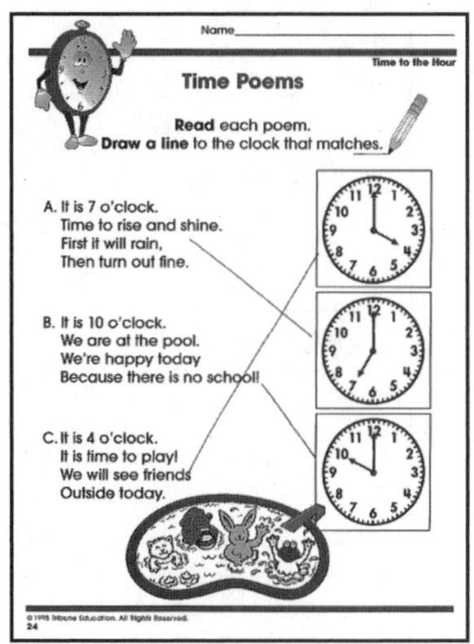

Name________

Time to the Hour

Time Poems

Read each poem.
Draw a line to the clock that matches.

A. It is 7 o'clock.
Time to rise and shine.
First it will rain,
Then turn out fine.

B. It is 10 o'clock.
We are at the pool.
We're happy today
Because there is no school!

C. It is 4 o'clock.
It is time to play!
We will see friends
Outside today.

Page 24

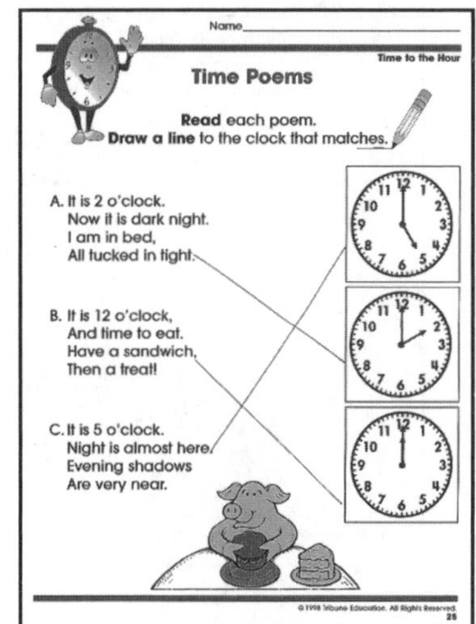

Name________

Time to the Hour

Time Poems

Read each poem.
Draw a line to the clock that matches.

A. It is 2 o'clock.
Now it is dark night.
I am in bed,
All tucked in tight.

B. It is 12 o'clock,
And time to eat.
Have a sandwich,
Then a treat!

C. It is 5 o'clock.
Night is almost here.
Evening shadows
Are very near.

Page 25

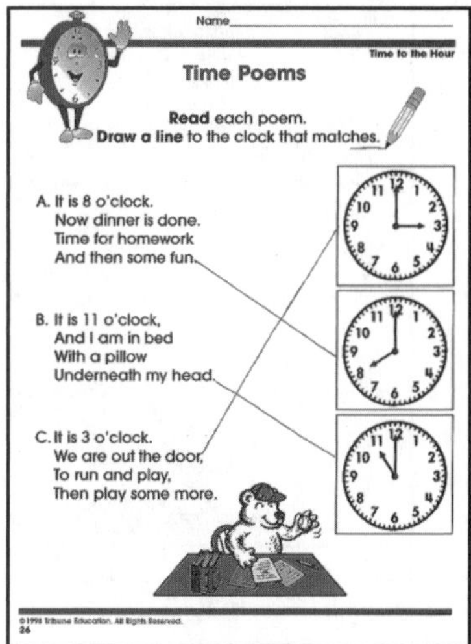

Name________

Time to the Hour

Time Poems

Read each poem.
Draw a line to the clock that matches.

A. It is 8 o'clock.
Now dinner is done.
Time for homework
And then some fun.

B. It is 11 o'clock,
And I am in bed
With a pillow
Underneath my head.

C. It is 3 o'clock.
We are out the door,
To run and play,
Then play some more.

Page 26

Name________

Time to the Hour

Digital Clocks: Introduction

Meet my friend **Digital Clock**.
He tells **time with numbers**.
First, he tells the **hour**, then the **minutes**.

10:00

Draw the little hour hand on this face clock below to read **10 o'clock**.

Both clocks show that it is **10 o'clock**.
Make a **green circle** around the kinds of clocks you have at home.
Answers will vary.

Page 27

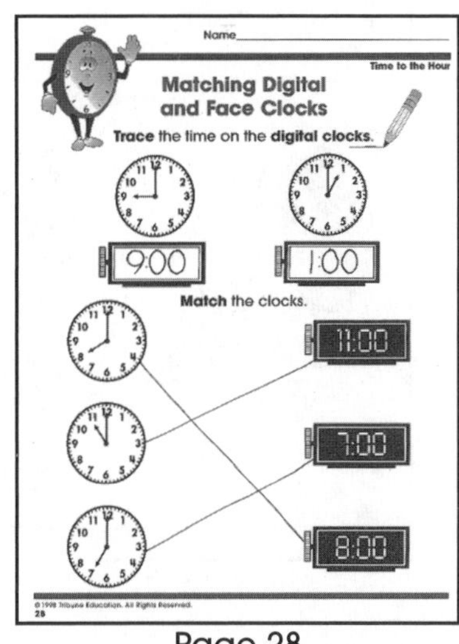

Name________

Time to the Hour

Matching Digital and Face Clocks

Trace the time on the **digital clocks**.

9:00 1:00

Match the clocks.

11:00 7:00 8:00

Page 28

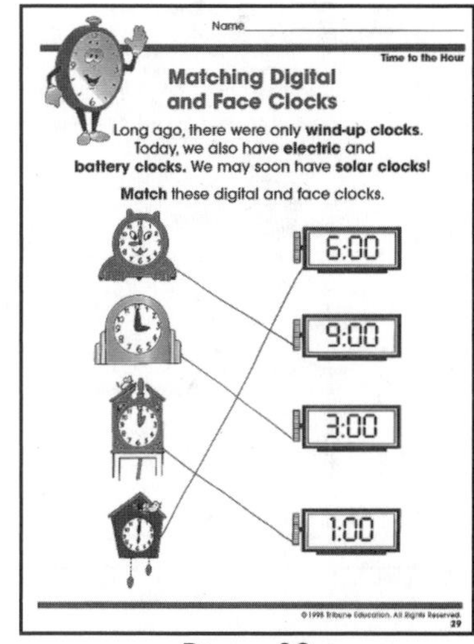

Name________

Time to the Hour

Matching Digital and Face Clocks

Long ago, there were only **wind-up clocks**. Today, we also have **electric** and **battery clocks**. We may soon have **solar clocks**!

Match these digital and face clocks.

6:00 9:00 3:00 1:00

Page 29

Name________

Time to the Hour

Digital Clocks

Write the time on the digital clocks.

4:00 11:00 9:00 7:00

Page 30

Name________

Time to the Hour

Digital Clocks

Write the time on the digital clocks.

5:00 12:00 8:00 3:00

Page 31

Name________

Time to the Hour

Digital Clocks

Write the time on the digital clocks.

2:00 10:00 6:00 1:00

Page 32

Name

Time to the Hour

Drawing the Hour Hand: Matching Digital and Face Clocks

Look at the digital clock.
Say the time.
Draw the **little hour hand** on each face clock.

4:00 2:00

8:00 6:00

33

Page 33

Name

Time to the Hour

Drawing the Hour Hand: Matching Digital and Face Clocks

Look at the digital clock.
Say the time.
Draw the **little hour hand** on each face clock.

11:00 3:00

10:00 1:00

34

Page 34

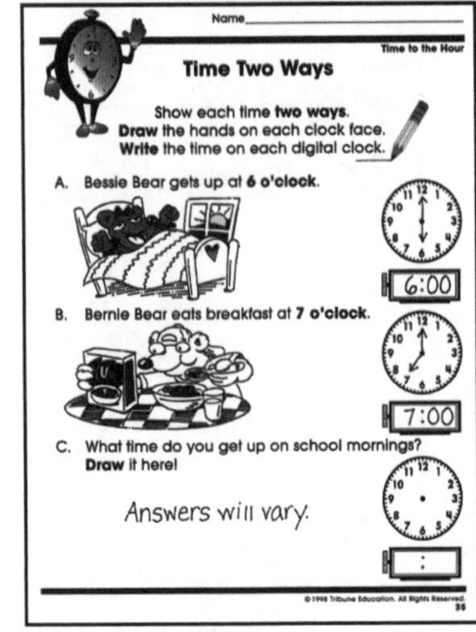
Name

Time to the Hour

Time Two Ways

Show each time **two ways.**
Draw the hands on each clock face.
Write the time on each digital clock.

A. Bessie Bear gets up at **6 o'clock.**

6:00

B. Bernie Bear eats breakfast at **7 o'clock.**

7:00

C. What time do you get up on school mornings? **Draw** it here!

Answers will vary.

35

Page 35

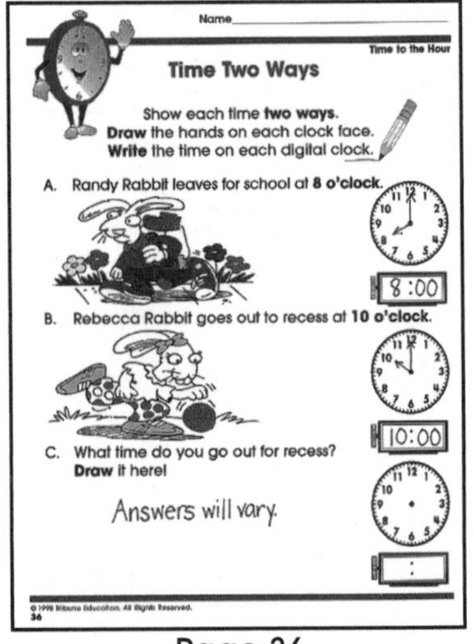
Name

Time to the Hour

Time Two Ways

Show each time **two ways.**
Draw the hands on each clock face.
Write the time on each digital clock.

A. Randy Rabbit leaves for school at **8 o'clock.**

8:00

B. Rebecca Rabbit goes out to recess at **10 o'clock.**

10:00

C. What time do you go out for recess? **Draw** it here!

Answers will vary.

36

Page 36

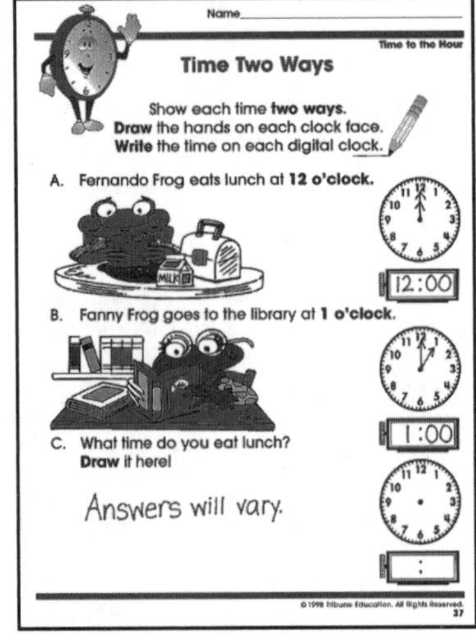
Name

Time to the Hour

Time Two Ways

Show each time **two ways.**
Draw the hands on each clock face.
Write the time on each digital clock.

A. Fernando Frog eats lunch at **12 o'clock.**

12:00

B. Fanny Frog goes to the library at **1 o'clock.**

1:00

C. What time do you eat lunch? **Draw** it here!

Answers will vary.

37

Page 37

Name

Time to the Hour

Time Two Ways

Show each time **two ways.**
Draw the hands on each clock face.
Write the time.

A. At **9 o'clock,** Frog goes for a swim.

9:00

B. At **11 o'clock,** Frog sits on a lily pad.

11:00

C. At **12 o'clock,** Frog eats a sandwich.

12:00

38

Page 38

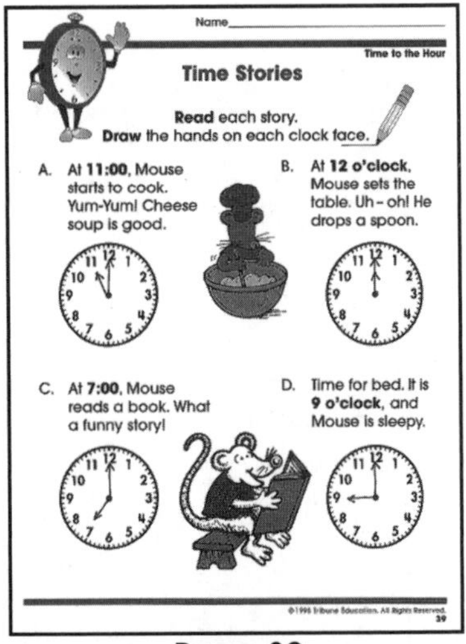
Name

Time to the Hour

Time Stories

Read each story.
Draw the hands on each clock face.

A. At **11:00,** Mouse starts to cook. Yum-Yum! Cheese soup is good.

B. At **12 o'clock,** Mouse sets the table. Uh-oh! He drops a spoon.

C. At **7:00,** Mouse reads a book. What a funny story!

D. Time for bed. It is **9 o'clock,** and Mouse is sleepy.

39

Page 39

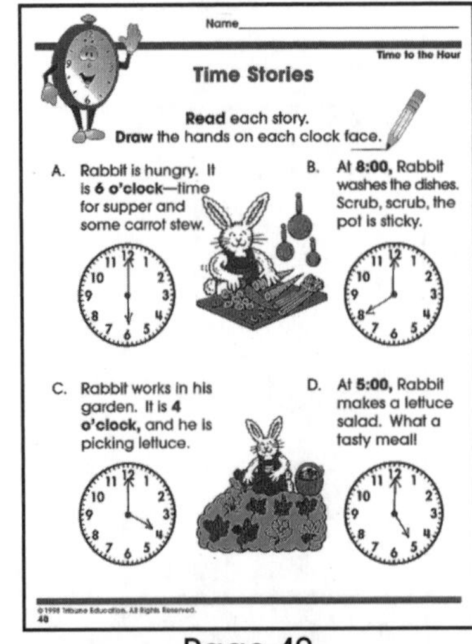
Name

Time to the Hour

Time Stories

Read each story.
Draw the hands on each clock face.

A. Rabbit is hungry. It is **6 o'clock**—time for supper and some carrot stew.

B. At **8:00,** Rabbit washes the dishes. Scrub, scrub, the pot is sticky.

C. Rabbit works in his garden. It is **4 o'clock,** and he is picking lettuce.

D. At **5:00,** Rabbit makes a lettuce salad. What a tasty meal!

40

Page 40

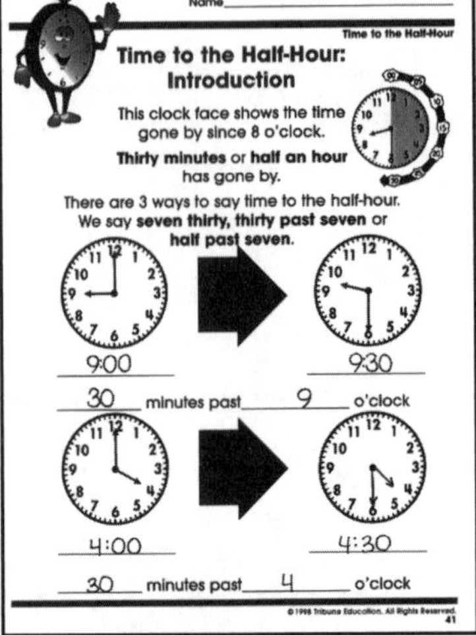
Name

Time to the Half-Hour

Time to the Half-Hour: Introduction

This clock face shows the time gone by since 8 o'clock.
Thirty minutes or **half an hour** has gone by.

There are 3 ways to say time to the half-hour.
We say **seven thirty, thirty past seven** or **half past seven.**

9:00 9:30

30 minutes past 9 o'clock

4:00 4:30

30 minutes past 4 o'clock

41

Page 41

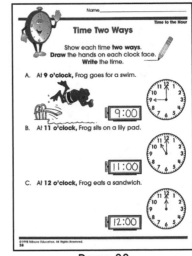

Answer Key - Time

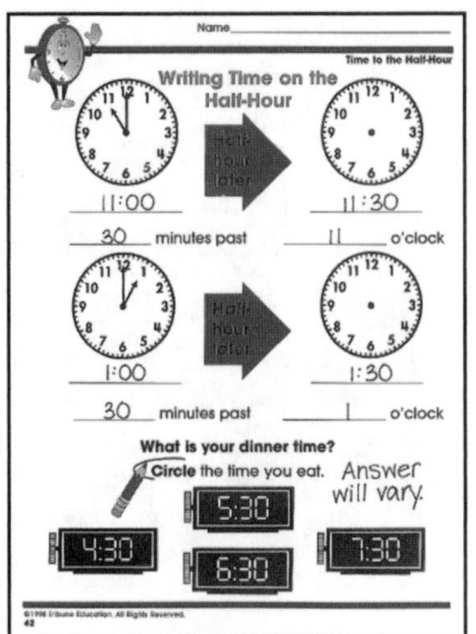

Name
Time to the Half-Hour
Writing Time on the Half-Hour
11:00
11:30
30 minutes past 11 o'clock
1:00
1:30
30 minutes past 1 o'clock
What is your dinner time?
Circle the time you eat.
Answer will vary.
4:30
5:30
6:30
7:30
©1998 Tribune Education. All Rights Reserved.
42

Page 42

Name

Time to the Half-Hour

Writing Time on the Half-Hour

What time is it?

half past 2 half past 9

half past 4 half past 12

half past 11 half past 1

©1998 Tribune Education. All Rights Reserved. 43

Page 43

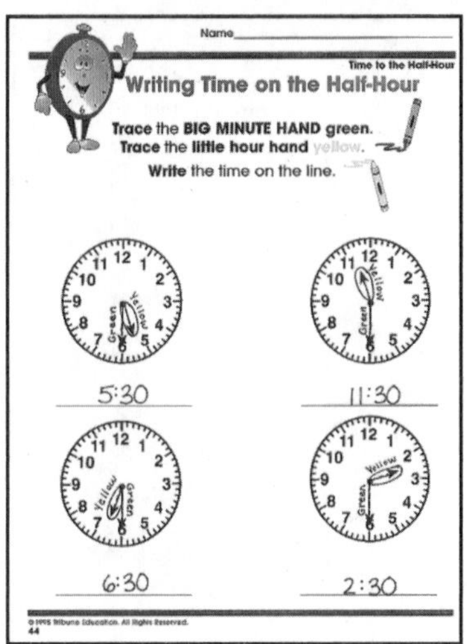

Name
Time to the Half-Hour
Writing Time on the Half-Hour
Trace the BIG MINUTE HAND green.
Trace the little hour hand yellow.
Write the time on the line.
5:30
11:30
6:30
2:30
©1998 Tribune Education. All Rights Reserved.
44

Page 44

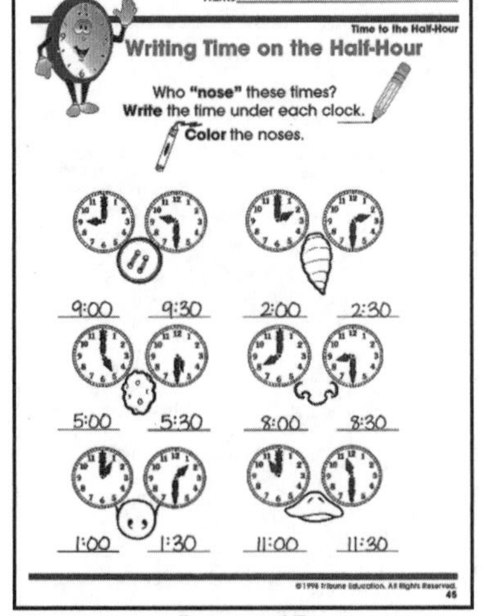

Name
Time to the Half-Hour
Writing Time on the Half-Hour
Who "nose" these times?
Write the time under each clock.
Color the noses.
9:00 9:30 2:00 2:30
5:00 5:30 8:00 8:30
1:00 1:30 11:00 11:30
©1998 Tribune Education. All Rights Reserved.
45

Page 45

Name
Time to the Half-Hour
Matching Digital and Face Clocks
These digital numbers got lost.
Put them in the right clocks on this page and page 47.
12:30
5:30

Page 46

Name

Time to the Half-Hour

Matching Digital and Face Clocks

8:30

3:30

6:30

9:30

©1998 Tribune Education. All Rights Reserved. 47

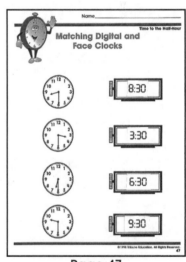

Page 47

Page 48

Page 49

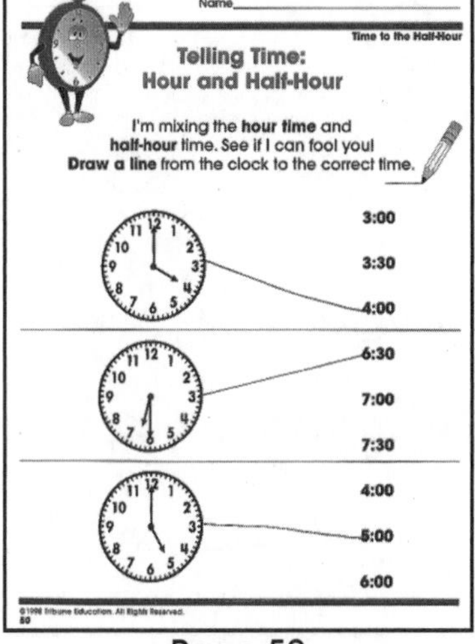

Page 50

Answer Key - Time

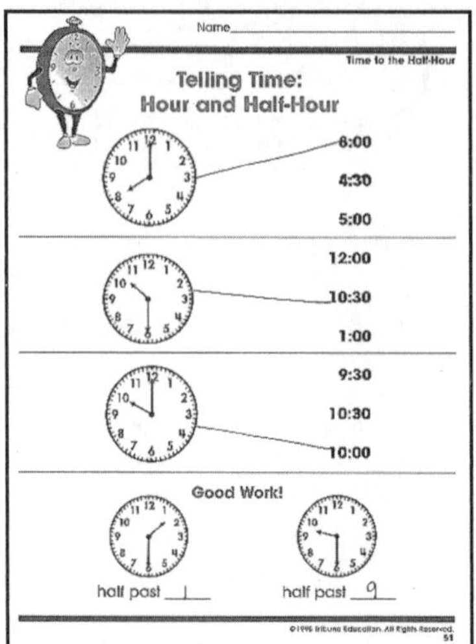
Name
Time to the Half-Hour
Telling Time: Hour and Half-Hour
6:00
4:30
5:00
12:00
10:30
1:00
9:30
10:30
10:00
Good Work!
half past 1
half past 9

Page 51

Name
Time to the Half-Hour
Writing the Time: Practice
Space Time
What time is it?
3:00 9:30 10:30 12:00
8:00 7:30 2:00 4:30
1:30 6:30
7:00 11:00

Page 52

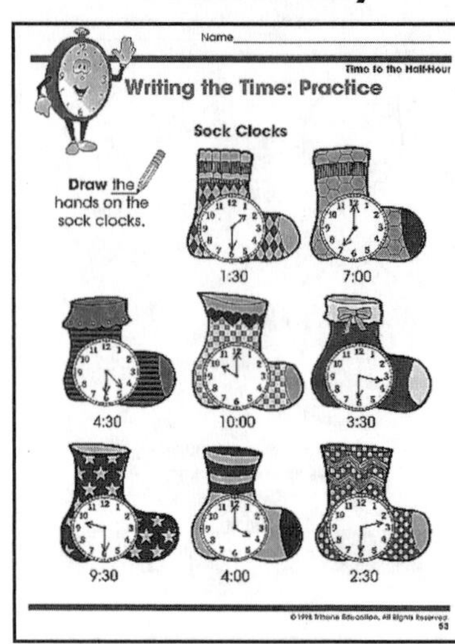
Name
Time to the Half-Hour
Writing the Time: Practice
Sock Clocks
Draw the hands on the sock clocks.
1:30 7:00
4:30 10:00 3:30
9:30 4:00 2:30

Page 53

Name
Time to the Half-Hour
Writing the Time: Practice
You Are My Sunshine
What time is it?
3:00 9:30 8:00 7:30
1:30 6:30 10:30 12:00
7:00 11:00 2:00 4:30

Page 54

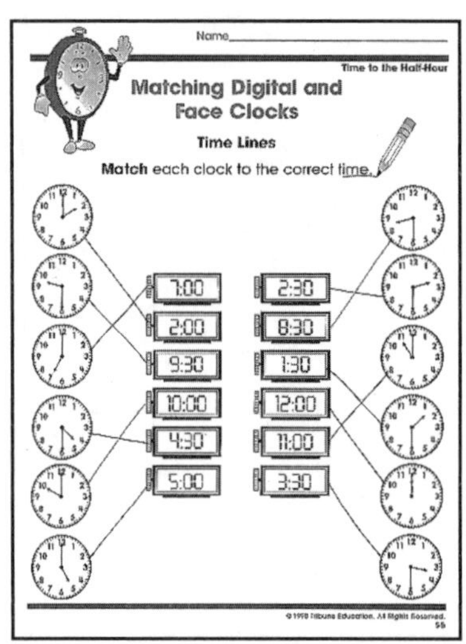
Name
Time to the Half-Hour
Matching Digital and Face Clocks
Time Lines
Match each clock to the correct time.
7:00 2:00 9:30 10:00 4:30 5:00
2:30 8:30 1:30 12:00 11:00 3:30

Page 55

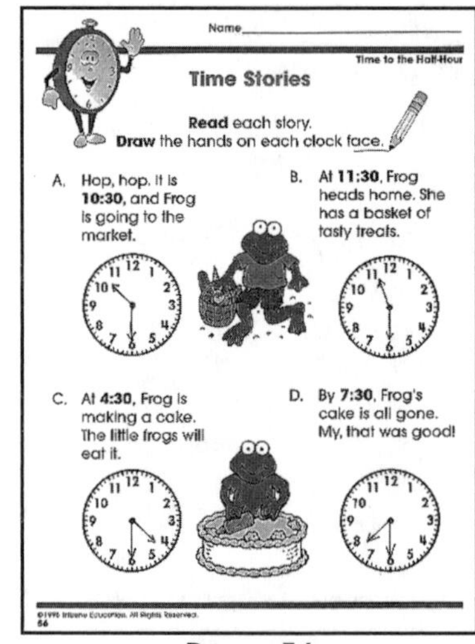
Name
Time to the Half-Hour
Time Stories
Read each story.
Draw the hands on each clock face.
A. Hop, hop. It is 10:30, and Frog is going to the market.
B. At 11:30, Frog heads home. She has a basket of tasty treats.
C. At 4:30, Frog is making a cake. The little frogs will eat it.
D. By 7:30, Frog's cake is all gone. My, that was good!

Page 56

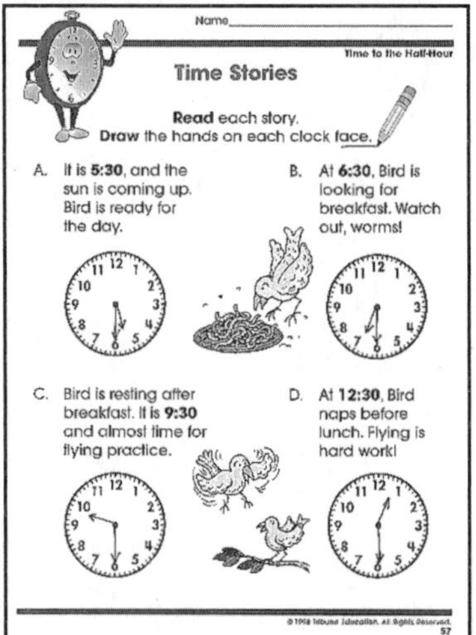
Name
Time to the Half-Hour
Time Stories
Read each story.
Draw the hands on each clock face.
A. It is 5:30, and the sun is coming up. Bird is ready for the day.
B. At 6:30, Bird is looking for breakfast. Watch out, worms!
C. Bird is resting after breakfast. It is 9:30 and almost time for flying practice.
D. At 12:30, Bird naps before lunch. Flying is hard work!

Page 57

Name
Time to the Half-Hour
Time Lapse: Hours
Can you tell how much time has passed?
3:00 6:00
If it started snowing at 3:00 and snowed until 6:00, it snowed 3 hours.
What time did the spider start spinning the web? 1:00
What time did she finish? 3:00
1:00 3:00
The spider took 2 hours to spin the web.

Page 58

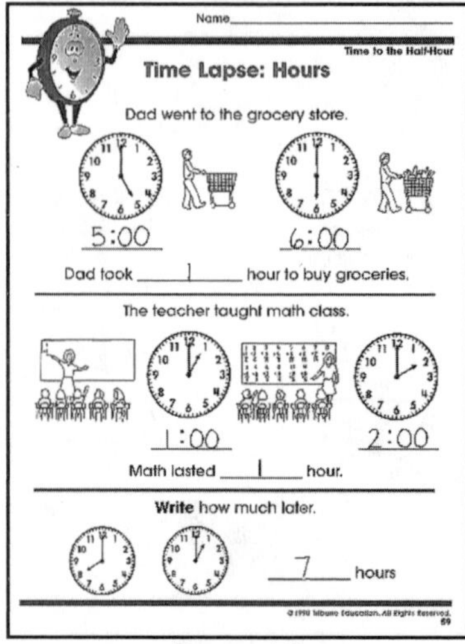
Name
Time to the Half-Hour
Time Lapse: Hours
Dad went to the grocery store.
5:00 6:00
Dad took 1 hour to buy groceries.
The teacher taught math class.
1:00 2:00
Math lasted 1 hour.
Write how much later.
7 hours

Page 59

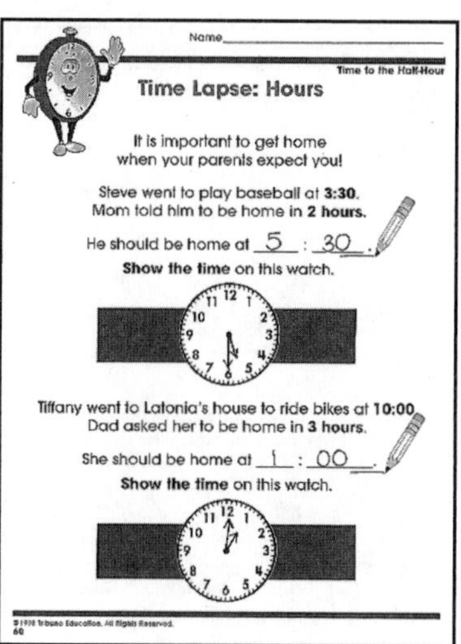

Name

Time to the Half-Hour

Time Lapse: Hours

It is important to get home when your parents expect you!

Steve went to play baseball at **3:30.** Mom told him to be home in **2 hours.**

He should be home at 5 : 30 .

Show the time on this watch.

Tiffany went to Latonia's house to ride bikes at **10:00.** Dad asked her to be home in **3 hours.**

She should be home at 1 : 00 .

Show the time on this watch.

©1998 Tribune Education. All Rights Reserved.
60

Page 60

Name

Time to the Half-Hour

Time Lapse: Hours

Kristen took her sister to the movies at **7:30.** Mom said she would meet them in **2 hours.**

She will meet them at 9 : 30 .

Show the time on this clock.

Latrissa went to the library for story hour. She got there at **1:00.** She stayed **1 hour.**

Story hour should be over at 2 : 00 .

Show the time Latrissa left for home.

©1998 Tribune Education. All Rights Reserved.
61

Page 61

Name

Time to the Half-Hour

Drawing the Hour Hand: A Half-Hour Later

Draw the hands on each clock face.

A. At **7:00,** Bill turns on the TV. — What time is it one half-hour later?

B. At **4:00,** we all jump in the car. — What time is it one half-hour later?

C. At **12:00,** Julio and Nathan are ready to eat. — What time is it one half-hour later?

©1998 Tribune Education. All Rights Reserved.
62

Page 62

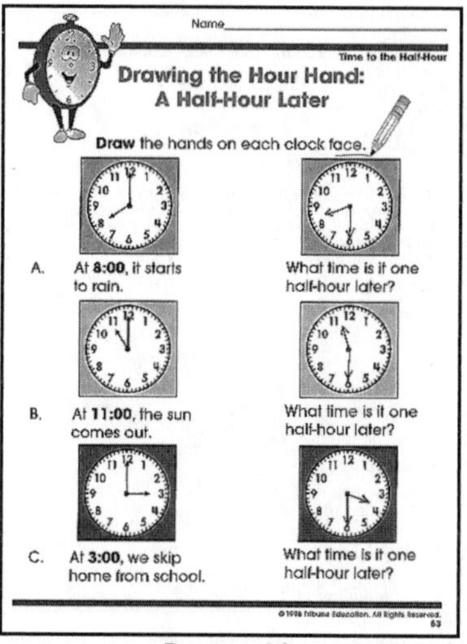

Name

Time to the Half-Hour

Drawing the Hour Hand: A Half-Hour Later

Draw the hands on each clock face.

A. At **8:00,** it starts to rain. — What time is it one half-hour later?

B. At **11:00,** the sun comes out. — What time is it one half-hour later?

C. At **3:00,** we skip home from school. — What time is it one half-hour later?

©1998 Tribune Education. All Rights Reserved.
63

Page 63

Name

Time to the Half-Hour

Drawing the Hour Hand: A Half-Hour Later

Draw the hands on each clock face.

A. At **6:30,** a fire engine roars down the street. — What time is it one half-hour later?

B. At **11:30,** everyone is playing in the schoolyard. — What time is it one half-hour later?

C. At **5:30,** my dog gets out of the yard. — What time is it one half-hour later?

©1998 Tribune Education. All Rights Reserved.
64

Page 64

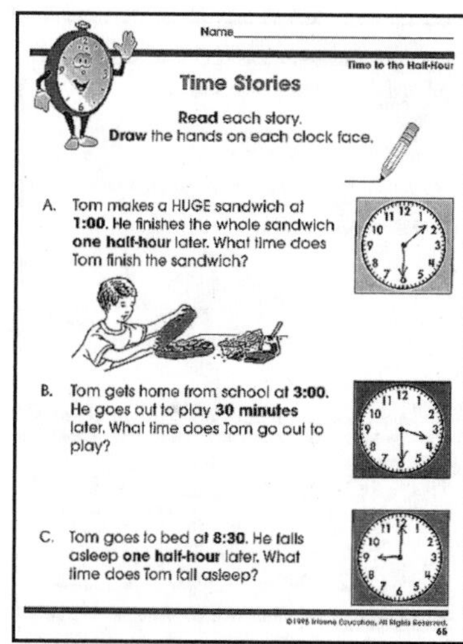

Name

Time to the Half-Hour

Time Stories

Read each story.
Draw the hands on each clock face.

A. Tom makes a HUGE sandwich at **1:00.** He finishes the whole sandwich **one half-hour** later. What time does Tom finish the sandwich?

B. Tom gets home from school at **3:00.** He goes out to play **30 minutes** later. What time does Tom go out to play?

C. Tom goes to bed at **8:30.** He falls asleep **one half-hour** later. What time does Tom fall asleep?

©1998 Tribune Education. All Rights Reserved.
65

Page 65

Name

Time to the Half-Hour

Time Stories

Read each story.
Draw the hands on each clock face.

A. Maria makes a lunch at **7:00.** She gets on the bus **30 minutes** later. What time does she get on the bus?

B. Maria helps make dinner at **5:30.** Everyone eats it **one half-hour** later. What time does everyone eat?

C. Maria's family plays a game at **8:30.** They stop playing **30 minutes** later. What time do they stop playing?

©1998 Tribune Education. All Rights Reserved.
66

Page 66

Name

Time to the Half-Hour

Time Stories

Read each story.
Draw the hands on each clock face.

A. Li goes for a walk at **10:30.** He comes back with three friends **30 minutes** later. What time does he come back with his friends?

B. Li gets on his bike at **3:30.** He reaches the library **one half-hour** later. What time does he get to the library?

C. Li starts home at **5:00.** He gets home **30 minutes** later. What time does he get home?

©1998 Tribune Education. All Rights Reserved.
67

Page 67

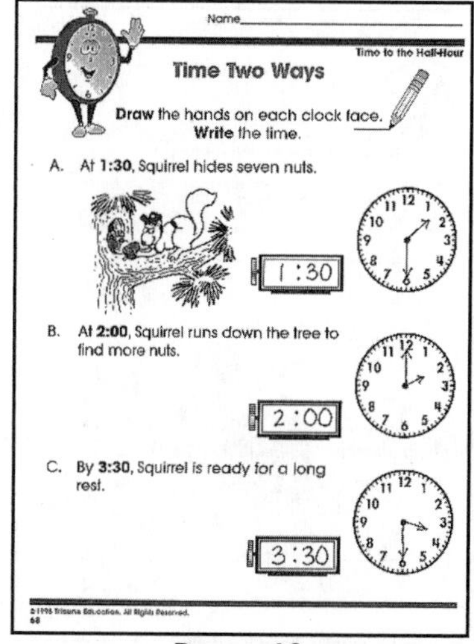

Name

Time to the Half-Hour

Time Two Ways

Draw the hands on each clock face.
Write the time.

A. At **1:30,** Squirrel hides seven nuts. — 1:30

B. At **2:00,** Squirrel runs down the tree to find more nuts. — 2:00

C. By **3:30,** Squirrel is ready for a long rest. — 3:30

©1998 Tribune Education. All Rights Reserved.
68

Page 68

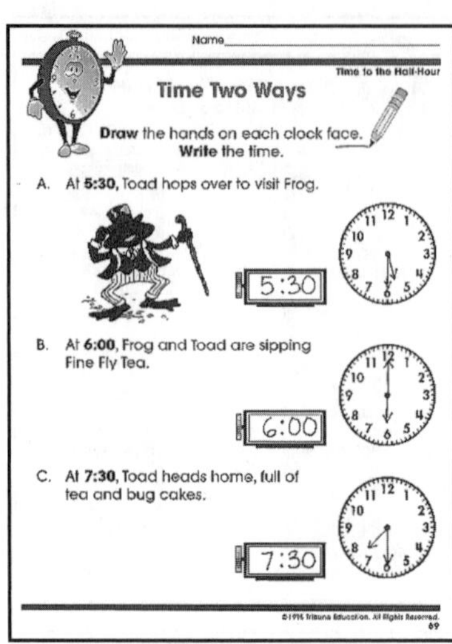
Name______

Time to the Half-Hour

Time Two Ways

Draw the hands on each clock face.
Write the time.

A. At **5:30**, Toad hops over to visit Frog. 5:30

B. At **6:00**, Frog and Toad are sipping Fine Fly Tea. 6:00

C. At **7:30**, Toad heads home, full of tea and bug cakes. 7:30

©1998 Tribune Education. All Rights Reserved. 69

Page 69

Name______

Time to the Half-Hour

Time Two Ways

Draw the hands on each clock face.
Write the time.

A. Maria Mouse gets to the library at **11 o'clock**. She leaves the library at **11:30**.

Gets to library 11:00 **Leaves the library** 11:30

B. Marcus Mouse gets to Pizza Palace at **3 o'clock**. He finishes his pizza at **3:30**.

Gets to Pizza Palace 3:00 **Finishes pizza** 3:30

©1998 Tribune Education. All Rights Reserved. 70

Page 70

Name______

Time to the Half-Hour

Time Two Ways

Draw the hands on each clock face.
Write the time.

A. Tim Toad begins planting the garden at **9 o'clock**. He finishes planting at **9:30**.

Begins planting 9:00 **Finishes planting** 9:30

B. Tara Toad starts roller-skating at **10 o'clock**. She stops roller-skating **30 minutes after 10 o'clock**.

Starts roller-skating 10:00 **Stops roller-skating** 10:30

©1998 Tribune Education. All Rights Reserved. 71

Page 71

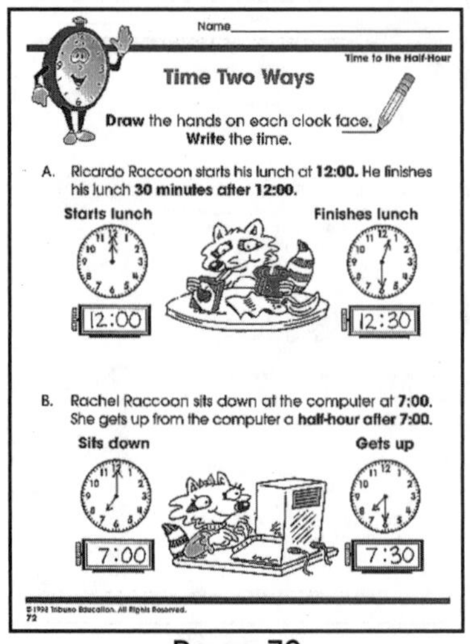
Name______

Time to the Half-Hour

Time Two Ways

Draw the hands on each clock face.
Write the time.

A. Ricardo Raccoon starts his lunch at **12:00**. He finishes his lunch **30 minutes after 12:00**.

Starts lunch 12:00 **Finishes lunch** 12:30

B. Rachel Raccoon sits down at the computer at **7:00**. She gets up from the computer a **half-hour after 7:00**.

Sits down 7:00 **Gets up** 7:30

©1998 Tribune Education. All Rights Reserved. 72

Page 72

Name______

Time to the Half-Hour

Time Stories

Read the story.
Write the time two ways.
Choose a time for everyone to eat lunch!

Bear is going on a picnic today with his brother and sister. They leave for the park at **9:00**. They get to the park at **10:00**. Bear helps carry the food to a picnic table. Then he gets out his kite. Bear flies his kite at **10:30**. Later, at (Answer will vary), everyone has a picnic lunch!

Put the story in order by writing what time Bear did each thing.

A. Leave for the park 9:00

B. Get to the park 10:00

C. Fly kite 10:30

D. Eat lunch Answer will vary.

©1998 Tribune Education. All Rights Reserved. 73

Page 73

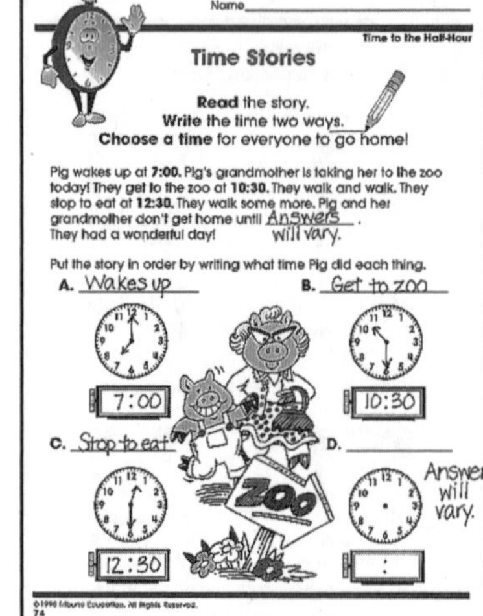
Name______

Time to the Half-Hour

Time Stories

Read the story.
Write the time two ways.
Choose a time for everyone to go home!

Pig wakes up at **7:00**. Pig's grandmother is taking her to the zoo today! They get to the zoo at **10:30**. They walk and walk. They stop to eat at **12:30**. They walk some more. Pig and her grandmother don't get home until Answers will vary. They had a wonderful day!

Put the story in order by writing what time Pig did each thing.

A. Wakes up 7:00

B. Get to zoo 10:30

C. Stop to eat 12:30

D. ______ Answer will vary.

©1998 Tribune Education. All Rights Reserved. 74

Page 74

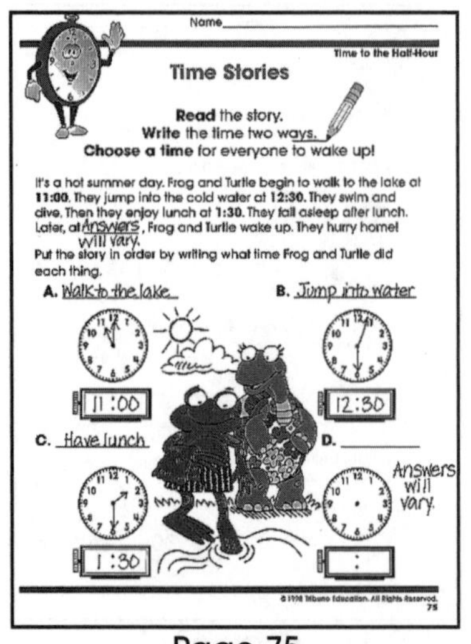
Name______

Time to the Half-Hour

Time Stories

Read the story.
Write the time two ways.
Choose a time for everyone to wake up!

It's a hot summer day. Frog and Turtle begin to walk to the lake at **11:00**. They jump into the cold water at **12:30**. They swim and dive. Then they enjoy lunch at **1:30**. They fall asleep after lunch. Later, at Answers will vary, Frog and Turtle wake up. They hurry home!

Put the story in order by writing what time Frog and Turtle did each thing.

A. Walk to the lake 11:00

B. Jump into water 12:30

C. Have lunch 1:30

D. ______ Answers will vary.

©1998 Tribune Education. All Rights Reserved. 75

Page 75

Name______

Time to the Half-Hour

Time Puzzles

Read each "time clue."
Draw the hands on each clock.
Write the time.

Answers will vary.

A. It's dark outside. Everyone is asleep.

B. Ring, ring! Time to get up.

C. Here comes the school bus. Run, so you won't be late!

D. I'm hungry! Soon it will be time for lunch.

©1998 Tribune Education. All Rights Reserved. 76

Page 76

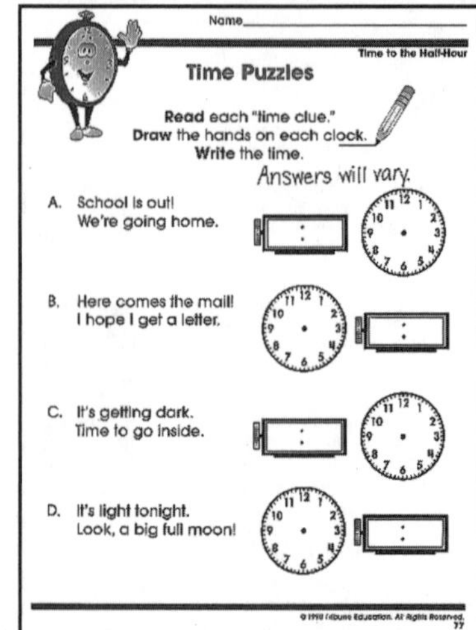
Name______

Time to the Half-Hour

Time Puzzles

Read each "time clue."
Draw the hands on each clock.
Write the time.

Answers will vary.

A. School is out! We're going home.

B. Here comes the mail! I hope I get a letter.

C. It's getting dark. Time to go inside.

D. It's light tonight. Look, a big full moon!

©1998 Tribune Education. All Rights Reserved. 77

Page 77

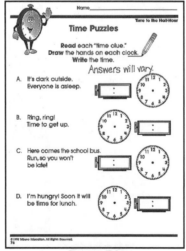

Name__________

Time to the Half-Hour

Time Puzzles

Read each "time clue."
Draw the hands on each clock.
Write the time.

Answers will vary.

A. Sometimes I have homework to do.

B. Sometimes I have jobs to do.

C. The best time is when I can do just what I want to do.

D. On Saturday and Sunday, I play with friends.

©1998 Tribune Education. All Rights Reserved. 78

Page 78

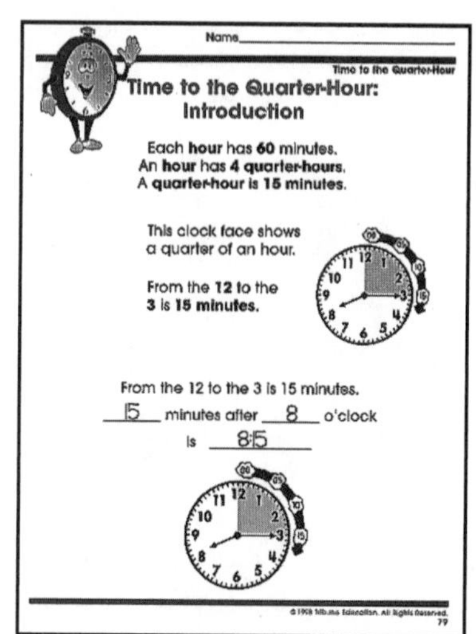

Name__________

Time to the Quarter-Hour

Time to the Quarter-Hour: Introduction

Each **hour** has **60** minutes.
An **hour** has **4 quarter-hours.**
A **quarter-hour is 15 minutes.**

This clock face shows a quarter of an hour.

From the **12** to the **3** is **15 minutes.**

From the 12 to the 3 is 15 minutes.
15 minutes after 8 o'clock
is 8:15

©1998 Tribune Education. All Rights Reserved. 79

Page 79

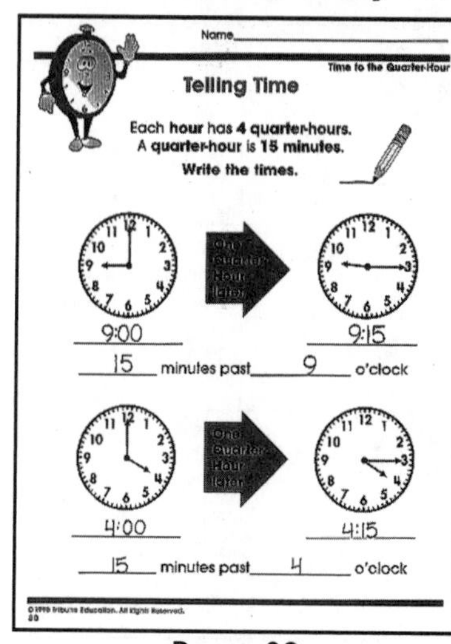

Name__________

Time to the Quarter-Hour

Telling Time

Each **hour** has **4 quarter-hours.**
A **quarter-hour** is **15 minutes.**
Write the times.

9:00 9:15
15 minutes past 9 o'clock

4:00 4:15
15 minutes past 4 o'clock

©1998 Tribune Education. All Rights Reserved. 80

Page 80

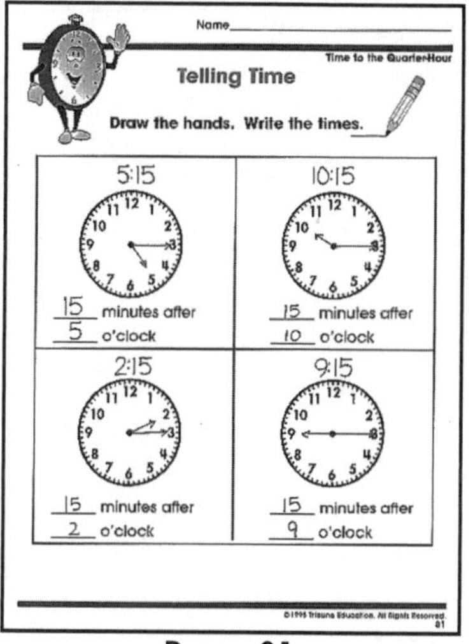

Name__________

Time to the Quarter-Hour

Telling Time

Draw the hands. Write the times.

5:15 15 minutes after 5 o'clock	10:15 15 minutes after 10 o'clock
2:15 15 minutes after 2 o'clock	9:15 15 minutes after 9 o'clock

©1998 Tribune Education. All Rights Reserved. 81

Page 81

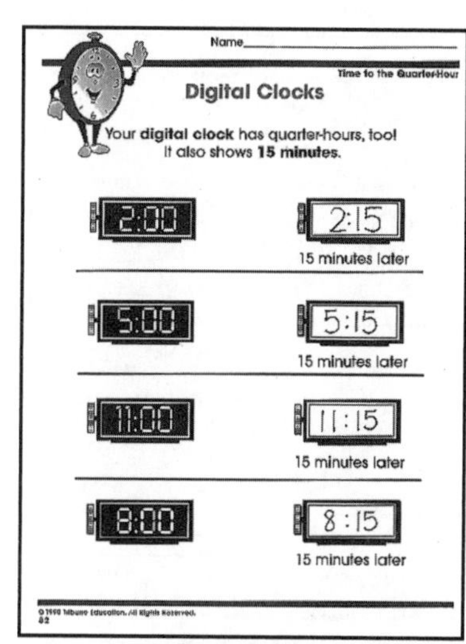

Name__________

Time to the Quarter-Hour

Digital Clocks

Your **digital clock** has quarter-hours, too!
It also shows **15 minutes.**

2:00 → 2:15 15 minutes later

5:00 → 5:15 15 minutes later

11:00 → 11:15 15 minutes later

8:00 → 8:15 15 minutes later

©1998 Tribune Education. All Rights Reserved. 82

Page 82

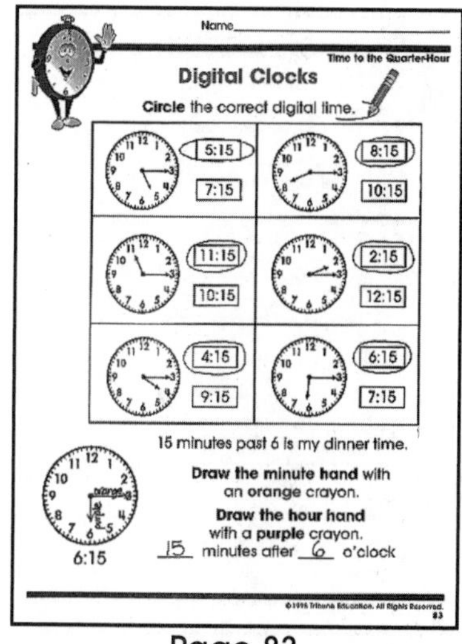

Name__________

Time to the Quarter-Hour

Digital Clocks

Circle the correct digital time.

5:15 / 7:15	8:15 / 10:15
11:15 / 10:15	2:15 / 12:15
4:15 / 9:15	6:15 / 7:15

15 minutes past 6 is my dinner time.

Draw the minute hand with an orange crayon.
Draw the hour hand with a **purple** crayon.
15 minutes after 6 o'clock

6:15

©1998 Tribune Education. All Rights Reserved. 83

Page 83

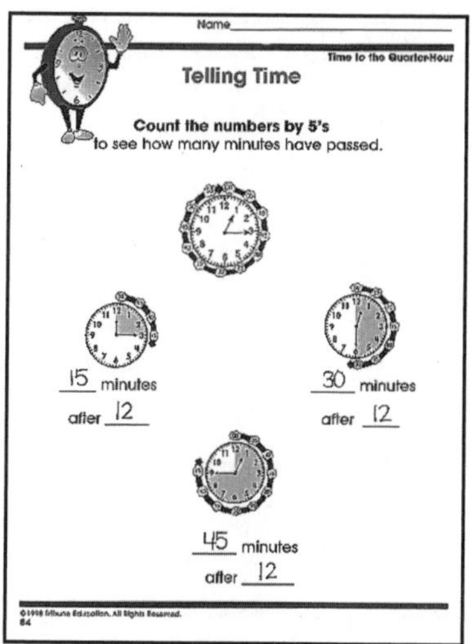

Name__________

Time to the Quarter-Hour

Telling Time

Count the numbers by 5's to see how many minutes have passed.

15 minutes after 12

30 minutes after 12

45 minutes after 12

©1998 Tribune Education. All Rights Reserved. 84

Page 84

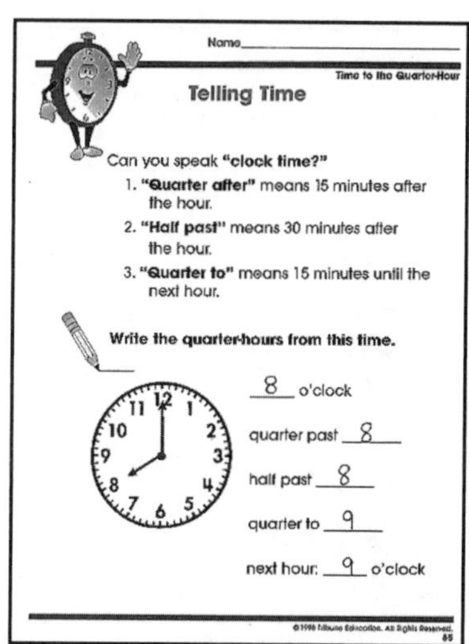

Name__________

Time to the Quarter-Hour

Telling Time

Can you speak **"clock time?"**

1. **"Quarter after"** means 15 minutes after the hour.
2. **"Half past"** means 30 minutes after the hour.
3. **"Quarter to"** means 15 minutes until the next hour.

Write the quarter-hours from this time.

8 o'clock
quarter past 8
half past 8
quarter to 9
next hour: 9 o'clock

©1998 Tribune Education. All Rights Reserved. 85

Page 85

Name__________

Time to the Quarter-Hour

Telling Time

Write the time on the digital clocks.

6:00 6:15

6:30 6:45

©1998 Tribune Education. All Rights Reserved. 86

Page 86

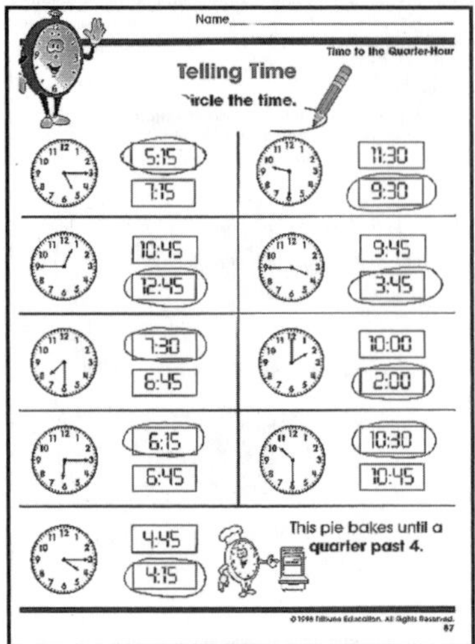
Page 87

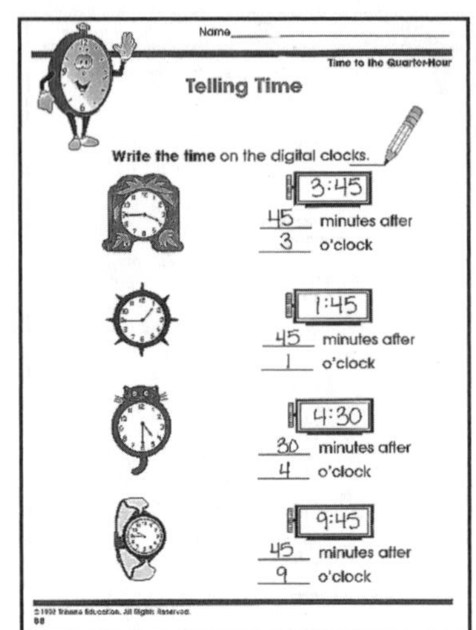
Page 88

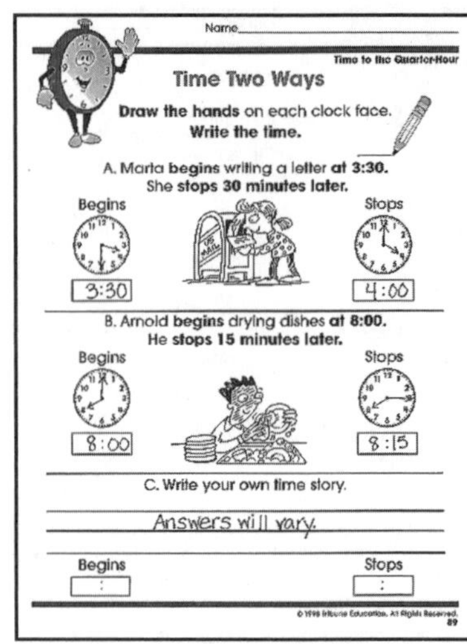
Page 89

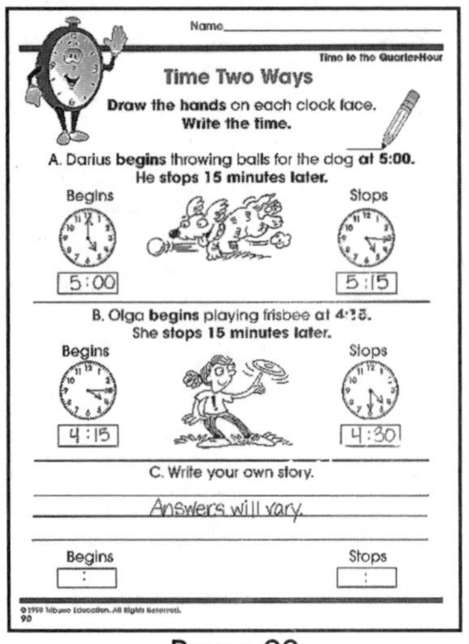
Page 90

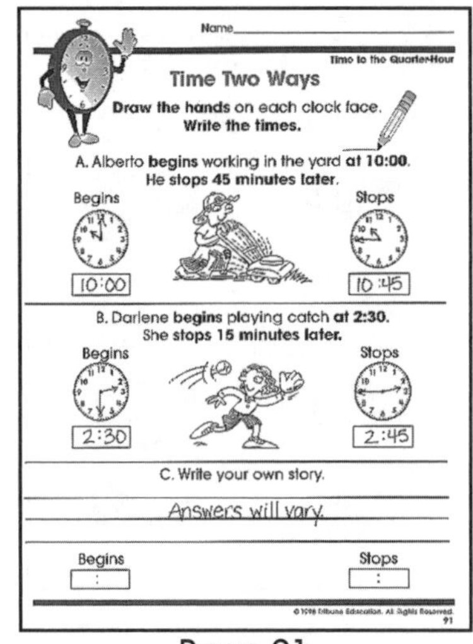
Page 91

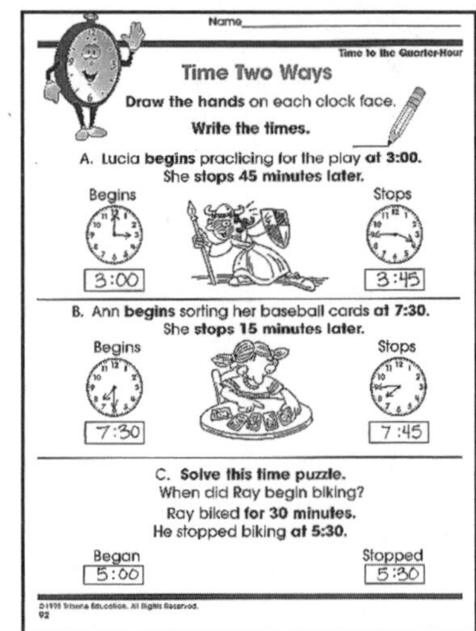
Page 92

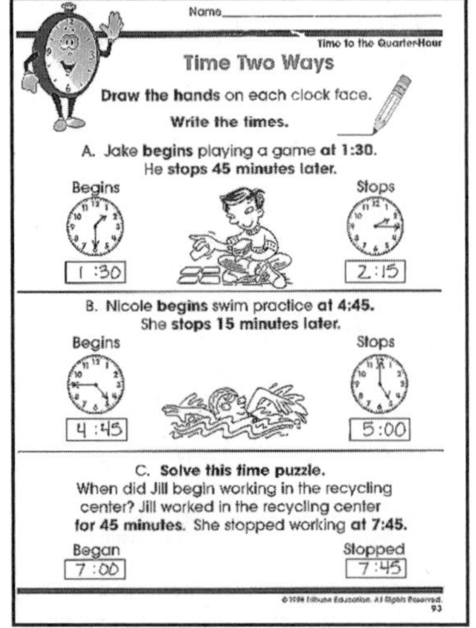
Page 93

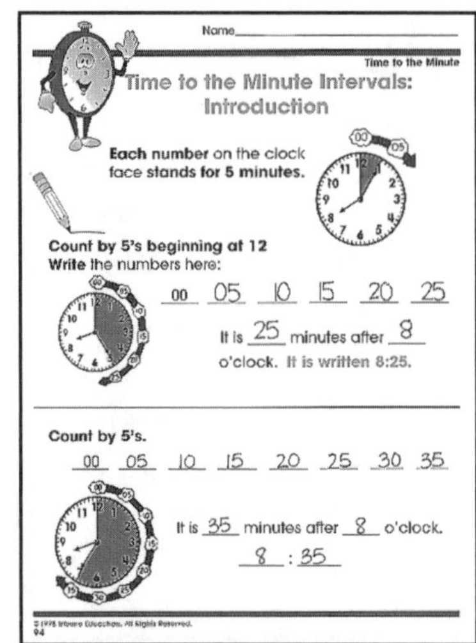
Page 94

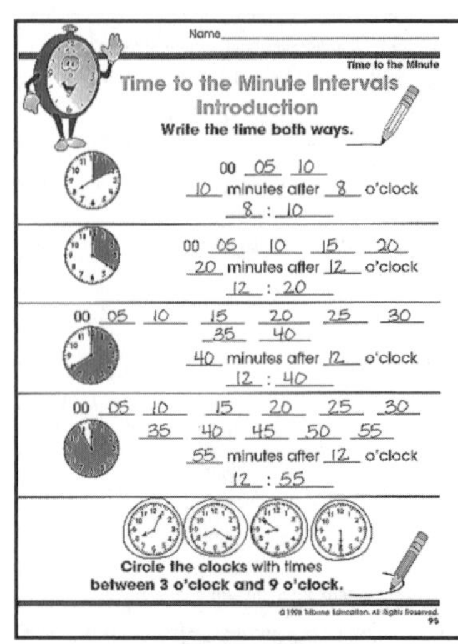
Page 95

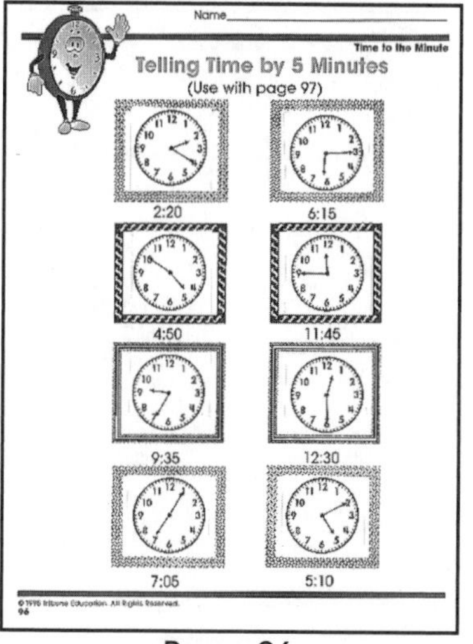

Page 96

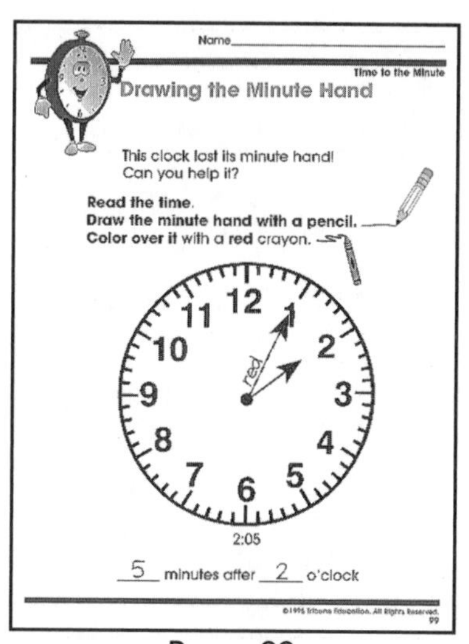

Page 99

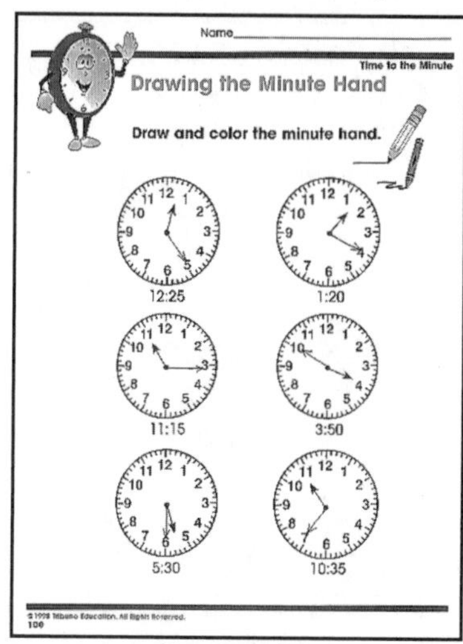

Page 100

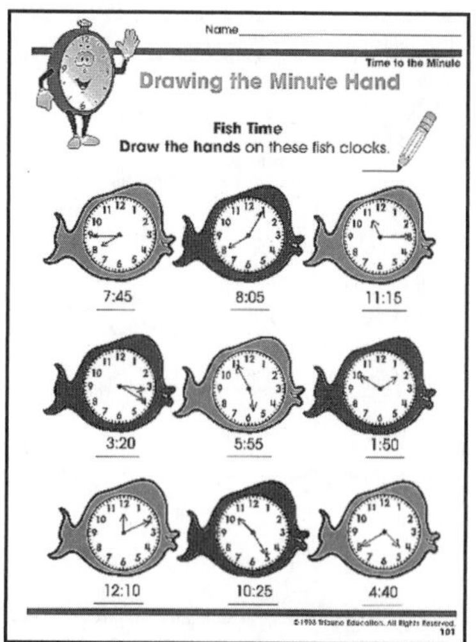

Name
Time to the Minute
Drawing the Minute Hand
Fish Time
Draw the hands on these fish clocks.
7:45
8:05
11:15
3:20
5:55
1:50
12:10
10:25
4:40

Page 101

Page 102

Name
Time to the Minute
Digital Clocks
Can you read a digital clock?
First read the hour.
Then read the minutes.
This clock is read four twenty or twenty minutes past 4 o'clock.
4:20
Match the digital and face clocks.
9:55
1:05
3:20
4:35

Page 103

Name
Time to the Minute
Digital Clocks
Circle the words to match the times.
five twenty
5:20
five fifty
six twenty-five
6:35
six thirty-five
seven ten
7:10
seven twenty
one fifty-five
11:55
eleven fifty-five

Page 104

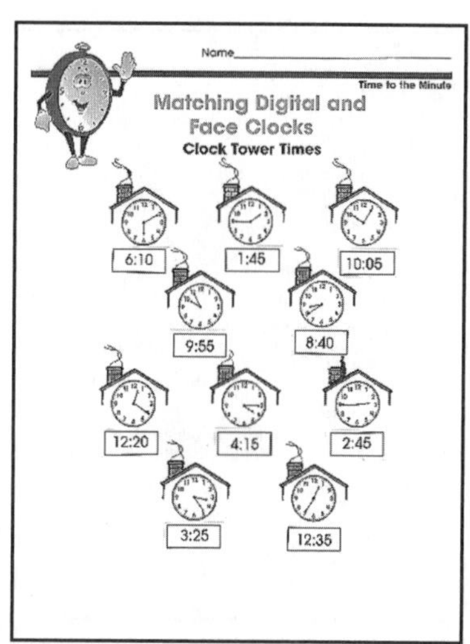

Page 105

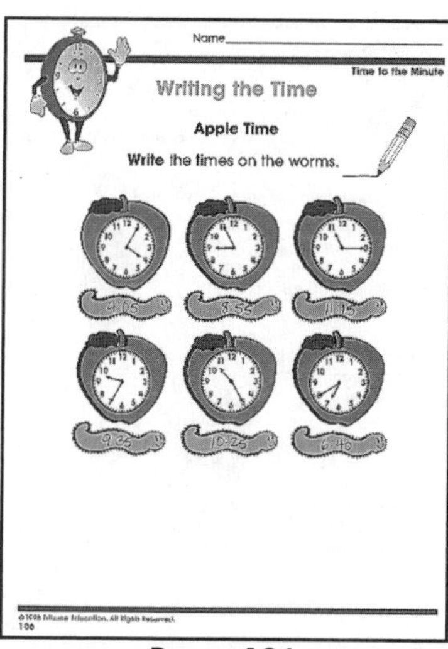

Name
Time to the Minute
Writing the Time
Apple Time
Write the times on the worms.

Page 106

Name________

Time to the Minute

Writing the Time

Turtle Time

What time is it?

9:10	8:25	
10:05	8:20	1:45
7:55	8:15	3:50
2:35	7:30	2:40

© 1998 Tribune Education. All Rights Reserved. 107

Page 107

Name________

Time to the Minute

Drawing Clock Hands

As Easy as 1, 2, 3!

Draw the hands. Write the time.

Three thirty	3:30
Five forty-five	5:45
Eleven twenty	11:20
Eight ten	8:10
Two fifty-five	2:55
Nine forty	9:40

© 1998 Tribune Education. All Rights Reserved. 108

Page 108

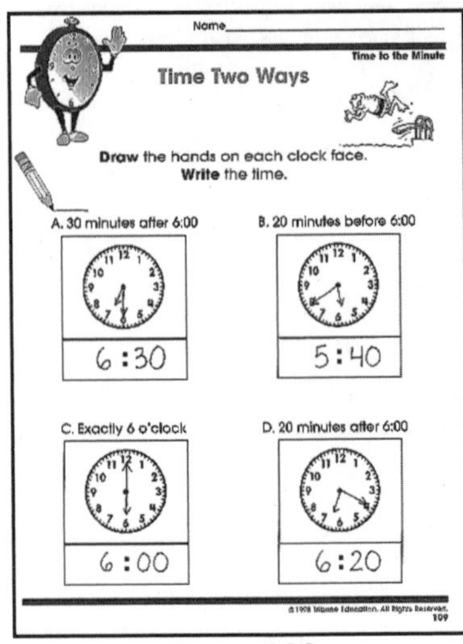
Name________

Time to the Minute

Time Two Ways

Draw the hands on each clock face.
Write the time.

A. 30 minutes after 6:00 — 6:30

B. 20 minutes before 6:00 — 5:40

C. Exactly 6 o'clock — 6:00

D. 20 minutes after 6:00 — 6:20

© 1998 Tribune Education. All Rights Reserved. 109

Page 109

Name________

Time to the Minute

Time Two Ways

Draw the hands on each clock face.
Write the time.

A. Exactly noon or midnight — 12:00

B. Quarter past 12:00 — 12:15

C. 15 minutes before 12:00 — 11:45

D. Half past 12:00 — 12:30

© 1998 Tribune Education. All Rights Reserved. 110

Page 110

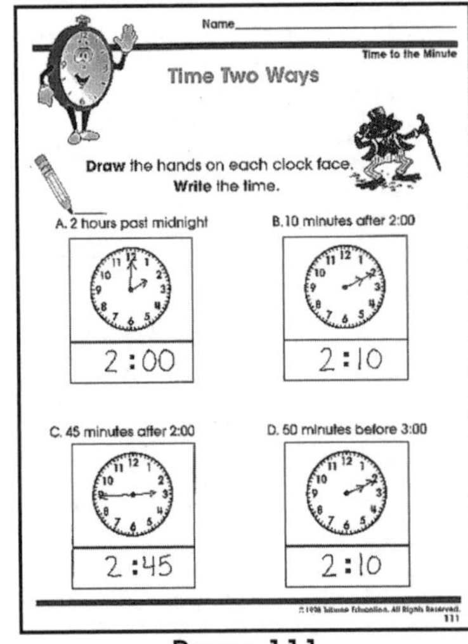
Name________

Time to the Minute

Time Two Ways

Draw the hands on each clock face.
Write the time.

A. 2 hours past midnight — 2:00

B. 10 minutes after 2:00 — 2:10

C. 45 minutes after 2:00 — 2:45

D. 50 minutes before 3:00 — 2:10

© 1998 Tribune Education. All Rights Reserved. 111

Page 111

Name________

Time to the Minute

Writing Familiar Times:
Family "Time Tree"

Answers will vary.

Write the time.
Draw the hands on each clock.

I get up at ______. I go to bed at ______. Lunch is at ______.

Dinner is at ______. School starts at ______. School ends at ______.

Recess is at ______. I play at ______.

© 1998 Tribune Education. All Rights Reserved. 112

Page 112

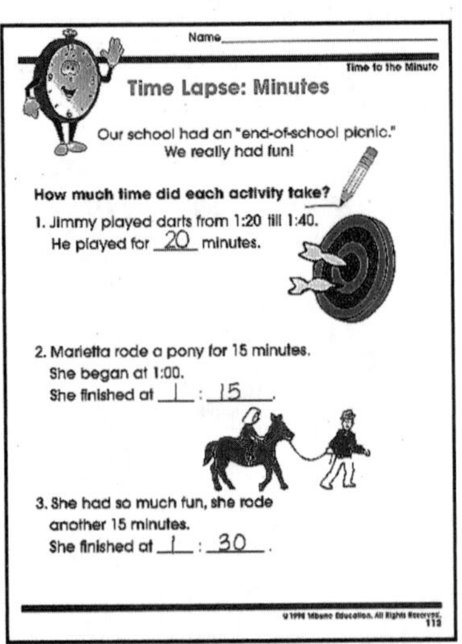
Name________

Time to the Minute

Time Lapse: Minutes

Our school had an "end-of-school picnic."
We really had fun!

How much time did each activity take?

1. Jimmy played darts from 1:20 till 1:40.
He played for 20 minutes.

2. Marietta rode a pony for 15 minutes.
She began at 1:00.
She finished at 1 : 15 .

3. She had so much fun, she rode another 15 minutes.
She finished at 1 : 30 .

© 1998 Tribune Education. All Rights Reserved. 113

Page 113

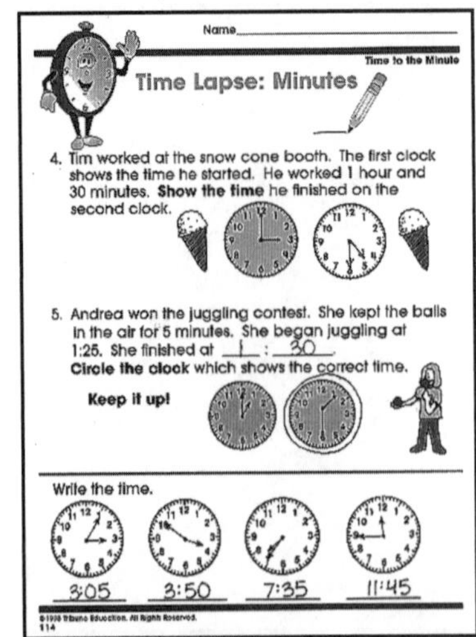
Name________

Time to the Minute

Time Lapse: Minutes

4. Tim worked at the snow cone booth. The first clock shows the time he started. He worked 1 hour and 30 minutes. Show the time he finished on the second clock.

5. Andrea won the juggling contest. She kept the balls in the air for 5 minutes. She began juggling at 1:25. She finished at 1 : 30 .
Circle the clock which shows the correct time.

Keep it up!

Write the time.

3:05 3:50 7:35 11:45

© 1998 Tribune Education. All Rights Reserved. 114

Page 114

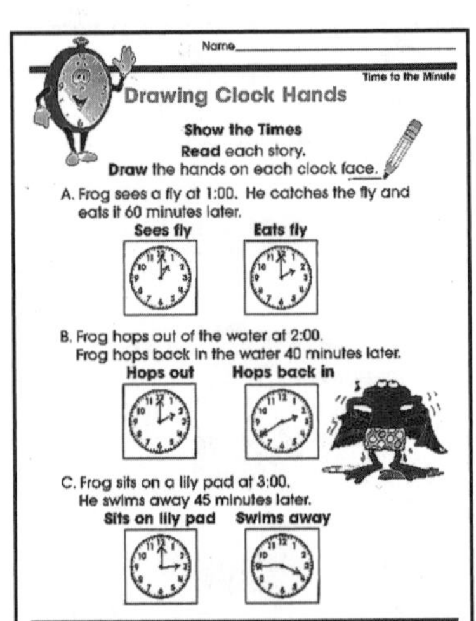
Name________

Time to the Minute

Drawing Clock Hands

Show the Times

Read each story.
Draw the hands on each clock face.

A. Frog sees a fly at 1:00. He catches the fly and eats it 60 minutes later.
Sees fly Eats fly

B. Frog hops out of the water at 2:00.
Frog hops back in the water 40 minutes later.
Hops out Hops back in

C. Frog sits on a lily pad at 3:00.
He swims away 45 minutes later.
Sits on lily pad Swims away

© 1998 Tribune Education. All Rights Reserved. 115

Page 115

Answer Key - Time

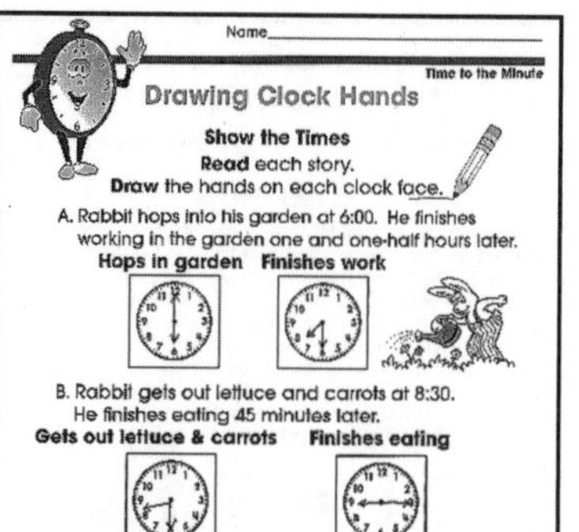
Name__________

Time to the Minute

Drawing Clock Hands

Show the Times

Read each story.
Draw the hands on each clock face.

A. Rabbit hops into his garden at 6:00. He finishes working in the garden one and one-half hours later.

Hops in garden **Finishes work**

B. Rabbit gets out lettuce and carrots at 8:30. He finishes eating 45 minutes later.

Gets out lettuce & carrots **Finishes eating**

C. Rabbit lies down for a nap at 4:00. He wakes up and hip-hops away 55 minutes later.

Lies down **Wakes up**

©1998 Tribune Education. All Rights Reserved.
116

Page 116

Name__________

Time to the Minute

Drawing Clock Hands

Show the Times

Read each story.
Draw the hands on each clock face.

A. Pig takes a mud bath at 9:00. Pig showers off 15 minutes later.

Takes mud bath **Showers off**

B. On Monday, Pig begins cleaning at noon. Her house is clean and neat 90 minutes later.

Begins cleaning **House is clean**

C. On Tuesday, Pig goes to the market at 12:45. She comes home with a basket full of goodies 30 minutes later.

Goes to market **Comes home**

©1998 Tribune Education. All Rights Reserved.
117

Page 117

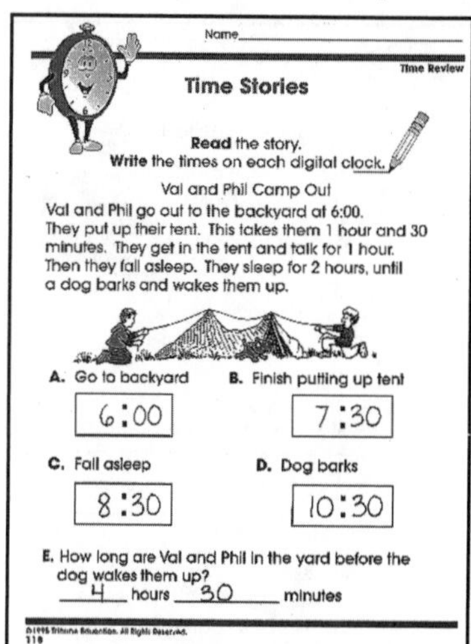
Name__________

Time Review

Time Stories

Read the story.
Write the times on each digital clock.

Val and Phil Camp Out

Val and Phil go out to the backyard at 6:00. They put up their tent. This takes them 1 hour and 30 minutes. They get in the tent and talk for 1 hour. Then they fall asleep. They sleep for 2 hours, until a dog barks and wakes them up.

A. Go to backyard 6:00
B. Finish putting up tent 7:30
C. Fall asleep 8:30
D. Dog barks 10:30

E. How long are Val and Phil in the yard before the dog wakes them up?
4 hours 30 minutes

©1998 Tribune Education. All Rights Reserved.
118

Page 118

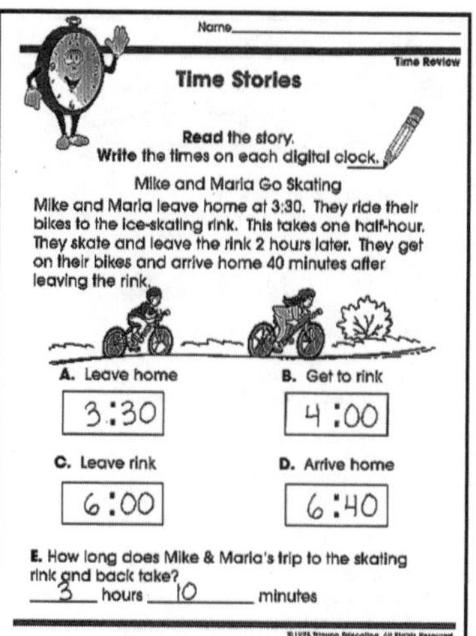
Name__________

Time Review

Time Stories

Read the story.
Write the times on each digital clock.

Mike and Maria Go Skating

Mike and Maria leave home at 3:30. They ride their bikes to the ice-skating rink. This takes one half-hour. They skate and leave the rink 2 hours later. They get on their bikes and arrive home 40 minutes after leaving the rink.

A. Leave home 3:30
B. Get to rink 4:00
C. Leave rink 6:00
D. Arrive home 6:40

E. How long does Mike & Maria's trip to the skating rink and back take?
3 hours 10 minutes

©1998 Tribune Education. All Rights Reserved.
119

Page 119

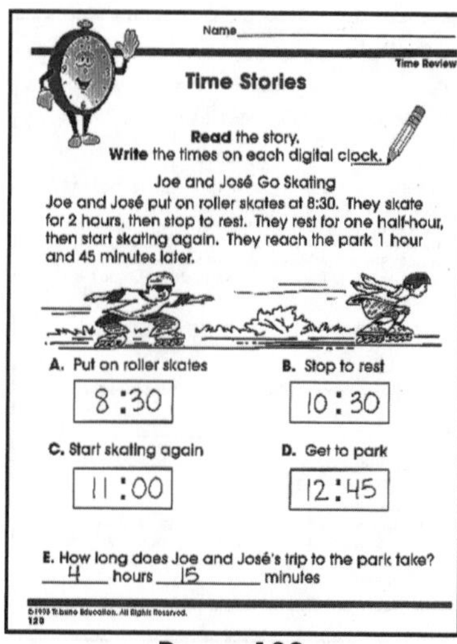
Name__________

Time Review

Time Stories

Read the story.
Write the times on each digital clock.

Joe and José Go Skating

Joe and José put on roller skates at 8:30. They skate for 2 hours, then stop to rest. They rest for one half-hour, then start skating again. They reach the park 1 hour and 45 minutes later.

A. Put on roller skates 8:30
B. Stop to rest 10:30
C. Start skating again 11:00
D. Get to park 12:45

E. How long does Joe and José's trip to the park take?
4 hours 15 minutes

©1998 Tribune Education. All Rights Reserved.
120

Page 120

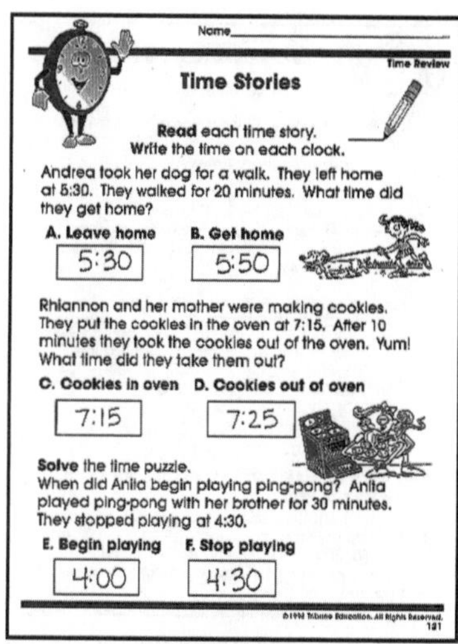
Name__________

Time Review

Time Stories

Read each time story.
Write the time on each clock.

Andrea took her dog for a walk. They left home at 5:30. They walked for 20 minutes. What time did they get home?

A. Leave home 5:30
B. Get home 5:50

Rhiannon and her mother were making cookies. They put the cookies in the oven at 7:15. After 10 minutes they took the cookies out of the oven. Yum! What time did they take them out?

C. Cookies in oven 7:15
D. Cookies out of oven 7:25

Solve the time puzzle.
When did Anita begin playing ping-pong? Anita played ping-pong with her brother for 30 minutes. They stopped playing at 4:30.

E. Begin playing 4:00
F. Stop playing 4:30

©1998 Tribune Education. All Rights Reserved.
121

Page 121

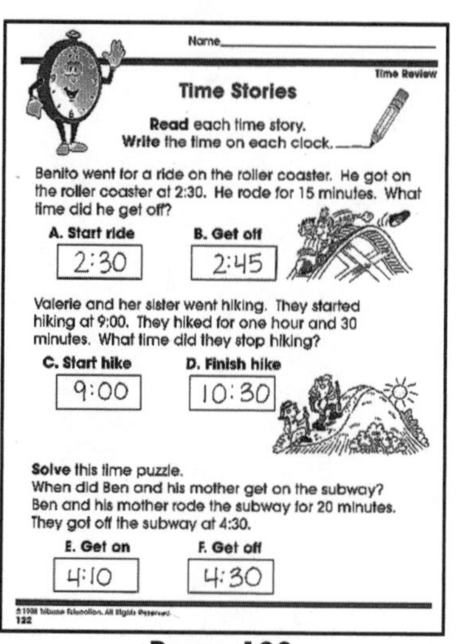
Name__________

Time Review

Time Stories

Read each time story.
Write the time on each clock.

Benito went for a ride on the roller coaster. He got on the roller coaster at 2:30. He rode for 15 minutes. What time did he get off?

A. Start ride 2:30
B. Get off 2:45

Valerie and her sister went hiking. They started hiking at 9:00. They hiked for one hour and 30 minutes. What time did they stop hiking?

C. Start hike 9:00
D. Finish hike 10:30

Solve this time puzzle.
When did Ben and his mother get on the subway? Ben and his mother rode the subway for 20 minutes. They got off the subway at 4:30.

E. Get on 4:10
F. Get off 4:30

©1998 Tribune Education. All Rights Reserved.
122

Page 122

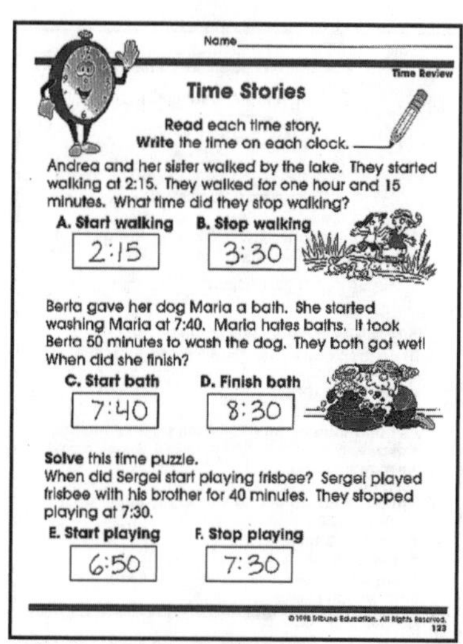
Name__________

Time Review

Time Stories

Read each time story.
Write the time on each clock.

Andrea and her sister walked by the lake. They started walking at 2:15. They walked for one hour and 15 minutes. What time did they stop walking?

A. Start walking 2:15
B. Stop walking 3:30

Berta gave her dog Maria a bath. She started washing Maria at 7:40. Maria hates baths. It took Berta 50 minutes to wash the dog. They both got wet! When did she finish?

C. Start bath 7:40
D. Finish bath 8:30

Solve this time puzzle.
When did Sergei start playing frisbee? Sergei played frisbee with his brother for 40 minutes. They stopped playing at 7:30.

E. Start playing 6:50
F. Stop playing 7:30

©1998 Tribune Education. All Rights Reserved.
123

Page 123

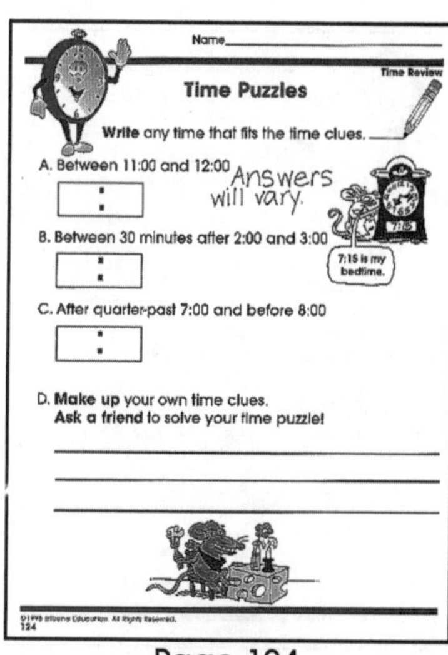
Name__________

Time Review

Time Puzzles

Write any time that fits the time clues.

A. Between 11:00 and 12:00 Answers will vary.

B. Between 30 minutes after 2:00 and 3:00

C. After quarter-past 7:00 and before 8:00

D. **Make up** your own time clues.
Ask a friend to solve your time puzzle!

©1998 Tribune Education. All Rights Reserved.
124

Page 124

Answer Key - Time

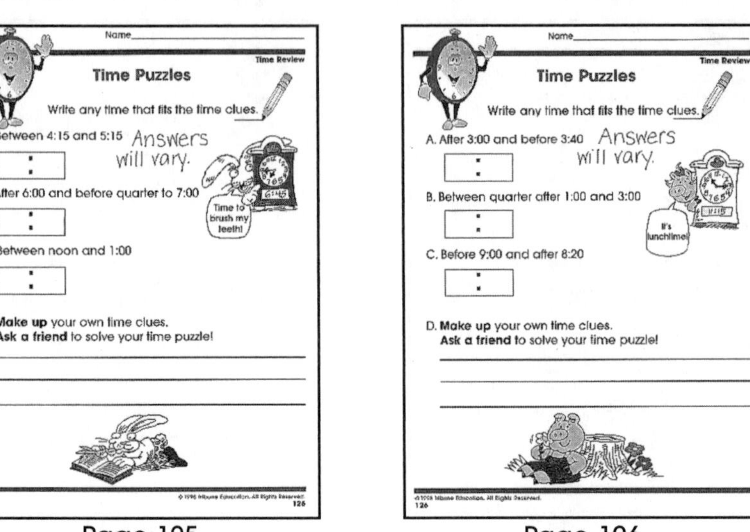

Name_______________ Time Review

Time Puzzles

Write any time that fits the time clues.

A. Between 4:15 and 5:15 [:] Answers will vary.

B. After 6:00 and before quarter to 7:00 [:]

C. Between noon and 1:00 [:]

D. **Make up** your own time clues. **Ask a friend** to solve your time puzzle!

Page 125

Name_______________ Time Review

Time Puzzles

Write any time that fits the time clues.

A. After 3:00 and before 3:40 [:] Answers will vary.

B. Between quarter after 1:00 and 3:00 [:]

C. Before 9:00 and after 8:20 [:]

D. **Make up** your own time clues. **Ask a friend** to solve your time puzzle!

Page 126

Name_______________ Time Review

Time Stories

Read the story. **Write** the time on each clock.

Story Times

Erin and her brother Harry were shopping for dinner. First they went into the bakery at 5:00 to buy fresh bread. This took 5 minutes. Next they walked to the market for vegetables and cereal. This took them 20 minutes. Then they walked next door for a treat at Fanny's Famous Fudge. This took them 15 minutes. Then they met their brother Andrew outside.

A. Go into bakery 5:00

C. Leave bakery 5:05

B. Leave market 5:25

D. See Andrew 5:40

E. How long had Erin and Harry been shopping when they saw Andrew? 40 minutes

F. Make up your own story about shopping. What do you do, and how long does each thing take? Make up a starting time. Use your clock to find the ending time.

Page 127

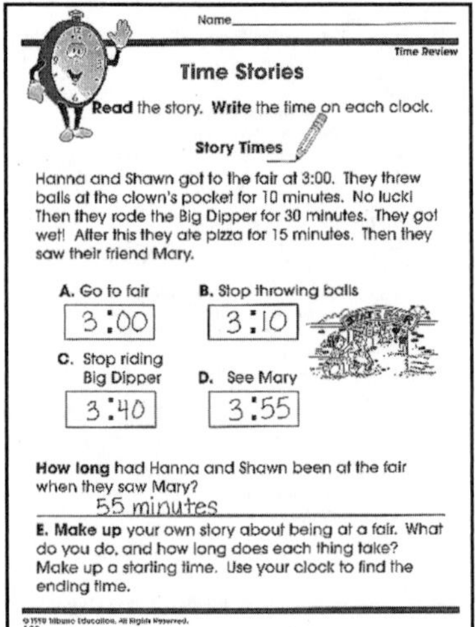

Name_______________ Time Review

Time Stories

Read the story. **Write** the time on each clock.

Story Times

Hanna and Shawn got to the fair at 3:00. They threw balls at the clown's pocket for 10 minutes. No luck! Then they rode the Big Dipper for 30 minutes. They got wet! After this they ate pizza for 15 minutes. Then they saw their friend Mary.

A. Go to fair 3:00

B. Stop throwing balls 3:10

C. Stop riding Big Dipper 3:40

D. See Mary 3:55

How long had Hanna and Shawn been at the fair when they saw Mary? 55 minutes

E. Make up your own story about being at a fair. What do you do, and how long does each thing take? Make up a starting time. Use your clock to find the ending time.

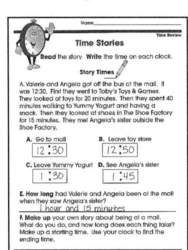

Page 128

Name_______________ Time Review

Time Stories

Read the story. **Write** the time on each clock.

Story Times

A. Valerie and Angela got off the bus at the mall. It was 12:30. First they went to Toby's Toys & Games. They looked at toys for 20 minutes. Then they spent 40 minutes walking to Yummy Yogurt and having a snack. Then they looked at shoes in The Shoe Factory for 15 minutes. They met Angela's sister outside the Shoe Factory.

A. Go to mall 12:30

B. Leave toy store 12:50

C. Leave Yummy Yogurt 1:30

D. See Angela's sister 1:45

E. How long had Valerie and Angela been at the mall when they saw Angela's sister? 1 hour and 15 minutes

F. Make up your own story about being at a mall. What do you do, and how long does each thing take? Make up a starting time. Use your clock to find the ending time.

Page 129

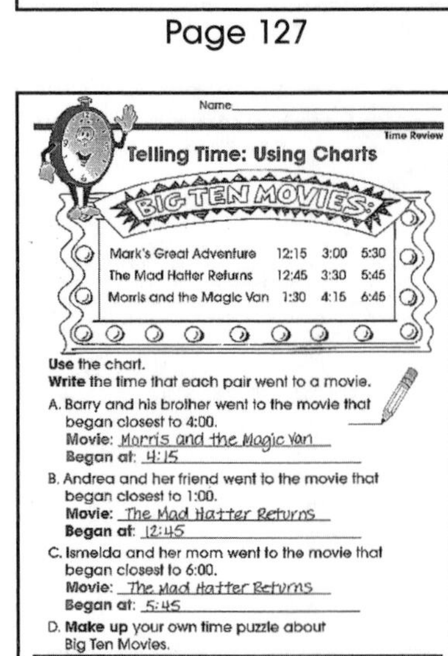

Name_______________ Time Review

Telling Time: Using Charts

BIG TEN MOVIES

Mark's Great Adventure	12:15	3:00	5:30
The Mad Hatter Returns	12:45	3:30	5:45
Morris and the Magic Van	1:30	4:15	6:45

Use the chart.
Write the time that each pair went to a movie.

A. Barry and his brother went to the movie that began closest to 4:00.
Movie: Morris and the Magic Van
Began at: 4:15

B. Andrea and her friend went to the movie that began closest to 1:00.
Movie: The Mad Hatter Returns
Began at: 12:45

C. Ismelda and her mom went to the movie that began closest to 6:00.
Movie: The Mad Hatter Returns
Began at: 5:45

D. **Make up** your own time puzzle about Big Ten Movies.

Page 130

Name_______________ Time Review

Telling Time: Using Charts

MAIN AIRPORT
MONDAY DEPARTURES:

Gull Air	10:45	12:10	1:45
Far West Airlines	9:25	10:10	11:40
Swift Flights	12:30	1:15	2:20

Use the chart.
Write the time that each pair took a flight.

A. Teresa and her aunt flew on the plane that left closest to 10:30.
Airline: Gull Air
Left at: 10:45

B. Kelly and her mother flew on the plane that left closest to 11:00.
Airline: Gull Air
Left at: 10:45

C. Leticia and her father flew on the plane that left closest to 12:15.
Airline: Swift Flights
Left at: 12:30

D. **Make up** your own time puzzle about the Main Airport.

Page 131

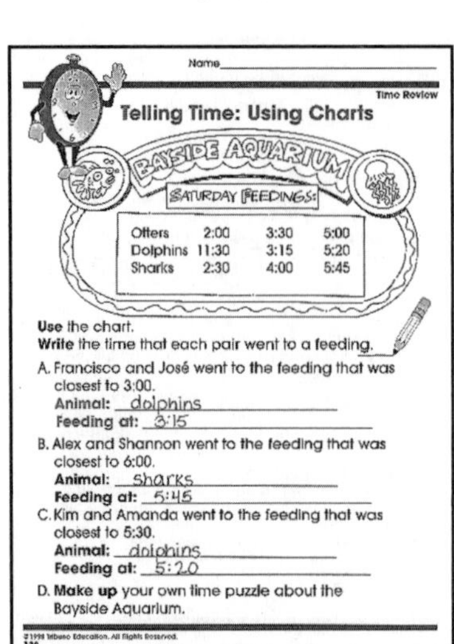

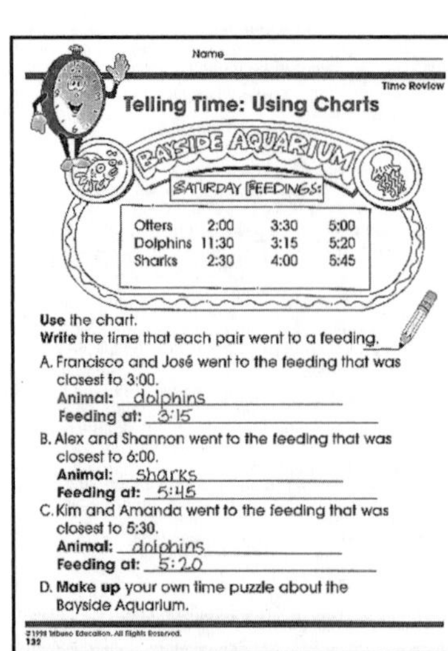

Name_______________ Time Review

Telling Time: Using Charts

BAYSIDE AQUARIUM
SATURDAY FEEDINGS:

Otters	2:00	3:30	5:00
Dolphins	11:30	3:15	5:20
Sharks	2:30	4:00	5:45

Use the chart.
Write the time that each pair went to a feeding.

A. Francisco and José went to the feeding that was closest to 3:00.
Animal: dolphins
Feeding at: 3:15

B. Alex and Shannon went to the feeding that was closest to 6:00.
Animal: sharks
Feeding at: 5:45

C. Kim and Amanda went to the feeding that was closest to 5:30.
Animal: dolphins
Feeding at: 5:20

D. **Make up** your own time puzzle about the Bayside Aquarium.

Page 132

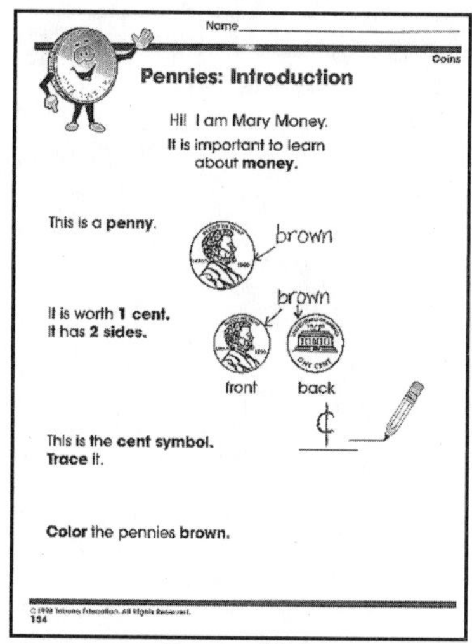

Name
Coins
Pennies: Introduction
Hi! I am Mary Money.
It is important to learn about money.
This is a penny.
brown
It is worth 1 cent.
It has 2 sides.
brown
front
back
This is the cent symbol.
Trace it.
¢
Color the pennies brown.

Page 134

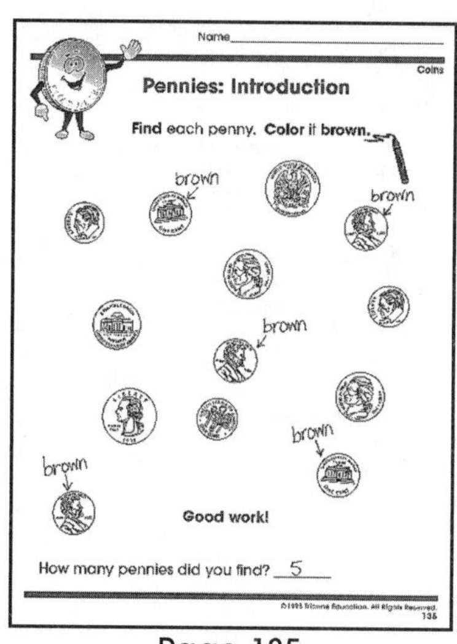

Name
Coins
Pennies: Introduction
Find each penny. Color it brown.
brown
brown
brown
brown
brown
Good work!
How many pennies did you find? 5

Page 135

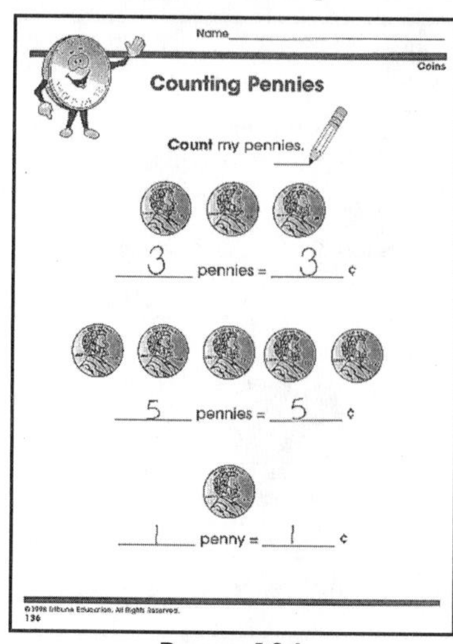

Name
Coins
Counting Pennies
Count my pennies.
3 pennies = 3 ¢
5 pennies = 5 ¢
1 penny = 1 ¢

Page 136

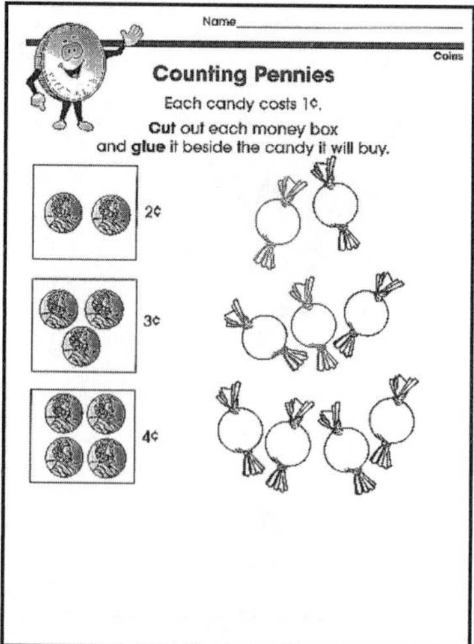

Name
Coins
Counting Pennies
Each candy costs 1¢.
Cut out each money box and glue it beside the candy it will buy.
2¢
3¢
4¢

Page 137

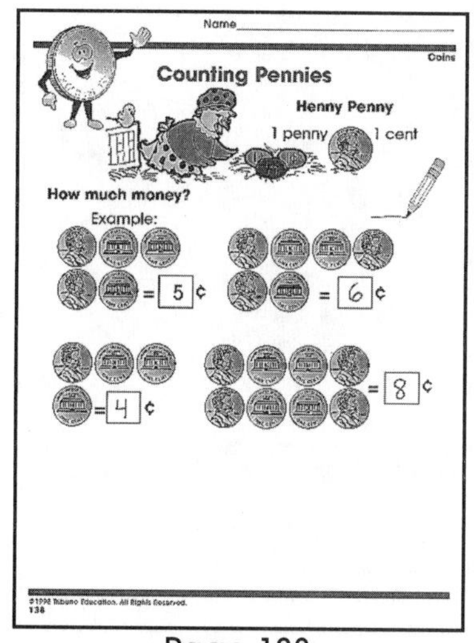

Name
Coins
Counting Pennies
Henny Penny
1 penny
1 cent
How much money?
Example:
5 ¢
6 ¢
4 ¢
8 ¢

Page 138

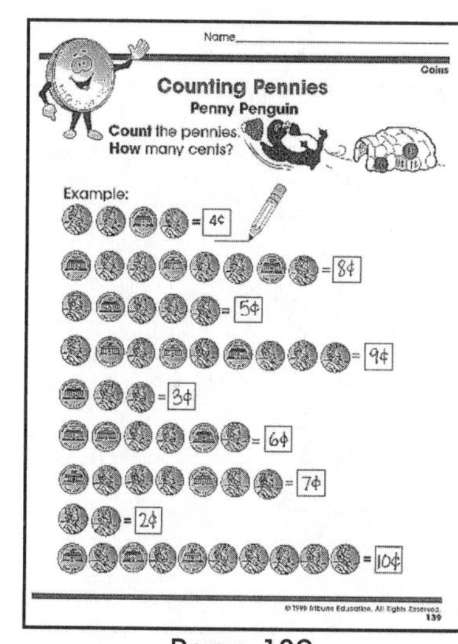

Name
Coins
Counting Pennies
Penny Penguin
Count the pennies.
How many cents?
Example:
4¢
8¢
5¢
9¢
3¢
6¢
7¢
2¢
10¢

Page 139

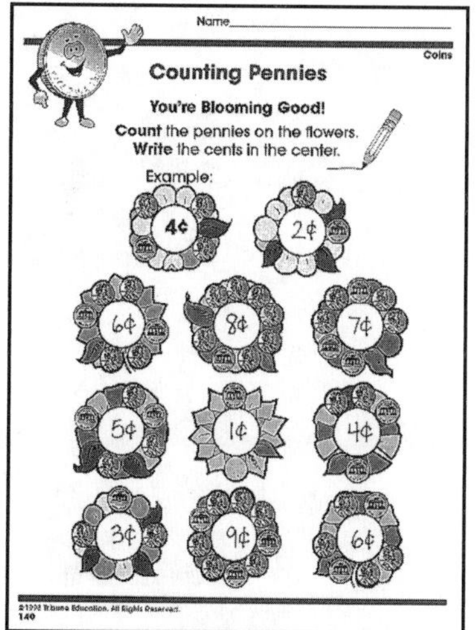

Name
Coins
Counting Pennies
You're Blooming Good!
Count the pennies on the flowers.
Write the cents in the center.
Example:
4¢
2¢
6¢
8¢
7¢
5¢
1¢
4¢
3¢
9¢
6¢

Page 140

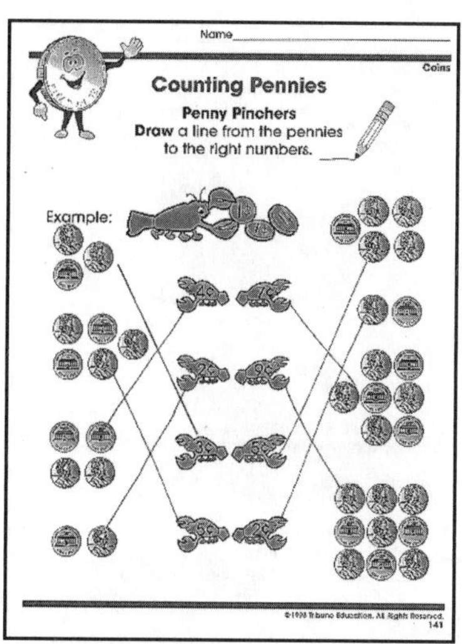

Name
Coins
Counting Pennies
Penny Pinchers
Draw a line from the pennies to the right numbers.
Example:

Page 141

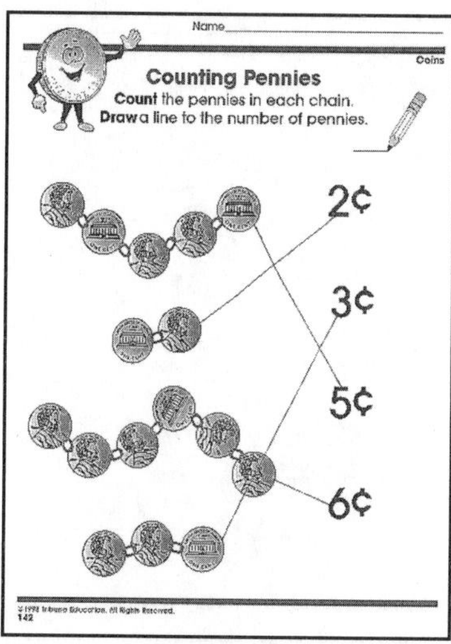

Page 142

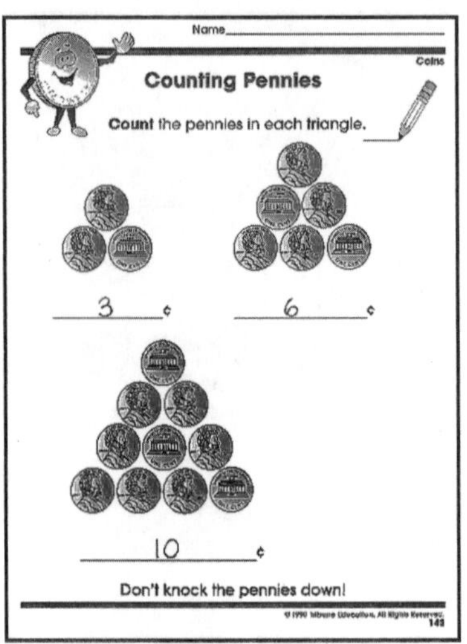
Name____

Coins

Counting Pennies

Count the pennies in each triangle.

3 ¢ 6 ¢

10 ¢

Don't knock the pennies down!

Page 143

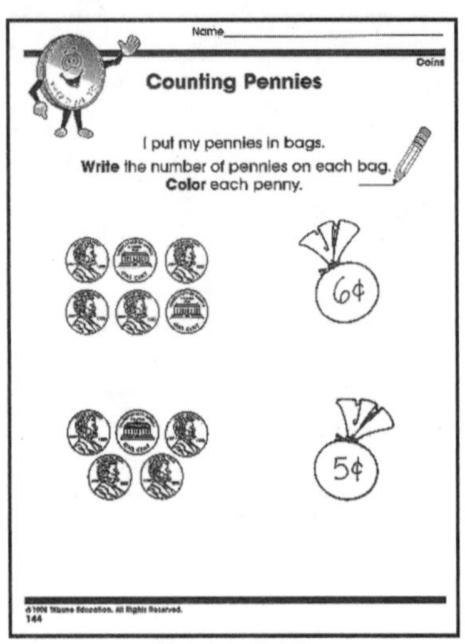
Name____

Coins

Counting Pennies

I put my pennies in bags.
Write the number of pennies on each bag.
Color each penny.

6¢

5¢

Page 144

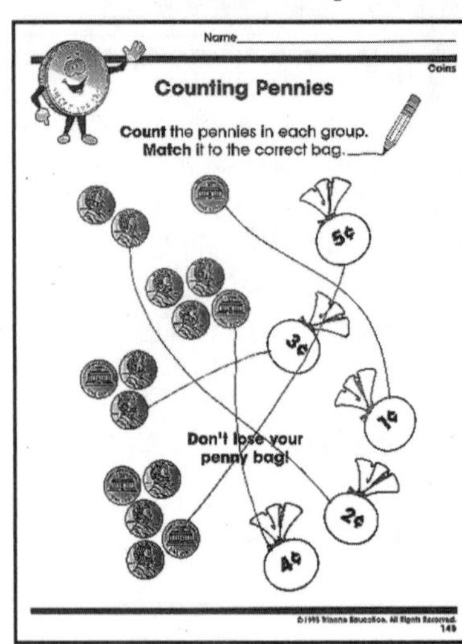
Name____

Coins

Counting Pennies

Count the pennies in each group.
Match it to the correct bag.

5¢ 3¢ 1¢ 2¢ 4¢

Don't lose your penny bag!

Page 145

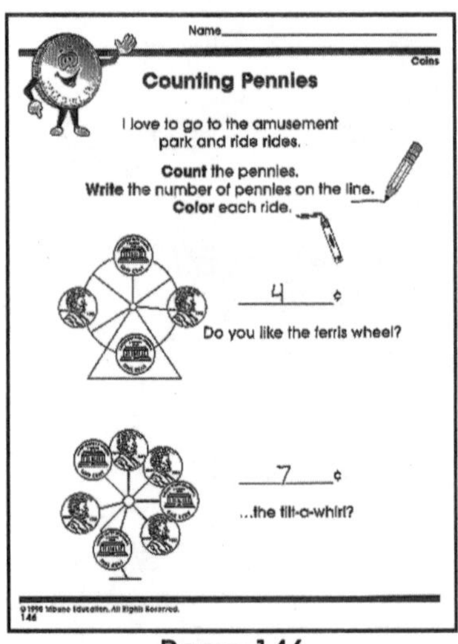
Name____

Coins

Counting Pennies

I love to go to the amusement park and ride rides.
Count the pennies.
Write the number of pennies on the line.
Color each ride.

4 ¢
Do you like the ferris wheel?

7 ¢
...the tilt-a-whirl?

Page 146

Name____

Coins

...the merry-go-round?
3 ¢

...the water flume?
5 ¢

...the bumper cars?
5 ¢

Page 147

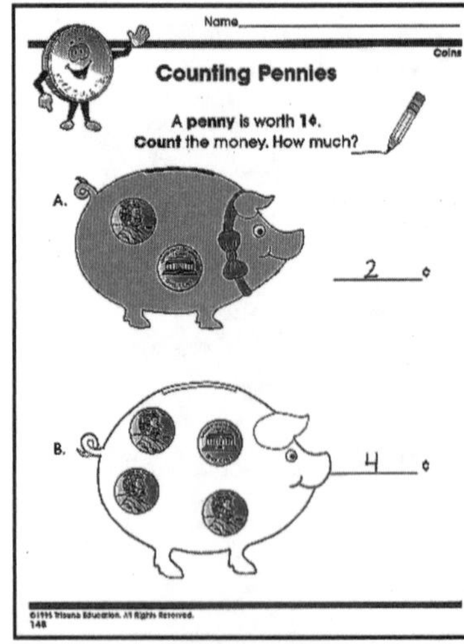
Name____

Coins

Counting Pennies

A **penny** is worth 1¢.
Count the money. How much?

A. 2 ¢

B. 4 ¢

Page 148

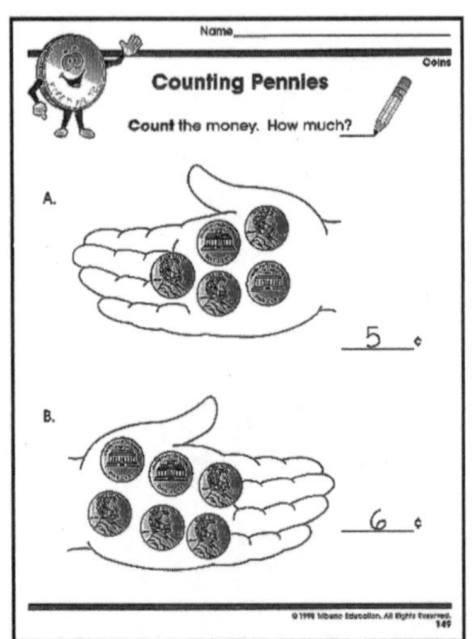
Name____

Coins

Counting Pennies

Count the money. How much?

A. 5 ¢

B. 6 ¢

Page 149

Name____

Coins

Counting Pennies
Who Has More Money?

Count the money.
Write the amount.

A. 3 ¢

B. 7 ¢

C. **Circle** the answer.
Who has more money?

Page 150

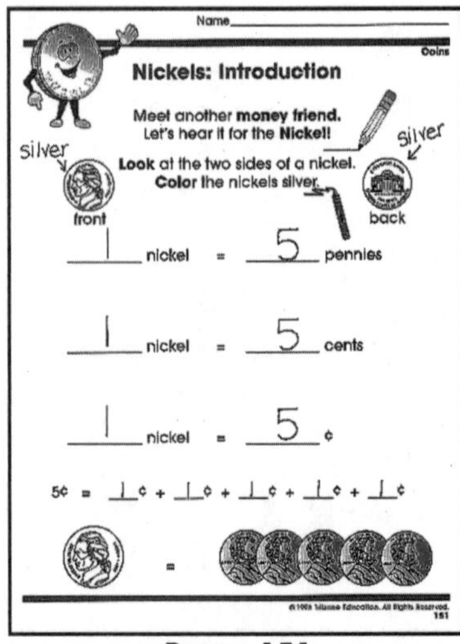
Name____

Coins

Nickels: Introduction

Meet another **money friend.**
Let's hear it for the **Nickel!**
Look at the two sides of a nickel.
Color the nickels silver.

silver front silver back

1 nickel = 5 pennies

1 nickel = 5 cents

1 nickel = 5 ¢

5¢ = 1¢ + 1¢ + 1¢ + 1¢ + 1¢

Page 151

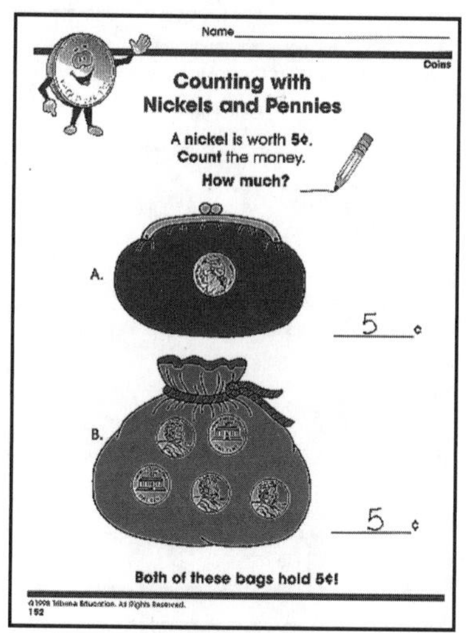
Name__________
Coins

Counting with Nickels and Pennies

A nickel is worth 5¢.
Count the money.
How much?

A. 5 ¢

B. 5 ¢

Both of these bags hold 5¢!

152

Page 152

Name__________
Coins

Counting with Nickels and Pennies

Here are my friends, **Penny** and **Nickel.**
You can count them together!

Remember: They both have a front and back!

Here is a **penny.**
Color it brown. brown

And here is a **nickel.**
Color it silver. silver

1 penny = 1 cent

1 penny = 1 ¢

1 nickel = 5 cents

1 nickel = 5 ¢

Make the cent symbol here: ¢

153

Page 153

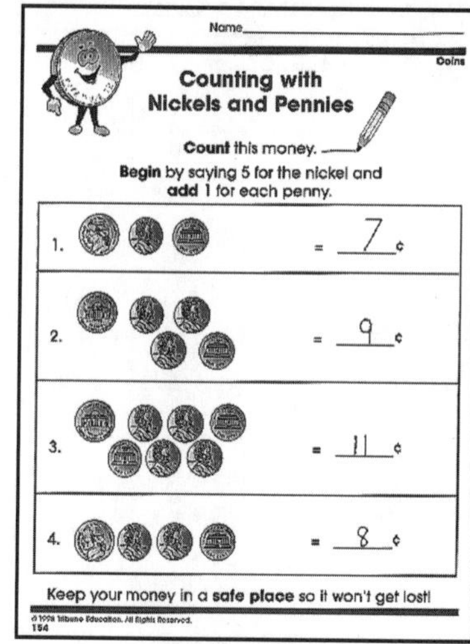
Name__________
Coins

Counting with Nickels and Pennies

Count this money.
Begin by saying 5 for the nickel and **add** 1 for each penny.

1. = 7 ¢

2. = 9 ¢

3. = 11 ¢

4. = 8 ¢

Keep your money in a **safe place** so it won't get lost!

154

Page 154

Name__________
Coins

Counting with Nickels and Pennies

Count the money.
Start with the nickel. Then **count** the pennies.
Write the amount.

5 ¢

8 ¢

4 ¢

7 ¢

10 ¢

4 ¢

155

Page 155

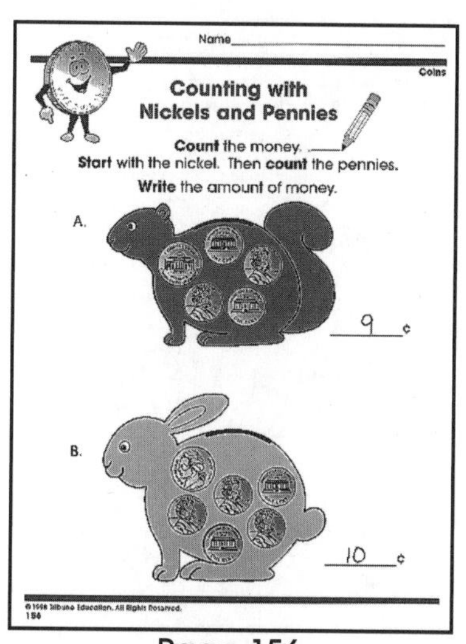
Name__________
Coins

Counting with Nickels and Pennies

Count the money.
Start with the nickel. Then **count** the pennies.
Write the amount of money.

A. 9 ¢

B. 10 ¢

156

Page 156

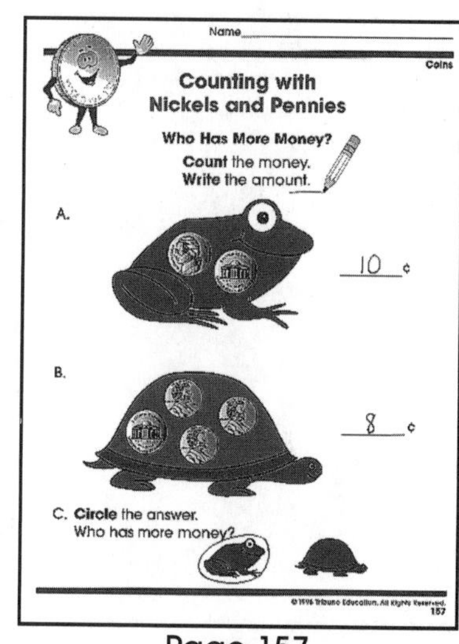
Name__________
Coins

Counting with Nickels and Pennies

Who Has More Money?
Count the money.
Write the amount.

A. 10 ¢

B. 8 ¢

C. **Circle** the answer.
Who has more money?

157

Page 157

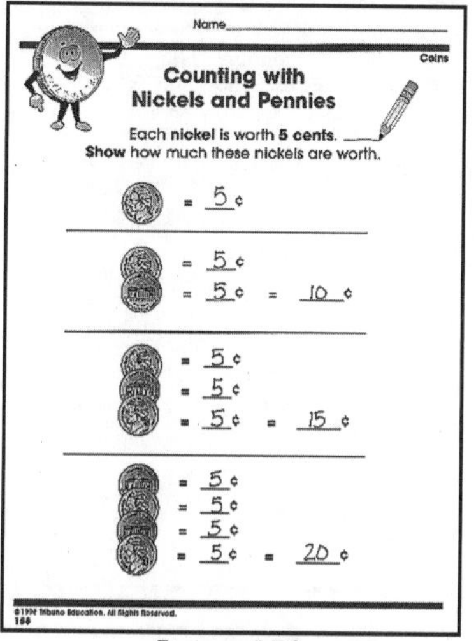
Name__________
Coins

Counting with Nickels and Pennies

Each **nickel** is worth **5 cents.**
Show how much these nickels are worth.

= 5 ¢

= 5 ¢
= 5 ¢ = 10 ¢

= 5 ¢
= 5 ¢
= 5 ¢ = 15 ¢

= 5 ¢
= 5 ¢
= 5 ¢
= 5 ¢ = 20 ¢

158

Page 158

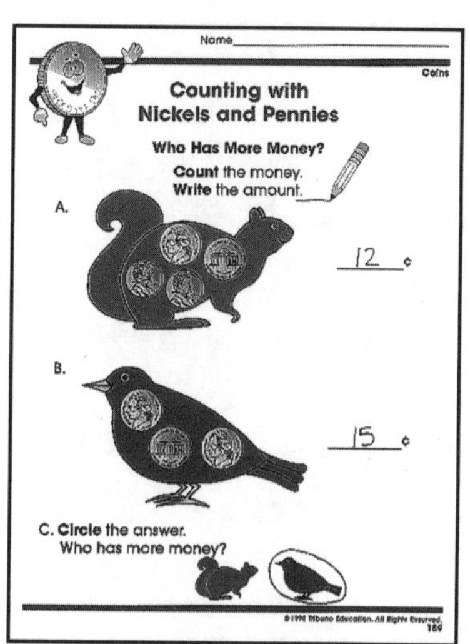
Name__________
Coins

Counting with Nickels and Pennies

Who Has More Money?
Count the money.
Write the amount.

A. 12 ¢

B. 15 ¢

C. **Circle** the answer.
Who has more money?

159

Page 159

Name__________
Coins

Nickels: Counting By Fives

Let's count my nickels to see if we have enough to buy something!

Count by 5's.
See how far you can count.

5, 10, 15, 20, 25,
30, 35, 40, 45, 50,
55, 60, 65, 70, 75,
80, 85, 90, 95, 100,

This is how to count nickels!

Practice counting by 5's!

160

Page 160

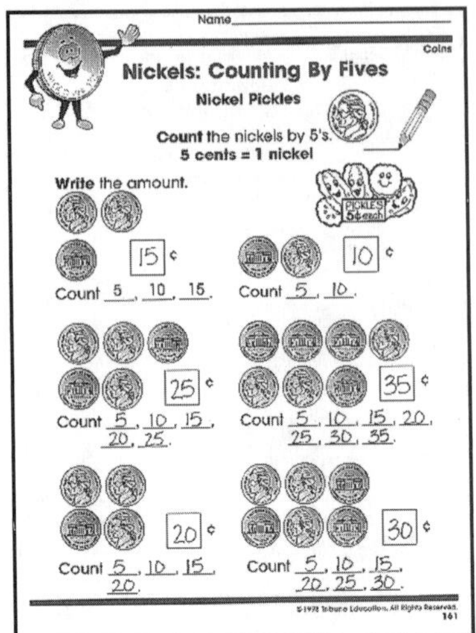
Name________________

Coins

Nickels: Counting By Fives

Nickel Pickles

Count the nickels by 5's.
5 cents = 1 nickel

Write the amount.

15 ¢ Count 5, 10, 15.

10 ¢ Count 5, 10.

25 ¢ Count 5, 10, 15, 20, 25.

35 ¢ Count 5, 10, 15, 20, 25, 30, 35.

20 ¢ Count 5, 10, 15, 20.

30 ¢ Count 5, 10, 15, 20, 25, 30.

©1998 Tribune Education. All Rights Reserved. 161

Page 161

Name________________

Coins

Nickels: Counting By Fives

Clowns

Count the nickels.
How much money is each clown worth?

10 ¢ 20 ¢

35 ¢ 45 ¢

©1998 Tribune Education. All Rights Reserved. 162

Page 162

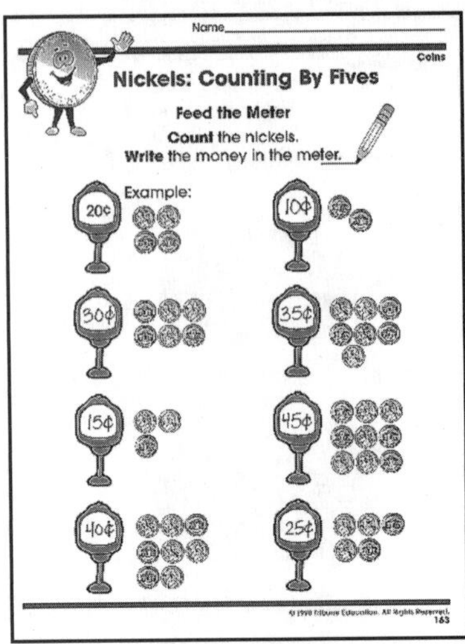
Name________________

Coins

Nickels: Counting By Fives

Feed the Meter

Count the nickels.
Write the money in the meter.

Example: 20¢

10¢

30¢

35¢

15¢

45¢

40¢

25¢

©1998 Tribune Education. All Rights Reserved. 163

Page 163

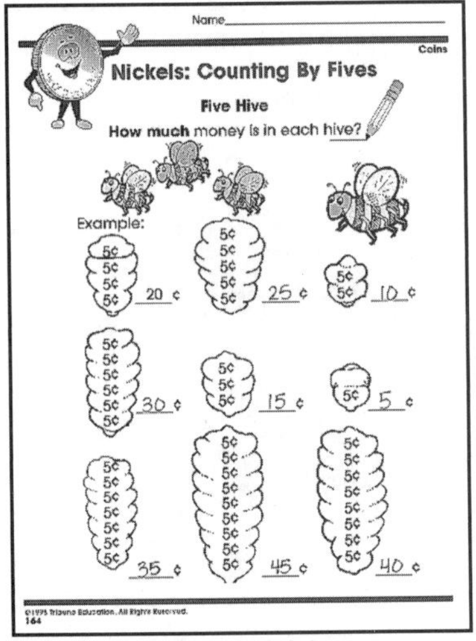
Name________________

Coins

Nickels: Counting By Fives

Five Hive

How much money is in each hive?

Example: 20 ¢

25 ¢

10 ¢

30 ¢

15 ¢

5 ¢

35 ¢

45 ¢

40 ¢

©1998 Tribune Education. All Rights Reserved. 164

Page 164

Name________________

Coins

Counting with Nickels and Pennies

Money Bunnies

Count the coins.
Write the amount under each bunny's carrot.

Example: 7 ¢

11 ¢

17 ¢

21 ¢

12 ¢

14 ¢

©1998 Tribune Education. All Rights Reserved. 165

Page 165

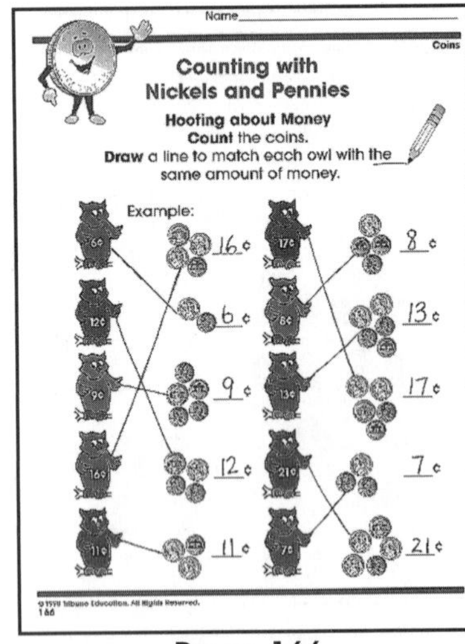
Name________________

Coins

Counting with Nickels and Pennies

Hooting about Money

Count the coins.
Draw a line to match each owl with the same amount of money.

Example: 16 ¢

6 ¢

9 ¢

12 ¢

11 ¢

8 ¢

13 ¢

17 ¢

7 ¢

21 ¢

©1998 Tribune Education. All Rights Reserved. 166

Page 166

Name________________

Coins

Counting with Nickels and Pennies

"Cent"-erpillars

Count the coins on each "cent"-erpillar.

Example: 17 ¢

14 ¢

21 ¢

9 ¢

13 ¢

27 ¢

18 ¢

16 ¢

31 ¢

19 ¢

©1998 Tribune Education. All Rights Reserved. 167

Page 167

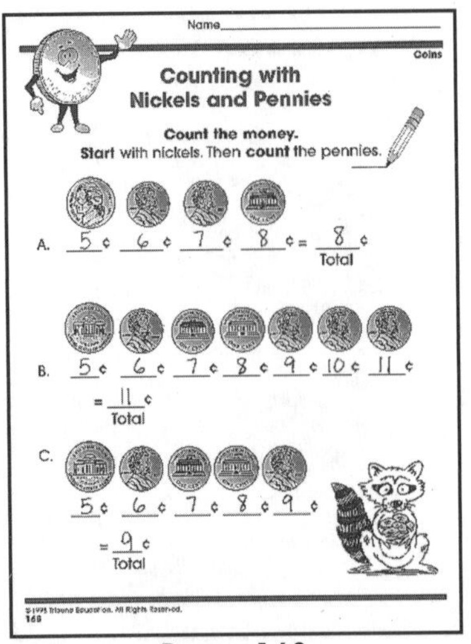
Name________________

Coins

Counting with Nickels and Pennies

Count the money.
Start with nickels. Then **count** the pennies.

A. 5 ¢ 6 ¢ 7 ¢ 8 ¢ = 8 ¢ Total

B. 5 ¢ 6 ¢ 7 ¢ 8 ¢ 9 ¢ 10 ¢ 11 ¢ = 11 ¢ Total

C. 5 ¢ 6 ¢ 7 ¢ 8 ¢ 9 ¢ = 9 ¢ Total

©1998 Tribune Education. All Rights Reserved. 168

Page 168

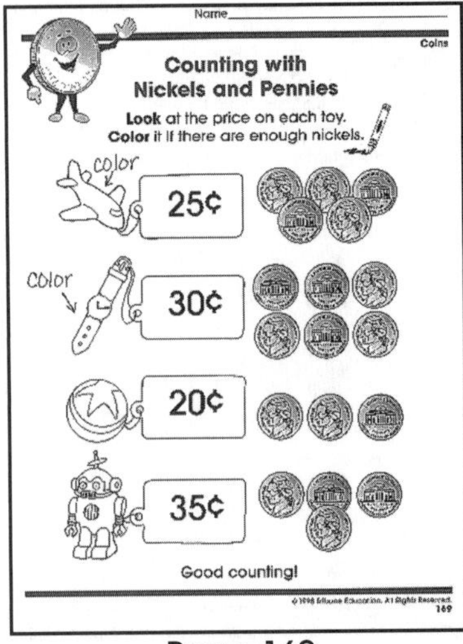
Name________________

Coins

Counting with Nickels and Pennies

Look at the price on each toy.
Color it if there are enough nickels.

color 25¢

color 30¢

20¢

35¢

Good counting!

©1998 Tribune Education. All Rights Reserved. 169

Page 169

Answer Key - Money

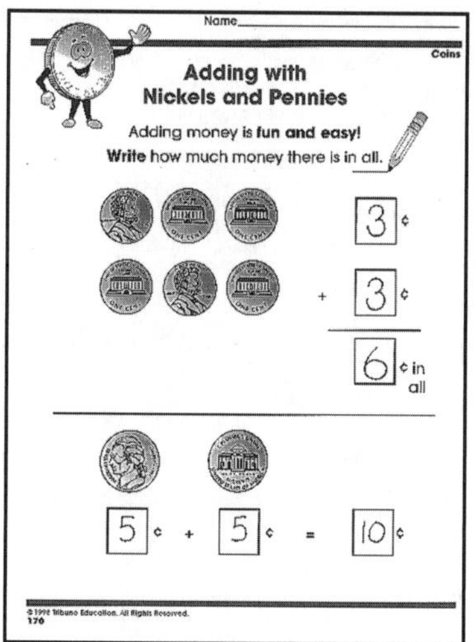
Name

Coins

Adding with Nickels and Pennies

Adding money is **fun and easy!**
Write how much money there is in all.

3¢ + 3¢ = 6¢ in all

5¢ + 5¢ = 10¢

©1998 Tribune Education. All Rights Reserved.
170

Page 170

Name

Coins

Adding with Nickels and Pennies

7¢ + 7¢ = 14¢

Draw groups of pennies and nickels here. **Write** an addition sentence using the coins you drew. **Color the coins.**

Answers will vary.

You are catching on!

©1998 Tribune Education. All Rights Reserved.
171

Page 171

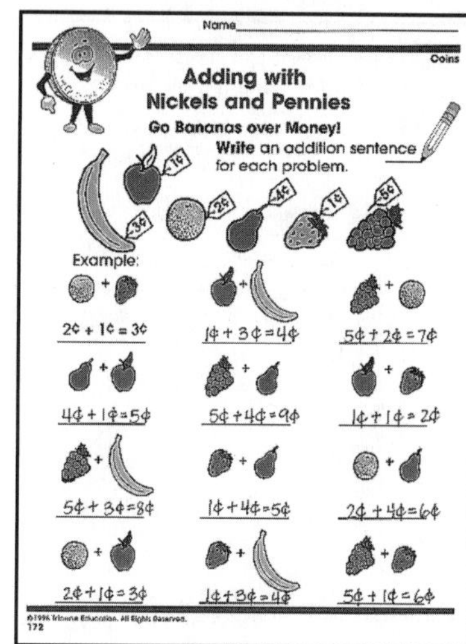
Name

Coins

Adding with Nickels and Pennies

Go Bananas over Money!

Write an addition sentence for each problem.

1¢ 3¢ 2¢ 4¢ 1¢ 5¢

Example:

2¢ + 1¢ = 3¢ | 1¢ + 3¢ = 4¢ | 5¢ + 2¢ = 7¢
4¢ + 1¢ = 5¢ | 5¢ + 4¢ = 9¢ | 1¢ + 1¢ = 2¢
5¢ + 3¢ = 8¢ | 1¢ + 4¢ = 5¢ | 2¢ + 4¢ = 6¢
2¢ + 1¢ = 3¢ | 1¢ + 3¢ = 4¢ | 5¢ + 1¢ = 6¢

©1998 Tribune Education. All Rights Reserved.
172

Page 172

Name

Coins

Adding with Nickels and Pennies

Kristen is having a birthday party. Let's see what she bought for her 3 friends.

5¢ 3¢ 2¢ 4¢ 2¢ 1¢

These are for her friends.

1. For Cassie, she bought the and the . She paid 4 ¢.
2. For Terri, she bought the and the . She paid 4 ¢.
3. For Lauren, she bought the and the . She paid 7 ¢.

©1998 Tribune Education. All Rights Reserved.
173

Page 173

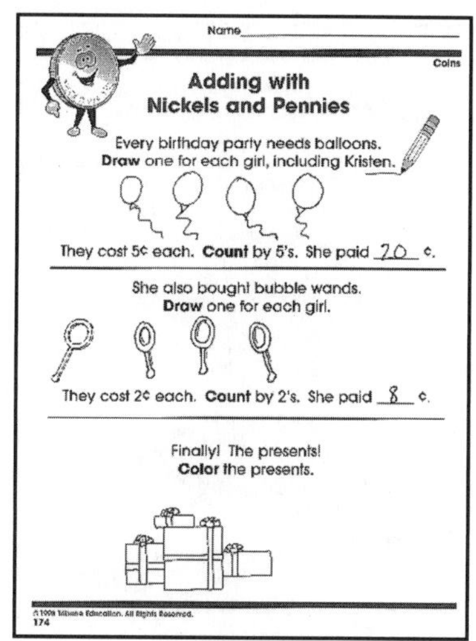
Name

Coins

Adding with Nickels and Pennies

Every birthday party needs balloons. **Draw** one for each girl, including Kristen.

They cost 5¢ each. **Count** by 5's. She paid 20 ¢.

She also bought bubble wands. **Draw** one for each girl.

They cost 2¢ each. **Count** by 2's. She paid 8 ¢.

Finally! The presents! **Color** the presents.

©1998 Tribune Education. All Rights Reserved.
174

Page 174

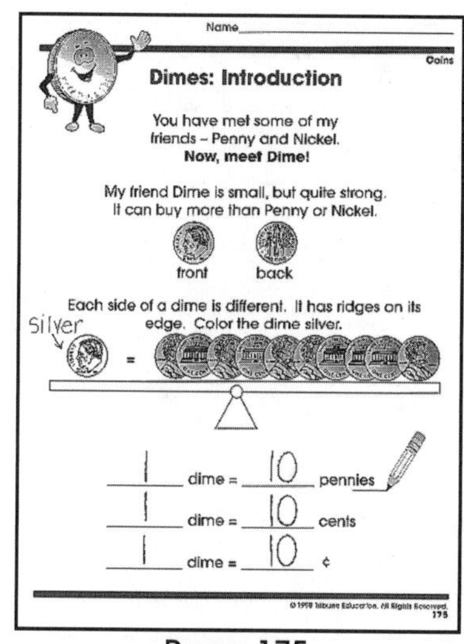
Name

Coins

Dimes: Introduction

You have met some of my friends – Penny and Nickel. **Now, meet Dime!**

My friend Dime is small, but quite strong. It can buy more than Penny or Nickel.

front back

Each side of a dime is different. It has ridges on its edge. Color the dime silver.

silver

1 dime = 10 pennies
1 dime = 10 cents
1 dime = 10 ¢

©1998 Tribune Education. All Rights Reserved.
175

Page 175

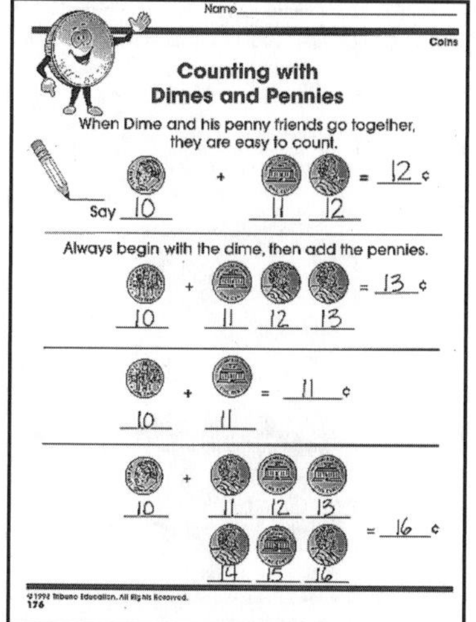
Name

Coins

Counting with Dimes and Pennies

When Dime and his penny friends go together, they are easy to count.

Say 10 + 11 12 = 12 ¢

Always begin with the dime, then add the pennies.

10 + 11 12 13 = 13 ¢

10 + 11 = 11 ¢

10 + 11 12 13 14 15 16 = 16 ¢

©1998 Tribune Education. All Rights Reserved.
176

Page 176

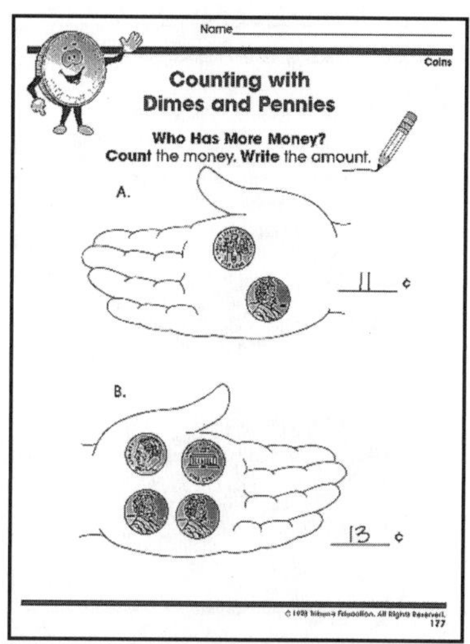
Name

Coins

Counting with Dimes and Pennies

Who Has More Money?
Count the money. **Write** the amount.

A. 11 ¢

B. 13 ¢

©1998 Tribune Education. All Rights Reserved.
177

Page 177

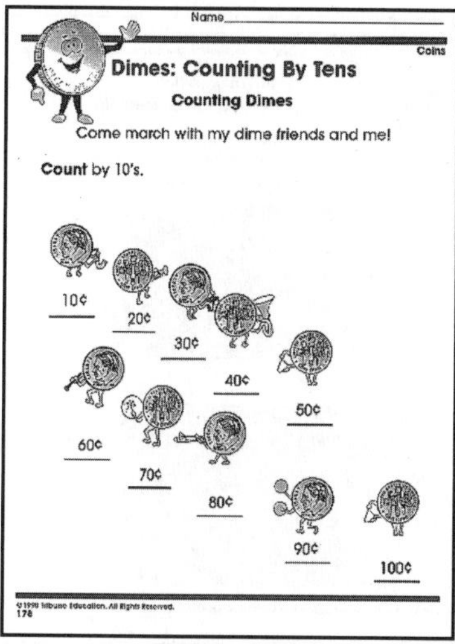
Name

Coins

Dimes: Counting By Tens

Counting Dimes

Come march with my dime friends and me!

Count by 10's.

10¢ 20¢ 30¢ 40¢ 50¢ 60¢ 70¢ 80¢ 90¢ 100¢

©1998 Tribune Education. All Rights Reserved.
178

Page 178

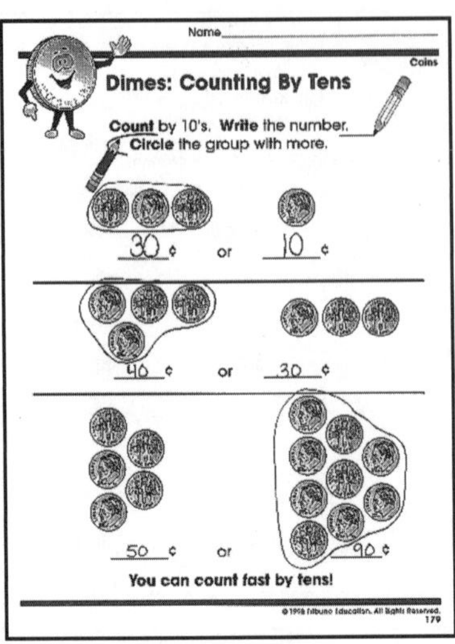

Name__________

Coins

Dimes: Counting By Tens

Count by 10's. **Write** the number.
Circle the group with more.

30 ¢ or 10 ¢

40 ¢ or 30 ¢

50 ¢ or 90 ¢

You can count fast by tens!

179

Page 179

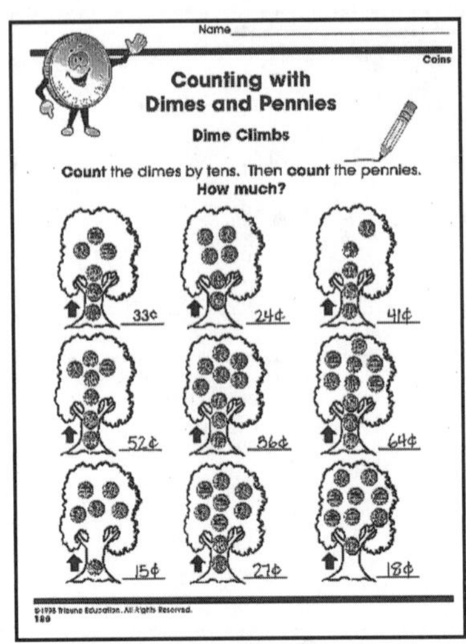

Name__________

Coins

Counting with Dimes and Pennies

Dime Climbs

Count the dimes by tens. Then **count** the pennies.
How much?

33¢ 24¢ 41¢

52¢ 86¢ 64¢

15¢ 27¢ 18¢

180

Page 180

Name__________

Coins

Counting with Dimes and Nickels

Do you like to do tricks?

I want to show you a trick about counting dimes and nickels.

Look carefully at these dimes and nickels.
Circle two nickels, then two more, until all the nickels are circled.

Then **count** by 10's to see how much money is here.

I see 90 ¢.

181

Page 181

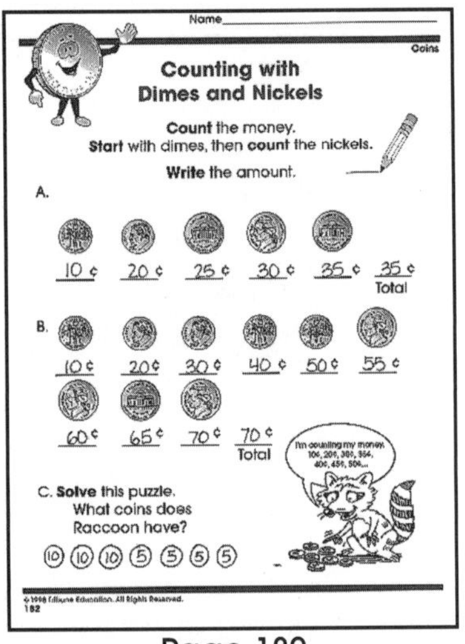

Name__________

Coins

Counting with Dimes and Nickels

Count the money.
Start with dimes, then **count** the nickels.
Write the amount.

A.
10 ¢ 20 ¢ 25 ¢ 30 ¢ 35 ¢ 35 ¢ Total

B.
10¢ 20¢ 30¢ 40 ¢ 50¢ 55 ¢
60¢ 65¢ 70¢ 70 ¢ Total

C. **Solve** this puzzle.
What coins does Raccoon have?

⑩ ⑩ ⑩ ⑤ ⑤ ⑤ ⑤

182

Page 182

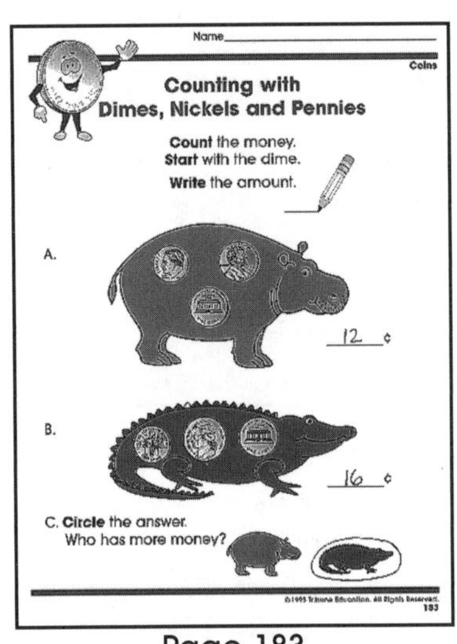

Name__________

Coins

Counting with Dimes, Nickels and Pennies

Count the money.
Start with the dime.
Write the amount.

A. 12 ¢

B. 16 ¢

C. **Circle** the answer.
Who has more money?

183

Page 183

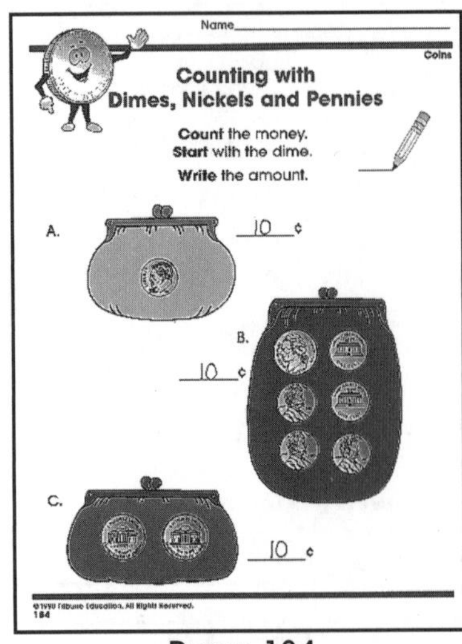

Name__________

Coins

Counting with Dimes, Nickels and Pennies

Count the money.
Start with the dime.
Write the amount.

A. 10 ¢

B. 10 ¢

C. 10 ¢

184

Page 184

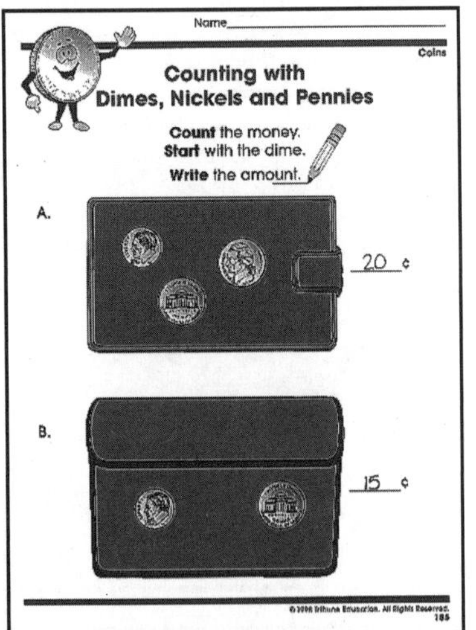

Name__________

Coins

Counting with Dimes, Nickels and Pennies

Count the money.
Start with the dime.
Write the amount.

A. 20 ¢

B. 15 ¢

185

Page 185

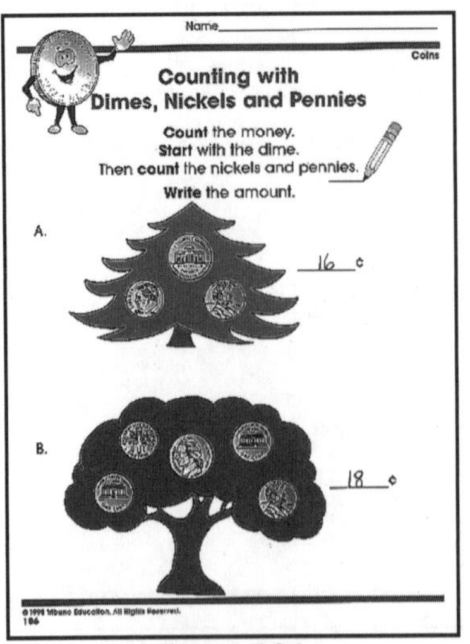

Name__________

Coins

Counting with Dimes, Nickels and Pennies

Count the money.
Start with the dime.
Then **count** the nickels and pennies.
Write the amount.

A. 16 ¢

B. 18 ¢

186

Page 186

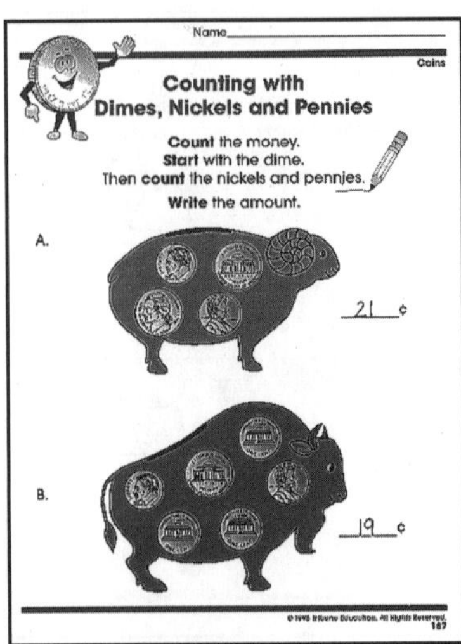

Name__________

Coins

Counting with Dimes, Nickels and Pennies

Count the money.
Start with the dime.
Then **count** the nickels and pennies.
Write the amount.

A. 21 ¢

B. 19 ¢

187

Page 187

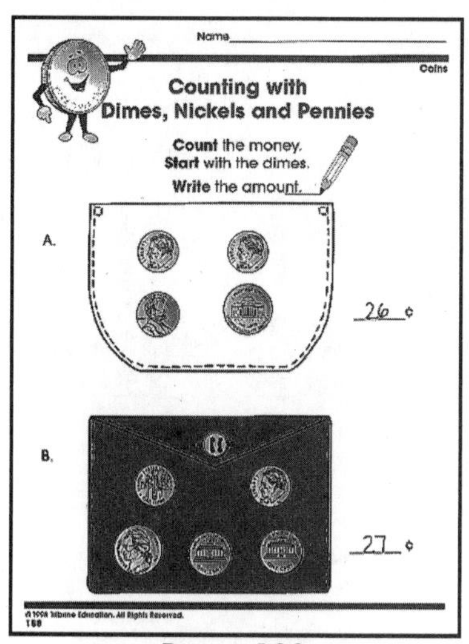
Name____________ Coins

Counting with Dimes, Nickels and Pennies

Count the money.
Start with the dimes.
Write the amount.

A. 26 ¢

B. 27 ¢

188

Page 188

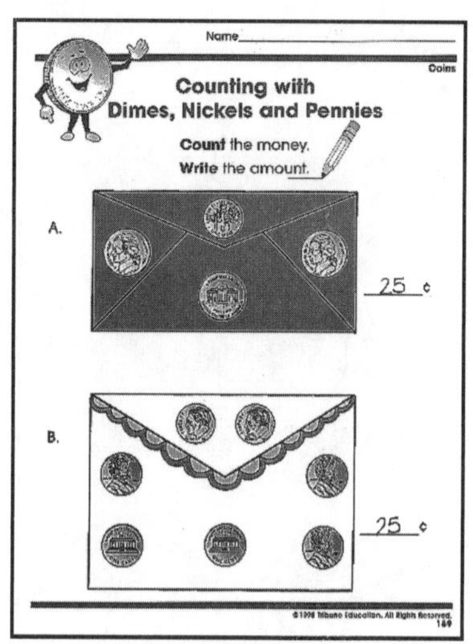
Name____________ Coins

Counting with Dimes, Nickels and Pennies

Count the money.
Write the amount.

A. 25 ¢

B. 25 ¢

189

Page 189

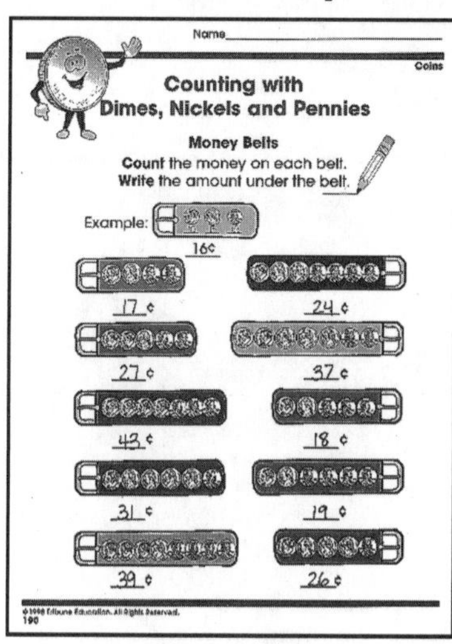
Name____________ Coins

Counting with Dimes, Nickels and Pennies

Money Belts
Count the money on each belt.
Write the amount under the belt.

Example: 16¢

17 ¢ 24 ¢
27 ¢ 37 ¢
43 ¢ 18 ¢
31 ¢ 19 ¢
39 ¢ 26 ¢

190

Page 190

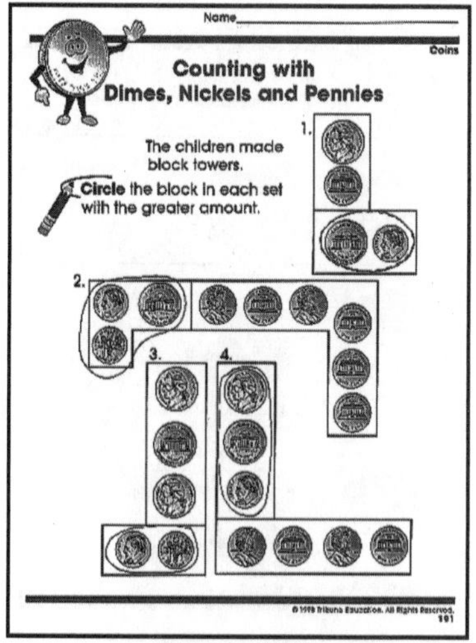
Name____________ Coins

Counting with Dimes, Nickels and Pennies

The children made block towers.
Circle the block in each set with the greater amount.

1. 2. 3. 4.

191

Page 191

Name____________ Coins

Counting with Dimes, Nickels and Pennies

Write how many cents.

1. 12 ¢
2. 16 ¢
3. 13 ¢

If you add 1 more penny to number 1, you will have 13 ¢
If you add 1 more penny to number 2, you will have 17 ¢
If you add 1 more penny to number 3, you will have 14 ¢

To count these cents takes a lot of sense!

192

Page 192

Name____________ Coins

Counting with Dimes, Nickels and Pennies

(Use with page 194)

There is a bake sale at school today.
Be sure to bring Mary Money along!

19¢ 12¢ 15¢ 9¢ 8¢

Decide which one you want.
In the space below, draw enough money to pay for it.

Answers will vary.

193

Page 193

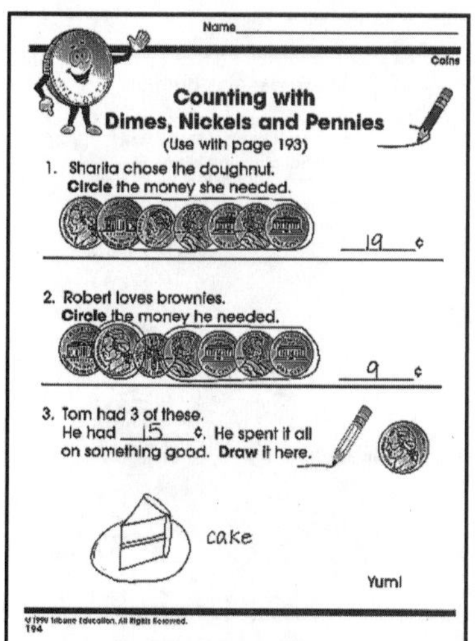
Name____________ Coins

Counting with Dimes, Nickels and Pennies

(Use with page 193)

1. Sharita chose the doughnut.
Circle the money she needed. 19 ¢

2. Robert loves brownies.
Circle the money he needed. 9 ¢

3. Tom had 3 of these.
He had 15 ¢. He spent it all on something good. **Draw** it here.

cake

Yum!

194

Page 194

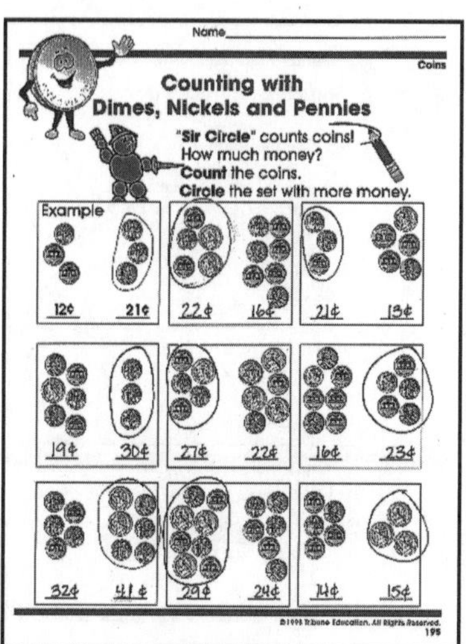
Name____________ Coins

Counting with Dimes, Nickels and Pennies

"**Sir Circle**" counts coins!
How much money?
Count the coins.
Circle the set with more money.

Example 12¢ 21¢ | 22¢ 16¢ | 21¢ 13¢
19¢ 30¢ | 27¢ 22¢ | 16¢ 23¢
32¢ 41¢ | 29¢ 24¢ | 14¢ 15¢

195

Page 195

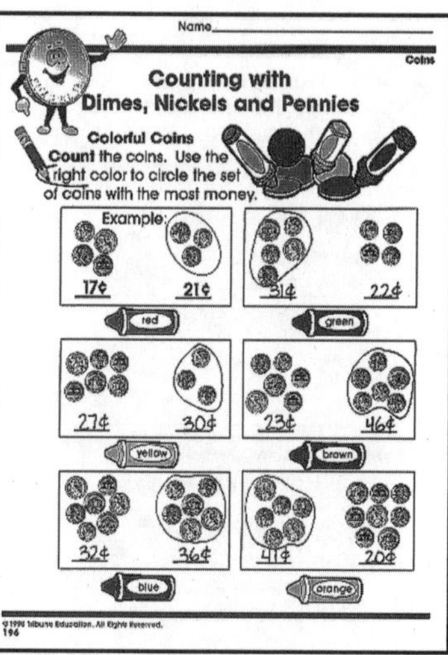
Name____________ Coins

Counting with Dimes, Nickels and Pennies

Colorful Coins
Count the coins. Use the right color to circle the set of coins with the most money.

Example: 17¢ 21¢ red | 31¢ 22¢ green
27¢ 30¢ yellow | 23¢ 46¢ brown
32¢ 36¢ blue | 41¢ 20¢ orange

196

Page 196

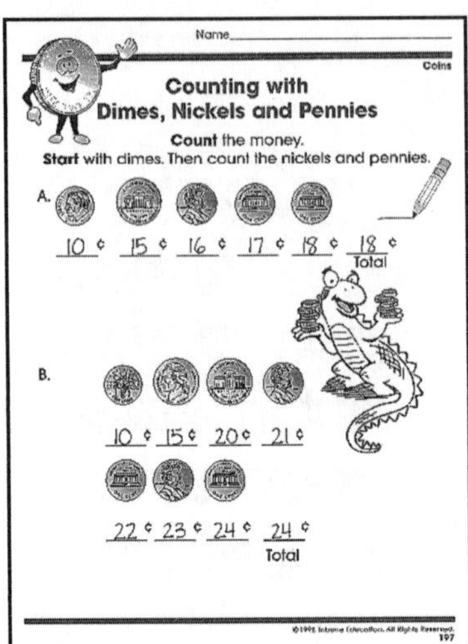

Name________

Coins

Counting with Dimes, Nickels and Pennies

Count the money.
Start with dimes. Then count the nickels and pennies.

A. 10¢ 15¢ 16¢ 17¢ 18¢ 18¢ Total

B. 10¢ 15¢ 20¢ 21¢

22¢ 23¢ 24¢ 24¢ Total

©1998 Tribune Education. All Rights Reserved. 197

Page 197

Name________

Coins

Counting with Dimes, Nickels and Pennies

Buy and Buy
Circle the coins to equal the right amount.

Example:

32¢ 26¢ 21¢ 14¢ 54¢ 31¢ 44¢ 42¢

©1998 Tribune Education. All Rights Reserved. 198

Page 198

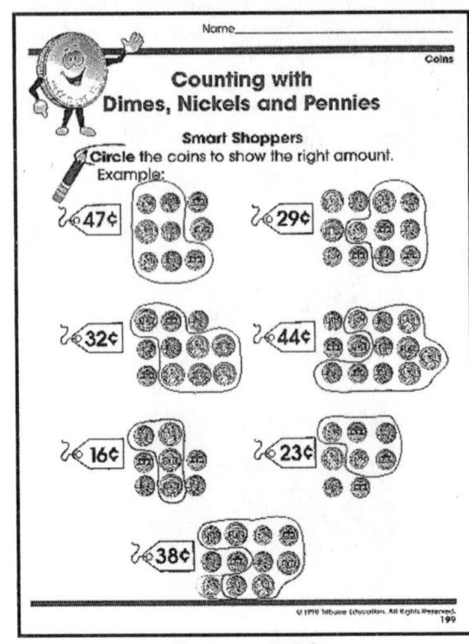

Name________

Coins

Counting with Dimes, Nickels and Pennies

Smart Shoppers
Circle the coins to show the right amount.

Example:

47¢ 29¢ 32¢ 44¢ 16¢ 23¢ 38¢

©1998 Tribune Education. All Rights Reserved. 199

Page 199

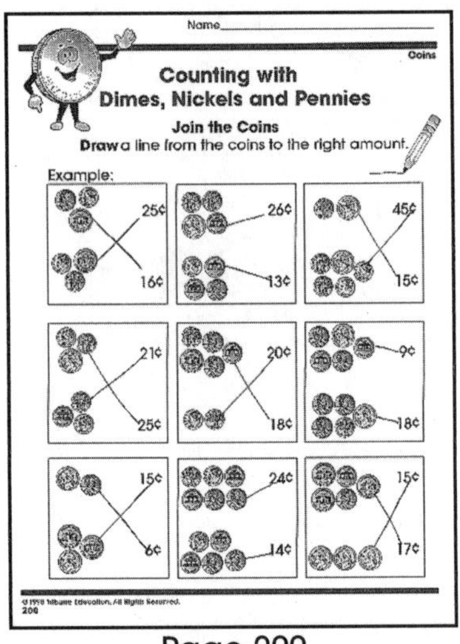

Name________

Coins

Counting with Dimes, Nickels and Pennies

Join the Coins
Draw a line from the coins to the right amount.

Example:

25¢ 16¢ 26¢ 13¢ 45¢ 15¢ 21¢ 25¢ 20¢ 18¢ 9¢ 18¢ 15¢ 6¢ 24¢ 14¢ 15¢ 17¢

©1998 Tribune Education. All Rights Reserved. 200

Page 200

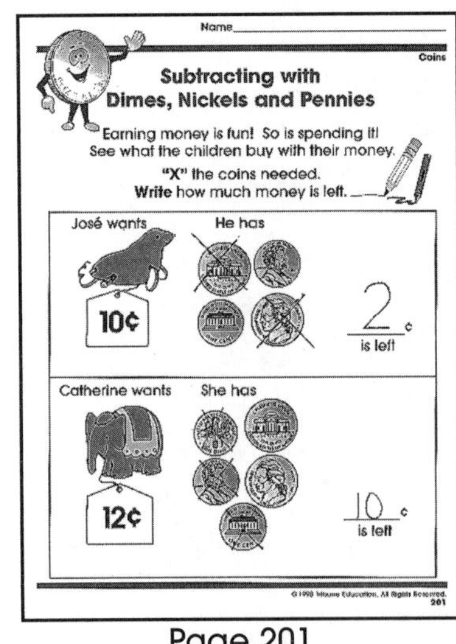

Name________

Coins

Subtracting with Dimes, Nickels and Pennies

Earning money is fun! So is spending it!
See what the children buy with their money.
"X" the coins needed.
Write how much money is left.

José wants He has 10¢ 2 ¢ is left

Catherine wants She has 12¢ 10 ¢ is left

©1998 Tribune Education. All Rights Reserved. 201

Page 201

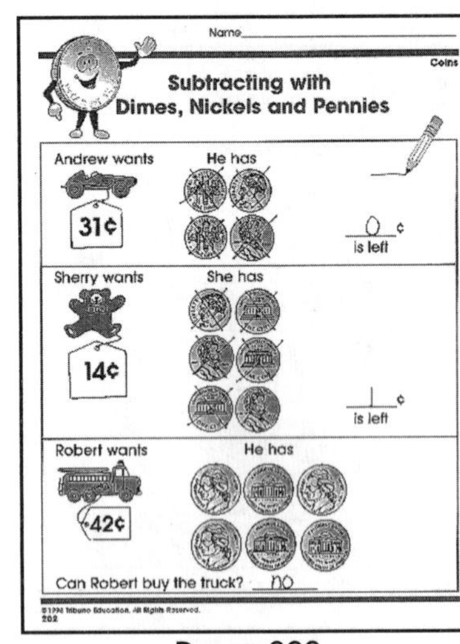

Name________

Coins

Subtracting with Dimes, Nickels and Pennies

Andrew wants He has 31¢ 0 ¢ is left

Sherry wants She has 14¢ 1 ¢ is left

Robert wants He has 42¢

Can Robert buy the truck? no

©1998 Tribune Education. All Rights Reserved. 202

Page 202

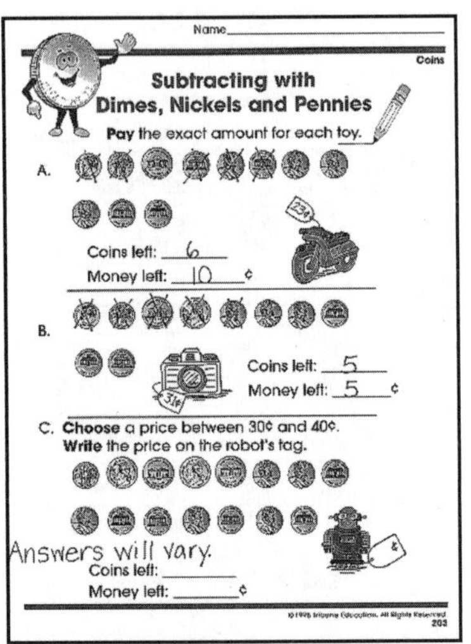

Name________

Coins

Subtracting with Dimes, Nickels and Pennies

Pay the exact amount for each toy.

A. Coins left: 6
Money left: 10 ¢

B. Coins left: 5
Money left: 5 ¢

C. **Choose** a price between 30¢ and 40¢.
Write the price on the robot's tag.

Answers will vary.
Coins left: ______
Money left: ______¢

©1998 Tribune Education. All Rights Reserved. 203

Page 203

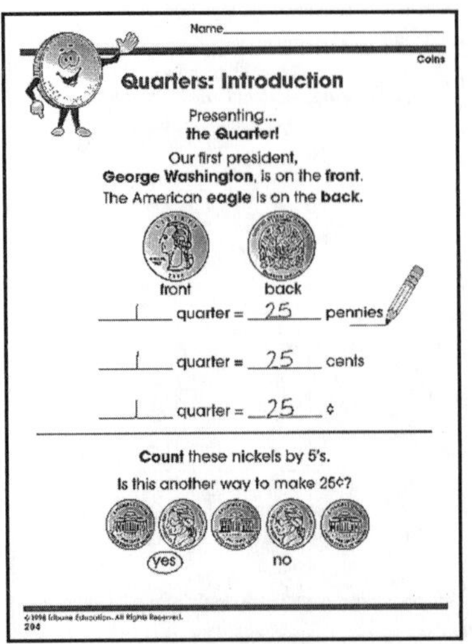

Name________

Coins

Quarters: Introduction

Presenting...
the Quarter!
Our first president,
George Washington, is on the **front**.
The American **eagle** is on the **back**.

front back

1 quarter = 25 pennies

1 quarter = 25 cents

1 quarter = 25 ¢

Count these nickels by 5's.
Is this another way to make 25¢?

(yes) no

©1998 Tribune Education. All Rights Reserved. 204

Page 204

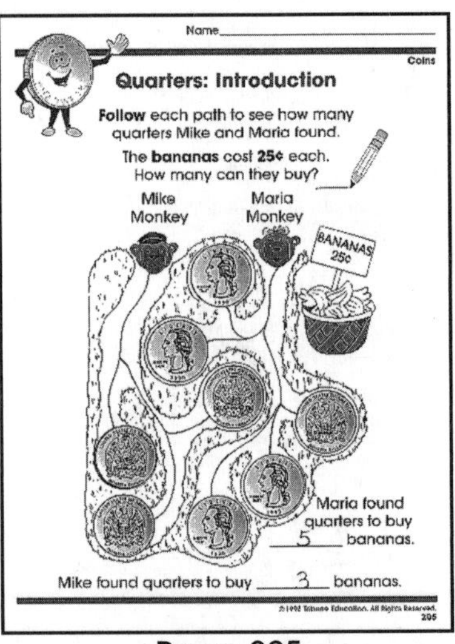

Name________

Coins

Quarters: Introduction

Follow each path to see how many quarters Mike and Maria found.
The **bananas** cost **25¢** each.
How many can they buy?

Mike Monkey Maria Monkey

BANANAS 25¢

Maria found quarters to buy 5 bananas.

Mike found quarters to buy 3 bananas.

©1998 Tribune Education. All Rights Reserved. 205

Page 205

Answer Key - Money

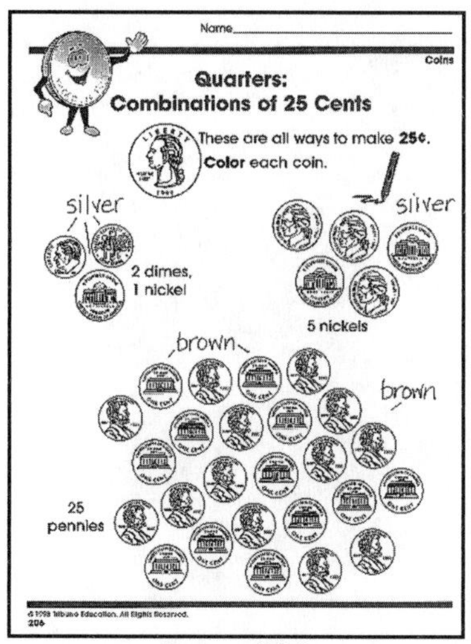

Name_______________

Coins

Quarters: Combinations of 25 Cents

These are all ways to make **25¢**. **Color** each coin.

silver

2 dimes, 1 nickel

silver

5 nickels

brown

brown

25 pennies

© 1998 Tribune Education. All Rights Reserved. 206

Page 206

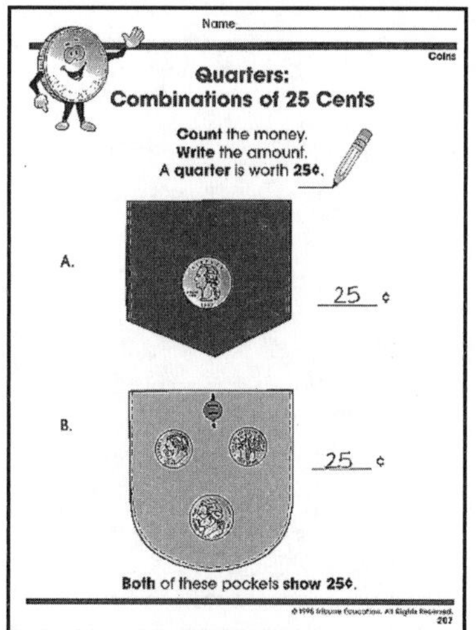

Name_______________

Coins

Quarters: Combinations of 25 Cents

Count the money. **Write** the amount. A **quarter** is worth **25¢**.

A. 25 ¢

B. 25 ¢

Both of these pockets **show 25¢**.

© 1998 Tribune Education. All Rights Reserved. 207

Page 207

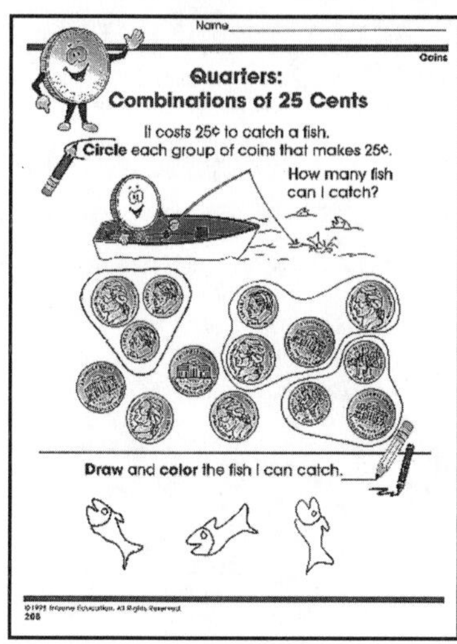

Name_______________

Coins

Quarters: Combinations of 25 Cents

It costs 25¢ to catch a fish. **Circle** each group of coins that makes 25¢.

How many fish can I catch?

Draw and **color** the fish I can catch.

© 1998 Tribune Education. All Rights Reserved. 208

Page 208

Name_______________

Coins

Quarters: More or Less Than 50 Cents

The tooth fairy left 2 quarters for your shiny baby tooth.

How much money do you have?

Each quarter is worth 25¢. Two quarters = 50¢

Color each toy you can buy.

color

color

49¢

25¢

72¢

39¢

color

5¢

color

45¢

60¢

color

© 1998 Tribune Education. All Rights Reserved. 209

Page 209

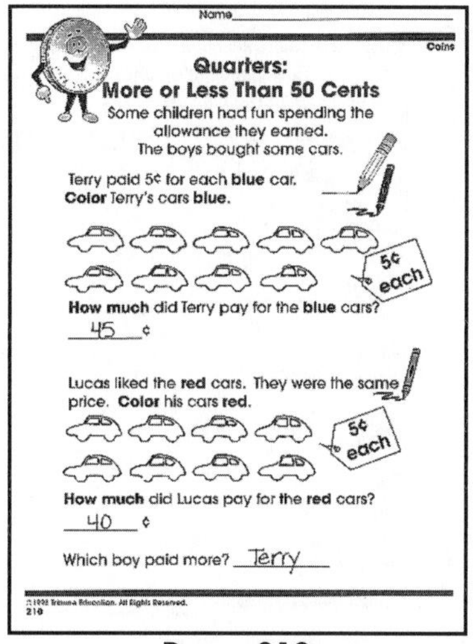

Name_______________

Coins

Quarters: More or Less Than 50 Cents

Some children had fun spending the allowance they earned. The boys bought some cars.

Terry paid 5¢ for each **blue** car. **Color** Terry's cars **blue**.

5¢ each

How much did Terry pay for the **blue** cars? 45 ¢

Lucas liked the **red** cars. They were the same price. **Color** his cars **red**.

5¢ each

How much did Lucas pay for the **red** cars? 40 ¢

Which boy paid more? Terry

© 1998 Tribune Education. All Rights Reserved. 210

Page 210

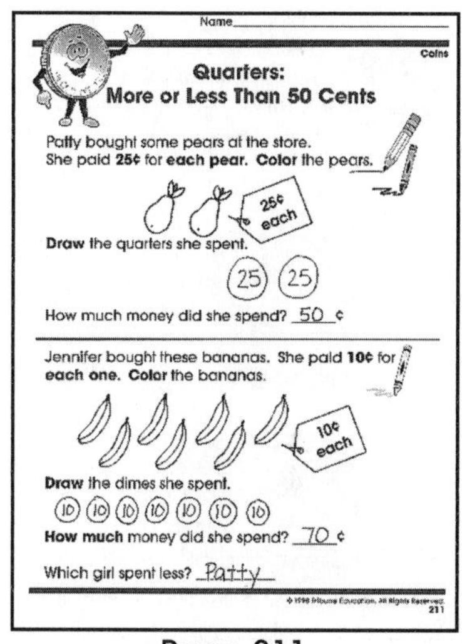

Name_______________

Coins

Quarters: More or Less Than 50 Cents

Patty bought some pears at the store. She paid **25¢** for **each pear**. **Color** the pears.

25¢ each

Draw the quarters she spent.

(25) (25)

How much money did she spend? 50 ¢

Jennifer bought these bananas. She paid **10¢** for **each one**. **Color** the bananas.

10¢ each

Draw the dimes she spent.

(10) (10) (10) (10) (10) (10) (10)

How much money did she spend? 70 ¢

Which girl spent less? Patty

© 1998 Tribune Education. All Rights Reserved. 211

Page 211

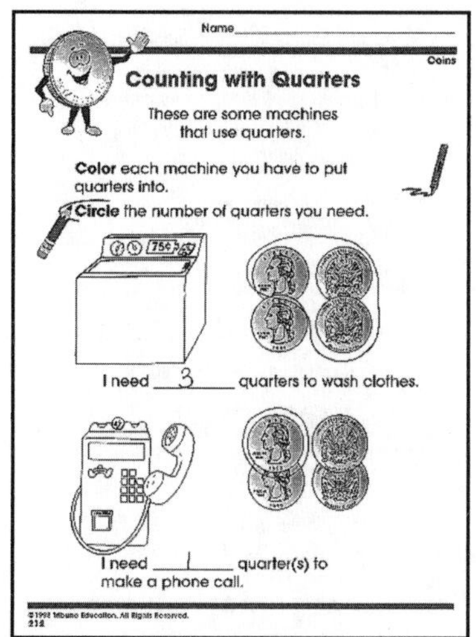

Name_______________

Coins

Counting with Quarters

These are some machines that use quarters.

Color each machine you have to put quarters into.

Circle the number of quarters you need.

75¢

I need 3 quarters to wash clothes.

I need 1 quarter(s) to make a phone call.

© 1998 Tribune Education. All Rights Reserved. 212

Page 212

Name_______________

Coins

Counting with Quarters

75¢

Drinks

I need 3 quarters to buy a drink.

Comic Books

$1.00

I need 4 quarters to buy a comic book.

50¢

I need 2 quarters to buy a frozen fruit bar.

Hurry! It's melting!

© 1998 Tribune Education. All Rights Reserved. 213

Page 213

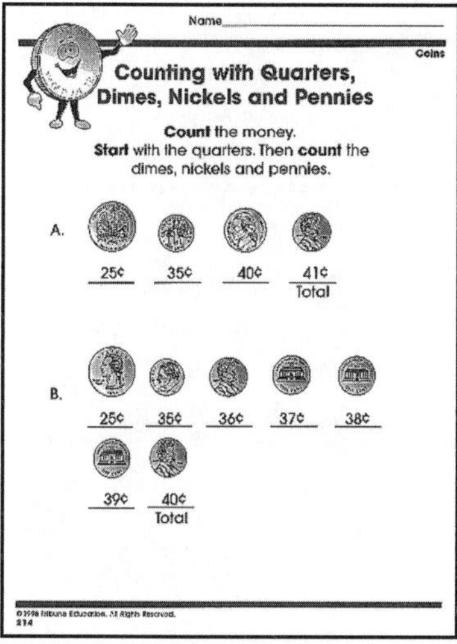

Name_______________

Coins

Counting with Quarters, Dimes, Nickels and Pennies

Count the money. **Start** with the quarters. Then **count** the dimes, nickels and pennies.

A. 25¢ 35¢ 40¢ 41¢ Total

B. 25¢ 35¢ 36¢ 37¢ 38¢ 39¢ 40¢ Total

© 1998 Tribune Education. All Rights Reserved. 214

Page 214

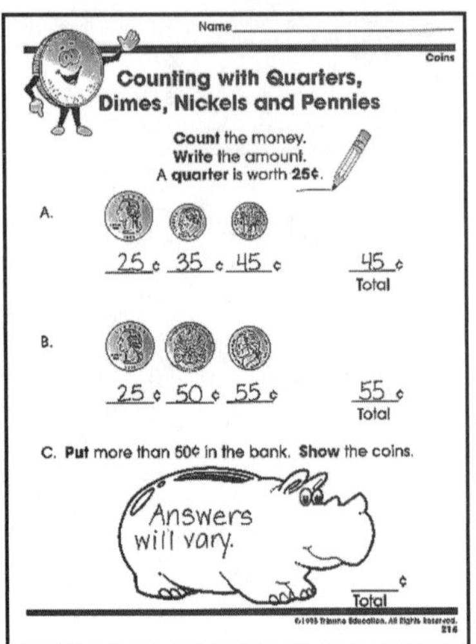
Name__________

Coins

Counting with Quarters, Dimes, Nickels and Pennies

Count the money. **Write** the amount. A **quarter** is worth **25¢**.

A. 25¢ 35¢ 45¢ — 45¢ Total

B. 25¢ 50¢ 55¢ — 55¢ Total

C. **Put** more than 50¢ in the bank. **Show** the coins.

Answers will vary.

___¢ Total

©1998 Tribune Education. All Rights Reserved. 215

Page 215

Name__________

Coins

Counting with Quarters, Dimes, Nickels and Pennies

Count the money. **Start** with the quarters. Then **count** the dimes, nickels and pennies.

A. 25¢ 35¢ 40¢ 41¢ 42¢ Total

B. 25¢ 35¢ 45¢ 50¢ 55¢ 56¢ 57¢ 58¢ Total

I'm counting my money. 25¢, 35¢, 45¢, 55¢, 60¢, 65¢, 66¢, 67¢.

C. **Solve** this puzzle. What coins does Lizard have?

(25) (10) (10) (10) (5) (5) (1) (1)

©1998 Tribune Education. All Rights Reserved. 216

Page 216

Name__________

Coins

Counting with Quarters, Dimes, Nickels and Pennies

Count the money. **Start** with the quarter. **Write** the amount.

A. 36¢

B. 31¢

©1998 Tribune Education. All Rights Reserved. 217

Page 217

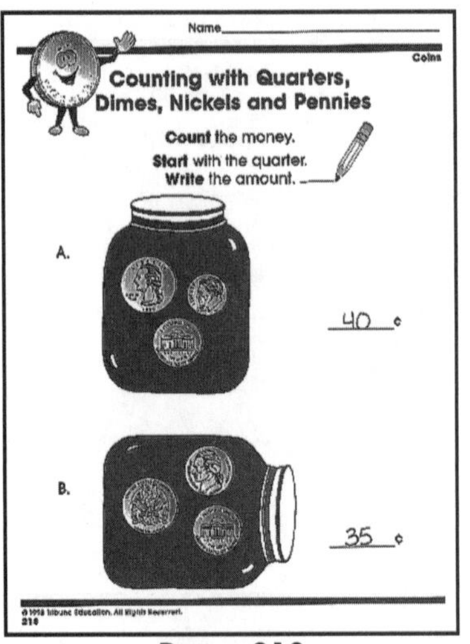
Name__________

Coins

Counting with Quarters, Dimes, Nickels and Pennies

Count the money. **Start** with the quarter. **Write** the amount.

A. 40¢

B. 35¢

©1998 Tribune Education. All Rights Reserved. 218

Page 218

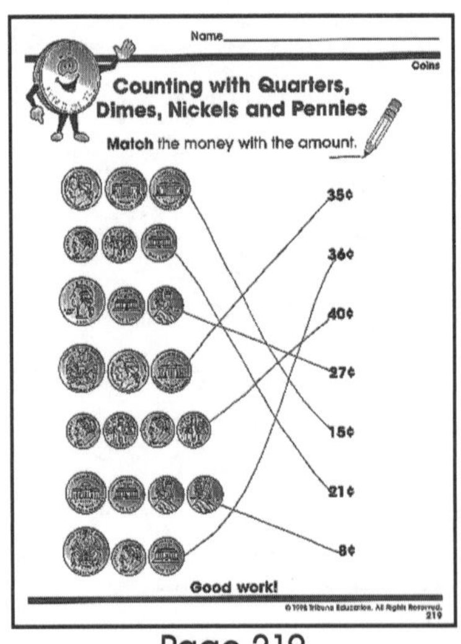
Name__________

Coins

Counting with Quarters, Dimes, Nickels and Pennies

Match the money with the amount.

35¢
36¢
40¢
27¢
15¢
21¢
8¢

Good work!

©1998 Tribune Education. All Rights Reserved. 219

Page 219

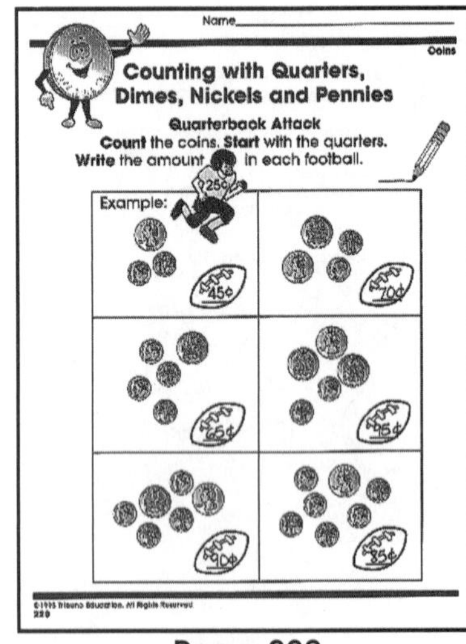
Name__________

Coins

Counting with Quarters, Dimes, Nickels and Pennies

Quarterback Attack

Count the coins. **Start** with the quarters. **Write** the amount in each football.

Example: 45¢

70¢

65¢

95¢

90¢

85¢

©1998 Tribune Education. All Rights Reserved. 220

Page 220

Name__________

Coins

Counting with Quarters, Dimes, Nickels and Pennies

(Use with page 222)

Carolyn and Marilyn are going to the beach for their vacation. The twins wanted to buy some things to take along. They emptied their piggy banks.

©1998 Tribune Education. All Rights Reserved. 221

Page 221

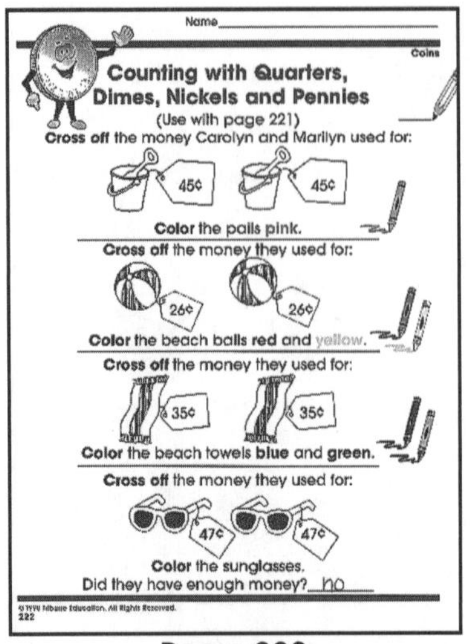
Name__________

Coins

Counting with Quarters, Dimes, Nickels and Pennies

(Use with page 221)

Cross off the money Carolyn and Marilyn used for: 45¢ 45¢

Color the pails **pink**.

Cross off the money they used for: 26¢ 26¢

Color the beach balls **red** and **yellow**.

Cross off the money they used for: 35¢ 35¢

Color the beach towels **blue** and **green**.

Cross off the money they used for: 47¢ 47¢

Color the sunglasses.

Did they have enough money? no

©1998 Tribune Education. All Rights Reserved. 222

Page 222

Name__________

Coins

Counting with Quarters, Dimes, Nickels and Pennies

You Make "Cents"

Count the coins.

Do you have enough money to buy each toy?

Toy price	You have...	yes or no
Example: 58¢	51¢	no
47¢	57¢	yes
75¢	76¢	yes
43¢	51¢	yes
98¢	$1.05	yes
32¢	25¢	no
26¢	29¢	yes
45¢	35¢	no

©1998 Tribune Education. All Rights Reserved. 223

Page 223

Answer Key - Money

Name____________
Coins

Counting with Quarters, Dimes, Nickels and Pennies

It is fun to buy things to keep your hair looking great!

13¢ 20¢ 29¢ 35¢ 32¢

How many of each coin do you need? **Write** 1, 2, 3 or 4.

	Quarters	Dimes	Nickels	Pennies
	1		1	2
	1	1		
	1			4
		1		3
		2		

©1998 Tribune Education. All Rights Reserved.
224

Page 224

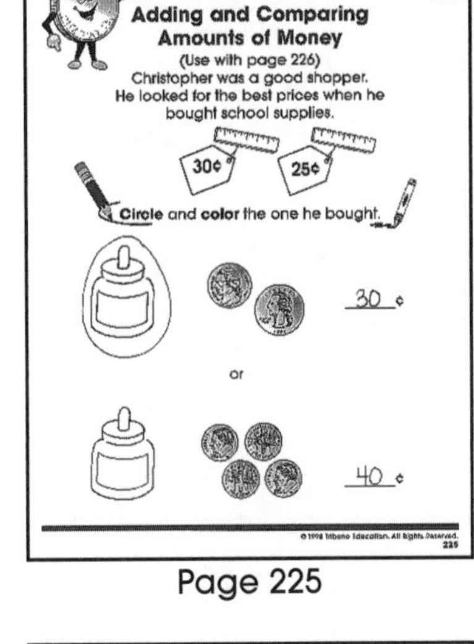
Name____________
Coins

Adding and Comparing Amounts of Money
(Use with page 226)

Christopher was a good shopper. He looked for the best prices when he bought school supplies.

30¢ 25¢

Circle and **color** the one he bought.

30 ¢

or

40 ¢

©1998 Tribune Education. All Rights Reserved.
225

Page 225

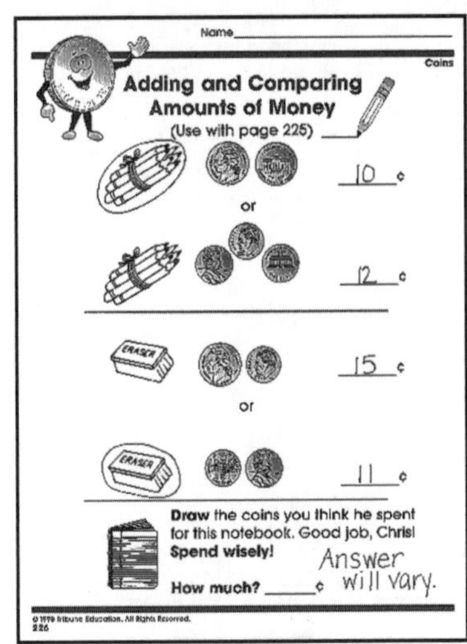
Name____________
Coins

Adding and Comparing Amounts of Money
(Use with page 225)

10 ¢
or
12 ¢

15 ¢
or
11 ¢

Draw the coins you think he spent for this notebook. Good job, Chris! **Spend wisely!**

How much? _____¢ Answer will vary.

©1998 Tribune Education. All Rights Reserved.
226

Page 226

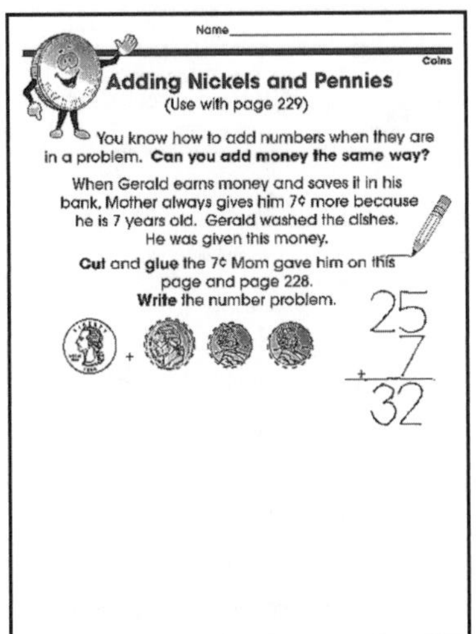
Name____________
Coins

Adding Nickels and Pennies
(Use with page 229)

You know how to add numbers when they are in a problem. **Can you add money the same way?**

When Gerald earns money and saves it in his bank, Mother always gives him 7¢ more because he is 7 years old. Gerald washed the dishes. He was given this money.

Cut and **glue** the 7¢ Mom gave him on this page and page 228.
Write the number problem.

25
+ 7
32

Page 227

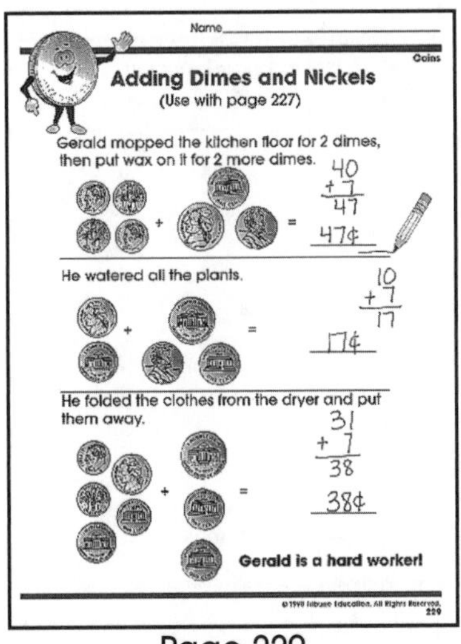
Name____________
Coins

Adding Dimes and Nickels
(Use with page 227)

Gerald mopped the kitchen floor for 2 dimes, then put wax on it for 2 more dimes.

40
+ 7
47

47¢

He watered all the plants.

10
+ 7
17

17¢

He folded the clothes from the dryer and put them away.

31
+ 7
38

38¢

Gerald is a hard worker!

©1998 Tribune Education. All Rights Reserved.
229

Page 229

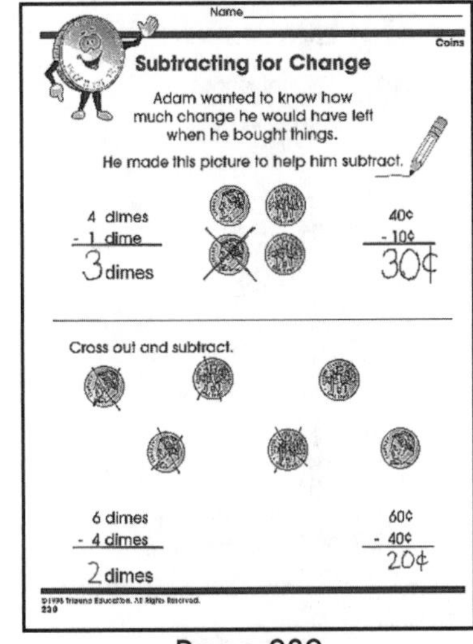
Name____________
Coins

Subtracting for Change

Adam wanted to know how much change he would have left when he bought things.

He made this picture to help him subtract.

4 dimes
- 1 dime
3 dimes

40¢
- 10¢
30¢

Cross out and subtract.

6 dimes
- 4 dimes
2 dimes

60¢
- 40¢
20¢

©1998 Tribune Education. All Rights Reserved.
230

Page 230

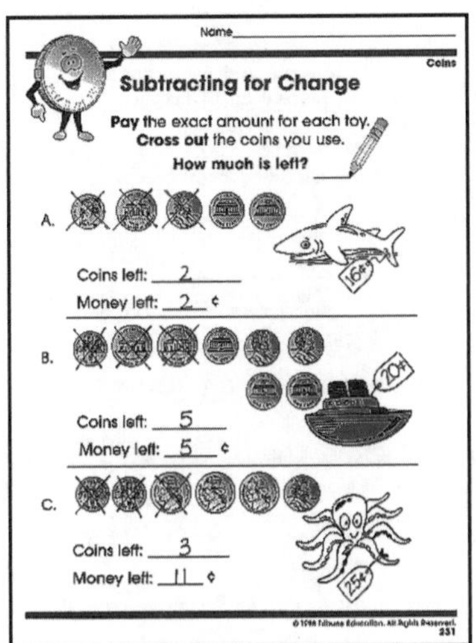
Name____________
Coins

Subtracting for Change

Pay the exact amount for each toy.
Cross out the coins you use.
How much is left?

A. 16¢
Coins left: 2
Money left: 2 ¢

B. 20¢
Coins left: 5
Money left: 5 ¢

C. 25¢
Coins left: 3
Money left: 11 ¢

©1998 Tribune Education. All Rights Reserved.
231

Page 231

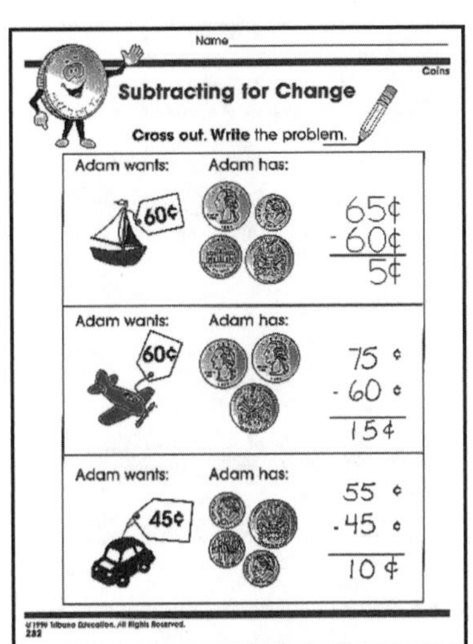
Name____________
Coins

Subtracting for Change

Cross out. Write the problem.

Adam wants: 60¢ Adam has:
65¢
- 60¢
5¢

Adam wants: 60¢ Adam has:
75 ¢
- 60 ¢
15¢

Adam wants: 45¢ Adam has:
55 ¢
- 45 ¢
10 ¢

©1998 Tribune Education. All Rights Reserved.
232

Page 232

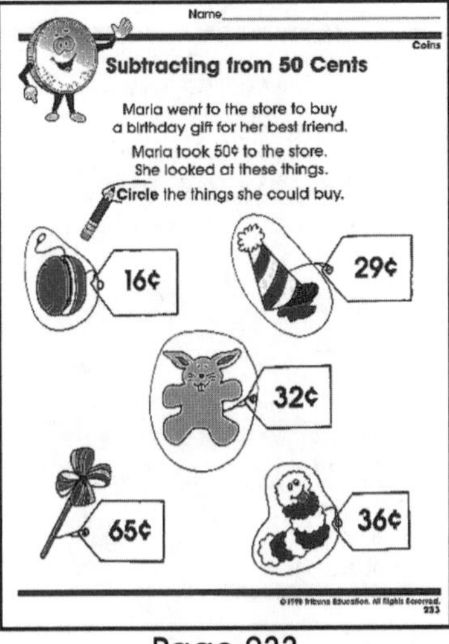
Name____________
Coins

Subtracting from 50 Cents

Maria went to the store to buy a birthday gift for her best friend.

Maria took 50¢ to the store. She looked at these things.

Circle the things she could buy.

16¢ 29¢ 32¢ 65¢ 36¢

©1998 Tribune Education. All Rights Reserved.
233

Page 233

Answer Key - Money

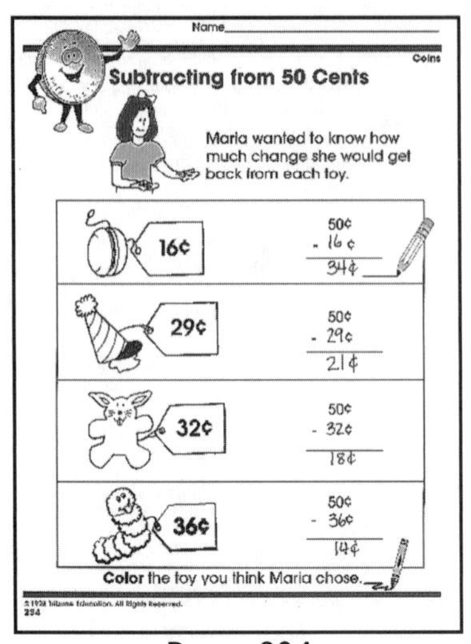

Name

Coins

Subtracting from 50 Cents

Maria wanted to know how much change she would get back from each toy.

16¢	50¢ - 16¢ = 34¢
29¢	50¢ - 29¢ = 21¢
32¢	50¢ - 32¢ = 18¢
36¢	50¢ - 36¢ = 14¢

Color the toy you think Maria chose.

Page 234

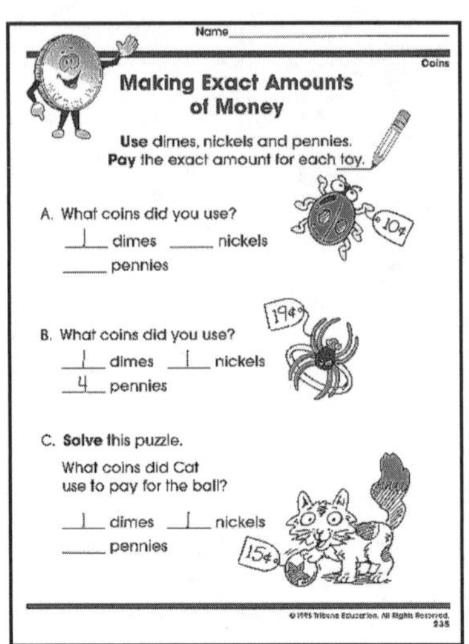

Name

Coins

Making Exact Amounts of Money

Use dimes, nickels and pennies. **Pay** the exact amount for each toy.

A. What coins did you use? 1 dimes ___ nickels ___ pennies (10¢)

B. What coins did you use? 1 dimes 1 nickels 4 pennies (19¢)

C. **Solve** this puzzle. What coins did Cat use to pay for the ball? 1 dimes 1 nickels ___ pennies (15¢)

Page 235

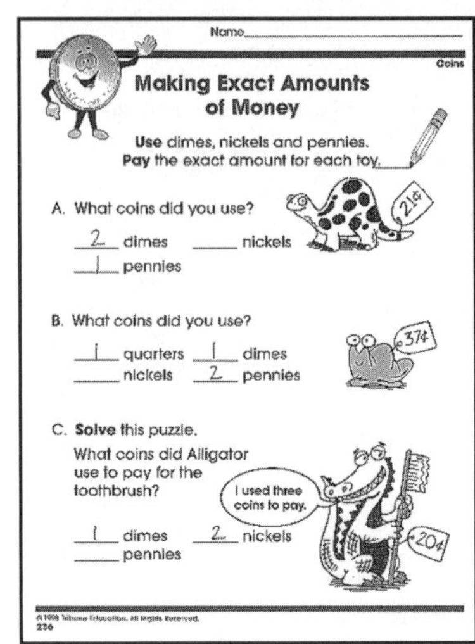

Name

Coins

Making Exact Amounts of Money

Use dimes, nickels and pennies. **Pay** the exact amount for each toy.

A. What coins did you use? 2 dimes ___ nickels 1 pennies (21¢)

B. What coins did you use? 1 quarters 1 dimes ___ nickels 2 pennies (37¢)

C. **Solve** this puzzle. What coins did Alligator use to pay for the toothbrush? 1 dimes 2 nickels ___ pennies (20¢)

I used three coins to pay.

Page 236

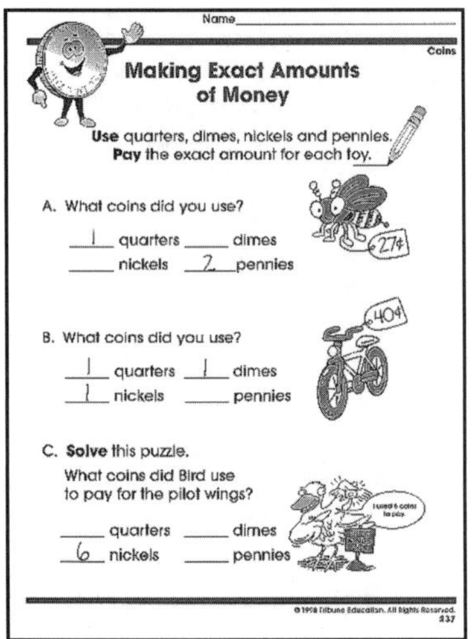

Name

Coins

Making Exact Amounts of Money

Use quarters, dimes, nickels and pennies. **Pay** the exact amount for each toy.

A. What coins did you use? 1 quarters ___ dimes ___ nickels 2 pennies (27¢)

B. What coins did you use? 1 quarters 1 dimes 1 nickels ___ pennies (40¢)

C. **Solve** this puzzle. What coins did Bird use to pay for the pilot wings? ___ quarters ___ dimes 6 nickels ___ pennies

Page 237

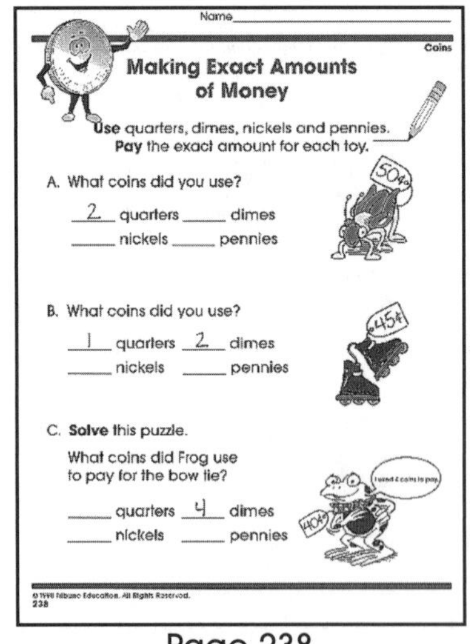

Name

Coins

Making Exact Amounts of Money

Use quarters, dimes, nickels and pennies. **Pay** the exact amount for each toy.

A. What coins did you use? 2 quarters ___ dimes ___ nickels ___ pennies (50¢)

B. What coins did you use? 1 quarters 2 dimes ___ nickels ___ pennies (45¢)

C. **Solve** this puzzle. What coins did Frog use to pay for the bow tie? ___ quarters 4 dimes ___ nickels ___ pennies (40¢)

Page 238

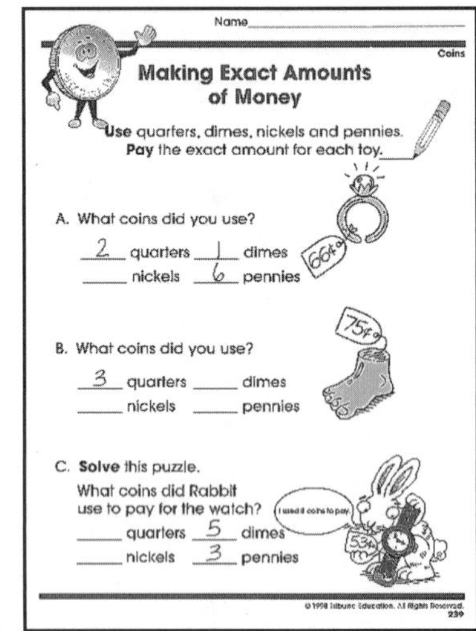

Name

Coins

Making Exact Amounts of Money

Use quarters, dimes, nickels and pennies. **Pay** the exact amount for each toy.

A. What coins did you use? 2 quarters 1 dimes ___ nickels 6 pennies (66¢)

B. What coins did you use? 3 quarters ___ dimes ___ nickels ___ pennies (75¢)

C. **Solve** this puzzle. What coins did Rabbit use to pay for the watch? ___ quarters 5 dimes ___ nickels 3 pennies (53¢)

Page 239

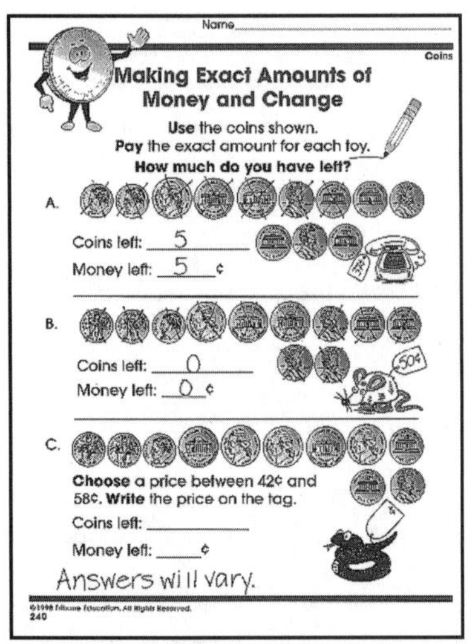

Name

Coins

Making Exact Amounts of Money and Change

Use the coins shown. **Pay** the exact amount for each toy. **How much do you have left?**

A. Coins left: 5 Money left: 5 ¢

B. Coins left: 0 Money left: 0 ¢ (50¢)

C. **Choose** a price between 42¢ and 58¢. **Write** the price on the tag. Coins left: ___ Money left: ___¢

Answers will vary.

Page 240

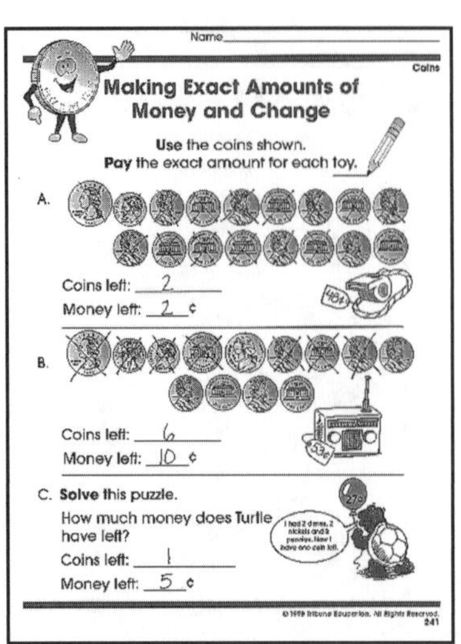

Name

Coins

Making Exact Amounts of Money and Change

Use the coins shown. **Pay** the exact amount for each toy.

A. Coins left: 2 Money left: 2 ¢ (48¢)

B. Coins left: 6 Money left: 10 ¢

C. **Solve** this puzzle. How much money does Turtle have left? Coins left: 1 Money left: 5 ¢

Page 241

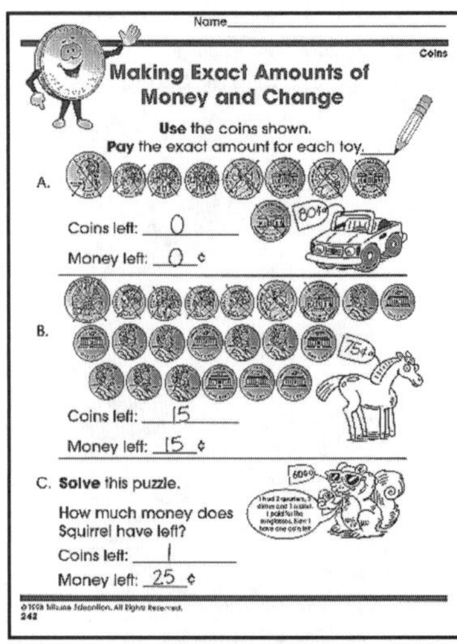

Name

Coins

Making Exact Amounts of Money and Change

Use the coins shown. **Pay** the exact amount for each toy.

A. Coins left: 0 Money left: 0 ¢ (80¢)

B. Coins left: 15 Money left: 15 ¢ (75¢)

C. **Solve** this puzzle. How much money does Squirrel have left? Coins left: 1 Money left: 25 ¢

Page 242

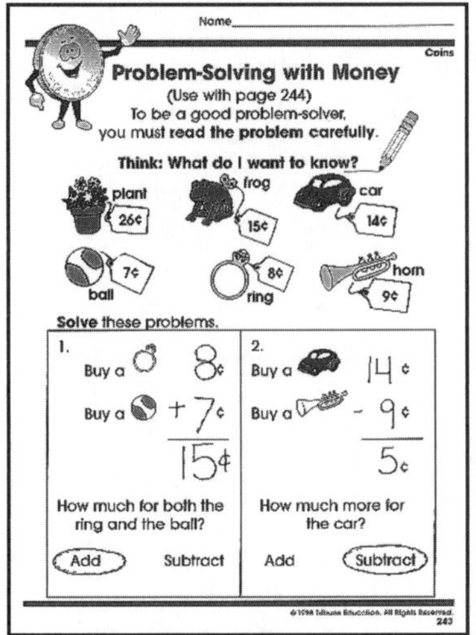

Name____

Coins

Problem-Solving with Money

(Use with page 244)

To be a good problem-solver, you must **read the problem carefully.**

Think: What do I want to know?

plant 26¢ frog 15¢ car 14¢ ball 7¢ ring 8¢ horn 9¢

Solve these problems.

1. Buy a ring 8¢
Buy a ball + 7¢
15¢
How much for both the ring and the ball?
(Add) Subtract

2. Buy a car 14¢
Buy a horn - 9¢
5¢
How much more for the car?
Add (Subtract)

© 1998 Tribune Education. All Rights Reserved. 243

Page 243

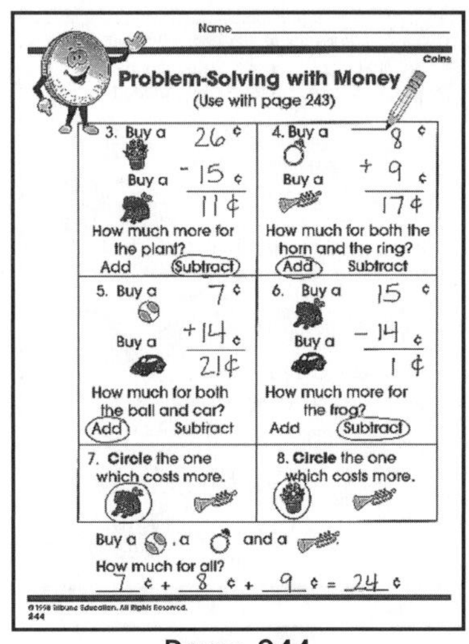

Name____

Coins

Problem-Solving with Money

(Use with page 243)

3. Buy a plant 26¢
Buy a frog - 15¢
11¢
How much more for the plant?
Add (Subtract)

4. Buy a ring 8¢
Buy a horn + 9¢
17¢
How much for both the horn and the ring?
(Add) Subtract

5. Buy a ball 7¢
Buy a car + 14¢
21¢
How much for both the ball and car?
(Add) Subtract

6. Buy a frog 15¢
Buy a car - 14¢
1¢
How much more for the frog?
Add (Subtract)

7. **Circle** the one which costs more.

8. **Circle** the one which costs more.

Buy a ball, a ring and a horn.
How much for all?
7¢ + 8¢ + 9¢ = 24¢

© 1998 Tribune Education. All Rights Reserved. 244

Page 244

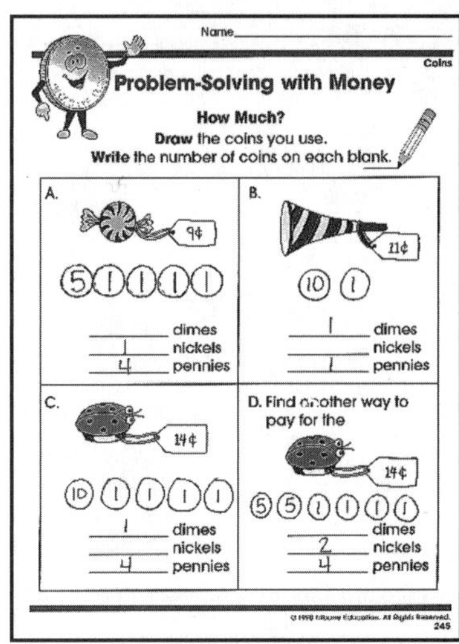

Name____

Coins

Problem-Solving with Money

How Much?

Draw the coins you use.
Write the number of coins on each blank.

A. 9¢ — (5)(1)(1)(1)(1)
___ dimes
1 nickels
4 pennies

B. 11¢ — (10)(1)
1 dimes
___ nickels
1 pennies

C. 14¢ — (10)(1)(1)(1)(1)
1 dimes
___ nickels
4 pennies

D. Find another way to pay for the 14¢ — (5)(5)(1)(1)(1)(1)
___ dimes
2 nickels
4 pennies

© 1998 Tribune Education. All Rights Reserved. 245

Page 245

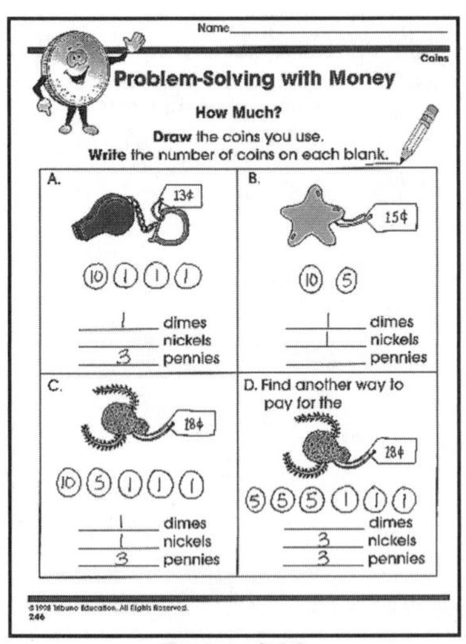

Name____

Coins

Problem-Solving with Money

How Much?

Draw the coins you use.
Write the number of coins on each blank.

A. 13¢ — (10)(1)(1)(1)
1 dimes
___ nickels
3 pennies

B. 15¢ — (10)(5)
1 dimes
1 nickels
___ pennies

C. 18¢ — (10)(5)(1)(1)(1)
1 dimes
1 nickels
3 pennies

D. Find another way to pay for the 18¢ — (5)(5)(5)(1)(1)(1)
___ dimes
3 nickels
3 pennies

© 1998 Tribune Education. All Rights Reserved. 246

Page 246

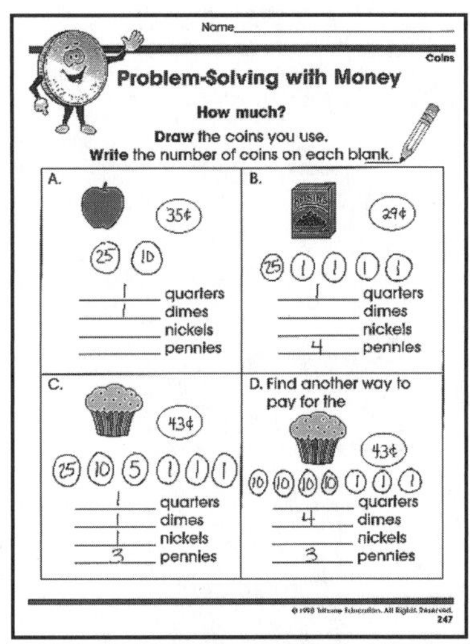

Name____

Coins

Problem-Solving with Money

How much?

Draw the coins you use.
Write the number of coins on each blank.

A. 35¢ — (25)(10)
1 quarters
1 dimes
___ nickels
___ pennies

B. 29¢ — (25)(1)(1)(1)(1)
1 quarters
___ dimes
___ nickels
4 pennies

C. 43¢ — (25)(10)(5)(1)(1)(1)
1 quarters
1 dimes
1 nickels
3 pennies

D. Find another way to pay for the 43¢ — (10)(10)(10)(10)(1)(1)(1)
___ quarters
4 dimes
___ nickels
3 pennies

© 1998 Tribune Education. All Rights Reserved. 247

Page 247

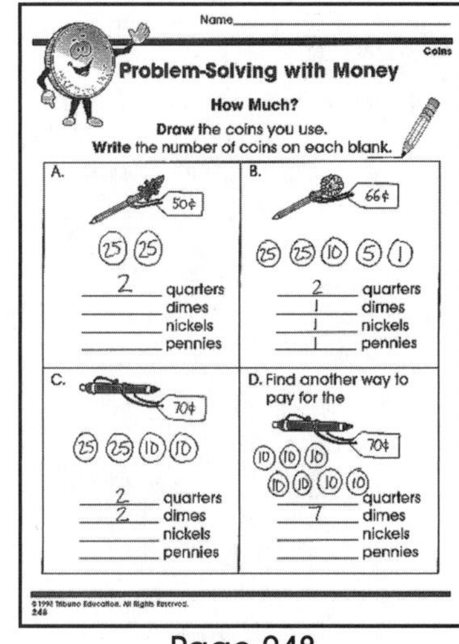

Name____

Coins

Problem-Solving with Money

How Much?

Draw the coins you use.
Write the number of coins on each blank.

A. 50¢ — (25)(25)
2 quarters
___ dimes
___ nickels
___ pennies

B. 66¢ — (25)(25)(10)(5)(1)
2 quarters
1 dimes
1 nickels
1 pennies

C. 70¢ — (25)(25)(10)(10)
2 quarters
2 dimes
___ nickels
___ pennies

D. Find another way to pay for the 70¢ — (10)(10)(10)(10)(10)(10)(10)
___ quarters
7 dimes
___ nickels
___ pennies

© 1998 Tribune Education. All Rights Reserved. 248

Page 248

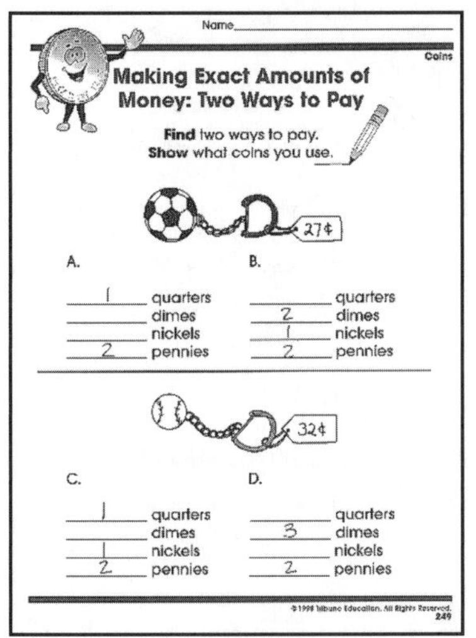

Name____

Coins

Making Exact Amounts of Money: Two Ways to Pay

Find two ways to pay.
Show what coins you use.

27¢

A.
1 quarters
___ dimes
___ nickels
2 pennies

B.
___ quarters
2 dimes
1 nickels
2 pennies

32¢

C.
1 quarters
___ dimes
1 nickels
2 pennies

D.
___ quarters
3 dimes
___ nickels
2 pennies

© 1998 Tribune Education. All Rights Reserved. 249

Page 249

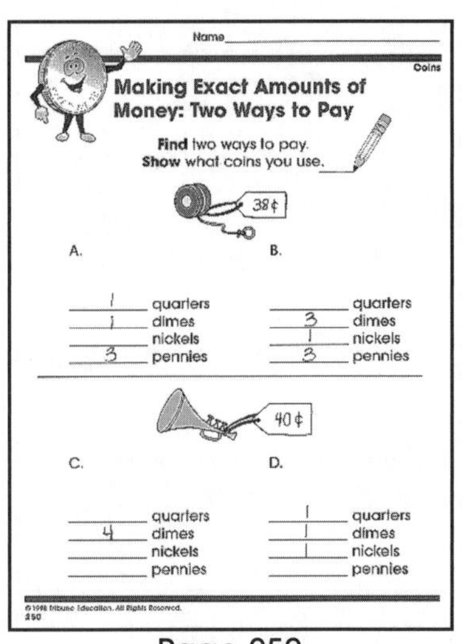

Name____

Coins

Making Exact Amounts of Money: Two Ways to Pay

Find two ways to pay.
Show what coins you use.

38¢

A.
1 quarters
1 dimes
___ nickels
3 pennies

B.
___ quarters
3 dimes
1 nickels
3 pennies

40¢

C.
___ quarters
4 dimes
___ nickels
___ pennies

D.
1 quarters
1 dimes
1 nickels
___ pennies

© 1998 Tribune Education. All Rights Reserved. 250

Page 250

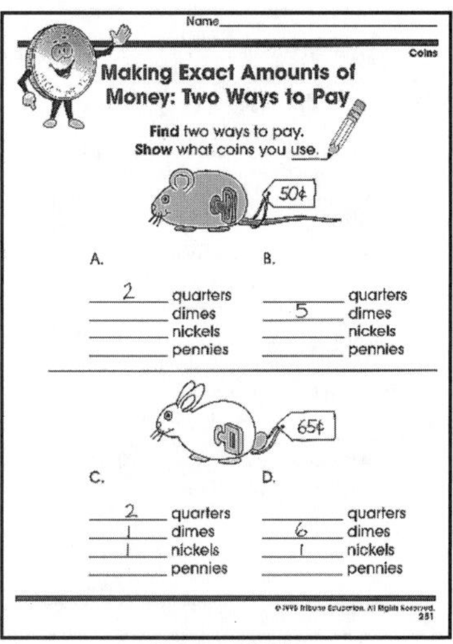

Name____

Coins

Making Exact Amounts of Money: Two Ways to Pay

Find two ways to pay.
Show what coins you use.

50¢

A.
2 quarters
___ dimes
___ nickels
___ pennies

B.
___ quarters
5 dimes
___ nickels
___ pennies

65¢

C.
2 quarters
1 dimes
1 nickels
___ pennies

D.
___ quarters
6 dimes
1 nickels
___ pennies

© 1998 Tribune Education. All Rights Reserved. 251

Page 251

Name__________ Coins

Making Exact Amounts of Money: How Much More?

Count the coins.
Find out how much more money you need to pay the exact amount.

A. How much money do you have? 15 ¢
How much more money do you need? 10 ¢

B. How much money do you have? 38 ¢
How much more money do you need? 7 ¢

C. **Solve** this puzzle.
How much more money does Frog need?
5 ¢

© 1998 Tribune Education. All Rights Reserved. 252

Page 252

Name__________ Coins

Making Exact Amounts of Money: How Much More?

Count the coins.
Find out how much more money you need to pay the exact amount.

A. How much money do you have? 25 ¢
How much more money do you need? 25 ¢

B. How much money do you have? 11 ¢
How much more money do you need? 49 ¢

C. **Solve** this puzzle.
How much more money does Monkey need?
10 ¢

© 1998 Tribune Education. All Rights Reserved. 253

Page 253

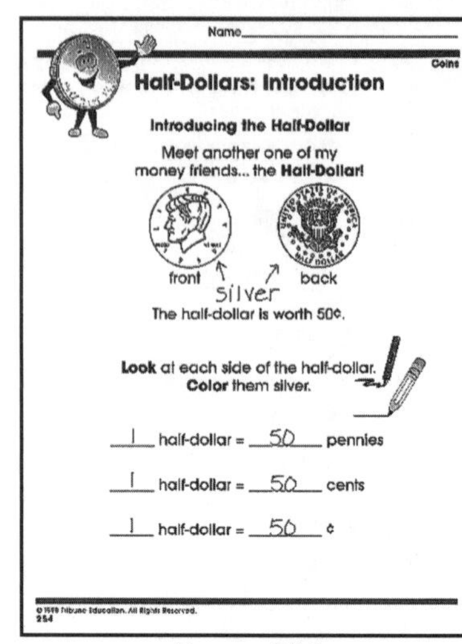
Name__________ Coins

Half-Dollars: Introduction

Introducing the Half-Dollar
Meet another one of my money friends... the **Half-Dollar!**

front back
silver

The half-dollar is worth 50¢.

Look at each side of the half-dollar.
Color them silver.

1 half-dollar = 50 pennies
1 half-dollar = 50 cents
1 half-dollar = 50 ¢

© 1998 Tribune Education. All Rights Reserved. 254

Page 254

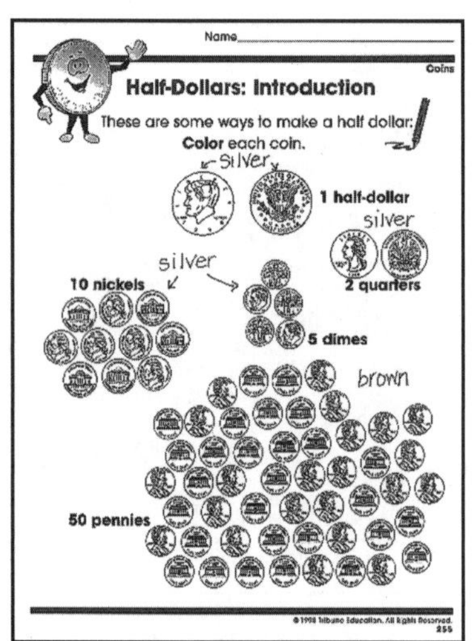
Name__________ Coins

Half-Dollars: Introduction

These are some ways to make a half dollar.
Color each coin.

silver
1 half-dollar
silver
2 quarters
silver
10 nickels
5 dimes
brown
50 pennies

© 1998 Tribune Education. All Rights Reserved. 255

Page 255

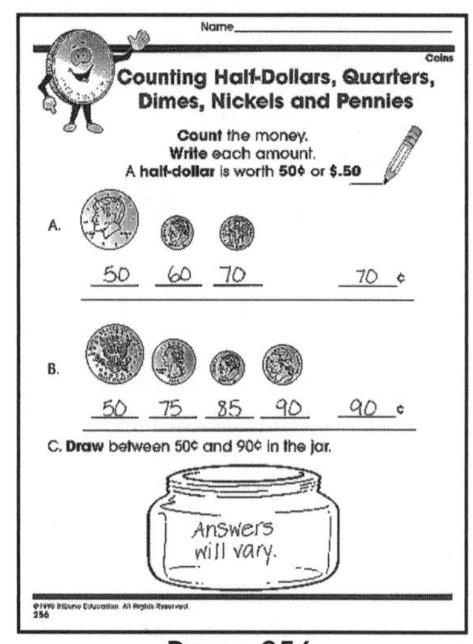
Name__________ Coins

Counting Half-Dollars, Quarters, Dimes, Nickels and Pennies

Count the money.
Write each amount.
A **half-dollar** is worth **50¢** or **$.50**

A. 50 60 70 — 70 ¢

B. 50 75 85 90 — 90 ¢

C. **Draw** between 50¢ and 90¢ in the jar.
Answers will vary.

© 1998 Tribune Education. All Rights Reserved. 256

Page 256

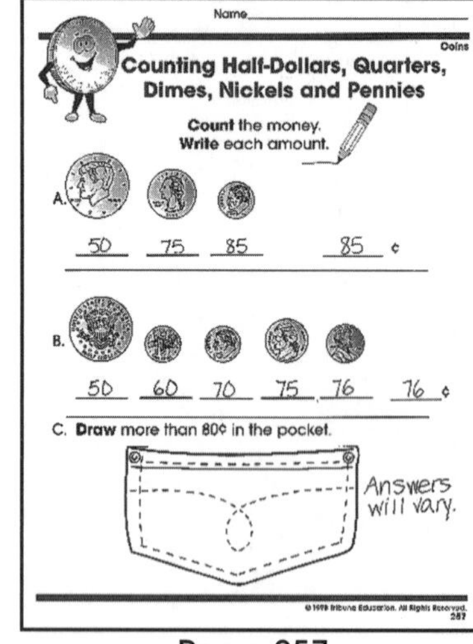
Name__________ Coins

Counting Half-Dollars, Quarters, Dimes, Nickels and Pennies

Count the money.
Write each amount.

A. 50 75 85 — 85 ¢

B. 50 60 70 75 76 — 76 ¢

C. **Draw** more than 80¢ in the pocket.
Answers will vary.

© 1998 Tribune Education. All Rights Reserved. 257

Page 257

Name__________ Coins

Counting Coins: How Much More?

Count the coins.
Find out how much more money you need to pay the exact amount.

A. How much money do you have? 75 ¢
How much more money do you need? 15 ¢

B. How much money do you have? 70 ¢
How much more money do you need? 29 ¢

C. **Solve** this puzzle.
How much more money does Alligator need?
1 ¢

© 1998 Tribune Education. All Rights Reserved. 258

Page 258

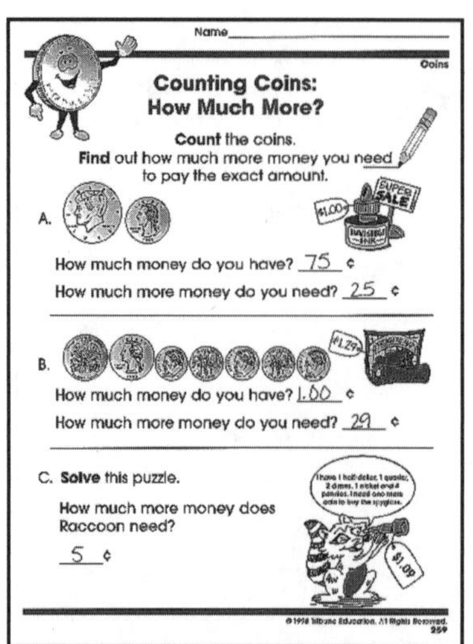
Name__________ Coins

Counting Coins: How Much More?

Count the coins.
Find out how much more money you need to pay the exact amount.

A. How much money do you have? 75 ¢
How much more money do you need? 25 ¢

B. How much money do you have? 1.00 ¢
How much more money do you need? 29 ¢

C. **Solve** this puzzle.
How much more money does Raccoon need?
5 ¢

© 1998 Tribune Education. All Rights Reserved. 259

Page 259

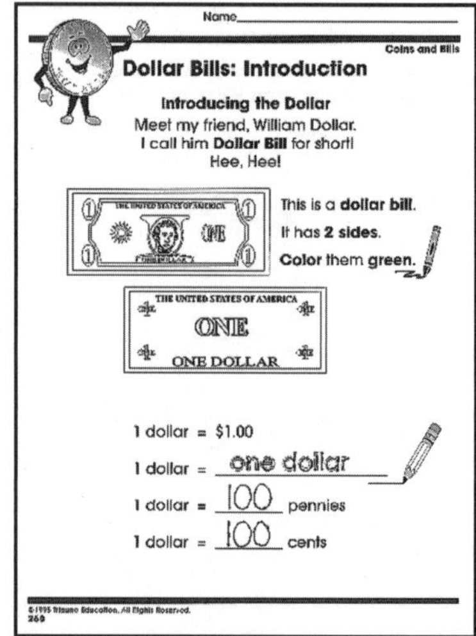
Name__________ Coins and Bills

Dollar Bills: Introduction

Introducing the Dollar
Meet my friend, William Dollar.
I call him **Dollar Bill** for short!
Hee, Hee!

This is a **dollar bill.**
It has **2 sides.**
Color them **green.**

1 dollar = $1.00
1 dollar = one dollar
1 dollar = 100 pennies
1 dollar = 100 cents

© 1998 Tribune Education. All Rights Reserved. 260

Page 260

Answer Key - Money

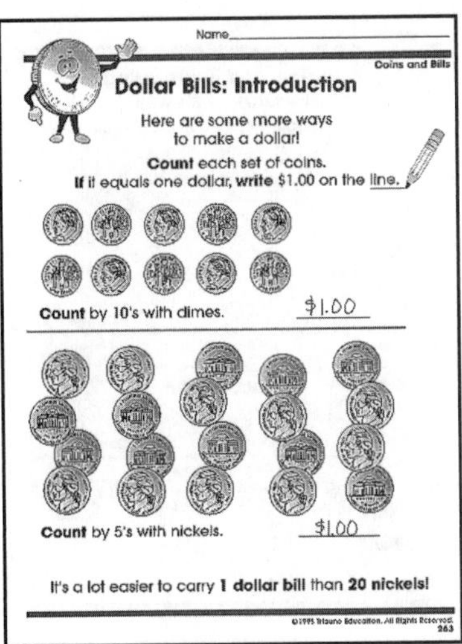

Name________

Coins and Bills

Dollar Bills: Introduction

Here are some more ways to make a dollar!

Count each set of coins.
If it equals one dollar, **write** $1.00 on the line.

Count by 10's with dimes. $1.00

Count by 5's with nickels. $1.00

It's a lot easier to carry **1 dollar bill** than **20 nickels!**

Page 263

Name________

Coins and Bills

Counting with Dollar Bills and Coins

Writing Dollar Amounts

A few **dollar tips** for you...

1. Drop the ¢ sign.
2. Add the $ sign.
3. Use a . (period) between the dollars and cents.

Write the amount of dollars and cents.

1. $ 1.08

2. $ 1.31

Page 264

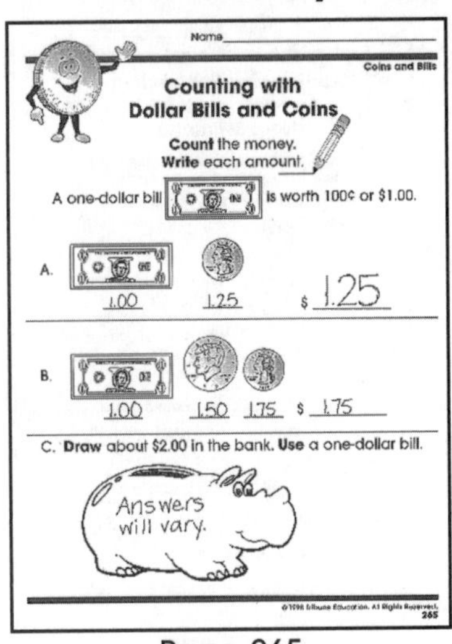

Name________

Coins and Bills

Counting with Dollar Bills and Coins

Count the money.
Write each amount.

A one-dollar bill is worth 100¢ or $1.00.

A. 1.00 1.25 $ 1.25

B. 1.00 1.50 1.75 $ 1.75

C. **Draw** about $2.00 in the bank. **Use** a one-dollar bill.

Answers will vary.

Page 265

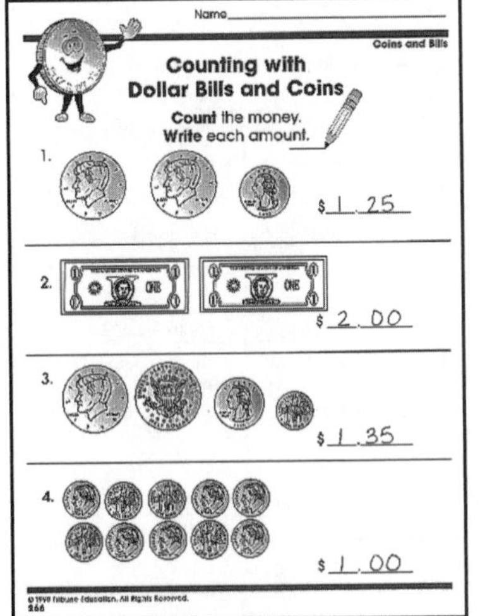

Name________

Coins and Bills

Counting with Dollar Bills and Coins

Count the money.
Write each amount.

1. $ 1.25
2. $ 2.00
3. $ 1.35
4. $ 1.00

Page 266

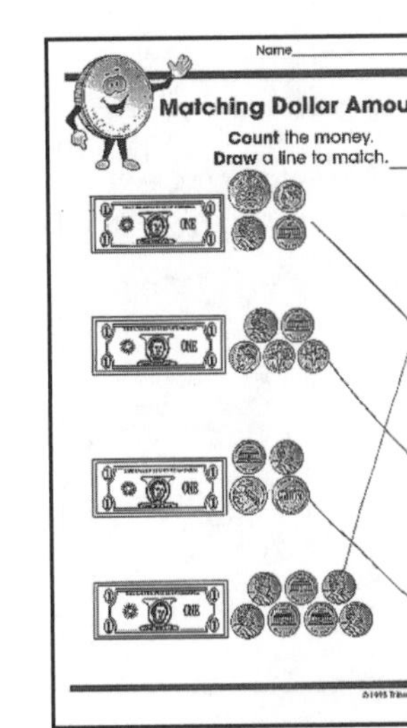

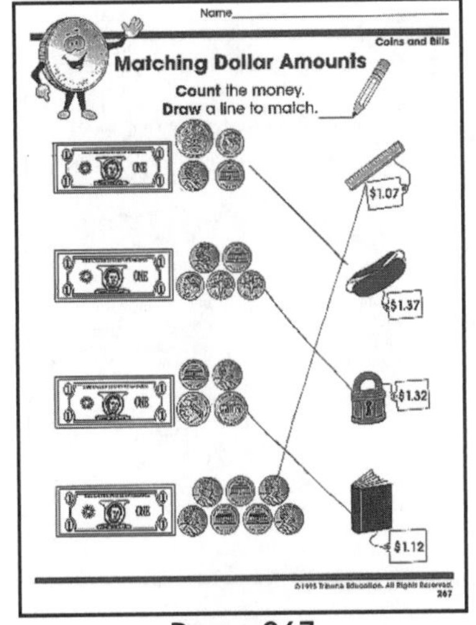

Name________

Coins and Bills

Matching Dollar Amounts

Count the money.
Draw a line to match.

Page 267

Name________

Coins and Bills

Matching Dollar Amounts

A Good Match

Count the money.
Draw a line to match.

$1.26 $1.27 .86 $1.21 Example $1.75 $1.61 $1.03 $1.25 $1.65 $1.10 $1.02 $1.06 $1.07 $1.01 .78

Page 268

Name________

Coins and Bills

Counting Dollar Bills and Coins: How Much More?

Count the coins and bills.
Find out how much more money you need to pay the exact amount.

A. How much money do you have? 1.27 ¢

How much more money do you need? 40 ¢

B. How much money do you have? 1.45

How much more money do you need? 30 ¢

C. **Solve** this puzzle.

How much more money does Anteater need?

25 ¢

Page 269

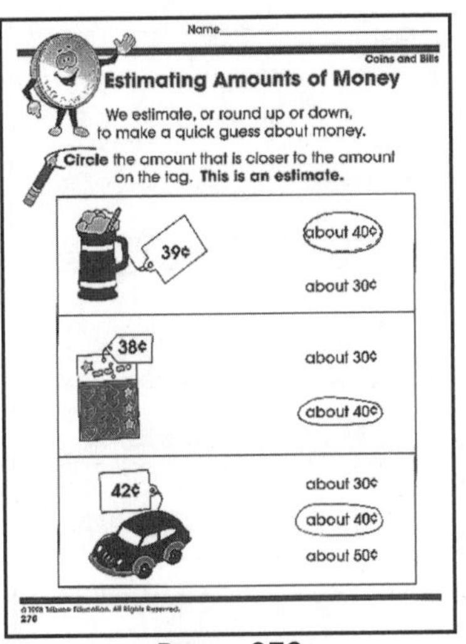

Name________

Coins and Bills

Estimating Amounts of Money

We estimate, or round up or down, to make a quick guess about money.

Circle the amount that is closer to the amount on the tag. **This is an estimate.**

39¢ — (about 40¢) about 30¢

38¢ — about 30¢ (about 40¢)

42¢ — about 30¢ (about 40¢) about 50¢

Page 270

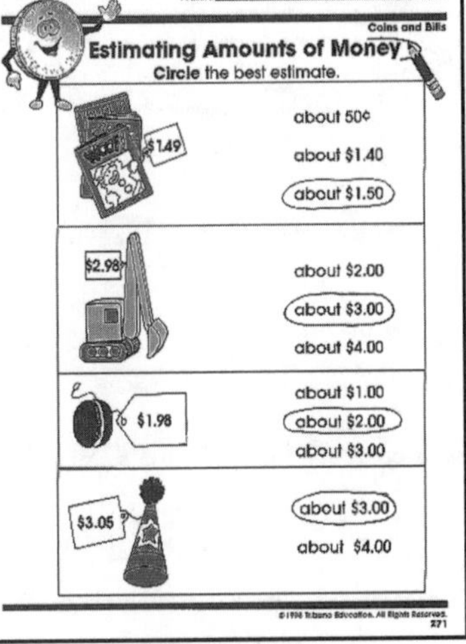

Name________

Coins and Bills

Estimating Amounts of Money

Circle the best estimate.

$1.49 — about 50¢, about $1.40, (about $1.50)

$2.98 — about $2.00, (about $3.00), about $4.00

$1.98 — about $1.00, (about $2.00), about $3.00

$3.05 — (about $3.00), about $4.00

Page 271

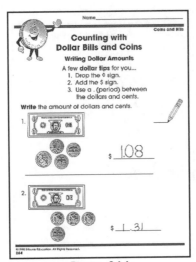

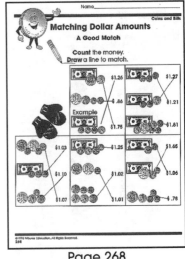

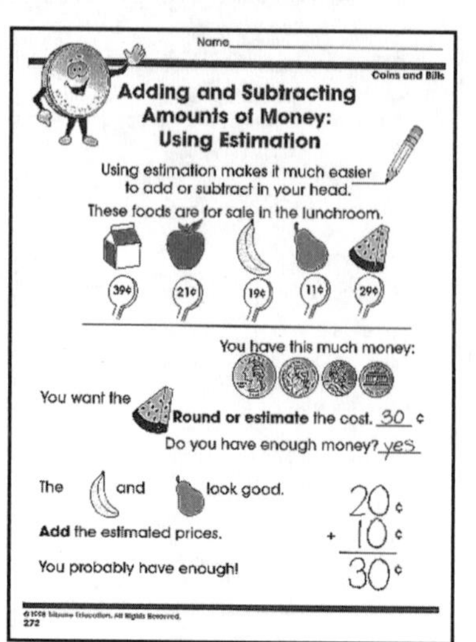
Name
Coins and Bills
Adding and Subtracting Amounts of Money: Using Estimation
Using estimation makes it much easier to add or subtract in your head.
These foods are for sale in the lunchroom.
39¢ 21¢ 19¢ 11¢ 29¢
You have this much money:
You want the [watermelon]. Round or estimate the cost. 30 ¢
Do you have enough money? yes
The [banana] and [pear] look good.
Add the estimated prices.
20¢ + 10¢ = 30¢
You probably have enough!
©1998 Tribune Education. All Rights Reserved. 272

Page 272

Name
Coins and Bills
Adding and Subtracting Amounts of Money: Using Estimation
You have this money:
You have 50 cents.
If you buy [milk], will you have enough left to buy a [banana]? yes (no)
money you have = 50 ¢
estimated milk = - 40 ¢
10 ¢
You have this money:
You want to buy [milk] and an [apple]. Estimate.
Do you have enough money? no
Which other fruit can you buy to have with your milk? a pear
©1998 Tribune Education. All Rights Reserved. 273

Page 273

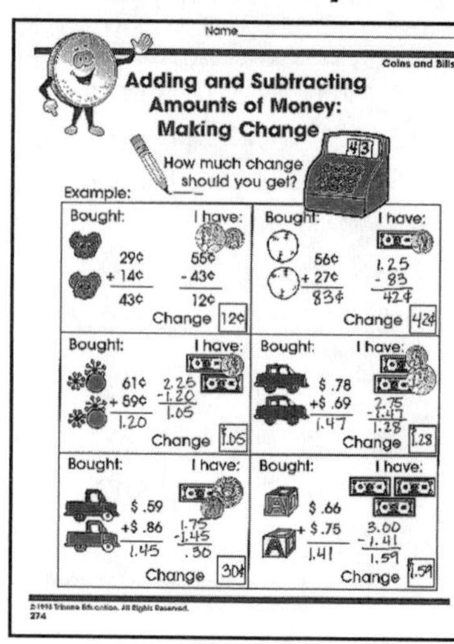
Name
Coins and Bills
Adding and Subtracting Amounts of Money: Making Change
How much change should you get?
Example:
Bought: 29¢ + 14¢ = 43¢ | I have: 55¢ - 43¢ = 12¢ | Change 12¢
Bought: 56¢ + 27¢ = 83¢ | I have: 1.25 - .83 = 42¢ | Change 42¢
Bought: 61¢ + 59¢ = 1.20 | I have: 2.25 - 1.20 = 1.05 | Change 1.05
Bought: $.78 + $.69 = 1.47 | I have: 2.75 - 1.47 = 1.28 | Change 1.28
Bought: $.59 + $.86 = 1.45 | I have: 1.75 - 1.45 = .30 | Change 30¢
Bought: $.66 + $.75 = 1.41 | I have: 3.00 - 1.41 = 1.59 | Change 1.59
©1998 Tribune Education. All Rights Reserved. 274

Page 274

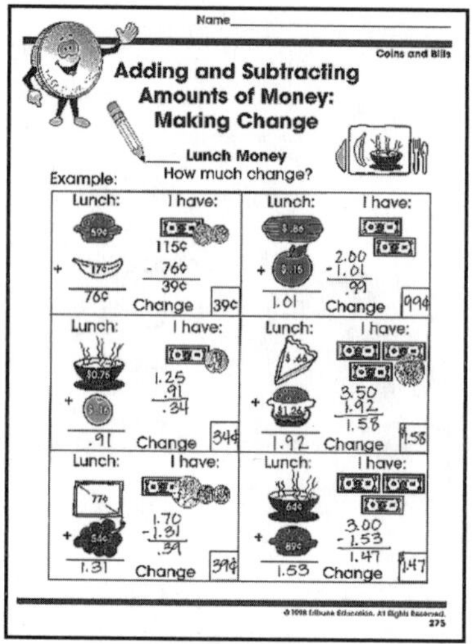
Name
Coins and Bills
Adding and Subtracting Amounts of Money: Making Change
Lunch Money
How much change?
Example:
Lunch: 76¢ | I have: 115¢ - 76¢ = 39¢ | Change 39¢
Lunch: 1.01 | I have: 2.00 - 1.01 = .99 | Change 99¢
Lunch: .91 | I have: 1.25 - .91 = .34 | Change 34¢
Lunch: 1.92 | I have: 3.50 - 1.92 = 1.58 | Change 1.58
Lunch: 1.31 | I have: 1.70 - 1.31 = .39 | Change 39¢
Lunch: 1.53 | I have: 3.00 - 1.53 = 1.47 | Change 1.47
©1998 Tribune Education. All Rights Reserved. 275

Page 275

Name
Coins and Bills
Making Change: Money Puzzles
Solve the puzzles. Show how much change you get.
A. Use 2 quarters. Pay 45¢. What change will you get? 5¢
B. Use 1 quarter, 2 dimes and 2 nickels. Pay 53¢. What change will you get? 2¢
C. Use 3 quarters and 1 dime. Pay 76¢. What change will you get? 9¢
D. Use 3 quarters and 2 nickels. Pay 82¢. What change will you get? 3¢
©1998 Tribune Education. All Rights Reserved. 276

Page 276

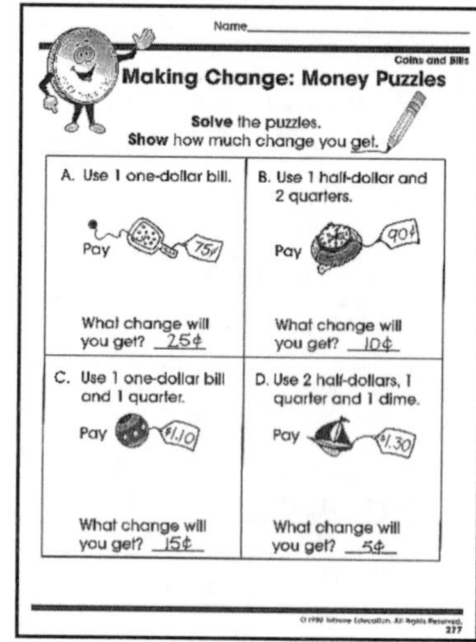
Name
Coins and Bills
Making Change: Money Puzzles
Solve the puzzles. Show how much change you get.
A. Use 1 one-dollar bill. Pay 75¢. What change will you get? 25¢
B. Use 1 half-dollar and 2 quarters. Pay 90¢. What change will you get? 10¢
C. Use 1 one-dollar bill and 1 quarter. Pay $1.10. What change will you get? 15¢
D. Use 2 half-dollars, 1 quarter and 1 dime. Pay $1.30. What change will you get? 5¢
©1998 Tribune Education. All Rights Reserved. 277

Page 277

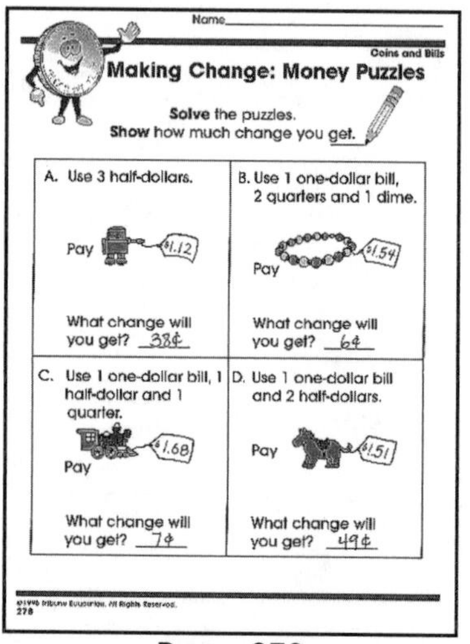
Name
Coins and Bills
Making Change: Money Puzzles
Solve the puzzles. Show how much change you get.
A. Use 3 half-dollars. Pay $1.12. What change will you get? 38¢
B. Use 1 one-dollar bill, 2 quarters and 1 dime. Pay $1.54. What change will you get? 6¢
C. Use 1 one-dollar bill, 1 half-dollar and 1 quarter. Pay $1.68. What change will you get? 7¢
D. Use 1 one-dollar bill and 2 half-dollars. Pay $1.51. What change will you get? 49¢
©1998 Tribune Education. All Rights Reserved. 278

Page 278

Name
Coins and Bills
Making Change: Money Puzzles
Solve the puzzles. Show how much change you get.
A. Use 2 one-dollar bills. Pay $1.59. What change will you get? 41¢
B. Use 2 one-dollar bills. Pay $1.85. What change will you get? 15¢
C. Use 3 one-dollar bills. Pay $2.65. What change will you get? 35¢
D. Use 3 one-dollar bills. Pay $2.06. What change will you get? 94¢
©1998 Tribune Education. All Rights Reserved. 279

Page 279

Name
Coins and Bills
Making Change: Money Puzzles
Solve the puzzles. Show how much change you get.
A. Use 4 one-dollar bills. Pay $3.55. What change will you get? 45¢
B. Use 5 one-dollar bills. Pay $4.15. What change will you get? 85¢
C. Use 3 one-dollar bills. Pay $2.80. What change will you get? 20¢
D. Use 2 one-dollar bills. Pay $1.95. What change will you get? 5¢
©1998 Tribune Education. All Rights Reserved. 280

Page 280

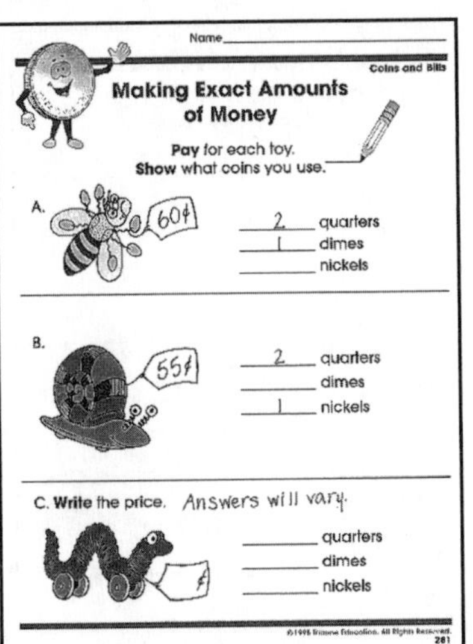

Name____________

Coins and Bills

Making Exact Amounts of Money

Pay for each toy.
Show what coins you use.

A. 60¢

2 quarters
1 dimes
____ nickels

B. 55¢

2 quarters
____ dimes
1 nickels

C. **Write** the price. Answers will vary.

____ quarters
____ dimes
____ nickels

©1998 Tribune Education. All Rights Reserved. 281

Page 281

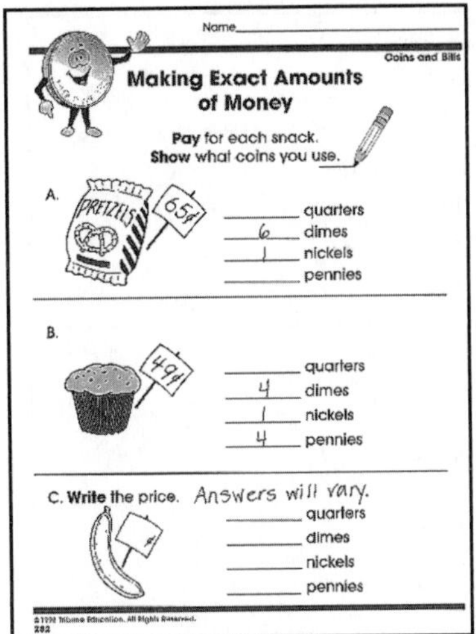

Name____________

Coins and Bills

Making Exact Amounts of Money

Pay for each snack.
Show what coins you use.

A. 65¢

____ quarters
6 dimes
1 nickels
____ pennies

B. 49¢

____ quarters
4 dimes
1 nickels
4 pennies

C. **Write** the price. Answers will vary.

____ quarters
____ dimes
____ nickels
____ pennies

©1998 Tribune Education. All Rights Reserved. 282

Page 282

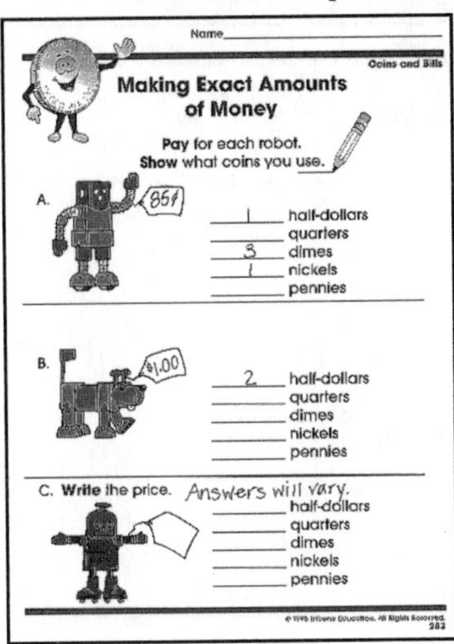

Name____________

Coins and Bills

Making Exact Amounts of Money

Pay for each robot.
Show what coins you use.

A. 85¢

1 half-dollars
____ quarters
3 dimes
1 nickels
____ pennies

B. $1.00

2 half-dollars
____ quarters
____ dimes
____ nickels
____ pennies

C. **Write** the price. Answers will vary.

____ half-dollars
____ quarters
____ dimes
____ nickels
____ pennies

©1998 Tribune Education. All Rights Reserved. 283

Page 283

Name____________

Coins and Bills

Making Exact Amounts of Money

Pay for each animal.
Show what coins you use.

A. $1.50

3 half-dollars
____ quarters
____ dimes
____ nickels
____ pennies

B. $1.35

2 half-dollars
____ quarters
3 dimes
1 nickels
____ pennies

C. **Write** the price. Answers will vary.

____ half-dollars
____ quarters
____ dimes
____ nickels
____ pennies

©1998 Tribune Education. All Rights Reserved. 284

Page 284

Name____________

Coins and Bills

Making Exact Amounts of Money

Pay for each toy.
Show what money you use.

A. $1.30

1 dollars
____ half-dollars
____ quarters
3 dimes
____ nickels
____ pennies

B. $1.55

1 dollars
1 half-dollars
____ quarters
____ dimes
1 nickels
____ pennies

C. **Write** the price. Answers will vary.

____ dollars
____ half-dollars
____ quarters
____ dimes
____ nickels
____ pennies

©1998 Tribune Education. All Rights Reserved. 285

Page 285

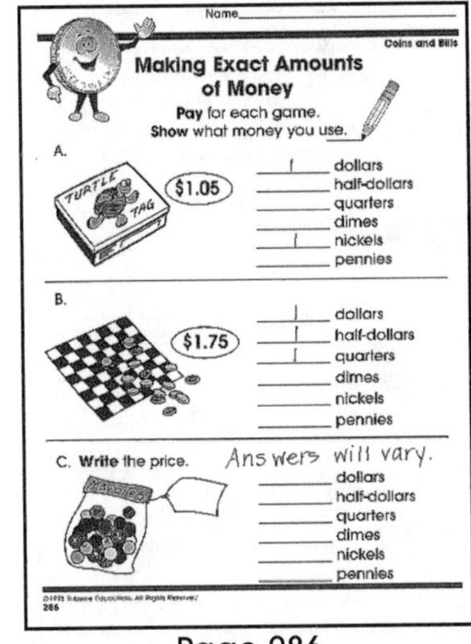

Name____________

Coins and Bills

Making Exact Amounts of Money

Pay for each game.
Show what money you use.

A. $1.05

1 dollars
____ half-dollars
____ quarters
____ dimes
1 nickels
____ pennies

B. $1.75

1 dollars
1 half-dollars
1 quarters
____ dimes
____ nickels
____ pennies

C. **Write** the price. Answers will vary.

____ dollars
____ half-dollars
____ quarters
____ dimes
____ nickels
____ pennies

©1998 Tribune Education. All Rights Reserved. 286

Page 286

Name____________

Review

Using Combinations of Coins to Pay

How Would You Pay?
Pay for each cookie.
Use as few coins as you can.

	(quarter)	(dime)	(nickel)	(penny)	Number of Coins Used
A. 28¢	1			3	4
B. 39¢	1	1		4	6
C. 49¢	1	2		4	7
D. Write the price. ¢	Answers will vary.				

©1998 Tribune Education. All Rights Reserved. 287

Page 287

Name____________

Review

Using Combinations of Coins to Pay

How Would You Pay?
Pay for each toy.
Use as few coins as you can.

	(quarter)	(dime)	(nickel)	(penny)	Number of Coins Used
A. 22¢		2		2	4
B. 37¢	1	1		2	4
C. 52¢	2			2	4
D. Write the price. ¢	Answers will vary.				

©1998 Tribune Education. All Rights Reserved. 288

Page 288

Name____________

Review

Using Combinations of Coins to Pay

How Would You Pay?
Pay for each book.
Use as few coins as you can.

	(quarter)	(dime)	(nickel)	(penny)	Number of Coins Used
A. 75¢	3				3
B. 80¢	3		1		4
C. 97¢	3	2		2	7
D. Write the price. ¢	Answers will vary.				

©1998 Tribune Education. All Rights Reserved. 289

Page 289

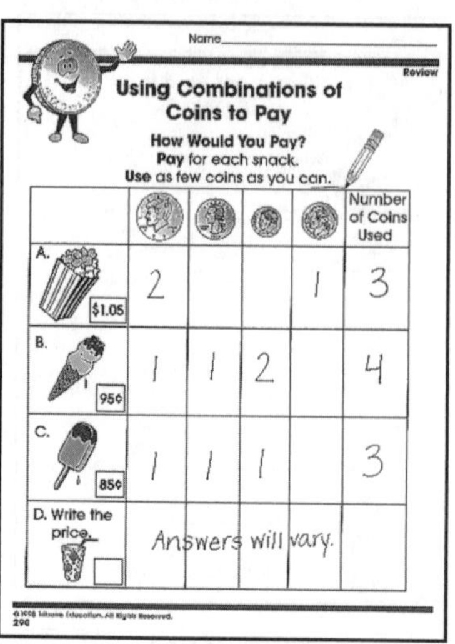

Review

Using Combinations of Coins to Pay

How Would You Pay?
Pay for each snack.
Use as few coins as you can.

					Number of Coins Used
A. $1.05	2			1	3
B. 95¢	1	1	2		4
C. 85¢	1	1	1		3
D. Write the price.	Answers will vary.				

Page 290

Review

Using Combinations of Coins to Pay

How Would You Pay?
Pay for each mask.
Use as few coins and bills as you can.

					Number of Coins Used
A. $1.75	1	3			4
B. $1.95	1	3	2		6
C. $2.50	2	2			4
D. Write the price.	Answers will vary.				

Page 291

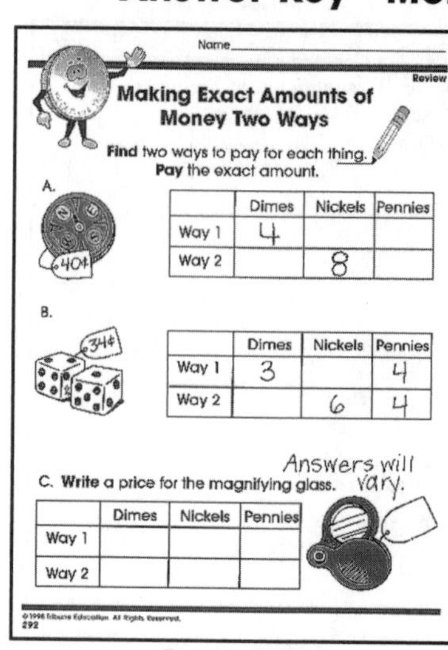

Review

Making Exact Amounts of Money Two Ways

Find two ways to pay for each thing.
Pay the exact amount.

A. 40¢

	Dimes	Nickels	Pennies
Way 1	4		
Way 2		8	

B. 34¢

	Dimes	Nickels	Pennies
Way 1	3		4
Way 2		6	4

C. Write a price for the magnifying glass. Answers will vary.

	Dimes	Nickels	Pennies
Way 1			
Way 2			

Page 292

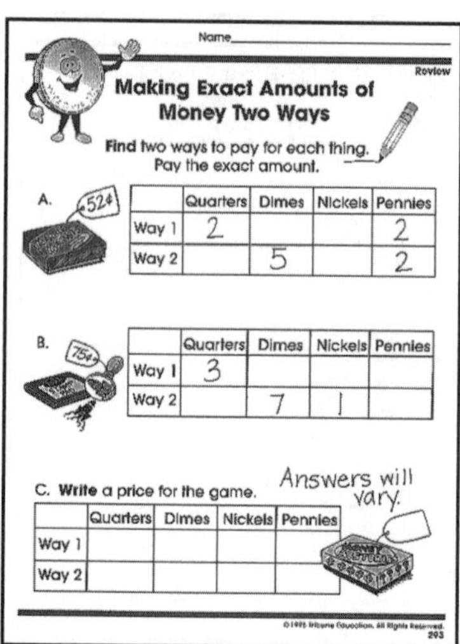

Review

Making Exact Amounts of Money Two Ways

Find two ways to pay for each thing.
Pay the exact amount.

A. 52¢

	Quarters	Dimes	Nickels	Pennies
Way 1	2			2
Way 2		5		2

B. 75¢

	Quarters	Dimes	Nickels	Pennies
Way 1	3			
Way 2		7	1	

C. Write a price for the game. Answers will vary.

	Quarters	Dimes	Nickels	Pennies
Way 1				
Way 2				

Page 293

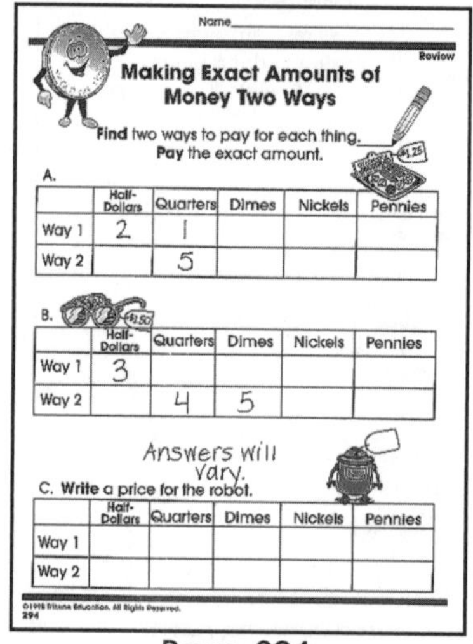

Review

Making Exact Amounts of Money Two Ways

Find two ways to pay for each thing.
Pay the exact amount.

A. $1.25

	Half-Dollars	Quarters	Dimes	Nickels	Pennies
Way 1	2	1			
Way 2		5			

B. $1.50

	Half-Dollars	Quarters	Dimes	Nickels	Pennies
Way 1	3				
Way 2		4	5		

Answers will vary.
C. Write a price for the robot.

	Half-Dollars	Quarters	Dimes	Nickels	Pennies
Way 1					
Way 2					

Page 294

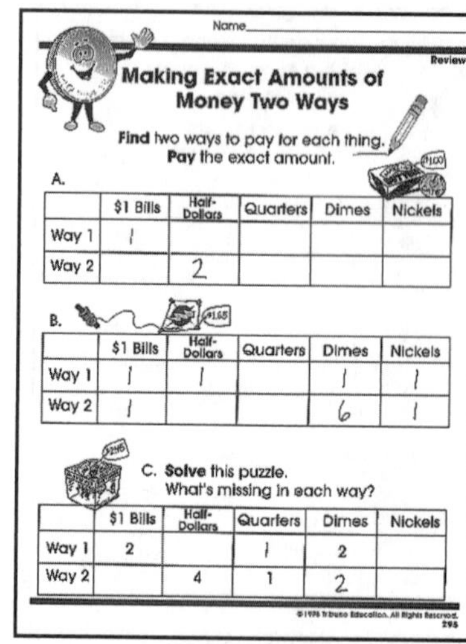

Review

Making Exact Amounts of Money Two Ways

Find two ways to pay for each thing.
Pay the exact amount.

A. $1.00

	$1 Bills	Half-Dollars	Quarters	Dimes	Nickels
Way 1	1				
Way 2		2			

B. $1.55

	$1 Bills	Half-Dollars	Quarters	Dimes	Nickels
Way 1	1	1		1	1
Way 2	1			6	1

C. Solve this puzzle.
What's missing in each way?

	$1 Bills	Half-Dollars	Quarters	Dimes	Nickels
Way 1	2		1	2	
Way 2		4	1	2	

Page 295

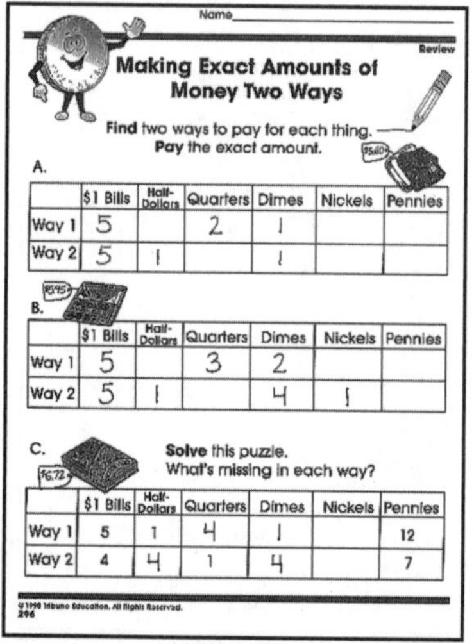

Review

Making Exact Amounts of Money Two Ways

Find two ways to pay for each thing.
Pay the exact amount.

A. $5.60

	$1 Bills	Half-Dollars	Quarters	Dimes	Nickels	Pennies
Way 1	5		2	1		
Way 2	5	1		1		

B. $5.95

	$1 Bills	Half-Dollars	Quarters	Dimes	Nickels	Pennies
Way 1	5		3	2		
Way 2	5	1		4	1	

C. $6.72 Solve this puzzle.
What's missing in each way?

	$1 Bills	Half-Dollars	Quarters	Dimes	Nickels	Pennies
Way 1	5	1	4	1		12
Way 2	4	4	1	4		7

Page 296

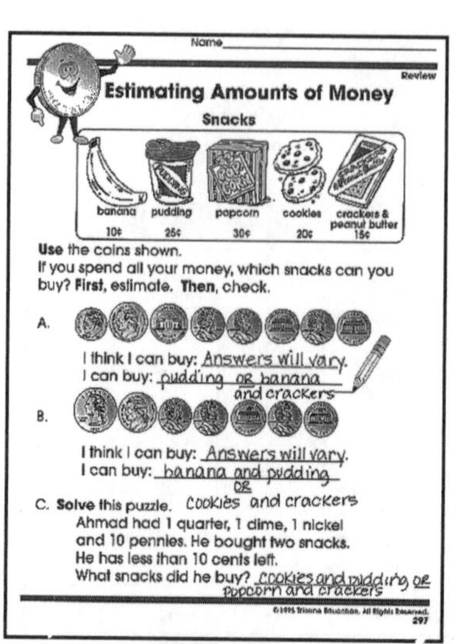

Review

Estimating Amounts of Money

Snacks

banana 10¢, pudding 25¢, popcorn 30¢, cookies 20¢, crackers & peanut butter 15¢

Use the coins shown.
If you spend all your money, which snacks can you buy? First, estimate. Then, check.

A. I think I can buy: Answers will vary.
I can buy: pudding or banana and crackers

B. I think I can buy: Answers will vary.
I can buy: banana and pudding or cookies and crackers

C. Solve this puzzle.
Ahmad had 1 quarter, 1 dime, 1 nickel and 10 pennies. He bought two snacks. He has less than 10 cents left. What snacks did he buy? cookies and pudding or popcorn and crackers

Page 297

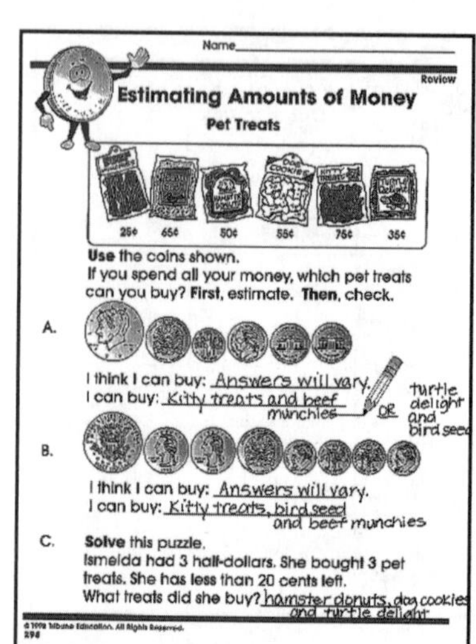

Review

Estimating Amounts of Money

Pet Treats

25¢ 65¢ 50¢ 55¢ 75¢ 35¢

Use the coins shown.
If you spend all your money, which pet treats can you buy? First, estimate. Then, check.

A. I think I can buy: Answers will vary.
I can buy: Kitty treats and beef munchies or turtle delight and bird seed

B. I think I can buy: Answers will vary.
I can buy: Kitty treats, bird seed and beef munchies

C. Solve this puzzle.
Ismelda had 3 half-dollars. She bought 3 pet treats. She has less than 20 cents left. What treats did she buy? hamster donuts, dog cookies and turtle delight

Page 298

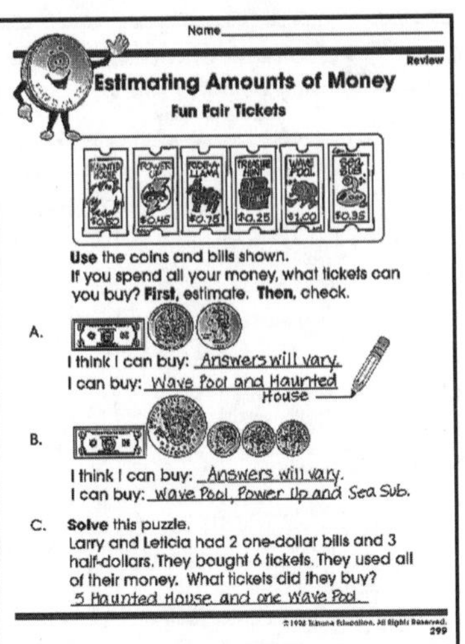
Name__________

Review

Estimating Amounts of Money

Fun Fair Tickets

Use the coins and bills shown.
If you spend all your money, what tickets can you buy? **First**, estimate. **Then**, check.

A. I think I can buy: Answers will vary.
I can buy: Wave Pool and Haunted House

B. I think I can buy: Answers will vary.
I can buy: Wave Pool, Power Up and Sea Sub.

C. **Solve** this puzzle.
Larry and Leticia had 2 one-dollar bills and 3 half-dollars. They bought 6 tickets. They used all of their money. What tickets did they buy?
5 Haunted House and one Wave Pool

©1998 Tribune Education. All Rights Reserved. 299

Page 299

Name__________

Review

Estimating Amounts of Money

Kassie's Cafe

Hamburger	65¢	Milk	35¢
Cheeseburger	75¢	Chocolate Milk	45¢
Burrito	60¢	Apple Juice	50¢
Small Pizza	60¢	Berry Juice	55¢
Super Salad	40¢	Dream Bar	25¢

Use the coins and bills shown.
If you spend all your money, what can you buy?
First, estimate. **Then**, check.

A. I think I can buy: Answers will vary.
I can buy: Answers will vary.

B. I think I can buy: Answers will vary.
I can buy: Answers will vary.

C. **Solve** this puzzle.
Tina had 1 one-dollar bill, 1 half-dollar and 2 quarters. She bought three things. She has less than 25 cents left. What did Tina buy? Answers must add up to an answer between $1.76 and $2.00.

©1998 Tribune Education. All Rights Reserved. 300

Page 300

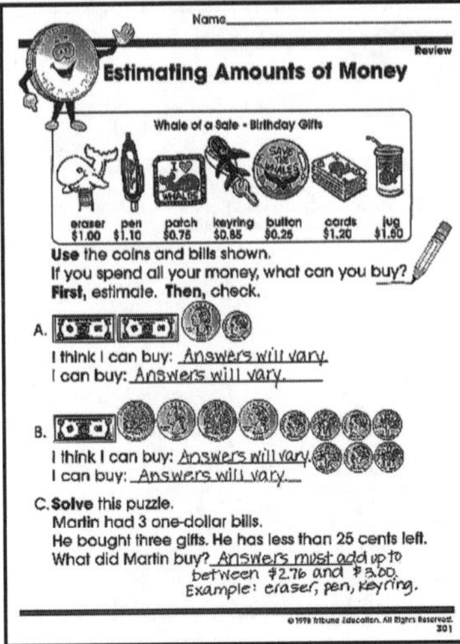
Name__________

Review

Estimating Amounts of Money

Whale of a Sale • Birthday Gifts

eraser $1.00, pen $1.10, patch $0.75, keyring $0.85, button $0.25, cards $1.20, jug $1.50

Use the coins and bills shown.
If you spend all your money, what can you buy?
First, estimate. **Then**, check.

A. I think I can buy: Answers will vary.
I can buy: Answers will vary.

B. I think I can buy: Answers will vary.
I can buy: Answers will vary.

C. **Solve** this puzzle.
Martin had 3 one-dollar bills.
He bought three gifts. He has less than 25 cents left.
What did Martin buy? Answers must add up to between $2.76 and $3.00.
Example: eraser, pen, keyring.

©1998 Tribune Education. All Rights Reserved. 301

Page 301

Name__________

Review

Making Exact Amounts and Change

Pay the exact amount.
What change do you get back?

A. Amount you get back: 9 ¢

B. Amount you get back: 17 ¢

C. Amount you get back: 30 ¢

©1998 Tribune Education. All Rights Reserved. 302

Page 302

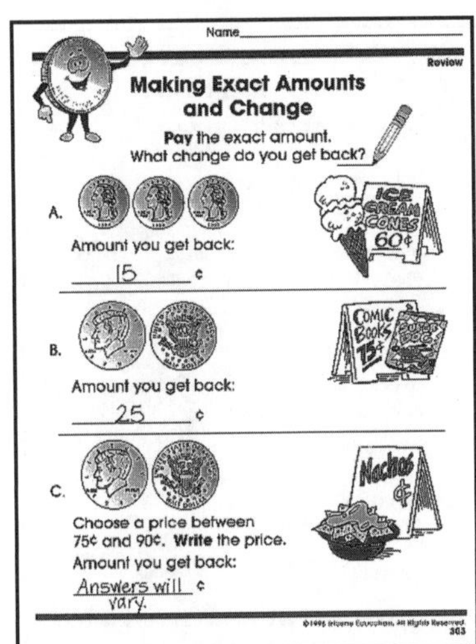
Name__________

Review

Making Exact Amounts and Change

Pay the exact amount.
What change do you get back?

A. Amount you get back: 15 ¢

B. Amount you get back: 25 ¢

C. Choose a price between 75¢ and 90¢. **Write** the price.
Amount you get back: Answers will vary. ¢

©1998 Tribune Education. All Rights Reserved. 303

Page 303

Name__________

Review

Making Exact Amounts and Change

Pay the exact amount.
What change do you get back?

A. Amount you get back: 19 ¢

B. Amount you get back: 20 ¢

C. **Choose** a price between $1.15 and $1.28. **Write** the price.

Amount you get back: Answers will vary. ¢

©1998 Tribune Education. All Rights Reserved. 304

Page 304

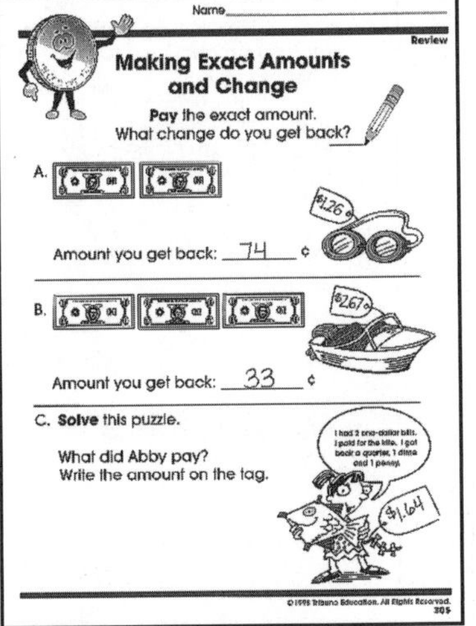
Name__________

Review

Making Exact Amounts and Change

Pay the exact amount.
What change do you get back?

A. Amount you get back: 74 ¢

B. Amount you get back: 33 ¢

C. **Solve** this puzzle.
What did Abby pay?
Write the amount on the tag.

$1.64

©1998 Tribune Education. All Rights Reserved. 305

Page 305

Name__________

Review

Making Exact Amounts and Change

Pay the exact amount.
What change do you get back?

A. Amount you get back: $ .66

B. Amount you get back: $ 2.25

C. **Solve** this puzzle.
What did Dominic pay?
Write the amount on the tag.

2.72

©1998 Tribune Education. All Rights Reserved. 306

Page 306

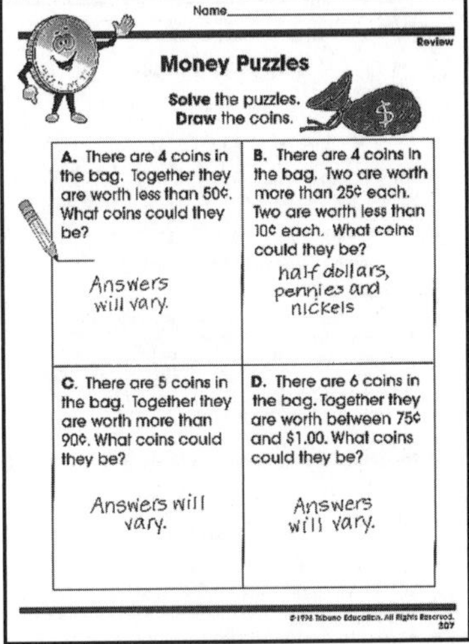
Name__________

Review

Money Puzzles

Solve the puzzles.
Draw the coins.

A. There are 4 coins in the bag. Together they are worth less than 50¢. What coins could they be? Answers will vary.	**B.** There are 4 coins in the bag. Two are worth more than 25¢ each. Two are worth less than 10¢ each. What coins could they be? half dollars, pennies and nickels
C. There are 5 coins in the bag. Together they are worth more than 90¢. What coins could they be? Answers will vary.	**D.** There are 6 coins in the bag. Together they are worth between 75¢ and $1.00. What coins could they be? Answers will vary.

©1998 Tribune Education. All Rights Reserved. 307

Page 307

Name________________

Review

Money Puzzles

Solve the puzzles.
Draw the coins.

A. There are 5 coins in the bank. Together they are worth \$1.00 exactly. What coins could they be? (50) (25) (10) (10) (5)	**B.** There are 6 coins in the bank. Together they are worth between 80¢ and \$1.20. What coins could they be? Answers will vary.
C. There are 6 coins in the bank. Two are worth more than 10¢ each. Four are worth less than 10¢ each. All together they are worth more than \$1.00. What coins could they be? (50) (50) (50) (5) (5) (5)	**D.** There are 6 coins in the bank. Four are worth more than 10¢ each. Two are worth less than 25¢ each. All together they are worth less than \$1.50. What coins could they be? Answers will vary.

©1998 Tribune Education. All Rights Reserved. 308

Page 308

Name________________

Review

Using Combinations of Coins to Pay

Use the coins shown to make each amount.

A. Use 3 of the coins to make 25¢. What coins did you use?			2	1	
B. Use 4 of the coins to make 50¢. What coins did you use?		1	2	1	
C. Use 4 of the coins to make 66¢. What coins did you use?	1		1	1	1
D. Use 5 of the coins to make 96¢. What coins did you use?	1	1	2		1

©1998 Tribune Education. All Rights Reserved. 309

Page 309

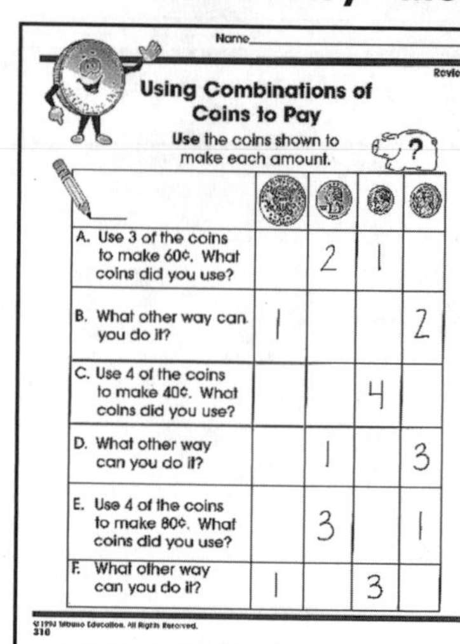
Name________________

Review

Using Combinations of Coins to Pay

Use the coins shown to make each amount.

A. Use 3 of the coins to make 60¢. What coins did you use?		2	1	
B. What other way can you do it?	1			2
C. Use 4 of the coins to make 40¢. What coins did you use?			4	
D. What other way can you do it?		1		3
E. Use 4 of the coins to make 80¢. What coins did you use?		3		1
F. What other way can you do it?	1		3	

©1998 Tribune Education. All Rights Reserved. 310

Page 310

Name________________

Review

Money Story Puzzles

Solve the money story puzzles.

A. Sean sees a box of magnets on sale for 50 cents. He takes 10 coins out of his pocket and buys the magnets.
What coins could they be?
nickels

B. Tonia sees a small bag of jacks for 58 cents. She takes 9 coins out of her pocket to pay.
What coins could they be?
(10) (10) (10) (10) (10) (5) (1) (1) (1)

C. Dustin sees a toy hammer. He wants to buy it for his little brother. He pulls six coins out of his pocket and pays 75 cents.
What coins could they be?
(25) (10) (10) (10) (10) (10)

©1998 Tribune Education. All Rights Reserved. 311

Page 311

Name________________

Review

Money Story Puzzles

Solve the money story puzzles.

A. Matt buys a box of things for doing magic tricks. He takes an even number of coins out of his pocket and pays 65 cents.
What coins could they be?
Answers will vary.

B. Stacey buys a poster for 70 cents. She uses an odd number of coins to buy it.
What coins could they be?
Answers will vary.

C. **Write** a money story puzzle about buying the stuffed whale.
Answers will vary.

©1998 Tribune Education. All Rights Reserved. 312

Page 312

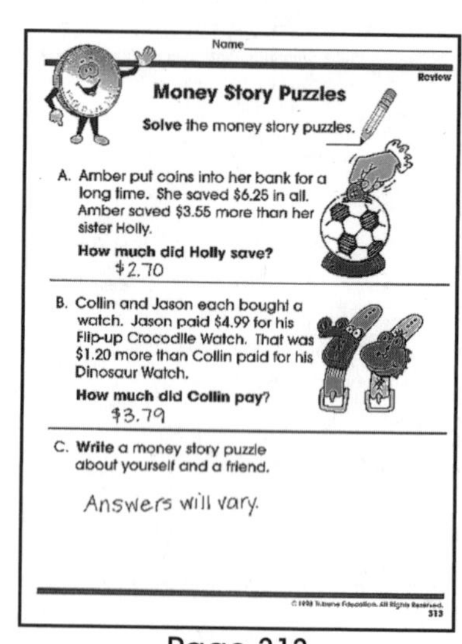
Name________________

Review

Money Story Puzzles

Solve the money story puzzles.

A. Amber put coins into her bank for a long time. She saved \$6.25 in all. Amber saved \$3.55 more than her sister Holly.
How much did Holly save?
\$2.70

B. Collin and Jason each bought a watch. Jason paid \$4.99 for his Flip-up Crocodile Watch. That was \$1.20 more than Collin paid for his Dinosaur Watch.
How much did Collin pay?
\$3.79

C. **Write** a money story puzzle about yourself and a friend.
Answers will vary.

©1998 Tribune Education. All Rights Reserved. 313

Page 313

Name________________

Review

Money Story Puzzles

Solve the money story puzzles.

A. Darci and Kara fed the horses at the fair. Kara's mother gave the girls 3 one-dollar bills, 3 quarters, 5 dimes and 3 nickels. Darci and Kara divided the money equally.
How much money did each of them get?
\$2.20

B. Josh and Ben washed cars one Saturday. When they finished, they had 3 one-dollar bills, 1 half dollar, three quarters, 2 dimes and 1 nickel in their money box. The boys divided the money fairly.
How much money did each of them get?
\$2.25

C. **Write** a money story puzzle about earning money and dividing it equally.
Answers will vary.

©1998 Tribune Education. All Rights Reserved. 314

Page 314

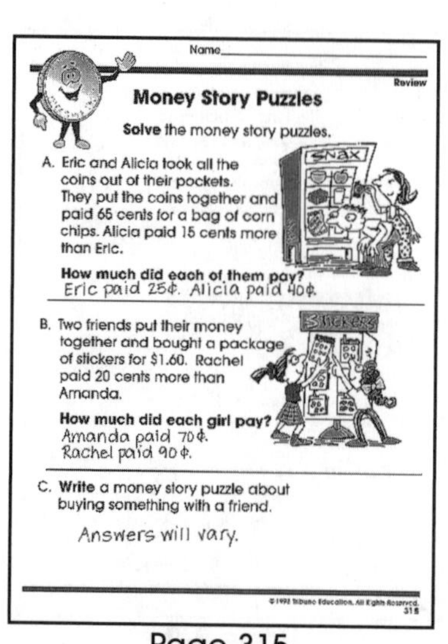
Name________________

Review

Money Story Puzzles

Solve the money story puzzles.

A. Eric and Alicia took all the coins out of their pockets. They put the coins together and paid 65 cents for a bag of corn chips. Alicia paid 15 cents more than Eric.
How much did each of them pay?
Eric paid 25¢. Alicia paid 40¢.

B. Two friends put their money together and bought a package of stickers for \$1.60. Rachel paid 20 cents more than Amanda.
How much did each girl pay?
Amanda paid 70¢.
Rachel paid 90¢.

C. **Write** a money story puzzle about buying something with a friend.
Answers will vary.

©1998 Tribune Education. All Rights Reserved. 315

Page 315

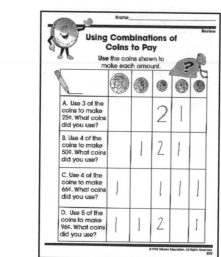